D0893276

PERSON MEMORY:
The Cognitive Basis of Social Perception

PERSON MEMORY:
The Cognitive Basis of Social Perception

Edited by **REID HASTIE**
Harvard University

THOMAS M. OSTROM
Ohio State University

EBBE B. EBBESEN
University of California, San Diego

ROBERT S. WYER, JR.
University of Illinois at Urbana-Champaign

DAVID L. HAMILTON
University of California, Santa Barbara

DONAL E. CARLSTON
University of Iowa

LEA LAWRENCE ERLBAUM ASSOCIATES, PUBLISHERS
1980   Hillsdale, New Jersey

Lawrence Erlbaum Associates, Inc., Publishers
365 Broadway
Hillsdale, New Jersey 07642

Library of Congress Cataloging in Publication Data

Main entry under title:

Person memory.

Bibliography: p.
Includes index.
1. Social perception—Addresses, essays, lectures.
2. Cognition—Addresses, essays, lectures.
3. Memory—Addresses, essays, lectures.
I. Hastie, Reid.
HMI32.P42   302   80-10327
ISBN 0-89859-024-8

H M 132 P42 (handwritten)

Contents

Preface

In the summer of 1974, five authors of this volume met at a 3-week workshop on Mathematical Approaches to Person Perception at the University of California, San Diego. The workshop was designed by Norman Anderson and Seymour Rosenberg to promote the development of formal models for the process of impression formation and for long-term social knowledge structures. One explicit goal of the workshop was to explore connections between Anderson's algebraic process models of information integration and Rosenberg's geometric structural models of implicit personality theory.

The living accommodations at the workshop were ideal for informal, after-hours discussions. Although we had known one another casually before this time, these late evening conversations allowed each of us to explore more fully the research aims and theoretical dispositions of the others. At that time we were just beginning to appreciate the relevance of the cognitive processing methods and theory for traditional problems of impression formation and person perception. We were dissatisfied with past approaches, feeling that they had run their course, and we were eager to search out new research strategies that would focus on the dynamic processes involved in impression organization.

In the years since 1974, we began meeting to discuss the new research directions we each, individually, were exploring in our laboratories. A mutual interest emerged in the development of cognitive information processing metaphors for human thought and their application to problems of social perception, memory, and judgment. Within the context of modern research on social cognition, the most distinctive aspects of our work are its empirical focus on how people cognitively represent people in memory, and its theoretical emphasis on models of cognitive organization and process. In a sense, we had concluded that an adequate theory of social memory was the necessary foundation for solutions to many of the questions concerning social perception and judgment that had dominated the 1974 workshop.

The present volume summarizes the work conducted between 1974 and 1979 on social memory by the original members of our "Person Memory Group," with the addition of Donal Carlston, who joined the group in 1977. He had just finished his dissertation (which won the 1978 Society of Experimental Social Psychology Dissertation Award) and was in the process of initiating some follow-up work. His chapter summarizes this research.

In addition to six chapters summarizing individual research programs, the volume includes a general introduction and a concluding theoretical integration. The introduction (Hastie & Carlston) is organized around a social perception and memory system that closely resembles model frameworks from traditional experimental psychology. This system introduces the reader to the information-processing approach that underlies the theoretical discussions found in each of the chapters covering individual research programs. The introductory chapter is also designed to acquaint the reader with concepts that dominate theorizing in current experimental psychology, as well as research methods and major empirical findings in that field. The concluding integrative chapter (Wyer & Srull) presents one specific information-processing model that is designed to integrate the main findings from the individual research programs.

We hope that the present volume will serve several purposes. First, we are eager to present the results of our research on social memory to our fellow scientists, interested students, and the general public. Second, we want to promote the development of the information-processing metaphor as a common theoretical vehicle for psychological sciences. Third, the volume may serve as a text for advanced undergraduate and graduate courses on social cognition. (Title page editorship order was determined by a lottery conducted by Reid Hastie.)

REID HASTIE
THOMAS M. OSTROM
EBBE B. EBBESEN
ROBERT S. WYER, JR.
DAVID L. HAMILTON
DONAL E. CARLSTON

PERSON MEMORY:
The Cognitive Basis of Social Perception

1 Theoretical Issues in Person Memory

Reid Hastie
Harvard University

Donal Carlston
University of Iowa

PRELIMINARIES

The shared concern of the authors of this volume is the development of an adequate theoretical account for the perception , retention, and utilization of social information. For many of us, the goal of developing models for person memory grew out of our desire to extend accounts of the formation, representation, and retrieval of first impressions of other people. The pioneering work of Solomon Asch and Norman Anderson stimulated our interest in person perception. But, as these authors were quick to acknowledge, thoroughgoing process accounts of the mental events and structures underlying algebraic models for information integration are an important extension of those models. The theoretical analyses in this volume all borrow extensively from recent developments in cognitive psychology. This first review chapter is an attempt to acknowledge some of these sources, to introduce concepts that are relatively new to social psychology, and to show some original applications of cognitive principles in social cognition.

Although the chapters in this volume are evidence for the upsurge of research on the topic of person memory, there are actually only about 20 to 30 papers in the literature directly relating to the topic. We cite some of this related work on person memory, but the primary function of this introduction is to outline the framework of a model for memory and to specify the distinctions that give the model its structure. This framework is based almost exclusively on cognitive research on nonsocial memory tasks.

It is important to warn the reader of our theoretical biases and goals. First, we are unabashedly mentalistic. We believe that the most coherent and most useful psychological theories will bridge the gap between stimulus and response with a span of unobservable mental links. We call these intervening processes cognition and believe that eventually a proper theory of the mind will be in the form of a computational model expressed in abstract logical or Automata Theory terms and embodied in an operating computer program. Furthermore, we believe that the major task in cognitive psychology is to discover empirical constraints on the classes of mentalistic models that are plausible.

Sometimes it will be impossible to distinguish between certain classes of cognitive models when only limited observations of stimulus-response pairings are available. The recent results of Townsend (1971, 1974) and J. R. Anderson (1976, 1978) concerning the basic indeterminancy of certain models are some of the most important conclusions from cognitive psychology. The identifiability problem raised in these analyses is a demonstration that under some conditions the cognitive endeavor is hopeless. The Townsend and Anderson papers provide clear examples of cases where *different* abstractly specified process models can mimic one another, producing identifiability problems.

However, we reject the methodological agnosticism preached by Townsend and Anderson and do *not* believe that identifiability problems will turn our models into empirically indistinguishable ghost ships. Similar problems have been raised in other sciences but have not led to the abandonment of the theoretical enterprise. Our faith is that as the models grow more elaborate, the data base against which they are tested will expand, presenting more challenging tests that will wreck less sophisticated models and provide ever more discriminating tests between similar models. We believe that standards of parsimony, plausibility, and completeness in conjunction with a rich data base of behavioral and (eventually) physiological facts will prevent model indistinguishability problems from stopping our theoretical venture. In any case, we feel that it is premature to worry about model identifiability problems in research on person memory. At present, we need to work toward proposing *any* models that are sufficient to account for human performance in social memory tasks.

What must a minimally sufficient cognitive model for person memory accomplish? First, there is almost uniform agreement that any memory process may be divided into at least three major substages: acquisition, retention, and retrieval (Crowder, 1976). Thus, at the very minimum a sufficient memory model must specify the representation, transformation, and processing of information in each substage. Second, our conception of the mind as an active information-processing computer includes the assumption that our environment is organized or structured and that the mind selects and seeks structure in its world. Thus, we must have a theoretical vocabulary to summarize the structure within and between to-be-remembered events. Third, we must make some theoretical decisions about which aspects of the subject's responses we will measure. These issues are often glossed over and solved by reference to traditional practice, but it is important to realize that measurement is strongly determined by our cognitive theory. It seems obvious that we make critical choices when we count number of sentences correct, number of words correct, design measures of organization in recall output sequences, or measure discrimination sensitivity with signal detection theory's d' rather than with an index of percent correct. In fact, we suspect that historically more theoretical progress has resulted from the introduction of new, differentially sensitive dependent variables than when developments occur in stimulus description or new mental constructs are proposed. For example, the recent widespread use of chronometric dependent variables has focused theoretical analyses on the structural form of mental representations and produced dramatic advances in our characterization of the stimulus, the organism, and the response (Anderson & Bower, 1973; Posner, 1978; Shepard & Metzler, 1971).

General Model

Let us consider a prototypical acquaintance situation in which one person (observer) watches a second person (target) acting in a social context (e.g., talking to a third person at a cocktail party). We would like to have a theory that accounts for the manner in which our observer perceives action by the target, stores information in memory, utilizes portions of that information to make inferences about the target (e.g., forming an abstract impression of the target, explaining the target's past actions, predicting the target's future actions), and recalls information later in time.

Figure 1.1 is a schematic diagram of the minimum components for a memory system. Even this simplified system makes clear that any sufficient model must include at least six component substages:

1. Devices to parse and encode information from the ongoing social behavior stream that is available to the observer's sense organs. For example, the social psychologist Newtson's (Newtson, 1976; Newtson, Engquist, & Bois, 1977) experiments to identify the perceptual units within sequences of behavior are a straightforward effort to develop a behavior-stream parsing theory (see Chapter 6, Ebbesen this volume).

2. An account of the encoding transformations that convert raw perceptual information into mentally significant symbol structures. To our knowledge, no research on social perception has directly addressed this issue, although there is considerable research by cognitive psychologists on the

FIG. 1.1. Schematic diagram depicting the major substages in a cognitive model of memory. Arrows represent the flow of information.

initial representation and transformation of visual (Conrad, 1964; Sperling, 1963, 1967; Wickelgren, 1965, 1966) and auditory (Crowder, 1972; Crowder & Morton, 1969; Massaro, 1972) stimulus information.

3. A description of the symbols and relations that are primitives in the "mental language" in which social information is represented and retained. Cognitive theorists have been primarily concerned with differences between representation formats for propositional verbal material and analogue visual material (Anderson, 1978; Kosslyn & Pomerantz, 1977). Social psychologists are beginning to address these issues in their formulation of process models for social judgment (Taylor & Fiske, 1978; Wyer & Srull, Chapter 7, this volume). But again there is no research using social stimulus materials on the topic.

4. An account of the action of events occurring during the retention internal on the mental representation to render some information inaccessible (forgotten) whereas other information is still accessible. There has been a lively argument between proponents of trace decay and retrieval interference process theories of forgetting. *Trace decay* theorists (Brown, 1958; Peterson & Peterson, 1959; Posner & Konick, 1966) argue that the simple passage of time results in the fading or deterioration of the memory trace representation of information. *Trace interference* theorists (Waugh & Norman, 1965; Wickelgren, 1965, 1966) also argue that the locus of forgetting is the loss or destruction of memory traces, but they assign the cause to mental events intervening between the encoding of the original trace and efforts to retreive it. Finally, retrieval *cue interference* theorists (Anderson & Bower, 1973; Tulving, 1974) argue that trace information is virtually undisturbed by the passage of time or occurrence of mental events but that particular traces become difficult to locate or cue as the retention interval lengthens.

5. An account of the decoding transformations that probe, search, or interrogate the memory structure. Cognitive theories separate over whether processes at this stage occur in serial (e.g., Sternberg, 1966) or in parallel (e.g., J. R. Anderson, 1976; Collins & Loftus, 1975), and there is disagreement over the function of memory probes or retrieval cues in accessing and evaluating information (Brown, 1976; Kintsch, 1970; Tulving & Thomson, 1973; Watkins & Tulving, 1975).

6. Finally, the model must specify the nature of decisions that are made when a response is generated and performed (Anderson & Bower, 1972; Atkinson & Juola, 1974; Broadbent, 1971).

We have now taken the first two steps toward a cognitive analysis by positing a variety of mental symbol structures and operations that transform them and by breaking the vast flow of information processes into stages or subroutines. It should be clear that the system in Fig. 1.1 will require elaboration before it can account for mental events occurring during our simple cocktail party scenario. These elaborations take three forms. First, we want to distinguish between the storage in memory of long-term conceptual information about people and new information about the people immediately observed. Second, we will need to postulate a collection of inference procedures, in the long-term conceptual store, that allow the observer to reason about specific actors or about abstract classes of actors. Third, we must have a vocabulary to describe the behavior of an Executive system that orders and monitors events in the memory system we have outlined. In particular, this Executive has the capacity to implement the individual's motives, intentions, and goals by activating and sequencing elementary information processes.

Figure 1.2 presents a division of a social cognition system into six subsystems. First, there is a Sensory Buffer through which all information that is perceived in the environment must pass. Second, information flows through a Short-Term Memory store that interacts with a perceptual lexicon in long-term memory to yield conceptual representations of the incoming information. Presumably this limited short-term channel includes selection mechanisms that are experienced as conscious focal attention. Third, the cognitive system includes a Working Memory that selects information from Short-Term Memory and controls the attention mechanisms in the short-term subsystem. The Working Memory also houses an abbreviated model or schema representing the perceiver's immediate environment as well as inference procedures that have been placed in Working Memory by the system's Executive. Fourth, there is an Executive that is chiefly responsible for interactions between the other subsystems. The Executive maintains a representation of the system's current goals as well as plans or lists of instructions to be executed in attaining those goals. Fifth, the system includes a Long-Term Memory that is divided into an Event Memory Store and a Conceptual Memory Store. The Event Store contains almost exclusively declarative knowledge, specific factual information about social events and individual persons. The Conceptual Store contains an extensive lexicon of declarative information about social categories and generic events or individuals. We have already indicated that this lexicon will be consulted when information in Short-Term Memory is interpreted or comprehended. It also contains all of the procedural information that is used to guide social inferences. These procedures are copied into Working Memory when they are to be executed. Finally, there is an Output Buffer that is the source of signals to the motoric systems when vocal or muscular responses are initiated. (Bower [1975] presents a similar overview of the cognitive system.)

Declarative Versus Procedural Representations. One distinction that will be central in our framework for social memory is between declarative and procedural representations of knowledge. This distinction is often introduced

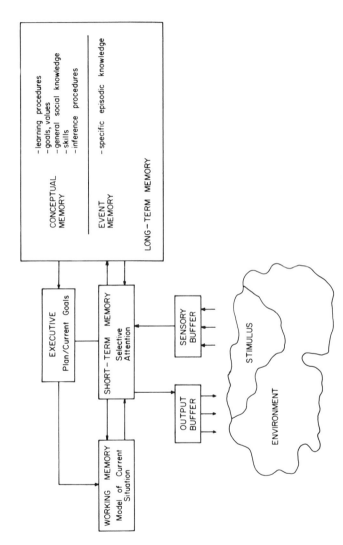

CONCEPTUAL MEMORY
- learning procedures
- goals, values
- general social knowledge
- skills
- inference procedures

EVENT MEMORY
- specific episodic knowledge

LONG - TERM MEMORY

EXECUTIVE
Plan/Current Goals

SHORT - TERM MEMORY
Selective Attention

WORKING MEMORY
Model of Current Situation

SENSORY BUFFER

OUTPUT BUFFER

STIMULUS

ENVIRONMENT

FIG. 1.2. Flowchart representing the major subparts of a cognitive information-processing system for social perception and memory.

7

as the focus of a debate between theorists who believe that most knowledge is "knowing that" (declarativists) and theorists who believe that knowledge is primarily "knowing how" (proceduralists) (Winograd, 1975). Proceduralists argue that an appropriate psychological model would be an operating program device with world knowledge embedded in its programs. What the program knows about the English language, the social world, or arithmetic is part of the programs for operating on those domains (Minsky, 1975).

In contrast, declarativists do not believe that knowledge of a domain is inextricably bound to procedures for its use. Intelligence rests on two bases: a general set of procedures for manipulating facts of all types, and a set of particular facts describing each knowledge domain. A model for the declarativist approach is axiomatic mathematics. Facts correspond to axioms, and mental processes correspond to the proof procedures that are applied to draw conclusions from each particular axiom system (McCarthy & Hayes, 1969).

From a strictly formal point of view, the two positions are indistinguishable. Programming languages of comparable power are available that provide either proceduralist or declarativist representations.

In developing a framework for a theory of person memory, we take a declarativist orientation distinguishing explicit knowledge from procedures that operate on it. Our primary motivation is ease of expression. Within the context of current research and theory on social perception and judgment, it seems easier to separate structure and process than to attempt to represent all knowledge as procedures. For example, many current models for social judgment are represented as algebraic equations in which variable values are supplied as "scale values" (e.g., N. H. Anderson, 1974b). It is relatively easy to think of a common data base (the social knowledge of an individual) that supplies "scale values" for a variety of judgments. For example, information about the covariation of two personality traits represented in a static Implicit Personality Theory structure would be accessed to provide "scale values" for an attribution judgment, a unitary impression judgment, or a decision about occupational suitability. It is the fact that we need not specify all of the possible uses of a piece of information in its basic representation that makes declarative representation seem economical and easy to communicate.

Conceptual Versus Event Memory.   The motivations for a distinction between a Conceptual Knowledge store and an episodic Event Memory store are similar to the grounds Tulving (1972) advanced for a distinction between semantic and episodic memory stores. The Event Memory store is hypothesized to serve as a storehouse for descriptions of temporally located events and individuals. For the example of our cocktail party conversation, information characterizing the appearance and identities of the speakers and a record of the content of the social interaction (actions and verbal remarks) would be represented in our observer's Event Memory store. Furthermore, inferences that the observer makes about the characteristics of the speakers, their motives, their future actions, etc., would also be stored in Event Memory. However, the reasoning procedures or strategies that actually generated these inferences would be located in the observer's Conceptual Memory store. Thus, the social Conceptual Memory store would contain procedures to perform any complex reasoning task as well as containing general categories for the description of people, social actions, and events.

If the observer at our example cocktail party were to learn that one of the speakers was employed as a computer programmer, the observer might make the inference that the speaker was also likely to enjoy playing chess and store this conclusion along with directly observed information in an Event Memory representation of the speaker. The derivation of the conclusion that the speaker enjoys chess would occur when the Conceptual Memory lexicon was accessed to comprehend the fact that the speaker's occupation was a computer programmer. The category, computer programmer, would be connected to a network of related attributes and categories. The observer would be able to use this network of *general* relationships and a set of inference procedures to reach conclusions about a specific individual's preferences, motives, probable future actions, and countless other unobserved attributes. The event-specific facts would stimulate the action of general reasoning procedures and the structure and, to some extent, the content of the Event Memory representation would be determined by principles of organization from the Conceptual Memory store.

One set of inference procedures that has received a tremendous amount of attention from social psychologists is routines to integrate several sources of information about a single individual into a unitary impression. These impression formation procedures have often been described as algebraic averaging rules. In fact, some theoreticians would characterize all inference procedures as algebraic combination rules. For example, Norman Anderson has suggested that social inference tasks as diverse as impression formation (N.H. Anderson, 1974b), causal attribution (N.H. Anderson, 1974a), and evaluative balance judgments (N.H. Anderson, 1977) are all characterized by cognitive algebra. We will remain open-minded on the issue of procedural representation. It seems that some types of social inference can be more easily represented in propositional or set theoretical notation than in algebraic equations.

Executive Subroutine. In this review, we will not attempt to specify the nature of the Executive monitoring system. It is obvious that the Executive would be the locus of control over memory encoding and retrieval procedures, would call and order the operation of Conceptual Memory inference procedures, and would determine the timing, information utilization, and combination rule selection in information integration procedures when impression formation occurs. We assume that the Executive can be characterized by a list of current goals (e.g., to evaluate a person as a potential roommate, employee, or lover; to explain the persons's past behavior; or to predict the person's future behavior) and a set of plans that organize the goals into a hierarchy of superordinate and subordinate goal states and order the activation, interaction, and termination of elementary information processes in the Conceptual and Event Memory stores. These elementary processes may be already organized into cognitive skills or procedures such as the conceptual inference procedures that we have introduced. Execution of the elmentary information processes will be limited by the state of arousal of the person and by structural limits on Working Memory, Short-Term Memory, and the channels connecting subparts of the cognitive system (represented by distinct boxes in Fig. 1.2).

Short-Term Memory Versus Working Memory. The postulation of multiple memory stores with distinct locations, functions, and capacities is probably the best-known characteristic of the cognitive approach. Although the notion of a compartmentalized mind is an old one (e.g., Freud, 1900/1953; James, 1890/1950), cognitive psychologists have taken the divide-and-analyze tactic farther than other students of memory and attention (e.g., Norman, 1970). In the present analysis, we have gone beyond the usual distinction between a very large long-term store and a very limited short-term store to distinguish between the short-term store, the long-term store, and an intermediate-term (Working Memory) store.

The Short-Term Memory in the present system is conceptualized along traditional lines (Atkinson & Shiffrin, 1971; Broadbent, 1958; Waugh & Norman, 1965). A mental representation of a physical stimulus event in the environment is passed from the Sensory Buffer to the limited capacity Short-Term Memory where, with reference to semantic information in Long-Term Memory, it is recoded into a more meaningful mental presentation. We might describe the symbolic representation as being held in a limited capacity "location," or alternately as being in the "active" portion of the larger memory system, or as being in the focus of current conscious attention. These alternate descriptions of Short-Term Memory would be equivalent in a computational representation, and it is probably easiest to think of Short-Term Memory as a short list of immediately available symbols. A summary of the Short-Term Memory's characteristics would include four features:

1. Short-Term Memory is the currently active portion of memory. Active might be defined with reference to recoding or comparison operations, or with reference to the potential activation of (production system) procedures.

2. Processing systems in the Executive or Working Memory (see following) have extremely rapid access to symbols in Short-Term Memory.
3. Temporal order information and physical stimulus surface structure information are relatively prominent in Short-Term Memory.
4. Short-Term Memory capacity is limited to six or seven symbols.

Functionally Short-Term Memory is the "staging area" in which recently perceived or retrieved information is "chunked" into meaningful, useful, or durable ensembles and in which information is translated from one representation code into another code (Posner, 1972; Posner & Boies, 1971; Posner & Klein, 1973; Prytulak, 1971). The other major function of Short-Term Memory is to maintain information in a state of activation to be readily available for utilization by other subsystems, the so-called rehearsal function (Atkinson & Shiffrin, 1968; Craik, 1977; Rundus, 1971).

The concept of an intermediate-term Working Memory is relatively recent. The label Working Memory was introduced by Baddeley and Hitch (1974) because they believed that at least two classes of results (the recency effect in free recall and memory span results), usually explained with reference to the Short-Term Store concept, should be distinguished. The present concept of a Working Memory is not identical with the Baddeley and Hitch system but rather has more in common with Klatzky's (1975) concept of a short-term "workbench" or Bower's (1975) concept of Working Memory.

The primary function of Working Memory in the present system is to represent information about the actor's immediate environment. Such a model would include information about the relative location of physical objects in the immediate setting and information about functional relations between the objects and the actor (see Gibson, 1977, on affordances). Arguments for the existence of a subjective environmental model are based chiefly on intuitive impressions. We do not have a sense of "recreating" our setting every time we blink our eyes or turn our heads. We are able to quickly anticipate the immediate consequences of simple physical changes (e.g., moving a chair, switching on a radio, etc.). We are able to follow or maintain the thread of a convoluted series of conversational propositions. Phenomena such as these increase the plausibility of an intermediate-term, fringe-of-consciousness memory store.

A second major function of Working Memory is to house inference procedures (see following) that have been retrieved from Conceptual Memory for use to achieve current goals. These procedures generate logical, geometric, physical, and causal inferences about events in the actor's physical and social worlds. We postulate that these procedures operate in a limited-capacity Working Memory because our ability to generate inferences simultaneously is limited.

Example Inference. Before we move on to characterize some of the subparts of the Fig. 1.2 flowchart in more detail, we will work through an example inference, impression formation judgment, in the cocktail party scenario. Suppose that our observer has set the goal of evaluating the intelligence of one of the speakers in our hypothetical conversation. This goal is registered in the Executive portion of the cognitive system, and the goal is explicated by consulting the inference procedure for impression formation in the Conceptual Memory store. This procedure is copied into Working Memory, and the Executive initiates attention routines that seek information relevant to the evaluation of intelligence in the ongoing interaction being observed. The Executive also initiates a search of Event Memory at the locus of the speaker's representation in that store. Information coming from the sense organs via Short-Term Memory and from Event Memory is evaluated with reference to the lexicon of social information in Conceptual Memory. For instance, a search of Event Memory might yield the fact that the speaker was an accomplished pianist. Reference to the lexicon of social attributes in Conceptual Memory would produce an evaluation of high intelligence based on the instantiation of the category of generic behaviors "skillful musician." Evaluations of the speaker's personal characteristics and actions would be passed on to the impression formation procedure in Working Memory. The Executive monitors the perceptual and mnemonic search and terminates information seeking when sufficient evaluations have been received to yield a judgment of intelligence. Search may vary in thoroughness as a function of the gravity of the judgment, time pressure to render a judgment, etc. The final evaluation of intelligence might then be entered into the observer's Event Memory representation of the speaker, or it might be passed to yet another procedure to produce further evaluations or to initiate a response such as a verbal comment about the speaker's apparent intelligence.

The point of this example is to show how Fig. 1.2 separates subprocesses underlying the complex impression judgment into distinct subsystems. The behavior of the subsystems can be "unpacked" to reveal theoretically elementary information processes. The notion of an elementary process only makes sense within a very complete theoretical framework. Anderson and Bower (1973), Newell and Simon (1972), and Norman and Rumelhart (1975) all provide example theoretical vocabularies with elementary processes such as "retrieve one proposition," "compare element *a* with element *b*," "write one proposition," and so forth. The interaction of subsystems (e.g., copying the impression formation procedure from Conceptual Memory into Working Memory under the control of the executive) can then be discussed in relatively clear terms.

A complete cognitive theoretical analysis would result in a computational process model comprised of elementary information processes and an elementary representational vocabulary. In the ideal, the primitive operations and primitive vocabulary in the model would be necessary and sufficient to provide accounts for a wide range of cognitive phenomena; they would be mental constructs rather than physiological or physical entities; and they would be minimally powerful computationally to provide a complete but simple model. The best-known attempt to define an economical but sufficient set of elementary information processes and symbols is the Newell and Simon model of the mind (Chase, 1978; Newell & Simon, 1972). These theorists systematically outline the components of a human Information Processing System consisting of a sensory system, a memory, a central processor, and a response generator. Elementary symbol structures are defined for several problem-solving tasks (e.g., theorem proving, cryptarithmetic, chess playing) and a basic set of general elementary information processes (e.g., reading, writing, same-different comparisons) are combined to produce task-specific models. Obviously, the present analysis borrows heavily from Newell and Simon. However, detailed Information Processing System models are not presented here nor is the task of establishing the set of sufficient, economical, and general processes and symbols to account for social cognition completed.

For the purposes of this review, we have tried to present a general, uncontroversial cognitive system that can serve as a table of contents to organize a survey of recent theoretical analyses of social perception, social memory, and social inference. Other chapters in this volume (e.g., Wyer & Srull's conclusion) present detailed models and defend controversial assumptions about the structure of memory representations, the order in which information is retrieved, or the particular inference procedures that are activated in rendering a single judgment.

CONCEPTUAL SOCIAL MEMORY

The Conceptual Memory Store of knowledge about people in general resides in a durable, richly linked and multiply accessible long-term store. The Conceptual Memory Store for social information is analogous to the semantic or lexical memory stores that are hypothesized to underlie language production and comprehension (Smith, 1979; Tulving, 1972). Researchers in cognitive psychology (Collins & Loftus, 1975; Meyer, 1970; Smith, Shoben, & Rips, 1974), have developed detailed set theoretical and network models for the representation of the referential and relational meanings of words. Miller and Johnson-Laird (1976) review current research and theory on the manner in which perceptual routines link the referent of a word to its semantic representation, and Smith (1979) reviews the major theoretical analyses of the representation of semantic *relationships* among lexical entries. A complete characterization of Conceptual Social Memory would specify both the referential and relational "definitions" of all important social concepts, events, and generic individuals.

Some differences between lexical memory models and our proposed general social memory store derive from differences in acquisition and the functions of the two types of memory. First, we think that the lexical memory structure is quite stable across individual members of a language community. If there were a technique to compare the structures of mature English-speakers' lexical memory stores, we would expect to find high similarity across individuals. However, we suspect that social memory structures vary dramatically, even across individuals from a single cultural community. For example, members of different social classes, racial groups, and genders possess similar language habits and would doubtless exhibit extremely similar lexical memory structures. The perception of social behavior would be expected to vary considerably as a function of class, race, and gender, implying that the underlying Conceptual Social Memory also varies greatly. Second, it seems that categorical syllogistic reasoning dominates inferences in lexical or semantic memory; however, causal reasoning appears to be more important in social memory. Thus, a catalogue of the inference procedures in lexical memory would be dominated by principles of categorical reasoning, whereas causal reasoning procedures would be most common in social memory.

The Structure of Conceptual Social Memory

Spatial Models. In social psychology, representations of Implicit Personality Theory (Rosenberg & Sedlak, 1972a; Schneider, 1973) have led discussions of Conceptual Social Memory. Models of Implicit Personality Theory have taken the form of multidimensional spatial domains closely tied to the scaling and clustering methods that have been used to derive them from subjects' co-occurrence, conditional probability, and similarity judgments (Rosenberg & Sedlak, 1972b). The elementary concepts in these spaces are trait adjectives (e.g., hostile, friendly, intelligent, stupid, etc.) and the elementary relations are distances along fundamental dimensions in the space (e.g., social good-bad intellectual good-bad). There are two major failings of the spatial representation that limit its utility as a general social memory structure. First, the spatial models have not been developed to perform their primary function in our overview flowchart, the parsing and comprehension of events in the stream of perceived social action. Most of the research to validate these models has concerned individual differences in social perception (Rosenberg, 1976) rather than the functions of Implicit Personality Theory in social judgment. Second, the structural Implicit Personality Theory models have not been closely connected to process models for social inference such as Integration Theory (N. H. Anderson, 1974b), Balance Theory (Gollob, 1974b; Wyer, 1975), and causal attribution theories (Kelley, 1973; Shaver, 1975).

Set Theoretical Models. Efforts to develop an alternative to the spatial models for Implicit Personality Theory have been heavily influenced by recent theoretical statements in cognitive psychology. The work by Smith and his students on process models for semantic categorical reasoning and by Rosch (Rosch & Lloyd, 1978) on the representation of categorical concepts has stimulated the development of set theoretical, feature-based models of social concepts (Cantor & Mischel, 1977, 1979; Ebbesen & Allen, 1979; and Markus, 1977). Smith and his students (e.g., Smith, Shoben & Rips, 1974) have proposed a model to represent the semantic structures of noun categories and to account for category membership judgments (e.g., "Is a penguin a bird?"). The model assumes that each noun category is represented as a list of perceptual and conceptual features that are ordered with reference to their importance (criteriality) in defining the category. A feature such as "has feathers" may be ranked high in the feature lists of both "robin" and "bird" categories, whereas "can fly" is ranked somewhat lower, at least for the "bird" category where it is associated but not criterial. Category membership judgments are *computed,* when required, by an elaborate two-stage match process that counts feature overlap between the two categories compared. Cantor, Ebbesen, and Markus have all hypothesized that personality trait categories are represented by conceptual and perceptual feature lists, that features are ranked in criteriality, and that category membership judgments (e.g., "Is a generous man an honest man?") are determined by a match process. All three theorists suggest that the features of trait categories will be behavioral, connecting the Conceptual social knowledge Store to perception.

The featural category models are all new and virtually untested, but they directly address the two major weaknesses of the spatial Implicit Personality Theory models: The categories are defined with reference to perceptually available behavioral features, and explicit processing routines have been proposed to account for simple social inferences. The notion of defining a category by listing the features or attributes of the category's members and then describing perceptual routines that would be applied to test for the presence of each feature was suggested by philosophers and linguists more than fifty years ago (Carnap, 1928, 1956). Miller and Johnson-Laird (1976) have recently elaborated this verificationist theory of semantics by describing perceptual mechanisms and conceptual structures that would be sufficient to represent the meanings of color terms and selected verbs and adjectives. Social psychologists (e.g., Cantor & Mischel, 1979) have outlined a similar analysis of the meanings of personality trait terms in which perceptual verification would involve testing for the presence of behavioral attributes.

Script Models. A third point of view is emerging in the domain of general Conceptual Memory Store models. This approach is associated with the computer models for language comprehension proposed by Schank and Abelson (1977). If the categorical model approach focuses on the *noun* category as the fundamental entity in knowledge, the Schank and Abelson focus is on the *verb* as the central carrier of meaning.

The Schank and Abelson analysis begins with the assumption that knowledge about familiar situations is stored as a description of the events that are expected to occur in the situations. This ordered list of events is called a *script.* Scripts group and order the events within a situation and are hypothesized to guide the formation of Event Memory traces. For instance, a script for "Restaurants" would be activated in Conceptual Memory when the perceiver believes it is relevant to his or her experience. The script would serve as a form or mold that determines the ordering of restaurant-related events as they are perceived and stored in Event Memory. One problem with the application of scripts to person memory is that they are designed to structure sequences of events, especially events that are causally related. To date, Schank and Abelson and their colleagues have not discussed the application of script structures to static, individual person information. However, it seems quite plausible to speak of scripts for types of people that would include stereotyped sequences of generic behaviors. Person scripts (e.g., extravert) or perhaps social role scripts (e.g., trial judge) would be stored in Conceptual Memory and activated by contextual cues in the same manner as situation scripts (e.g., restaurant script). Once activated, the script would be copied into Working Memory to direct comprehension, information seeking, inference generation, and the storage of information in Event Memory.

To date, some applications of script or schema theories have extended the notion of a script beyond the situation description functions described by Schank and Abelson (1977). For example, Spiro (1977) and Langer and Abelson (1972) have applied the script vocabulary to characterize inferences drawn in social interaction outside of stereotyped settings such as restaurants, doctor's offices, etc. In addition, Wyer and Srull (Chapter 7, this volume) attempt to characterize schematic aspects of person memory with reference to scriptlike concepts. However, a definitive extension of the script analysis to account for Conceptual or Event Memory in social settings has not yet appeared.

Social Inference

One of the major motivations for postulating a Conceptual Memory is to isolate a collection of inference procedures contained in that long-term store. The reasoning tasks performed by procedures can be divided into six categories: (1) referential and relational reasoning about the meanings of entities and events; (2) causal or attributional reasoning about events; (3) categorical membership reasoning; (4) transitive relational reasoning about entities; (5) social balance reasoning about relationships between individuals; (6) integration of information to form an impression.

We have divided our mental inference procedures in this manner because these categories reflect the division of research paradigms and models in experimental psychology. Also, to some extent, our classes of inference procedures reflect the classes of normative models that have been proposed by philosophers and scientists. Thus, for example, psychological research on syllogistic categorical reasoning has clustered around a unique set of distinctive experimental tasks, psychological models, and normative logical models. Furthermore, models for categorical reasoning have not borrowed from research and theory on "semantic reasoning," causal reasoning, transitive reasoning, balance reasoning, or impression formation.

Of course, this classification of inference procedures is not ironclad. The level of generality of the classification may be uneven. Perhaps from the perspective of a perfect psychological model of the mind, transitive reasoning and balance reasoning are products of the same mental procedures, whereas causal reasoning to infer an actor's intentions might be very different from causal reasoning about moods or traits. It may also be that this system excludes certain important types of inferences (e.g., moral judgments or equity judgments) and includes classes of reasoning (e.g., causal attribution) that may be eliminated by generalizing the functions of other procedures.

It is also important to note that the various procedures would be expected to "call" one another. For instance, causal attribution inferences might occur during impression formation; the results of applying the causal procedures could then become input for the impression procedure. At present, we are still developing characterizations of many of the elementary procedures, and it is too soon to make sensible predictions about the manner in which these as-yet-unspecified procedures will interact.

Referential and Relational Meaning. Almost no research has been conducted on the first class of reasoning abilities, the "semantics" of social behavior. This class of reasoning concerns the referential meaning of behaviors and individuals. How are features, attributes, or perceptual patterns of social behavior used to identify an action? For example, what characteristics of an act lead to its identification as aggression or altruism? How do we identify individuals with whom we are acquainted? On an even more molecular level, how do we decide that someone is reading a newspaper, shaking hands, or combing his hair? Ebbesen's Chapter 6 in this volume addresses some of these questions in its concern with the manner in which the perceiver parses the ongoing stream of behavior to comprehend it. Newtson's (Newtson, 1976; Newtson, Engquist, & Bois, 1977) empirical investigations of social perception are among a few directed at this issue. Newtson's approach has been to show subjects a videotaped sequence of events and then to ask for a subjective parse of the sequence. His focus is on the identification of event boundaries. He has had some success demonstrating that his subjective parsing method locates boundaries between acts that have mnemonic and perceptual consequences for the observer. However, for the present there is no coherent theory of social perception that accounts for our ability to recognize and distinguish actions and individuals.

The second semantic reasoning ability, involving relational meaning, has been studied quite extensively at the level of personality trait terms. Dozens of studies in the literature have researched the semantic relations between trait adjectives, and we have reviewed the models of these relationships (trait space, hierarchical trait categories, scripts) previously. It may be important to distinguish between abstract reasoning about classes of traits, moods, behaviors, etc., and concrete, specific reasoning about particular individuals. We refer to the abstract case as relational reasoning (Is an intelligent person a cynical person? Is a person who plays chess the type of person who reads *Playboy* magazine? Is a happy person a nervous person?) and to the concrete case as referential reasoning (Is Jane intelligent? Does Jane play chess? Is Jane happy?). The conceptual difference between the two types of reasoning is clear; one concerns abstract categories or collections, each of which may have many members, whereas the other concerns category membership or the nature of a particular individual. For the moment, we think that the distinction is worth preserving, but it is clear that general categorical reasoning will occur in what are ostensibly particularistic reasoning tasks. For example, the generic characteristics of an individual's racial or gender categories may influence our reasoning about that individual (Hamilton, 1979), and our attitudes about the desirability of general issues or generic classes of events may influence our reasoning about specific events (Janis & Frick, 1943; McGuire, 1960). The reverse may happen as well with referential reasoning strategies occurring in relational reasoning tasks. For example, cognitive psychologists have demonstrated that particularistic instance-based reasoning strategies may appear in what are ostensibly abstract categorical judgment tasks (Brooks, 1978; Medin & Schaffer, 1978; Tversky & Kahneman, 1973).

It is important to realize that the models for mental structures in Conceptual Memory outlined in the preceding section of this chapter require additional theoretical development before they make clear commitments on processing issues such as performance on relational reasoning tasks. For example, the spatial representation associated with Implicit Personality Theory models may seem to include commitments to specific relational reasoning strategies, but it does not. In this case, there are dozens of plausible algebraic combination rules that might prescribe the manner in which spatial coordinates should be combined to yield similarity, likelihood of co-occurrence, and other judgments. Until a specific relational reasoning procedure is proposed that operates on information stored in the static declarative knowledge structures in Conceptual Memory, the cognitive model for reasoning is incomplete.

Categorical Reasoning. Reasoning about an individual person's membership in categories or about the person's attributes can be reduced to three conceptual types or procedures. First, reasoning deductively by *inclusion:* James Bartlett is a university professor implies that James Bartlett has several unmentioned attributes or properties—for instance, that he has a middle-class salary, lives near a university, has advanced academic degrees, is literate, and so forth. We are using the notion of category loosely here, and these attributes are not criterial but rather are characteristic of individuals in the category. Therefore, although we would expect members of the category "university professor" to have these attributes, lack of the attributes does not disqualify an individual as a member. Nonetheless, we expect individuals to possess these attributes and would doubtless reason accordingly until specific exceptions were noticed.

Second, we reason deductively by *exclusion.* We know that membership in one category may imply nonmembership in another category. For example, if we know that James Bartlett is a university professor, we infer that he is not a rock musician. Again, the logic is not irresistible. The exclusion principle usually operates on "fuzzy" natural categories, and we do not "short-circuit" when an exception appears.

Third, we reason inductively by *instantiation.* When we learn that an individual with certain properties is a member of a category, we infer that some members of the category possess those properties. For example, if we learn that James Bartlett is a university professor and we know that he has blond hair, we conclude that some university professors have blond hair.

Relatively little research has been performed to isolate membership reasoning strategies of these types in social inference tasks. McGuire's (e.g., McGuire, 1960) pioneering studies of social syllogistic reasoning and the recent developments of this work by Wyer (Wyer, 1974) account for most of the literature. The models proposed by these theoreticians combine probability theory with the rules of syllogistic logic. The weakness of this approach is that it does not yield dynamic process models that mimic human mental reasoning processes. Recent work by cognitive psychologists (J. R. Anderson, 1976; Erickson, 1974; Johnson-Laird & Steedman, 1978; Revlis, 1975; and Smith, 1979) has produced process models for categorical reasoning tasks. The application of these models to social reasoning is an obvious next step.

Transitive Reasoning. The third class of reasoning principles that has been studied in social judgment concerns inferences about linear orderings or transitive relationships. For example, if we know that Dick is taller than Jerry and that Jerry is taller than Jimmie, we can infer that Dick is also taller than Jimmie. Some of the earliest psychological research on transitive orderings was conducted with social judgment materials by DeSoto and his colleagues (DeSoto, 1960; DeSoto, London, & Handel, 1965). The spatial reasoning heuristic that DeSoto proposed is still one of the popular models for transitive reasoning tasks (Huttenlocker, 1968; Potts, 1974). However, Clark has argued persuasively that linguistic factors also influence transitive inferences (Clark, 1969).

Transitive reasoning is doubtless important in many social inferences; however, at present we are unaware of research on the conditions that elicit transitive reasoning. For example, to what extent would a social perceiver reason transitively when evaluating the relative strengths of athletes, business competitors, or beauty queens in empirical situations where transitivity may not apply? On the other hand, cognitive psychologists (e.g., Grether & Plott, 1977; Lichtenstein & Slovic, 1971; Tversky, 1969) have identified a number of judgment situations in which intransitivity will appear and have proposed process models to account for this apparent irrationality.

Balance Reasoning. A fourth class of reasoning principles, studied almost exclusively by social psychologists, was introduced by Heider (1958) who called them balance principles. These principles apply to the emotional valences of social relationships. They were originally applied to triadic social relationships (Insko, Songer, & McGarvey, 1974; Zajonc, 1968), but they have been generalized to larger groups (Cartwright & Harary, 1956). There has been some dispute over whether it is necessary to consider constellations of three individuals as a unit or whether the triadic case can be reduced to one or two dyadic relationships (Zajonc, 1968). It seems that most of the balance principle effect is due to a positivity bias and an agreement bias (triads in which there are several positive relationships are seen as pleasant or consistent, and triads in which two individuals agree about an object are seen as pleasant or consistent) acting in concert.

Gollob (1974a) has generalized the Heiderian balance principle to include seven sources of influence on many types of global judgments of sentences in a subject-verb-object form. Gollob has developed a systematic classification of inferences (Which subpart of the sentence is the focus of the judgment?) and a rigorous methodological framework to evaluate the influence of each of the seven "cues" in the sentence. Within this framework Gollob (1974a, 1974b; Wyer, 1975) and his colleagues have studied a broad range of content domains and types of inferences. Neither Heider's balance theory nor

Gollob's subject-verb-object framework provides a cognitive model of the mental processes underlying balance biases in judgment. However, the two approaches provide clear predictions about performance and a vocabulary to describe relevant judgment tasks.

Causal Reasoning. The fifth class of reasoning procedures involves causal reasoning or attribution. Most psychological research on causal reasoning has been conducted by social psychologists, although some pioneering work was conducted by developmental researchers (Mischotte, 1963; Piaget, 1954), and recently some theorists have recognized that causal reasoning is fundamental to many situations of judgment under uncertainty (Tversky & Kahneman, 1980).

There are currently four theoretical orientations toward social causal reasoning. Unfortunately the experimental tasks, causal domains, and available data to which the four orientations have been applied vary considerably, and so comparative evaluation is difficult.

Schemata Models. Kelley (1972, 1973) and Jones and Davis (1965; see also Jones & McGillis, 1976) have departed from Heider's seminal monograph on social judgment to develop typologies of causal schemata for causal reasoning. Kelley's models are called ANOVA attribution models and causal schemata models; the framework developed by Jones and his colleagues is called Correspondence Theory. Both approaches attempt to specify reasoning principles or procedures that accept certain types of evidence or data and produce conclusions about causal relations between events.

McArthur's research (1972, 1976) evaluating Kelley's ANOVA Model exemplifies the type of causal reasoning to which this class of models applies. The subject is given information about an event, for example:

1. Paul likes a particular painting in the art museum.
2. Almost no one likes this painting.
3. Paul likes almost all paintings.
4. In the past Paul has always liked this particular painting.

Then the subject is asked to explain the first event: Why did Paul like the painting in the art museum? Was it something about the painting (entity), about Paul (person), about the circumstances (time), or a specific combination of these factors? The ANOVA Model uses the implicit pattern of covariation in the set of facts to predict the subject's attribution. Essentially the theory views the subject as a "naive scientist" who attributes responsibility for an outcome to the cue that is most highly correlated with the outcome. In the example, Paul is the "cue" with the highest correlation, and McArthur found that about 85% of her subjects attributed his liking to his person rather than to the painting or to the museum setting.

Jones and Davis' Correspondence Theory is similar to the ANOVA Model in its focus on covariation, but it emphasizes the number and desirability of the consequences of an action as well as the action's expectedness. Kelley's Schemata Theory was developed to account for causal attribution in situations where less information is available than in the preceding example based on McArthur's (1972) stimulus materials.

Bayesian Model. A second approach accepts Bayes' theorem as the fundamental attribution principle and evaluates the relative likelihood that one or another causal hypothesis is true, using evidence summarized as probability statements (Ajzen & Fishbein, 1975). The Bayesian Model might be applied to our example in which "Paul likes a particular painting in the art museum" is the to-be-explained event. Ajzen and Fishbein (1975) would represent the behavior ("Paul likes the painting") as B and a possible causal attribution ("Paul has a disposition to like paintings") as H. The likelihood ratio (L) determines the subject's attribution.

$$L = \frac{P(B/H)}{P(B/\bar{H})} .$$

If L is greater than 1, the behavior will be attributed to H rather than $\bar{H}$. If Paul has a greater disposition to like paintings rather than not to like paintings, the event of his liking a painting will tend to be attributed to his disposition. Ajzen and Fishbein show that many of the predictions generated by alternate attribution models (e.g., Kelley's [1973] formulations) can be encompassed by the likelihood ratio principle. Of course, the Bayesian Model is not universally popular (e.g., Fischhoff & Lichtenstein, 1978), but it is still a plausible causal reasoning procedure.

Cognitive Algebra. The third approach is an application of Norman Anderson's Integration Theory that hypothesizes that certain simple algebraic judgment models will characterize causal reasoning (Anderson, 1974a). In this instance, Anderson and Butzin (1974) asked subjects to estimate the extent to which motivation and ability factors caused an athletic performance. They concluded that a simple multiplying rule described the combination of motivation and ability to causally predict performance. However, in cases parallel to the McArthur task example ("Paul likes the painting...") subtractive, compensatory algebraic rules appeared to be more appropriate (Anderson, 1974b).

Cognitive Heuristics.   The fourth general approach to causal reasoning is less formal than the others. Theorists such as Jones and Nisbett (1972), McArthur and Post (1977), Ross (1977), and Taylor and Fiske (1978) have argued that a limited set of "cognitive heuristics" can account for most causal reasoning. The focus of this theoretical approach is on the mechanisms that control attention. For instance, Jones and Nisbett (1972), McArthur and Post (1977), Storms (1973), and Taylor and Fiske (1975) argued that the focal person in an observer's field of view dominates causal attribution (is seen as setting the tone of a conversation, as dominating the conversation, and so forth) because any entity that dominates attention will be judged to be causal. The cognitive heuristics approach is different from the other theoretical orientations because it alone has not made a commitment to a general causal vocabulary or proposed a format for mental representation.

Summary.   There are other approaches to attribution, but these four points of view span the theoretical field. The first three points of view, Schemata models, Bayesian models, and Cognitive Algebra models, have quite a bit in common. All three perspectives describe data structures that accept certain classes of evidence or cues and, when enough information is available, yield causal attributions to entities in the domain of judgment. It is easy to relate these approaches to the process models we have cited when describing relational meaning, categorical reasoning, transitive reasoning, and balance reasoning. However, no single approach, including the very general Integration Theory algebraic models, spans all of these reasoning tasks.

Impression Formation.   Research on social judgment processes has been dominated by impression formation tasks. Norman Anderson (1974b) has conducted a massive research program using the Asch (1946) impression task as his focal method. Anderson distinguishes between *valuation* and *integration* stages of the overall impression formation process. Valuation involves comprehending and evaluating component cues (e.g., trait objectives) that are relevant to the impression. Presumably valuation stage processes would be sensitive to variations in the response scale. If the observer is attempting to form an impression of a target person's likeability, the valuation stage would yield one evaluation of an ensemble of cues; however, a very different evaluation would be produced if a judgment of intelligence were the goal. Asch (1946) hypothesized that there would be considerable stimulus cue interaction in the valuation stage (change of meaning processes). Anderson has argued convincingly that rather little semantic interaction occurs at this stage in the Asch task (N. H. Anderson, 1974b), but he has also emphasized the importance of configural effects in the valuation stage in other tasks (e.g., Anderson, 1977). The present framework would locate valuation phenomena in the procedures for referential and relational reasoning (see preceding discussion).

Following the valuation stage, Anderson postulated the information integration stage that has been the focus of most of his research. In this stage cue information, represented as scale values or quantitative magnitudes produced in the valuation stage, is combined to yield a unitary impression. Anderson has proposed a family of algebraic equations to characterize the integration rules. Anderson's empirical research provides strong support for an averaging model as the usual integration rule:

$$R = w_1s_1 + w_2s_2 + \ldots \quad .$$

Where R is the output of the integration stage (e.g., unitary impression of likeability); s_1, s_2, etc., are the scale values for each cue output from the valuation stage, and w_1, w_2, etc., are weights that represent the importance or impact of each cue on the unitary impression (R). (The w's are constrained to sum to 1, making the model an averaging rule.) In the present framework, the averaging rule would correspond to the impression formation procedure stored in Conceptual Memory.

There are two clear differences between our summary of the impression procedure and Anderson's Integration Theory averaging model. First, we have separated the valuation stage from the integration stage and located valuation in a separate set of semantic inference procedures. Second, Anderson has assumed that the integration rule operates only on cue information immediately available in the subject's stimulus field. This assumption may hold in the versions of the Asch task studied by Anderson, but a general model for impression formation should assume that inferred information and information retrieved from long-term Event Memory will also enter into the integration stage.

Concluding Remarks on Inference Procedures. Obviously, the present taxonomy of six types of inference procedures is a first effort. We have attempted to make the most important distinctions between conceptually different classes of reasoning. We think that this particular classification separates reasoning capacities that are in some sense distinct mental procedures; that, for example, categorical reasoning procedures are "qualitatively different" from causal reasoning procedures. At the moment, it is difficult to be clear about what "qualitatively different" might mean. On the conceptual level, the notion of a qualitative difference would only be sensible within the context of a detailed theory of the mind. This chapter does not pretend to be such a theory. On an empirical level, an argument for qualitative differences becomes even more difficult. The particular taxonomy outlined here is based on our intuitions and on apparent distinctions in the research literature. For the most part, papers on causal attribution do not cite papers on balance principles, etc. Ultimately the test will be: Do successful models of human performance on the two types of hypothetically different inference tasks require postulation of distinct representation structures and process routines?

The theoretical models we have cited tend to be task specific, at least with reference to the classes of reasoning procedures that we feel must be included in any complete characterization of long-term social memory. (Actually, at least two of the approaches are more general than we have indicated. Anderson has applied Integration Theory models to a considerable number of judgment tasks besides impression formation and causal attribution. The Bayesian approach has also been applied to several other social judgments— in addition to its broad use in decision-making research [Edwards, 1968].) There are two important reasons to review these models in a paper on person *memory*. First, all of these reasoning tasks may occur when we think about people. Probably all social judgments can be characterized as combinations of these six types of relatively simple inferences. Therefore, any adequate model of social judgment will have to specify how these inference procedures are acquired, retained in a long-term Conceptual Memory store, and called-up to be utilized in judgment. Thus, any characterization of memory for information about people will have to describe the system of social categories and the procedures that operate on them when concrete person information is perceived, used, or remembered. Second, often we retrieve information about a particular person from memory and then reason with that information using these hypothetical judgment routines. Thus, any ambitious theory of person memory would need to specify these routines to account for the retrieval and utilization of information about people.

In conclusion, we should indicate that there are at least two radically different approaches to the characterization of social inference. One view, espoused by Schank and Abelson (1977), is that any effort to summarize inference making with a small number of generic procedures or principles is doomed. To capture the full complexity of natural reasoning, thousands of distinct situation-specific procedures need to be postulated. Thus, for example, we need separate procedures (scripts) to reason about restaurants, drug stores, doctors' offices, dentists' offices, etc. In addition, these theoreticians propose a general set of procedures for causal reasoning (inferences about plans and intentions). The contrast with the present analysis, limited to six general procedures, is quite dramatic.

We might move even further in the direction of multiplicity of procedures underlying reasoning and hypothesize that all reasoning is episodic or based on a review of specific events. Brooks (1978) and Medin and Schaffer (1978) have made a suggestion in this direction that would account for categorical inferences by assuming that the reasoner samples memories of specific previously encountered instances and makes inferences using elementary judgments of similarity. This approach must assume that the reasoner stores and retains general attributes of instances and that human nature endows each of us with a common sense of which attributes are relevant to judgments of similarity in various contexts. However, these authors make a strong case that instance-based strategies may account for results that have been frequently cited as evidence for general inference principles such as our categorical reasoning procedure.

SOCIAL EVENT MEMORY

We have made the distinction between Conceptual Social Memory and Social Event Memory on the basis of the functions of the two types of memory. The Conceptual Memory Store has three major functions: (1) to contain perceptual routines that are applied to parse and comprehend the stream of social experience; (2) to contain a stable, general, abstract lexicon of social concepts such as trait, mood, and generic behavior categories; and (3) to contain procedures that generate inferences from abstract representations, especially from abstract structures that serve as the forms or frames for specific event information.

Our concept of Social Event Memory refers to the representation of information about specific social events that occur in particular temporal and spatial locations. Obviously, the two stores are inextricably bound together in our framework. Traces are not laid down in the Event Store unless the perceptual routines in the Conceptual Store have been applied. Inferences do not occur in the Event Store unless reasoning procedures in the Conceptual Store are activated and applied. And presumably, learning a social lexicon and even inference procedures requires abstracting from information stored in Event Memory.

An important question concerns the extent to which memory processes in the two stores exhibit similar encoding, retention, and retrieval characteristics. Do the two stores "obey the same laws of memory?" Our answer is a tentative "probably." Smith and his colleagues have addressed this question most directly in research on semantic and episodic memory (Shoben, Wescourt, & Smith, 1978; Smith, Adams, & Schorr, 1978). They find that patterns of inter-item inference are different when sentences are retrieved from semantic memory or from episodic memory or when facts are integrated semantically rather than stored as an unintegrated list. However, they argue that a single, albeit complex, representation code can account for all their results.

A superficial examination of learning, forgetting, and retrieval in Conceptual and Event memories would suggest that learning is slower, forgetting is slower, and retrieval is faster from Conceptual Memory. Thus far these differences do not force us to postulate distinct laws for the dynamic properties of the two systems. A single representation format with one set of writing, transformation, and utilization rules appears to be sufficient to model both systems. However, we will maintain the distinction between the two stores because we ascribe such different functions to Conceptual and Event Memories.

Attributes of Social Stimuli. We have loaded Conceptual Social Memory with general principles and inference procedures. The discussion of Conceptual Memory representation format, the structure of the mental language, has been motivated by considerations of the types of inferences and transformations that are expected to occur in social reasoning tasks. Our discussion of memory for specific social events, an episodic social memory, requires more careful consideration of representation formats. The motivation for alternate formats stems from an examination of the nature of the external stimulus events that we wold like to represent. What classes of objective social information are important in the real social world? What forms must a mental language take to represent these classes of information in a psychologically plausible manner?

We have argued that a sufficient theory of social judgment and social memory must provide a consistent, precise description of mental structures and processes intervening between a stimulus and the relevant responses. We have also argued that such a theory must provide a characterization of the stimulus and the response. This task is especially difficult because one of the distinctive features of social psychological research is the willingness to study behavior in rich, dynamic environments and to attempt to account for a wide range of behaviors.

Ostrom (1975) has reviewed the literature on person information and produced a useful taxonomy of attribute categories. He breaks up the classes of person information into character traits and general habits; physical and biological characteristics; behaviors and affilitative memberships; attitudes, feelings, and beliefs; and social, financial, medical, and family characteristics.

Fiske and Cox (1979) performed a similar analysis and produced a slightly different breakdown of person descriptions based on principles of language development. Fiske's conceptual categories included: physical appearance, behaviors, relationships to the perceiver, characteristic situational contexts, origins, and "functional properties." The Ostrom and the Fiske and Cox nomenclatures overlap greatly, but the Fiske and Cox system is especially rich in categories for behavioral information, whereas the Ostrom system emphasizes cognitive or mental characteristics (such as attitudes). These categories need to be extended to explicitly provide formats or categories to represent verbal information about people. We learn a considerable amount about people in conversations that communicate verbal summaries of trait, mood, and intention information. Some of this verbal information may be treated in the same ways as other behavioral information about a person. That is, similar representations would be established in Event Memory based on observing someone "stealing a wallet" or based on a verbal report that the person "stole a wallet." However, there will certainly be important differences beween the representation of directly observed and indirectly reported events (e.g., when the credibility of the reporter is in doubt or when characteristics of the action are not easily verbalized).

The Ostrom and the Fiske and Cox categorization schemes are products of a blunt empirical attack on the problem of summarizing written impression protocols. These schemes probably include almost all of the types of information that we must represent in Event Memory. However, we would like to provide a more general characterization of the dimensions along which person information varies.

Cantor (Cantor & Mischel, 1979), and Ebbesen (Chapter 6, this volume) have emphasized the distinction between behavior-specific and abstract-predispositional person information. We might posit a continuum ranging from concrete behavioral and physionomic detail through more abstract generic behaviors to highly abstract personality traits. This continuum of information "forms" is important because we would probably propose different representational formats for information at the ends of the continuum. For instance, a script or Conceptual Dependency representation (Schank & Abelson, 1977) seems appropriate for concrete actions, whereas an associative network would be more suitable for abstract trait attributes.

A second dimension that occurs frequently in discussions of person information involves the emotional or moral evaluation of personal attributes. Almost any social attribute elicits an immediate and enduring evaluative reaction from a perceiver. The pervasiveness of these reactions and their significance in controlling the perceiver's behavior lead us to suggest that evaluative valence is associated with almost any perceived social attribute.

Representational Format. Three types of mental codes need to be considered in the representation of social information: propositional formats (the only format considered in our discussion of Conceptual Memory), image formats, and affective formats. The first two codes have been examined extensively in the cognitive literature. A lively debate has flourished on the issue of whether or not a distinct pictorial, analogue code is necessary (or at least very convenient) to represent information presented in sentence and picture displays. For example, Kosslyn and Pomerantz (1977) and Shepard and Podgorny (1978) argue that distinct image and proposition codes are essentials in any psychological theory, whereas John Anderson (1978) and Pylyshyn (1973) have argued that a propositional code is sufficient. The conceptual distinction between the two types of code is fairly clear. Propositions resemble natural language sentences, but they are more abstract and follow certain conventions of form and function that do not necessarily apply to sentences. Three properties must be apparent before a representation can be considered to be a proposition (Frege, 1960): It must be abstract, it must have a truth value, and it must be associated with a system of rules of formation. These three requirements make it incorrect to strictly equate verbal representations with propositions, although they have much in common. Obviously, not all sentences in a language such as English are abstract enough to meet "invariance under transformation" requirements, to evaluate for "truthfulness," or to be considered well formed under the rules of English grammar. Examples of propositional representations in cognitive psychology are found in theoretical papers by Anderson and Bower (1973), Quillian (1969), Schank (1972), and Winograd (1975).

The concept of an image as a representational format is a bit looser. John Anderson (1978) and Pylyshyn (1973) have argued persuasively that an image representation is essentially pictorial: It is the product of perception of an object; it is a whole that may be compared to a percept in a templatelike manner; it is an anaologue structure that preserves the geometric relationships of the scene that produced it. (Note that Anderson and Pylyshyn do *not* advocate image formats as psychological models.) Kosslyn and Schwartz (1977) have proposed a computer model with the most concrete version of an image code in the literature. In their model, an image is represented by a set of points encoding the location in two-dimensional space of the contour points of the imaged object.

For the moment, we doubt that research on person memory can resolve the arguments between the propositionalists and the dual-code theorists. Social stimuli are extremely rich and varied, making it difficult to argue empirically that a specific class of information is representable only propositionally or only imaginally. Furthermore, social judgment responses typically require complex theoretical accounts, and it is usually fairly simple to conceive of alternate propositional or imaginal bases for most of these performances. For example, it is still an open question whether the averaging model for impression formation could be best represented as a logiclike inference from propositional axioms, as a visual montage of physionomic and behavioral images, or as the composite response elicited by several affective inclinations. In any case, our review of the attributes of social stimuli suggests that there is a considerable amount of information about people that can be conveniently represented pictorially. Thus, we would adopt the dual-code position when postulating representational codes for person memory.

In fact, we would go even further than the dual-code theorists and advocate the postulation of a third code to represent affective information. We think that affect can sensibly be included in an information-processing model and suspect that affective information is qualitatively different from visual and propositional information. Our motivation for the postulation of a third code is more conceptual than empirical. Historically, Western Psychologies have distinguished between cognitive and affective components of psychological functions, but there has been very little work within the information-processing tradition on the representation of affect (Deese, 1973). As with the distinction between propositional and image representation, it is doubtless true that a propositional format would be formally sufficient to represent the information we would like to put into an affective code. However, our argument is again that such an economy would become unwiedly and psychologically implausible in many cases.

The characteristics of affective information that lead to the postulation of a third code are subtle and have received relatively little study. First, there is research that implies that emotional information and semantic information are stored and accessed separately in memory (Anderson & Hubert, 1963; Dreben, Fiske, & Hastie, 1979; Moreland & Zajonc, 1977; Posner & Snyder, 1975). Second, there is research that suggests that emotional information is accessed early in the perception of events and that it has pervasive, automatic effects on processing subsequent events (Broadbent, 1977; Erdelyi, 1974). Finally, there is the subjective impression that the emotional significance of events is qualitatively different from perceiving geometric attributes or semantic content.

There are currently no proposals for a mental format to represent affective information. Recent theories of emotion imply that affect includes a motoric or visceral component that is absent from other experience (Cofer & Appley, 1964; Mandler, 1975). In the cognitive vernacular of this review, we would suggest that affective information is represented *procedurally* rather than *declaratively*. The notion that affective information is represented as automatic response tendencies fits the common characterization of emotions as immediate and difficult to modify. However, at present, the most common suggested format for affective or connotative information is as a set of coordinates in a multidimensional space (Izard & Tomkins, 1966; Osgood, Suci, & Tannenbaum, 1957).

Event Memory Structures. We have characterized classes of stimulus attributes and potential cognitive representation formats for Event Memory. To complete our description of the structure of Event Memory, we need to specify potential inter-event relationships. The possibilities for structuring Event Memory are fundamentally the same as the structures that we reviewed for Conceptual Memory.

If we consider the manner in which information about a single individual might be stored, theoretical cognitive psychology provides four plausible candidate structures: undifferentiated associative networks, ordered lists or stacks, hierarchical networks, and elaborate scripts or frames. The first three types of structures are best represented formally as graph structures (Flament, 1963; Harary, Norman, & Cartwright, 1965). An undifferentiated associative network is analogous to an unsigned, undirected graph where events correspond to *points* in the graph structure and associative pathways correspond to *edges*. An undirected graph is one where the relation between two points is symmetric and would correspond to a very simple association theory where associative habits between mental elements would be undirected. Some of the earliest research on serial learning (Ebbinghaus, 1885/1964) rejected this notion by distinguishing between forward and backward associations, and the simplest networks that are serious candidates for models of cognitive structure are both directed and signed. For instance, John Anderson's model, Free Recall by Associative Newtwork (J. R. Anderson, 1972), represents words or ideas as points and pathways between them as directed arcs. The arcs could be "tagged" or "untagged" depending on events during the study phase of a recall task. The "tagged–untagged" state corresponds to positive or negative *signed* relations.

An alternate structuring of memory for information about individuals is outlined by Wyer and Srull (Chapter 7, this volume). The authors postulate that social memory consists of a large number of storage "bins" connected by associative pathways. Bins correspond to the locations at which information about individuals (e.g., Richard Nixon), social entities (e.g., the Republican Party), or episodes (e.g., the 1972 Republican Convention) is stored. Within bins, information is ordered by time of occurrence; the most recent information to enter memory is stacked at the top of its bin, making it most easily accessible. Wyer and Srull also posit that optionally controlled processes such as rehearsal can operate to move information on the top of a within-bin stack or to copy information into other bins. This assumption gives the system flexibility and prevents simple recency principles from accounting for all memory phenomena in the model. The concept of an ordered stack or list has gained currency as a structure for memory since its application in computer science models. The transfer to cognitive psychology probably occurred when linguists noted the usefulness of the "pushdown stack" as a concept of short-term memory to account for certain sentence parsing performances (Anderson & Bower, 1973; Bever, Fodor, & Garrett, 1968).

The use of hierarchical network structures to store information about an individual person is illustrated in a paper by Hastie and Kumar (1979). The assumption was that access to the network is limited to entry at higher level nodes and that search proceeds downward, as though the search process is "climbing" an upsidedown tree. Higher level nodes in the tree represent more abstract information (e.g., trait and evaluative categories); lower nodes represent specific behavioral facts and inferences (which can also be stored in Event Memory). At the lowest levels of the tree, associative links break from the vertical pattern and concrete events are connected to one another. Formation of these low-level connections is governed by the simple associative principle of contiguity at encoding. The perceiver has some control over encoding contiguity in that two events may be linked if they are processed together in Short-Term Memory or Working Memory. Events may co-occur in these stores by occurring together in perception or they may be brought together by the operation of one of the inference procedures. Thus, for example, a new incoming event representation may be linked to an old event representation when the old event is retrieved and copied into Working Memory by a causal inference procedure called to explain the incoming event.

Ordered lists and hierarchical tree structures can be represented formally as unsigned graphs. The ordering of bins with respect to other bins in the Wyer and Srull model and the lowest level connections between concrete events in the Hastie and Kumar model could also be represented as directed unsigned graphs. However, arcs at this second level would not be ordered in a tree structure, but would form a more diffuse network, and bidirectional double links would be common, permitting movement back and forth between elements.

We have mentioned script and frame structures (Minsky, 1975; Schank & Abelson, 1977) in our discussion of Conceptual Memory. Complex structures such as these are candidates for Event Memory as well. For example, it is easy to think of a generic structure for "events in a restaurant" to act as a "mold" into which event-specific information is "poured." Thus, the memory trace in Event Memory would duplicate the basic form of the generic script, perhaps including the *reordering* of certain event-specific unexpected information or the *addition* of expected, but not experienced, information to the Event Memory trace.

Script and frame structures are too complex to be represented as graph structures. They include numerous labeled relations that represent causal, geometric, and categorical information, as well as simple proximity. Furthermore, scripts and frames have a procedural character such that expected default information is inferred when certain conditions are met. For example, subjects told that "John entered the restaurant, sat down, and ordered a cheeseburger" would probably infer that "John read the menu." For the present review, we have avoided the use of complex script structures. Schank and Abelson (1977) make a strong case that it is already time to move to complex representations, but we remain more conservative. The major advantage of the more elaborate representations is that they facilitate certain types of inference making. For example, storing information in a hierarchical structure encodes set membership information in the representation. Thus, certain categorical inferences may simply be read off of the memory trace structure. The alternative, one that we have emphasized in this review, is to "compute" categorical inferences using general inference procedures from Conceptual Memory that operate on specific Event Memory information. The suggestion is that relatively little set membership, sentiment *relationship,* or causal information is directly represented in Event Memory, but that these types of relationships can be inferred from Event Memory representations. Thus, for example, set membership of a perceived entity would be computed by comparing attributes of a specific instance in Event Memory with attributes of a general category in Conceptual Memory. The procedure that would actually be applied to yield the membership conclusion would be the referential meaning inference procedure described previously.

As an aside, we should note that the theoretician who would prefer to encode considerable relational information in Event Memory structures could easily do so. This would doubtless mean a shift to fewer types of inference procedures in Conceptual Memory and to more complex (hierarchical, script, or frame) structures in Event Memory.

Storage and Search Processes in Event Memory.   The characterization of Event Memory in this review is as a large repository for specific fact information. More active procedural knowledge was assigned to Conceptual Memory. We have indicated that this is a controversial choice and that other theoreticians might want to put considerably more inference machinery into Event Memory, or even to ignore the proposed Event–Conceptual distinction entirely. However, we will stay with our plan to keep Event Memory relatively homogeneous and separate from Conceptual Memory. Thus, the dynamic operations of Event Memory can be summarized fairly simply in procedures that record information and procedures that seek and retrieve information.

Cognitive psychologists have devoted considerable energy to specifying the encoding processes that occur as information is transmitted from sensory receptors to short-term stores. However, the processes underlying the registration of long-term memory traces have received scant attention since the all-or-none versus incremental learning controversy in animal and human learning (Restle, 1965).

On the other hand, retrieval processes have received a considerable amount of attention. Early research on the organization of memory (Bower, 1970; Mandler, 1967; Tulving, 1962) attempted to identify the higher-order secondary organizational structures of memory. Along with this effort to isolate Miller's (1956) "chunks" came the distinction between the retrieval of higher-order units and the retrieval of information from these units (Tulving

& Donaldson, 1972; Tulving & Pearlstone, 1966). Even early learning theory-based cognitive models such as the Atkinson and Shiffrin two-store model included analyses of memory search processes (e.g., Shiffrin, 1970). More recently the comparison of recall and recognition tasks has generated much research and theorizing (e.g., Brown, 1976). One point of view (Anderson & Bower, 1974; Kintsch, 1970) holds that recall is qualitatively more complex than recognition. Performance of a recall task requires at least two retrieval stages: a *search* for information followed by a *decision* about the appropriateness of the items uncovered by the search process. However, recognition tasks provide the subject with powerful cues (copies of to-be-remembered items), and the search process is bypassed, leaving only the decision stage to execute. Tulving and his associates have provided convincing empirical demonstrations that suggest that both stages are involved in either task (Tulving & Thomson, 1973; Watkins & Tulving, 1975).

The most recent controversy among cognitive psychologists concerning retrieval is over the operation of search processes seeking information in Long-Term Memory. One point of view argues that several search processes operate at once, racing across memory structures in parallel to reach the target information (J. R. Anderson, 1976; Collins & Loftus, 1975). The alternative is that only one process operates at a time, serially seeking stored information (J. R. Anderson, 1974).

The view of memory advanced in the present chapter would accord most easily with an all-or-none recording of stimulus information in Event Memory and a relatively simple serial search of hierarchical memory networks. Of course, a consistent, plausible Event Memory System could be constructed from almost any combination of the basic assumptions outlined earlier. The all-or-none assumption has become relatively uncontroversial recently; however, there is good reason to remain open on the parallel versus serial search process issue.

Describing the Response. One clear contribution of the cognitive approach has been the development of a much richer characterization of the response than had been available before. This appears to have come about for two reasons. First, efforts to solve the identifiability problem have led to richer characterizations of both the stimulus and the response in order to demonstrate the necessity for postulating many independent mental subroutines. Second, the goal of producing models sufficient to perform the tasks being studied has forced researchers to consider multiple aspects of responding in the task situations.

A history of research on memory could be written based on the evolution of the dependent variable. Early research in the associationist tradition concentrated on measures of accuracy such as the number of items correctly recalled. The primary theoretical device in the associationist approach concerned unitary item strength. The introduction of a distinction between Long-Term and Short-Term Memory stores was accompanied by a breakdown of the measure of total amount recalled into an input serial position curve summary (Atkinson & Shiffrin, 1971; Glanzer, 1972). The serial-position measure allowed researchers to separate recall from the Short-Term Store and recall from the Long-Term Store.

The development of multistore models occurred at the same time as theoretical analyses of the organization of memory became popular. Organization theory brought new measures of clustering (Bousfield & Bousfield, 1966) and subjective organization (Tulving, 1962). More recently, confidence ratings have been introduced and analyzed using techniques from signal detection theory to reduce performance in recognition tasks to sensitivity components (d', discriminability measures) and strategic motivational components (β, threshold measures). Even more recently, chronometric, reaction-time measures have been introduced and used to isolate independent subroutine processing systems (Anderson & Bower, 1973; Collins & Quillian, 1969; Posner, 1978). Currently, there is an emphasis on developing models to account for several response dimensions at once, especially where measures of both accuracy and speed are available (Pachella, 1974; Wickelgren, 1977). A final class of cognitive measures, one that has not been used extensively in research on memory, includes the various self-report protocols that have been collected to study higher cognitive functions such as decision making (Payne, 1976) and problem solving (Newell & Simon, 1972).

Measures of Accuracy. Students of memory have always focused on accounting for the subject's ability to accurately reproduce to-be-remembered material. In traditional free-recall, cued-recall, and serial-recall tasks, most of these dependent variables have been variations on the theme of "probability of responding correctly." Number of items and proportion of items correctly recalled are the obvious measures of item information (Bahrick, 1964; Crowder, 1976; Luh, 1922; Murdock, 1974). Alternate measures have included number correct within a fixed response time or cumulative items-recalled curves (Roediger, 1978). Measures of savings in relearning or number of learning trials to a performance criterion were common in paired-associate and serial-learning paradigms (Postman, 1971).

In standard free recall and cued recall methods, the problem of measuring the rate of intrusions, "recall" of nonpresented items, has rarely been addressed because intrusion rates are typically quite low. However, measures of accuracy in recognition memory tasks have been designed to index both "hit" rates (correct identification of to-be-remembered items) and "correct rejection" rates (correct rejection of new lure items that appear on the memory test, but that were not present in the original study set). An important advance in the analysis of recognition data occurred when the Signal Detection Theory model, developed in research on perception, was applied to memory tasks (Banks, 1970; McNicol, 1972). The Signal Detection model summarizes overall performance with two conceptually distinct indices: an index of memory sensitivity (d') based on differential responding to "old" and "new" test items, and an index of strategic or motivational thresholds (β) based on differential rates of "yes" and "no" responding. A separate line of development, applied chiefly to data from free recall tasks, provides separate indices for recall from Short-Term and Long-Term Memory stores (Watkins, 1974). These analyses are usually based on serial position curve summaries and attempt to separate the recency component (presumed to depend on Short-Term store capacity) from asymptote and primacy components (presumed to depend on Long-Term store transfer rates).

Measures of Structure.   Miller (1956) suggested that the proper unit of memory was the subject-defined chunk, not the experimenter-defined item. This suggestion was followed by a number of efforts to identify the chunk, or higher-order unit of memory organization (Tulving, 1968). Most of this research used order of output at recall in free recall tasks, where subjects are instructed to order recall at will. Two families of indices have been developed to summarize structure in recall output order. First, there are clustering measures that index the extent to which the subject's recall reflects the structure of experimenter-defined categories or the orderings of items in the original list. For example, the experimenter might select words from ten conceptual categories (e.g., animal names, articles of clothing, carpenter's tools, etc.) and then use a clustering measure to index the extent to which recalled items are ordered by category—i.e., with items from each category recalled next to other items from that cateogry (Bousfield & Bousfield, 1966; Hubert & Levin, 1976; Shuell, 1969). The second class of indices attempts to measure the extent to which a subject imposes a personal, idiosyncratic organization on the set of recalled words. Most of these indices require the use of multitrial tasks and depend on the appearance of regularities in recall order from trial to trial. The assumption is that the extent to which recall order is stereotyped is a measure of subjective organization of the list. If the recall order on trial two is similar to the recall order on trial three, then the list has been organized by the subject (Pellegrino & Battig, 1974; Sternberg & Tulving, 1977; Tulving, 1962).

Variants on this approach use subject ratings or sortings of the to-be-remembered items as the basis for analysis (Friendly, 1977; Mandler, 1967).

Chronometric Measures.   Cognitive psychologists have recently started to use measures of events that occur at the time of hypothetical mental processes as well as measures of the products of those processes collected after the critical mental events have occurred. The primary process measure is time to respond. Interestingly, measures of rate of responding in subject-paced tasks such as free recall have not yielded important theoretical advances (Indow & Tagano, 1970; Murdock & Okada, 1970). However, the use of reaction times in discrete trial procedures has produced a flood of theoretical speculations about memory processes (e.g., Collins & Loftus, 1975; Posner, 1969; Sternberg, 1966, 1969) and memory representation (e.g., Anderson & Bower, 1973; Kintsch, 1974; Posner, 1972; Shepard, 1975). There are several special technical problems that arise with the use of reaction-time measures. First, reaction times for a single subject in a single experimental condition are typically not symmetrically distributed around the mean reaction time. This makes it difficult to apply parametric, confirmatory statistical methods with confidence. Several procedures are available to cope with this problem. Nonparametric procedures coupled with a thorough display of the skewed distributions are one possibility. An alternative is to achieve approximate normality by discarding the very slowest responses. This is sensible if there is reason to believe that many of the slowest responses are produced by the subject's failure to prepare for a trial, faulty stimulus displays, or other conditions that are not considered in the theoretical analysis of the task. A third possibility is to transform the raw reaction times (usually to logarithm of reaction time) to produce a roughly normal distribution of transformed values. The major drawback with this procedure is that the conceptual analysis is usually based on the theoretical duration of mental events in real time, and it is possible for the logarithmic transformation to alter the apparent relationships between experimental conditions (Estes, 1956; Stevens, 1955). The most sophisticated analyses of reaction-time data in psychology have gone beyond the focus on mean or median indices of central tendency to summarize the entire distribution of reaction times (Green & Luce, 1974; Ratcliff, 1978). However, this level of sophistication requires the postulation of detailed process models as well as considerable technical expertise at data analysis.

One issue that has recently dominated the use of reaction-time data concerns the speed-accuracy trade-off. The basic problem is straightforward: it is not reasonable to compare reaction times between conditions where accuracy of performance also varies. For example, a mean reaction time of 3 seconds has one meaning when accompanied by an error rate of 5% and has a very different meaning when associated with an error rate of 50%. Unfortunately, the only sensible procedures to deal with this problem are complex and demand theoretical sophistication and large experimental designs (Pachella, 1974; Wickelgren, 1977). A partial, but often practical, solution to the problem is provided if error rates can be fixed at a moderate level (e.g., 10%-30%) across critical experimental conditions, whereas reaction times vary considerably. It is also often the case that reaction times and error rates are positively related (i.e., slower responses are more likely to be in error). This usually simplifies interpretation, at least in comparison to the negative correlation, speed-accuracy trade-off case. The general lesson from a review of the reaction-time literature is that sophisticated theories that predict both speed of response and probability of error are needed before either speed or accuracy data can be interpreted properly.

One interesting chronometric approach is exemplified by the work of Posner and his associates (Posner, 1978). The novel feature of this research is the use of measures of brain responses as well as overt behavioral responses. The research does not attempt to reduce behavioral phenomena to its physical substrate, but the correlations between behavioral and physical systems are used to motivate distinct conceptual analyses of brain and behavior. For example, the discovery of a discontinuity in electrical activity 150 milliseconds after stimulation would encourage the experimenter to study behavioral variables especially carefully at that point in time. Or the detection of extremely similar patterns of electrical activity in two very different tasks would suggest that the tasks share some subroutine processing stages. To date, Posner's approach has attracted only a small following, but advances in psychophysiology are sure to promote more widespread study of brain-behavior correlations. It is still early to look for models that account for both brain and behavior events.

Verbal Self-Report Protocols. It is important to be explicit about the major types of verbal protocols that have been used as data. There are at least three general classes of self-report data: (1) traditional introspective reports of mental events intervening between the stimulus and the response given after the response is produced, usually by experienced introspectors and often using standardized vocabularies (Boring, 1953); (2) post-response reports of events intervening between stimulus and response given by untrained self-observers and often elicited by an experimenter-conducted interrogation (Maier, 1931; Nisbett & Wilson, 1977) (3) talk-aloud protocols collected during the stimulus-response interval to report currently experienced mental events, usually given by untrained self-observers (Duncker, 1945; Newell & Simon, 1972). None of these process measures have been used extensively to study memory. They are usually applied to perceptual, free association, or complex problem-solving tasks. Social psychologists have used analogues of these self-report methods to study "cognitive responding" in attitude-change situations (Greenwald, Brock, & Ostrom, 1968; Petty, Ostrom, & Brock, in press), and some research on person perception has attempted to reduce complex verbal protocols, elicited as person descriptions, to manageable data (Asch, 1946; McGuire & Padawer-Singer, 1976; Pepitone & Hayden, 1955). Within the domain of memory taks, self-report protocols would seem to offer one of the few avenues to measure encoding stage events as they occur. The chapter by Hastie (Chapter 5, this volume) includes an example of such an analysis.

Summary. We have included this catalogue of dependent variables from cognitive psychology because we feel that theorizing about person memory can be advanced by considering more aspects of responding in social tasks. We are particularly keen on increasing the use of reaction-time methodologies in social tasks. In fact, any effort to consider the *process* of producing the terminal response with the goal of decomposing intervening events into substages is a major step in the cognitive analysis.

CONCLUDING REMARKS

Summary of the Framework for a Model of Person Memory. The goal of this chapter is to outline the framework of a cognitive model for person memory. The framework illustrates the assumption that the mental processes underlying a complex performance such as encoding and utilizing social information or forming an impression can be decomposed into subsets of processes or subroutines.

Figures 1.1. and 1.2 provide a graphic rendering of this decomposition in two general flow-charts. The first figure merely serves as a reminder that any *memory* task performance can be decomposed into three stages: acquisition, retention, and retrieval. In addition, the figure indicates that a *minimally* complete mentalistic (i.e., cognitive) model must characterize five features of the performance:

1. provide a vocabulary to describe the stimulus;
2. characterize encoding transformations of stimulus information that occur during acquisition;
3. describe the structure of the mental representation that is created and retained in memory;
4. characterize the decoding function that operates during retrieval; and
5. provide a vocabulary to describe to-be-measured responses.

Figure 2 is a complex but conventional characterization of a memory model as a set of interacting subroutines. Six major subroutines were distinguished:

1. a Sensory Buffer;
2. a limited-capacity Short-Term Memory;
3. a large capacity Long-Term Memory subdivided into Conceptual Memory and Event Memory stores;

4. an Executive Processor;
5. a limited capacity Working Memory; and
6. an Output Buffer.

A major portion of the discussion in this chapter concerned the elaboration of subsystems within the Long-Term Memory store.

The Conceptual Memory system was developed by distinguishing between primarily *declarative* knowledge structures in a lexicon of social categories and events and primarily *procedural* knowledge manifested in computation mechanisms that were identified with classes of social inferences. Conceptual Memory was assigned three general capacities: first, to perform referential meaning tasks to identify and classify social entities and events. This requires the application of referential meaning inference procedures to link incoming perceptual information to addresses in the social lexicon. Second, to make semantic inferences using relational meaning inference procedures. Third, to make categorical, transitive, social balance, causal, and integration inferences.

Our discussion of the Event Memory system concentrated on the manner in which information about unique individuals would be utilized. A brief review of taxonomies for person stimulus information was provided as a first answer to our theoretical requirement to provide a vocabulary for stimulus information. Three formats for the mental representation of person information in Event Memory were introduced: propositional format, image formats, and affect formats. Four structural possibilities were outlined: undifferentiated associative networks, ordered lists or stacks, hierarchical networks, and complex script or frame knowledge structures. Finally, alternative parallel and serial search processes were described.

Relatively little discussion was given to other subroutine systems in the overall cognitive framework. It would take us far from the central thread uniting the research programs summarized in this volume to elaborate our discussion of Working Memory, the Output Buffer, the Sensory Buffers, and the Executive.

This chapter attempted to remain as noncommittal as possible within the range of process and structure alternatives advanced by cognitive theorists. Our goal is to develop a theoretical *framework* that introduces important principles and distinctions from cognitive psychology but that does not settle on specific answers to controversial modeling questions. Our hope is that social psychologists who are unfamiliar with the cognitive approach advanced by the authors of this volume will be able to use this chapter as an outline of critical choice points in the formulation of a specific model for person memory. For example, the decision to make an ordered list the primary structure in a memory store for information about individual persons (see Wyer & Srull, Chapter 7 in this volume) is only meaningful in the context of alternative formulations. This chapter attempted to communicate both the locations of such theoretical choice points and the possible avenues leading away from them.

OVERVIEW OF INDIVIDUAL CHAPTERS

Chapter 2 by Ostrom, Lingle, Pryor, and Geva focuses on the relationship between memory and decision making. Two questions organize the research program: First, to what extent does making a decision thematically organize the factual information on which the decision is based? Second, to what extent is an initial decision the basis of subsequent decisions? This research used trait adjectives as descriptions of an individual and asked subjects to make occupational successfulness judgments. An elaborate network of rating, recall, decision time, and recognition time measures is employed in the research. The research concludes that judgments made at the time of initial encoding exert a powerful organizing influence on information attributed to a person. Furthermore, the initial judgment dominates factual information in subsequent decisions. However, the authors argue that the use of inferred (judgment) or given (factual) information is optional. Alternate instructions or task definitions would presumably increase the use of fact information in a series of decisions. This research addresses issues that have only been foreshadowed by cognitive research and theory. Recent research on judgment and choice (Slovic, Fischhoff, & Lichtenstein, 1977; Tversky & Kahneman, 1973) has only started to characterize the influence of "availability" on decision making.

Chapter 3 by Carlston reports research on the generation of inferences during the initial perception and encoding of behavioral information. The experimental program, using written descriptions of behaviors as stimulus materials, makes a strong case that both experimenter-*given* factual information and *new* perceiver-generated inferences influence impression ratings and the recall of behavioral information. This conclusion suggests that previous analyses of impression fomation that implicitly assume that only experimenter-given information is integrated to render an impression judgment are too simple. The research also makes contact with cognitive research on the *given–new* (Haviland & Clark, 1974) and *fact–inference* (Kintsch, 1974) distinctions in text comprehension.

Chapter 4 by Hamilton, Katz, and Leirer also focuses on events during the encoding process. Subjects were given descriptions of behaviors preceded by an instruction to form an impression of the individual depicted or to attempt to recall the sentences. Interestingly, subjects given the impression task recalled more behavioral information than memory-task subjects. Further manipulations of the structure of the to-be-remembered materials, combined with dependent variable indices of clustering by experimenter-defined categories and of idiosyncratic subjective organization, yield a strong case that the two instruction conditions lead to different Event Memory structures. These structural differences are revealed in differential patterns of clustering and subjective organization as well as in overall amount recalled. These experiments are in the tradition of cognitive research on subjective organization and clustering (Shuell, 1969; Sternberg & Tulving, 1977; Tulving & Donaldson, 1972).

Chapter 5 by Hastie concentrates on the recall of specific factual information that supports or contradicts an abstract initial impression of an individual. The research varied the structure of behavioral information, presented in written or filmed media, that subjects utilized to make a series of impression judgments. The focal empirical issue concerned the relative recall of behavior descriptions that were congruent or incongruent with an inital trait impression. A theoretical interpretation for the results was developed that emphasized differential processing of congruent and incongruent events during the encoding process. The research addresses issues raised by cognitive theoreticians involving levels of processing (Craik & Lockhart, 1972; Posner, 1969) during acquisition and the structure of episodic memory (Anderson & Bower, 1973).

Chapter 6 by Ebbesen is concerned with the perception and comprehension of ongoing behavior. A series of experiments is described in which subjects view videotaped sequences of behaviors while performing the button-press unitizing task introduced by Newtson (1973). Ebbesen proposes two information-processing models to account for the unitizing results and evaluates them with recognition accuracy, judgment reaction time, and button-press data. The conclusion of the paper is that performance of the unitizing task does not mediate memory and judgment performances. The research makes contact with cognitive research on memory scanning (Sternberg, 1966, 1969) and semantic memory structure (Smith, 1978) as well as traditional research on information theory and perception (e.g., Garner, 1976).

Wyer and Srull close the volume in Chapter 7 by proposing a model for person memory that addresses the general issues raised in this introductory chapter. The Wyer and Srull model is much more detailed than the present framework, and it includes specific commitments to alternative structural and processing systems. Thus, the model is precise enough to be the plan for computer programs that would yield explicit, falsifiable predictions of human behavior in person memory tasks. In addition, Wyer and Srull summarize the results of recent research to study the effects of primary memory on impression judgments and retrieval processes to illustrate the power of their theoretical analysis.

These diverse research programs exhibit several common characteristics, in addition to the commitment to develop a cognitive theory to account for the acquisition, retention, and utilization of social information. First, although the experimental tasks are all modeled on Asch's classic method (Asch, 1946), the stimulus material is typically sentential behavioral descriptions or even filmed behaviors rather than unitary trait adjectives. Thus, the research uses rich, concrete, representative materials to characterize to-be-evaluated individuals. Second, there is a heavy emphasis on identifying processes occurring during the encoding and initial comprehension of social information. Although traditional accounts for impression formation have cited attentional processes, (N. H. Anderson, 1974b), little effort was made to discuss qualitative differences in processing or to characterize the structure of impression and factual information stores in Event Memory. Third, the research programs have utilized a variety of dependent variables to index impression judgments, accuracy of recall, organization of recall and time to decide or recall. This is a notable departure from the exclusive focus on a one-dimensional (e.g., likeability) impression rating that characterizes the vast bulk of research on social judgment. Fourth, the research has focused exclusively on how information about individual persons is remembered and utilized. Obviously, research on person memory might start by studying multiple person interactions or groupings of individuals. The focus on individuals seems justified in that more complex cases can be accounted for with reference to simpler cases. However, this approach will doubtless miss some types of information and some organizational structures. For example, research on memory for isolated individuals will underestimate the extent to which inter-individual relational information is represented in memory or the extent to which information is structured in distinctive *episodes* or *attribute* categories rather than by *individuals*.

Is There a Field of Person Memory?.   An important question concerns the extent to which research on person memory is independent of more traditional research on verbal learning, memory and attention, and person perception. Of course, there is no definite answer to the question. None of the fields neighboring the infant subfield of person memory is sharply bounded, and it remains to be seen what directions research on person memory will take. Nonetheless, it is useful to identify the distinctive features of person memory research.

One illustrative comparison is between a standard verbal learning task such as free recall learning and the tasks in the present research programs. In the typical free recall task, the experimental subject is instructed to study and recall a list of common English words. In a typical person memory task, the subject is told to study a list of written behavior descriptions attributed to a single individual with the goal of forming a clear impression of that individual's personality. The instruction to recall behavioral descriptions is of subordinate importance.

First, it is obvious that the person memory task stimuli (sentences) are richer, more complex materials than the list of English words in the free recall task. Second, the dependent variables in the person memory task are more numerous, including measures of impression formation as well as accuracy of recall and organization of recall. Third, we expect considerable between-subject variation in perception of the to-be-remembered behavior descriptions, whereas perception of to-be-remembered words in the verbal learning task is expected to exhibit little individual difference variation. Fourth, although we believe that immediate evaluative responses occur during word perception, these reactions are weak. However, we expect dramatic between-event affective differences for behavior descriptions with some acts eliciting strong positive emotions and others eliciting strong negative emotions.

Fifth, we expect a considerable amount of egocentric review to occur in the social memory task. Subjects are constantly engaged in self-relevance comparative evaluations while comprehending and encoding behavior descriptions. Questions, such as "Would I act in this fashion?", "Would I like a person who behaves in this manner?", "Is this behavior similar to my own actions yesterday?", constantly occur to us as we observe others. These reactions are elicited by lists of behavior descriptions, and they are not elicited by lists of unconnected words.

Sixth, a considerable amount of causal reasoning occurs when we observe another person's actions. Conclusions, such as "He is in a foul temper.", "He is an introverted person.", or "He is unintelligent.", are reached while observing or mentally reviewing another's behavior. Questions, such as "What events might have caused his behavior?", or "What will he do next?", are asked and answered. In fact, we suspect that the most distinctive aspect of social memory processes is the rich flood of causal inferences generated and encoded in memory along with the perceptions that gave rise to them. However, it is very unlikely that causal inferences underlie perceived inter-item relations in to-be-remembered lists of words.

Aside from the unique or distinctive qualities of memory research using social judgment tasks or social stimulus materials, person memory research would seem to provide several major benefits to its intellectual forebears. One contention of the authors of this volume is that research and theorizing about person perception and social judgment will be impeded until an adequate foundation in person memory is laid. Furthermore, the time seems ripe to extend the powerful memory models developed to account for results in traditional verbal learning tasks to new, more complex domains. This strategy will surely lead to the development of more complete theories of memory, and it is a straightforward response to the criticism that cognitive theories are task specific and lack generality (Neisser, 1976; Newell, 1973). Furthermore, social perception and social judgment tasks approach the real-world situations in which we would like to solve practical problems. Development of an adequate theory of person memory is an important step toward a practical, useful psychological science.

ACKNOWLEDGMENTS

The authors are grateful to Robert S. Wyer, Jr. and Thomas Ostrom for useful comments on earlier versions of this chapter. The writing of this chapter was supported in part by a research grant to the first author from N.I. M. H. (MH 28928).

REFERENCES

Ajzen, I., & Fishbein, M. A Bayesian analysis of attribution processes. *Psychological Bulletin,* 1975, *82,* 261–277.

Anderson, J. R. FRAN: A simulation model of free recall. In G. H. Bower (Ed.), *The psychology of learning and motivation* (Vol. 5). New York: Academic Press, 1972.

Anderson, J. R. Retrieval of propositional information from long-term memory. *Cognitive Psychology,* 1974, *5,* 451–574.

Anderson, J. R. *Language, memory, and thought.* Hillsdale, N.J.: Lawrence Erlbaum Associates, 1976.

Anderson, J. R. Arguments concerning representations for mental imagery. *Psychological Review,* 1978, *85,* 249–277.

Anderson, J. R., & Bower, G. H. Recognition and retrieval processes in free recall. *Psychological Review,* 1972, *79,* 97–123.

Anderson, J. R., & Bower, G. H. *Human associative memory.* Washington, D.C.: Winston, 1973.

Anderson, J. R., & Bower, G. H. A propositional theory of recognition memory. *Memory & Cognition,* 1974, *2,* 405–412.

Anderson, N. H. Cognitive algebra. In L. Berkowitz (Ed.), *Advances in experimental social psychology* (Vol. 7). New York: Academic Press, 1974. (a)

Anderson, N. H. Information integration theory: A brief survey. In D. H. Krantz, R. C. Atkinson, R. D. Luce, & P. Suppes (Eds.), *Contemporary developments in mathematical psychology* (Vol. 2). San Francisco: Freeman, 1974. (b)

Anderson, N. H. Some problems in using analysis of variance in balance theory. *Journal of Personality and Social Psychology,* 1977, *35,* 140–158.

Anderson, N. H., & Butzin, C. A. Performance = motivation × ability: An integration theoretical analysis. *Journal of Personality and Social Psychology,* 1974, *30,* 598–604.

Anderson, N. H., & Hubert, S. Effects of concomitant verbal recall on order effects in personality impression formation. *Journal of Verbal Learning and Verbal Behavior,* 1963, *2,* 379–391.

Asch, S. E. Forming impressions of personality. *Journal of Abnormal and Social Psychology*. 1946, *41*, 258–290.

Atkinson, R. C., & Juola, J. F. Search and decision processes in recognition memory. In D. H. Krantz, R. C. Atkinson, R. D. Luce, & P. Suppes (Eds.), *Contemporary developments in mathematical psychology* (Vol. 1). San Francisco: Freeman, 1974.

Atkinson, R. C., & Shiffrin, R. M. Human memory: A proposed system and its control processes. In K. Spence (Ed.), *The psychology of learning and motivation* (Vol. 2). New York: Academic Press, 1968.

Atkinson, R. C., & Shiffrin, R. M. The control of short-term memory. *Scientific American*, 1971, *225*(2), 82–90.

Baddeley, A. D, & Hitch, G. Working memory. In G. H. Bower (Ed.), *The psychology of learning and motivation* (Vol. 8). New York: Academic Press, 1974.

Bahrick, H. P. Methods of measuring retention. In E. A. Bilodeau (Ed.), *Acquisition of skill*. New York: Academic Press, 1964.

Banks, W. P. Signal detection theory and human memory. *Psychological Bulletin*, 1970, *74*, 81–99.

Bever, T. G., Fodor, J. A., & Garrett, M. A formal limitation of associationism. In T. R. Dixon & D. L. Horton (Eds.), *Verbal behavior and general behavior theory*. Englewood Cliffs, N.J.: Prentice-Hall, 1968.

Boring, E. G. A history of introspection. *Psychological Bulletin*, 1953, *50*, 169–189.

Bousfield, A. K., & Bousfield, W. A. Measurement of clustering and of sequential constancies in repeated free recall. *Psychological Reports*, 1966, *19*, 935–942.

Bower, G. H. Organizational factors in memory. *Cognitive Psychology*, 1970, *1*, 18–46.

Bower, G. H. Cognitive psychology: An introduction. In W. K. Estes (Ed.), *Handbook of learning and cognitive processes* (Vol. 1). Hillsdale, N.J.: Lawrence Erlbaum Associates, 1975.

Broadbent, D. E. *Perception and communication*. London: Pergammon Press, 1958.

Broadbent, D. E. *Decision and stress*. New York: Academic Press, 1971.

Broadbent, D. E. The hidden preattentive processes. *American Psychologist*, 1977, *32*, 109–118.

Brooks, L. Nonanalytic concept formation and memory for instances. In E. Rosch & B. Lloyd (Eds.), *Cognition and categorization*. Hillsdale, N.J.: Lawrence Erlbaum Associates, 1978.

Brown, J. Some tests of the decay theory of immediate memory. *Quarterly Journal of Experimental Psychology*, 1958, *10*, 12–21.

Brown, J. *Recall and recognition*. New York: Wiley, 1976.

Cantor, N., & Mischel, W. Traits as prototypes: Effects on recognition memory. *Journal of Personality and Social Psychology*, 1977, *35*, 38–48.

Cantor, N., & Mischel, W. Prototypicality and personality: Effects on free recall and personality impressions. *Journal of Research in Personality*, 1979, *13*, 187–205.

Cantor, N., & Mischel, W. Categorization processes in the perception of people. L. Berkowitz (Ed.), *Advances in experimental social psychology*. New York: Academic Press, 1979.

Carnap, R. *Der logische aufbau der welt*. Leipzig: Meiner, 1928.

Carnap, R. *Meaning and necessity: A study in semantics and modal logic*. Chicago: University of Chicago, 1956.

Cartwright, D., & Harary, F. Structural balance: A generalization of Heider's theory. *Psychological Review*, 1956, *63*, 277–293.

Chase, W. G. Elementary information processes. In W. K. Estes (Ed.), *Handbook of learning and cognitive processes* (Vol. 5). Hillsdale, N.J.: Lawrence Erlbaum Associates, 1978.

Clark, H. H. Linguistic processes in deductive reasoning. *Psychological Review*, 1969, *76*, 387–404.

Cofer, C. N., & Appley, M. H. *Motivation: Theory and research*. New York: Wiley, 1964.

Collins, A. M., & Loftus, E. F. A spreading-activation theory of semantic processing. *Psychological Review*, 1975, *82*, 407–428.

Collins, A. M., & Quillian, M. R. Retrieval time from semantic memory. *Journal of Verbal Learning and Verbal Behavior*, 1969, *8*, 240–247.

Conrad, R. Acoustic confusions in immediate memory. *British Journal of Psychology*, 1964, *55*, 75–84.

Craik, F. I. M. Depth of processing in recall and recognition. In S. Dornic (Ed.), *Attention and performance VI*. Hillsdale, N.J.: Lawrence Erlbaum Associates, 1977.

Craik, F. I. M., & Lockhart, R. S. Levels of processing: A framework for memory research. *Journal of Verbal Learning & Verbal Behavior*, 1972, *11*, 671–684.

Crowder, R. G. Visual and auditory memory. In J. F. Kavanagh & I. G. Mattingly (Eds.), *Language by ear and by eye: The relationship between speech and reading*. Cambridge, Mass.: MIT Press, 1972.

Crowder, R. G. *Principles of learning and memory*. Hillsdale, N. J.: Lawrence Erlbaum Associates, 1976.

Crowder, R. G., & Morton, J. Precategorical acoustic storage (PAS). *Perception and psychophysics*, 1969, *5*, 365–373.

Deese, J. Cognitive structure and affect. In P. Pliner, L. Krames, & T. Alloway (Eds.), *Communication and affect*. New York: Academic Press, 1973.

DeSoto, C. B. Learning and social structure. *Journal of Abnormal and Social Psychology*, 1960, *60*, 417–421.

DeSoto, C. B., London, M., & Handel, S. Social reasoning and spatial paralogic. *Journal of Personality and Social Psychology*, 1965, *2*, 513–521.

Dreben, E. K., Fiske, S. T., & Hastie, R. The independence of evaluative and item information: Impression and recall order effects in behavior-based impression formation. *Journal of Personality and Social Psychology*, 1979, *37*, 1758–1768.

Duncker, K. On problem solving. *Psychological Monographs*, 1945, *58* (5, Whole No. 270).

Ebbinghaus, H. E. *Memory: A contribution to experimental psychology*. New York: Dover, 1964. (Originally published, 1885; translated, 1913.)

Ebbesen, E., & Allen, R. B. Cognitive processes in implicit personality trait inferences. *Journal of Personality and Social Psychology*, 1979, *37*, 471–488.

Edwards, W. Conservatism in human information processing. In B. Kleinmuntz (Ed.), *Formal representation of human judgment*. New York: Wiley, 1968.

Erdelyi, M. H. A new look at the New Look: Perceptual defense and vigilance. *Psychological Review*, 1974, *81*, 1–25.

Erickson, J. R. A set analysis theory of behavior in formal syllogistic reasoning tasks. In R. L. Solso (Ed.), *Theories in cognitive psychology: The Loyola Symposium*. Hillsdale, N.J.: Lawrence Erlbaum Associates, 1974.

Estes, W. K. The problem of inference from curves based on group data. *Psychological Bulletin*, 1956, *53*, 134–140.

Fischhoff, B., & Lichtenstein, S. Don't attribute this to Reverend Bayes. *Psychological Bulletin*, 1978, *85*, 239–243.

Fiske, S. T., & Cox, M. G. Person concepts: The effect of target familiarity and descriptive purpose on the process of describing others. *Journal of Personality*, 1979, *47*, 136–161.

Flament, C. *Applications of graph theory to group structure*. Englewood Cliffs, N.J.: Prentice-Hall, 1963.

Frege, G. Über Sinn und Bedeutung. Zeitschrift für Philosophie und Philosophische Kritik. In P. Greach and M. Black (Eds.), *Translations from the philosophical writings of Gottlieb Frege*. Oxford, England: Blackwell, 1960.

Freud, S. Die Traumdeutung. In J. Strachey (Ed. and trans.) *The interpretation of dreams* (Vol. IV and V of the Standard Edition). London: Hogarth Press, 1953. (Originally published, 1900, Vienna: Franz Deutcke.).

Friendly, M. L. In search of the M-Gram: The structure of organization in free recall. *Cognitive Psychology*, 1977, *9*, 188–249.

Garner, W. R. *The processing of information and structure.* Hillsdale, N.J.: Lawrence Erlbaum Associates, 1976.

Gibson, J. J. The theory of affordances. In R. Shaw & J. Bransford (Eds.), *Perceiving, acting, and knowing.* Hillsdale, N.J.: Lawrence Erlbaum Associates, 1977.

Glanzer, M. Storage mechanisms in recall. In G. H. Bower & J. T. Spence (Eds.), *The psychology of learning and motivation* (Vol. 5). New York: Academic Press, 1972.

Gollob, H. F. Some tests of a social inference model. *Journal of Personality and Social Psychology,* 1974, *29,* 157–172. (a)

Gollob, H. F. The subject-verb-object approach to social cognition. *Psychological Review,* 1974, *81,* 286–321. (b)

Green, D. M., & Luce, R. D. Counting and timing mechanisms in auditory discrimination and reaction time. In D. H. Krantz, R. C. Atkinson, R. D. Luce, & P. Suppes (Eds.), *Contemporary developments in mathematical psychology* (Vol. 2). San Francisco: Freeman, 1974.

Greenwald, A. G., Brock, T. C, & Ostrom, T.M. (Eds.). *Psychological foundations of attitudes.* New York: Academic Press, 1968.

Grether, D. M., & Plott, C. R. *Economic theory of choice and the preference reversal phenomenon.* California Institute of Technology Social Science Working Paper No. 152, March, 1977.

Hamilton, D. L. A cognitive-attributional analysis of stereotyping. In L. Berkowitz (Ed.), *Advances in experimental social psychology* (Vol. 12). New York: Academic Press, 1979.

Harary, F., Norman, R., & Cartwright, D. *Structural models: An introduction to the theory of directed graphs.* New York: Wiley, 1965.

Hastie, R., & Kumar, P. A. Person memory: Personality traits as organizing principles in memory for behaviors. *Journal of Personality and Social Psychology,* 1979, *37,* 25–38.

Haviland, S. E., & Clark, H. H. What's new? Acquiring new information as a process in comprehension. *Journal of Verbal Learning and Verbal Behavior,* 1974, *13,* 512–521.

Heider, F. *The psychology of interpersonal relations.* New York: Wiley, 1958.

Hubert, L. J., & Levin, J. R. A general statistical framework for assessing categorical clustering in free recall. *Psychological Bulletin,* 1976, *15,* 459–470.

Huttenlocher, J. Constructing spatial images: A strategy in reasoning. *Psychological Review,* 1968, *75,* 550–560.

Indow, T., & Togano, K. On retrieving sequence from long-term memory. *Psychological Review,* 1970, *77,* 317–331.

Insko, C. A., Songer, E., & McGarvey, W. Balance, positivity, and agreement in the Jordan paradigm: A defense of balance theory. *Journal of Experimental Social Psychology,* 1974, *10,* 53–83.

Izard, C. E., & Tompkins, S. S. Affect and behavior: Anxiety as a negative affect. In C. D. Spielberger (Ed.), *Anxiety and behavior.* New York: Academic Press, 1966.

James, W. *The principles of psychology.* New York: Henry Holt, 1890. (Dover Books edition, 1950.) (Originally published, 1890. New York: Henry Holt.)

Janis, I. L., & Frick, F. The relationship between attitudes toward conclusions and errors in judging logical validity of syllogisms. *Journal of Experimental Psychology,* 1943, *33,* 73–77.

Johnson-Laird, P. N., & Steedman, M. The psychology of syllogisms. *Cognitive Psychology,* 1978, *10,* 64–66.

Jones, E. E., & Davis, K. E. From acts to dispositions: The attribution process in person perception. In L. Berkowitz (Ed.), *Advances in experimental social psychology* (Vol. 2). New York: Academic Press, 1965.

Jones, E. E., & McGillis, D. Correspondent inferences and the attribution cube: A comparative reappraisal. In J. H. Harvey, W. J. Ickes, & R. F. Kidd (Eds.), *New directions in attribution research.* Hillsdale, N.J.: Lawrence Erlbaum Associates, 1976.

Jones, E. E., & Nisbett, R. E. The actor and the observer: Divergent perceptions of the causes of behavior. In E. E. Jones, D. E. Kanouse, H. H. Kelley, R. E. Nisbett, S. Valins, & B. Weiner (Eds.), *Attribution: Perceiving the causes of behavior*. Morristown, N. J.: General Learning Press, 1972.

Kelley, H. H. Causal schemata and the attribution process. In E. E. Jones, D. E. Kanouse, H. H. Kelley, R. E. Nisbett, S. Valins, & B. Weiner (Eds.), *Attribution: Perceiving the causes of behavior*. Morristown, N.J.: General Learning Press, 1972.

Kelley, H. H. The processes of causal attribution. *American Psychologist*, 1973, *28*, 107–128.

Kintsch, W. *Learning, memory, and conceptual processes*. New York: Wiley, 1970.

Kintsch, W. *The representation of meaning in memory*. Hillsdale, N.J.: Lawrence Erlbaum Associates, 1974.

Klatzky, R. L. *Human memory: Structures and processes*. San Francisco: Freeman, 1975.

Kosslyn, S. M., & Pomerantz, J. R. Imagery, propositions, and the form of internal representations. *Cognitive Psychology*, 1977, *9*, 52–76.

Kosslyn, S. M., & Schwartz, S. P. A data-driven simulation of visual imagery. *Cognitive Science*, 1977, *1*, 265–296.

Langer, E. J., & Abelson, R. P. The semantics of asking a favor: How to succeed in getting help without really dying. *Journal of Personality and Social Psychology*, 1972, *24*, 26–32.

Lichtenstein, S., & Slovic, P. Reversal of preferences between bids and choices in gambling decisions. *Journal of Experimental Psychology*, 1971, *89*, 46–55.

Luh, C. W. The conditions of retention. *Psychological Monographs*, 1922, *31*, Whole No. 142.

Maier, N. R. F. Reasoning in humans II: The solution of a problem and its appearance in consciousness. *Journal of Comparative Psychology*, 1931, *12*, 181–194.

Mandler, G. Organization and memory. In K. W. Spence & J. T. Spence (Eds.), *The psychology of learning and motivation* (Vol. 1). New York: Academic Press, 1967.

Mandler, G. *Mind and emotion*. New York: Wiley, 1975.

Markus, H. Self-schemata and processing information about the self. *Journal of Personality and Social Psychology*, 1977, *35*, 63–78.

Massaro, D. W. Perceptual images, processing time, and perceptual units in auditory perception. *Psychological Review*, 1972, *79*, 124–145.

McArthur, L. Z. The how and the what of why: Some determinants and consequences of causal attribution. *Journal of Personality and Social Psychology*, 1972, *22*, 171–193.

McArthur, L. Z. The lesser influence of consensus than distinctiveness information on causal attributions: A test of the person-thing hypothesis. *Journal of Personality and Social Psychology*, 1976, *33*, 733–742.

McArthur, L. Z., & Post, D. L. Figural emphasis and person perception. *Journal of Experimental Social Psychology*, 1977, *13*, 520–535.

McCarthy, J., & Hayes, P. Some philosophical problems from the standpoint of artificial intelligence. In B. Meltzer & D. Michie (Eds.), *Machine intelligence 4*. Edinburgh, 1969.

McGuire, W. J. A syllogistic analysis of cognitive relationships. In M. J. Rosenberg, C. I. Hovland, W. J. McGuire, R. P. Abelson, & J. W. Brehm (Eds.), *Attitude organization and change*. New Haven: Yale University, 1960.

McGuire, W. J., & Padawer-Singer, A. Trait salience in the spontaneous self-concept. *Journal of Personality and Social Psychology*, 1976, *33*, 743–754.

McNicol, D. *A primer of signal detection theory*. London: George Allen, 1972.

Medin, D. L., & Schaffer, M. M. Context theory of classification learning. *Psychological Review*, 1978, *85*, 207–238.

Meyer, D. E. On the representation and retrieval of stored semantic information. *Cognitive Psychology*, 1970, *1*, 242–290.

Miller, G. A. The magical number seven plus or minus two: Some limits on our capacity for processing information. *Psychological Review*, 1956, *63*, 81–97.

Miller, G. A., & Johnson-Laird, P. N. *Language and perception*. Cambridge, Mass.: Harvard University, 1976.

Minsky, M. A framework for representing knowledge. In P. H. Winston (Ed.), *The psychology of computer vision*. New York: McGraw-Hill, 1975.

Mischotte, A. *The perception of causality*. New York: Basic Books, 1963.

Moreland, R. L., & Zajonc, R. B. Is stimulus recognition a necessary condition for the occurrence of exposure effects? *Journal of Personality and Social Psychology*, 1977, *35*, 191–199.

Murdock, B. B., Jr. *Human memory: Theory and data*. Hillsdale, N.J.: Lawrence Erlbaum Associates, 1974.

Murdock, B. B., Jr., & Okada, R. Inter-response times in single trial free recall. *Journal of Experimental Psychology*, 1970, *86*, 263–267.

Neisser, U. *Cognition and reality*. San Francisco: Freeman, 1976.

Newell, A. You can't play 20 questions with nature and win. In W. G. Chase (Ed.), *Visual information processing*. New York: Academic Press, 1973.

Newell, A., & Simon, H. A. *Human problem solving*. Englewood Cliffs, N.J.: Prentice-Hall, 1972.

Newtson, D. Attribution and the unit of perception of ongoing behavior. *Journal of Personality and Social Psychology*, 1973, *28*, 28–38.

Newtson, D. Foundations of attribution: The unit of perception of ongoing behavior. In J. H. Harvey, W. J. Ickes, & R. F. Kidd (Eds.), *New directions in attribution research* (Vol. 1). Hillsdale, N.J.: Lawrence Erlbaum Associates, 1976.

Newtson, D., Engquist, G., & Bois, J. The objective basis of behavior units. *Journal of Personality and Social Pscyhology*, 1977, *12*, 847–862.

Nisbett, R. E., & Wilson, T. D. Telling more than we can know: Verbal reports on mental processes. *Psychological Review*, 1977, *84*, 321–259.

Norman, D. A. (Ed.), *Models of human memory*. New York: Academic Press, 1970.

Norman, D. A., & Rumelhart, D. E. *Explorations in cognition*. San Francisco: Freeman, 1975.

Osgood, C. E., Suci, G. J., & Tannenbaum, P. H. *The measurement of meaning*. Urbana, Ill.: University of Illinois Press, 1957.

Ostrom, T. M. Cognitive representation of impressions. Ohio State University, *Social Psychology Bulletin*, 1975, *75*(4), (whole issue).

Pachella, R. G. The interpretation of reaction time in information processing research. In B. Kantowitz (Ed.), *Human information processing: Tutorials in performance and cognition*. Hillsdale, N.J.: Lawrence Erlbaum Associates, 1974.

Payne, J. W. Task complexity and contingent processing in decision making: An information search and protocol analysis. *Organizational Behavior and Human Performance*, 1976, *16*, 366–387.

Pellegrino, J. W., & Battig, W. F. Relationships among higher order organization measures and free recall. *Journal of Experimental Psychology*, 1974, *102*, 463–472.

Pepitone, A., & Hayden, R. G. Some evidence for conflict resolution in impression formation. *Journal of Abnormal and Social Psychology*, 1955, *51*, 302–307.

Peterson, L. R., & Peterson, M. G. Short-term retention of individual verbal items. *Journal of Experimental Psychology*, 1959, *58*, 193–198.

Petty, R. E., Ostrom, T. M., & Brock, T. C. (Eds.). *Cognitive responses in persuasion*. Hillsdale, N.J.: Lawrence Erlbaum Associates, in press.

Piaget, J. *The construction of reality in the child*. New York: Basic Books, 1954.

Posner, M. I. Abstraction and the process of recognition. In G. H. Bower & J. T. Spence (Eds.), *The psychology of learning and motivation*, (Vol. 3). New York: Academic Press, 1969.

Posner, M. I. Coordination of internal codes. In W. G. Chase (Ed.), *Visual information processing*. New York: Academic Press, 1972.

Posner, M. I. *Chronometric explorations of the mind.* Hillsdale, N.J.: Lawrence Erlbaum Associates, 1978.

Posner, M. I., & Boies, S. J. Components of attention. *Psychological Review*, 1971, *78*, 391–408.

Posner, M. I., & Klein, R. M. On the functions of consciousness. In S. Kornblum (Ed.), *Attention and performance IV*. New York: Academic Press, 1973.

Posner, M. I., & Konick, A. W. On the role of interference in short-term retention. *Journal of Experimental Psychology*, 1966, *72*, 221–231.

Posner, M. I., & Snyder, C. R. R. Attention and cognitive control. In R. L. Solso (Ed.), *Information processing and cognition: The Loyola Symposium*. Hillsdale, N.J.: Lawrence Erlbaum Associates, 1975.

Postman, L. Transfer, interference, and forgetting. In J. W. Kling and L. A. Riggs (Eds.), *Woodworth and Schlossberg's experimental psychology*. New York: Holt, Rinehart & Winston, 1971.

Potts, G. R. Storing and retrieving information about ordered relationships. *Journal of Experimental Psychology*, 1974, *103*, 431–439.

Prytulak, L. S. Natural language mediation. *Cognitive Psychology*, 1971, *2*, 1–56.

Pylyshyn, Z. W. What the mind's eye tells the mind's brain: A critique of mental imagery. *Psychological Bulletin*, 1973, *80*, 1–24.

Quillian, M. R. The teachable language comprehender. *Communications of the Association for Computing Machinery*, 1969, *12*, 459–476.

Ratcliff, R. A theory of memory retrieval. *Psychological Review*, 1978, *85*, 59–108.

Restle, F. Significance of all-or-none learning. *Psychological Bulletin*, 1965, *64*, 313–325.

Revlis, R. Syllogistic reasoning: Logical decisions from a complex data base. In R. Falmagne (Ed.), *Reasoning: Representation and processes in children and adults*. Hillsdale, N.J.: Lawrence Erlbaum Associates, 1975.

Roediger, H. L., Jr. Recall as a self-limiting process. *Memory & Cognition*, 1978, *6*, 54–63.

Rosch, E., & Lloyd, B. (Eds.). *Cognition and categorization*. Hillsdale, N.J.: Lawrence Erlbaum Associates, 1978.

Rosenberg, S. E. New approaches to the analysis of personal constructs in person perception. In J. K. Cole & A. W. Landfield (Eds.), *Nebraska Symposium on Motivation* (Vol. 23). Lincoln: University of Nebraska, 1976.

Rosenberg, S. E., & Sedlak, A. Structural representations of implicit personality theory. In L. Berkowitz (Ed.), *Advances in experimental social psychology* (Vol. 6). New York: Academic Press, 1972a.

Rosenberg, S. E., & Sedlak, A. Structural relationships of perceived personality trait relationships. In A. K. Romney, R. N. Shepard, & S. B. Nerlove (Eds.), *Multidimensional scaling: Theory and applications in the social sciences* (Vol. 2). New York: Seminar Press, 1972b.

Ross, L. The intuitive psychologist and his shortcomings: Distortion in the attribution process. In L. Berkowitz (Ed.), *Advances in experimental social psychology* (Vol. 10). New York: Academic Press, 1977.

Rundus, D. Analysis of rehearsal processes in free recall. *Journal of Experimental Psychology*, 1971, *89*, 63–77.

Schank, R. C. Conceptual dependency: A theory of natural language understanding. *Cognitive Psychology*, 1972, *3*, 552–631.

Schank, R. C., & Abelson, R. P. *Scripts, plans, goals, and understanding*. Hillsdale, N.J.: Lawrence Erlbaum Associates, 1977.

Schneider, D. J. Implicit personality theory: A review. *Psychological Bulletin*, 1973, *79*, 294–319.

Shaver, K. *An introduction to attribution processes.* Cambridge, Mass,: Winthrop, 1975.

Shepard, R. N. Form, formation, and transformation of internal representations. In R. L. Solso (Ed.), *Information processing and cognition: The Loyola Symposium.* Hillsdale, N.J.: Lawrence Erlbaum Associates, 1975.

Shepard, R. N., & Podgorny, P. Cognitive processes that resemble perceptual processes. In E. Rosch & B. Lloyd (Eds.), *Cognition and categorization.* Hillsdale, N. J.: Lawrence Erlbaum Associates, 1978.

Shepard, R. N., & Metzler, J. Mental rotation of three-dimensional objects. *Science,* 1971, *171,* 701-703.

Shiffrin, R. M. Memory search. In D. A. Norman (Ed.), *Models of human memory.* New York: Academic Press, 1970.

Shoben, E. J., Wescourt, K. T., & Smith, E. E. Sentence verification, sentence recognition, and the Semantic-Episodic distinction. *Journal of Experimental Psychology: Human Learning and Memory,* 1978, *4,* 304-317.

Shuell, T. J. Clustering and organization in free recall. *Psychological Bulletin,* 1969, *72,* 353-374.

Slovic, P., Fischhoff, B., & Lichtenstein, S. Behavioral decision theory. *Annual Review of Psychology,* 1977, *28,* 1-39.

Smith, E. E. Theories of semantic memory. In W. K. Estes (Ed.), *Handbook of learning and cognitive processes* (Vol. 6). Hillsdale, N.J.: Lawrence Erlbaum Associates, 1979.

Smith, E. E., Adams, N., & Schorr, D. Fact retrieval and the paradox of interference. *Cognitive Psychology,* 1978, *10,* 438-464.

Smith, E. E., Shoben, E. J., & Rips, L. J. Structure and process in semantic memory: A featural model for semantic decisions. *Psychological Review,* 1974, *81,* 214-241.

Sperling, G. A model for visual memory tasks. *Human Factors,* 1963, *5,* 19-31.

Spiro, R. J. Remembering information from text: Theoretical and empirical issues concerning the 'State of Schema' reconstruction hypothesis. In R. C. Anderson, R. J. Spiro, W. E. Montague (Eds.), *Schooling and the acquisition of knowledge,* Hillsdale, N.J.: Lawrence Erlbaum Associates, 1977.

Sternberg, R. J., & Tulving, E. The measurement of subjective organization in free recall. *Psychological Bulletin,* 1977, *84,* 539-556.

Sternberg, S. High-speed scanning in human memory. *Science,* 1966, *153,* 652-654.

Sternberg, S. The discovery of processing stages: Extensions of Donders' method. In W. G. Koster (Ed.), *Attention and performance II:* Amsterdam: North-Holland, 1969. (Reprinted from *Acta Psychologica,* 1969, *30.*)

Stevens, S. S. On the averaging of data. *Science,* 1955, *121,* 113-116.

Storms, M. D. Videotape and the attribution process: Reversing actors' and observers' point of view. *Journal of Personality and Social Psychology,* 1973, *27,* 165-175.

Taylor, S. E., & Fiske, S. T. Points of view and perceptions of causality. *Journal of Personality and Social Psychology,* 1975, *32,* 439-445.

Taylor, S. E., & Fiske, S. T. Salience, attention, and attribution: Top of the head phenomena. In L. Berkowitz (Ed.), *Advances in experimental social psychology* (Vol. 11). New York: Academic Press, 1978.

Townsend, J. T. A note on the identifiability of parallel and serial processes. *Perception and Psychophysics,* 1971, *10,* 161-163.

Townsend, J. T. Issues and models concerning the processing of a finite number of inputs. In B. Kantowitz (Ed.), *Human information processing: Tutorials in cognition and performance,* Hillsdale, N.J.: Lawrence Erlbaum Associates, 1974.

Tulving, E. Subjective organization in free recall of "unrelated" words. *Psychological Review,* 1962, *69,* 344-354.

Tulving, E. Theoretical issues in free recall. In T. R. Dixon & D. H. Horton (Eds.), *Verbal behavior & general behavior theory.* Englewood Cliffs, N.J.: Prentice-Hall, 1968.

Tulving, E. Episodic and semantic memory. In E. Tulving & W. Donaldson (Eds.), *Organization of memory*. New York: Academic Press, 1972.

Tulving, E. Cue-dependent forgetting. *American Scientist*, 1974, *62*, 74–82.

Tulving, E., & Donaldson, W. *Organization of memory*. New York: Academic Press, 1972.

Tulving, E., & Pearlstone, Z. Availability versus accessibility of information in memory for words. *Journal of Verbal Learning and Verbal Behavior*, 1966, *5*, 381–391.

Tulving, E., & Thomson, D. M. Encoding specificity and retrieval processes in episodic memory. *Psychological Review*, 1973, *80*, 352–373.

Tversky, A. Intransitivity of perferences. *Psychological Review*, 1969, *76*, 31–48.

Tversky, A., & Kahneman, D. Availability: A heuristic for judging frequency and probability. *Cognitive Psychology*, 1973, *5*, 207–232.

Tversky, A., & Kahneman, D. Causal schemata in judgments under uncertainty. In M. Fishbein (Ed.), *Progress in social psychology*. Hillsdale, N.J.: Lawrence Erlbaum Associates, 1980.

Watkins, M. J. The concept and measurement of primary memory. *Psychological Bulletin*, 1974, *81*(10), 695–711.

Watkins, M. J., & Tulving, E. Episodic memory: When recognition fails. *Journal of Experimental Psychology General*, 1975, *104*, 5–29.

Waugh, N. C., & Norman, D. A. Primary memory. *Psychological Review*, 1965, *72*, 89–104.

Wickelgren, W. A. Acoustic similarity and retroactive interference in short-term memory. *Journal of Verbal Learning and Verbal Behavior*, 1965, *4*, 53–61.

Wickelgren, W. A. Phonetic similarity and interference in short-term memory for single letters. *Journal of Experimental Psychology*, 1966, *71*, 396–404.

Wickelgren, W. A. Speed-accuracy tradeoff and information processing dynamics. *Acta Psychologica*, 1977, *41*, 67–85.

Winograd, T. Computer memories: A metaphor for memory organization. In C. N. Cofer (Ed.), *The structure of human memory*. San Francisco: Freeman, 1975.

Wyer, R. S., Jr. *Cognitive organization and change: An information processing approach*. Potomac, Md.: Lawrence Erlbaum Associates, 1974.

Wyer, R. S., Jr. Some informational determinants of one's own liking for a person and beliefs that others will like this person. *Journal of Personality and Social Psychology*, 1975, *31*, 1041–1053.

Zajonc, R. B. Cognitive theories in social psychology. In G. Lindzey & E. Aronson (Eds.), *The handbook of social psychology* (Vol. 1). Reading, Mass.: Addison-Wesley, 1968.

2

Cognitive Organization of Person Impressions

Thomas M. Ostrom
Ohio State University

John H. Lingle
Rutgers University,
Livingston College

John B. Pryor
University of Notre Dame

Nehemia Geva
University of Tel Aviv

Our thoughts about another person are rarely haphazard or completely jumbled. Nor are those thoughts usually itemized in a temporal or alphabetical fashion as might be the case with a grocery list or class roster. Rather, it seems that most of the things we know about a person fit together. The person's background, actions, friendships, possessions, and other personal characteristics all seem to follow from one another. The person impression makes sense. It appears to be organized.

Even though our intuitions and informal observations support the belief that impressions are organized, that they have a unity and coherence which distinguishes them from other cognitive arrays, the scientific documentation for this belief is rather skimpy. In this chapter we offer an analysis of impression organization. We review past work in social psychology on impresion organization and isolate the several features that appear to underlie most theoretical discussions of the problem. We next show how these fundamental concepts can be effectively represented in terms of modern associative network theory. Finally, we report several series of studies that examine some of the cognitive implications of impression organization.

THE STUDY OF IMPRESSION ORGANIZATION
IN SOCIAL PSYCHOLOGY

Concern with how people mentally organize information about social stimuli first emerged in social psychology through the influence of Gestalt theory (Koffka, 1935; Köhler, 1929). Early social psycholgists such as Heider (1944, 1946), Lewin (1951), and Kretch and Crutchfield (1948) assumed that many of the Gestalt principles that were known to influence the perception of physical objects also influenced social perception. Such organizational laws as figure-ground, continuation, set, pragnaz, part-whole relationships, past experience, proximity, and similarity are discussed in the theories of these authors. The Gestalt holistic view of perception emerged as a guiding principle for understanding nearly all social behavior in some of these early theoretical endeavors. For example, one of the central principles offered by Kretch and Crutchfield in their 1948 textbook on social psychology was that: "Man is an organizing animal. . . . As soon as we experience any facts, they will be perceived as organized into some sort of meaninful whole [p. 86]."

Fundamental Concepts in Impression Organization

A person impression is composed of a heterogeneous collection of elements. That collection may contain observations of the person's behavior, information about the person's likes and interests, knowledge about the person's memberships and possessions, and characterizations of the person's general traits and abilities. Each separate item that is discriminable from the others is termed a *cognitive element*. An impression, then, is made up of the cognitive elements that pertain to the person at the time impression-derived responses are being made. Our concern in this chapter is with how these cognitive elements come to be organized into a "meaningful whole."
      A number of different approaches have been proposed for understanding how people cognitively organize their social world. Indeed, an entire chapter in the 1968 *Handbook of Social Psychology* was devoted to this problem area (Zajonc, 1968). Only a subset of these approaches have been specifically applied to the organization of person impressions. Other applications have been to such cognitive domains as nations, social groupings, and a variety of other attitude objects.
      We do not attempt to review the differences that exist among the various approaches to the study of organization. These differences are discussed in other sources (e.g., Scott, 1963; Wyer, 1974a; Zajonc, 1968). Our concern, instead, is with identifying the concepts that are common to the several approaches. Fundamental to most analyses of the organization of cognitive elements are the concepts of interelement *association* and a grouping of

elements according to their content *theme*. These two concepts are elaborated in the following sections.

Interelement Associations. One of the earliest comprehensive treatments of interelement association was offered by Heider (1944, 1958) in his discussion of unit formation in social perception. Two cognitive elements form a cognitive unit if they are associated with one another. A person becomes associated with (or in some cases disassociated from) a variety of other features of our perceptual environment. A man forms a unit with his car, his wife, his job, his hobbies, his mannerisms, and a variety of traits that characterize his behavior. These associations typically vary in strength. A person may be viewed as very cooperative but only slightly aggressive.

The foregoing examples of cognitive units were restricted to associations between a person and a feature of the person. However, units can also be formed between two features. For example, the activity of parachute jumping stands in a unit relationship with the traits "daring and adventurous," and the occupation of librarian is associated with the traits "quiet and studious."

Asch (1946) was the first to study such associations in the context of impression organization. He used two kinds of tasks to assess the nature of the traits that are associated with the stimulus person. One task involved spontaneous associations that a person generated when asked to write a brief description of his or her impression. Presumably this instruction elicited the most salient or accessible of the person's associations. The second kind of task involved directed associations in which the subject was given a list of adjectives and asked to check those that best characterized the stimulus person. In this task, salience was held constant so that a person's impression response was due primarily to his or her beliefs regarding the strength of the cognitive unit between the stimulus person and the listed trait. (The implications of this task distinction for the study of cognitive response in general have been discussed by Ostrom, in press.)

The method of directed associations has been the one most widely adopted by researchers interested in impression organization in the years following Asch's initial work. In addition to its use in the study of person impressions, it has been employed to investigate the "implicit personality theory" through which people interrelate general personality traits (Bruner & Tagiuri, 1954). This early work has led in recent years to studying the dimensional structure that underlies the perceived similarities and differences between others in our social environment (Rosenberg & Sedlak, 1972).

Almost all research on interelement associations in social psychology has used the methods described previously. That is, subjects were asked to directly report their perceptions regarding the existence of (or magnitude of) an association between two elements. The subjects were invited to appraise their own cognitive world and describe relevant portions of it to the experimenter. There can be no question that this kind of data is important for understanding impression organization, especially for studying the beliefs people have about how their own perceptions are organized. However, the study of impressions should not be restricted solely to these few manifestations of organization.

We argue in this chapter that the time has come for social psychologists to begin exploring additional ways of assessing interelement associations. Our understanding of the nature of cognitive units has been limited in several ways due to the narrowness of this past emphasis on perceived associations. There are several limitations to the past approach.

First, there is no guarantee that people are conscious of all the associations they have to a person. Just as a computer can scan many memory locations in a fraction of a second, the human mind may also operate with comparable speed in reviewing associations to a person. If this is true, it certainly is not reflected in conscious experience. On most occasions, our thoughts about another person proceed at a much more sedate tempo, suggesting the possibility that many associations are filtered out before reaching consciousness. If such a filtering process exists (Erdelyi, 1974), it then becomes relevant to ask whether or not the filtered-out associations exert an influence on our responses that is independent of the associations that reach consciousness. Of course, such questions cannot be answered until alternative techniques are developed for detecting associations, techniques that are not dependent on the association being verbalized by the research subject.

A second problem with studying only those associations that are reported by subjects is that people may not be able to express all the thoughts that occur to them. The time and effort required to report one association could lead to forgetting of other associations that may have been temporarily stored in short-term memory (Roediger, 1978; Sperling, 1960).

A third problem is that even if people are consciously aware of all their activated associations, they may choose to not describe every one of them to the researcher. Some associations may be withheld because they are seen as irrelevant or unimportant to the aims of the research. Others may be withheld because they seem to be illogical or embarrassing. Even though such associations may not be expressed, it is quite possible that they influence impression-mediated responses to the target person.

A fourth problem is that the act of reporting an association may change the nature of its role in the organized impression (Whitten & Bjork, 1977). The strength, or even the very presence, of an association could be affected by having the experimenter call attention to it. By making it salient to the subject, the weight it carries in subsequent decision making could be altered.

We would like to study impression organization as it affects a variety of social responses—responses such as interpersonal judgments and communication patterns. Unfortunately, past research has studied only the manner in which the organization affects self-reports regarding the nature of interelement associations. Yet there is nothing inherent in the concept of association (or Heider's cognitive "unit") that requires it to be studied exclusively in that manner. A variety of alternative measures useful for studying associations (measures of accuracy, structure, chronometrics) are described in the introductory chapter to this volume. Several of these procedures are used in the research reported later in this chapter.

Thematic Grouping of Person Features. As mentioned earlier, cognitive elements are not only associated with a person, but also to each other. It is this fact that underlies the conception that person impressions are organized into a "meaningful whole." The associations we have about another person "fit together" in the sense that they follow from (or are congruent with one, or more) superordinate themes. In the terminology of Heider's balance theory (1944, 1958), such a theme would exist if a balanced set of unit relations existed among all the person descriptors, and between each of those elements and the person. It should be noted that this definition of a theme applies to balance among unit relations (Heider's most generic form of association) rather than the more restrictive sentiment relations. An internally balanced theme of "daring" would emerge, for example, if the person were known to engage in such activities as parachute jumping and mountain climbing and to avoid such activities as visiting libraries and watching television. The former activities have a unit relation with both the person and the theme "daring." The latter two are negatively associated with both the person and the theme. Also, the two activities in each pair are more similar to one another than to either of the activities in the other pair.

This concept of a theme is fundamental to all previous attempts in social psychology to examine how people organize their cognitive worlds. It is inherent in such theoretical terms as "attribute" (Zajonc, 1968), "category" (Bruner, 1957), "concept" (Harvey, Hunt, & Schroder, 1961), "construct" (Kelly, 1955), "dimension" (Osgood, Suci, & Tannenbaum, 1957), "schema" (Kuethe, 1962), and "stereotype" (Katz & Braly, 1933). Each of these several terms evolved within different conceptual frameworks and so differ somewhat in their definitions. However, they all share the concept of a "theme" as we have discussed it previously. This concept can also be found in work on learning and memory. A discussion of these ideas can be found in Lingle and Ostrom (in press).

Despite this abundance of theme-related concepts in social psychology, very little is known about how particular themes arise in impression organization. Why do we think of one person as intelligent, another as witty, and a third as adventuresome? When our information about a person can be organized in more than one way, why does one of the potential themes become dominant, whereas the remaining possibilities are ignored or subordinated?

Some answers to these questions were sought in Asch's (1946) work on first impressions. He presented his subjects with a person description composed of a list of trait adjectives. Some traits (or more generally, person features) were thought to be especially salient, vivid, or otherwise dominant so as to emerge as the focus of organization. In Asch's research, traits such as warm and cold appeared to occupy this central position, whereas traits like polite and blunt were more peripheral. Asch found that the order in which information items are presented could influence the nature of the theme. He found that the first items in the sequence tended to provide a thematic organization into which the later items were integrated (this was termed a "primacy" effect).

Most of the research on themes in person impressions that followed Asch's work examined the "structure" of impressions. Using the techniques of factor analysis and multidimensional scaling, investigators have studied the number of themes (or dimensions) people typically use when ascribing traits to others (e.g., Rosenberg & Sedlak, 1972). These procedures also allow the investigator to qualitatively label the dimensions. For example, Rosenberg, Nelson, and Vivekananthan (1968) found that two dimensions (one that discriminated good social from bad social and another that differentiated between good intellectual and bad intellectual) were used by their subjects when making impression ratings. Procedures also exist for measuring other structural properties such as complexity, degree of organization, differentiation, homogeneity, segmentation, unity, and valence (Zajonc, 1960, 1968).

Most of this "structuralist" research has been directed toward describing the themes people use (and in some cases, the relationships between themes) in their impressions of others. Unlike Asch's work, it has done little to establish the processes by which one theme rather than another becomes dominant. Perhaps one of the most valuable contributions of the "structuralist" approach was to establish that a single impression may be organized around more than one theme. This possibly was not emphasized in the research of Asch.

Effects of Thematic Organization

Most prior research on impression organization has been overly restrictive in the kinds of social behavior thought to be relevant to the study of organization. This work looked at the extent to which a theme was related to other cognitive elements, but only as subjectively perceived by the person. Although it certainly is of interest to understand how people perceive these associations, there are other classes of social behavior that are affected by the thematic organization of impressions. Not only should other kinds of social behavior be studied because of interest in the behaviors themselves, but also because such research should improve our understanding of the organizational process. The research reported later in this chapter studies the effects of organization on memory, repeated judgments, and decision time.

Memory is involved in a great deal of social interaction. In conversations we relate anecdotes, describe physical features, and provide character analyses of a variety of current and past acquaintances. It would be expected that an organizing theme should affect the kinds of information items available in memory; memory should be better for theme-relevant than theme-irrelevant information. Because the kind of information shared in conversation is dependent on what information can be remembered, knowing the effects of themes on memory is integral to understanding social communication.

Most of the people who are important to us are people with whom we have repeated contact and about whom we make repeated judgments. Those judgments involve such decisions as whether or not to seek help on a term paper or to extend an invitation to a party. The question of interest here is how themes influence repeated social decisions. Are later decisions independent of the earlier ones and based on a review of specific facts known about the person? Or do people sometimes generalize directly from the theme itself?

There are no doubt other important consequences of impression organization beyond the ones studied in this chapter. For example, do themes affect the kinds of information items we notice and attend to when learning more about the person? Do themes affect the nature of the information search we initiate when called upon to make an important decision about another (e.g., take on as a roommate)? Are we more resistant to changing our beliefs about a person's characteristics when those characteristics are theme relevant as opposed to theme irrelevant? All these questions are yet to be answered.

COGNITIVE ANALYSIS
OF IMPRESSION ORGANIZATION

It was argued in the preceding section that three concepts were at the core of most social psychological attempts to understand impression organization, namely, cognitive elements, interelement association, and themes. The second major point in that section was that future research on this problem should move away from exclusive dependence on data derived from subjective reports of associations. The purpose of the remainder of this chapter is to show how a cognitive analysis of impressions can substantially advance these social psychological concerns. Of course, a comprehensive understanding of impression organization would involve the many complexities of cognitive processing that are outlined in other chapters in this book (see especially Chapter 1 by Hastie & Carlston and Chapter 7 by Wyer & Srull). Our objective here is much more limited. We propose to illustrate how the previous social psychological concerns regarding impressions can be advanced by viewing them from a cognitive perspective.

In the early and middle 1970s, cognitive theorists began work on associative network models of memory (e.g., Anderson & Bower, 1973; Collins & Loftus, 1975; Wyer & Carlston, 1979). One of the goals of these theories is to understand sequential processes in human thought. Why, they ask, does one thought follow from another? Impression organization would be analyzed and explained by these theories in terms of the sequence of thoughts the perceiver has about the target person. This conceptual assumption is very different from the "holistic" Gestalt orientation that guided the early research on the problem in social psychology.

In our presentation of an associative network analysis of impression organization, we will not adhere strictly to any one of the models that have been proposed to date. Instead we draw upon the terminology and spatial metaphor that are common to all.

Cognitive elements are termed *nodes* by these theories. Many nodes correspond to concepts for which we have approximate semantic labels (e.g., run, face, or cloud); other nodes can't be labeled so precisely (e.g., the aesthetic experience of observing the setting sun from a deserted beach). Indeed, it is useful to posit the existence of a person node that cannot be labeled by using any feature of the person such as his name, race, or occupation. This is because each feature is represented in the system by a separate node of its own. The person node, then, represents the central person concept to which all nodes representing relevant cognitions about the person are associated.

Nodes are connected to one another by *pathways*. When one node is activated (e.g., we learn a friend has failed his psychology quiz), other nearby nodes will be activated (e.g., the friend failed his math quiz on the same day) and remote nodes will not (e.g., the friend has blue eyes). Nodes connected by short pathways are more closely associated (and therefore more likely to follow each other in thought) than those connected by long (or no) pathways.

Any person feature that stands in a unit relation (in Heider's terms) to a person would be represented by a pathway connecting the person node and the feature node. However, there may or may not be a direct pathway connecting any particular pair of feature nodes. Within this conceptual system, a feature node would become an "organizing theme" (or a theme node) to the extent that it is: (1) connected to the person by a very short pathway; and (2) connected to a large percentage of the other feature nodes by relatively short pathways. For example, the characteristic "belligerent" would become a theme node if all the behaviors one observed were seen as being of a hostile, aggressive, or threatening nature. Defined in this manner, a theme node will be readily activated once the person node is activated. Once the theme node is activated, the related feature nodes become immediately accessible.

There are several important implications of this approach for understanding themes. It leaves open the question of whether or not the person is aware of the strength (or existence) of an association. One need not be committed conceptually or methodologically to the assumption that people can accurately describe their cognitive associations.

Second, this orientation makes us aware of the possibility that almost any descriptor node could emerge as a theme. For one person it might be his race, for another his flowing red hair, for a third his polished and urbane manner, for a fourth a trait such as intelligence, and for a fifth his occupation (e.g., the typical professor). This abundance of possible themes suggests that the search for "fundamental" dimensions of person organization that has typified the structuralist approach is completely futile, at least in regard to how we organize our impressions of specific individuals.

Third, and most important, the associative network orientation offers some guidance in understanding how a node may come to serve as an organizing theme. To acquire that status, it must be linked to the person node, and pathways to other feature nodes of the person must be established. Next, we discuss several ways this could occur.

Determinants of Theme Nodes

A theme node might be based on a specific item of information received about a person. An example of this was when Asch (1946) directly informed his subjects of the traits *warm* or *cold.* In this case, the associative network representing the person would be collectively determined by the theme node, the other items received, and their semantic associates. It is of interest to note that the particular semantic associates brought to mind by a representation may be collectively determined by the particular theme and items that constitute the representation. For instance, the information item "determined" when presented in conjunction with "warm" may bring to mind "steadfast," but when presented in conjunction with "cold," "determined" may bring to mind "stubborn" (Ostrom & Essex, 1972; Wyer, 1974b; Zanna & Hamilton, 1977).

A theme node can also be derived by the perceiver and need not represent an explicit item of person information. Trait labels, such as extravert and intelligent, can represent abstractions from observed behavior. If each of several information items is closely linked to the same node, that node will be activated each time each of the descriptor nodes is activated and thereby come to take a central position in the network. For example, the "intelligent" node is activated three separate times upon learning the three facts that the person is a member of Phi Beta Kappa, solved a difficult puzzle, and beat Bobby Fisher in chess. Repeated activation of the "intelligent" node in conjunction with the person node would establish a short pathway between the two, allowing the theme of intelligent to emerge.

There is at least one more way theme nodes can be created. This third approach provides the basis of the empirical work we report later in the chapter. As indicated in the first chapter of this volume, most thought is purposive (or goal oriented) in nature. In most tasks (and many interaction settings), people expect to be making judgments and decisions regarding other people. When explicit judgments are required, judgments themselves may activate a theme node and create pathways to the other nodes representing items of person information. For example, employment managers must decide whether or not to hire an applicant for a specific job (e.g., an insurance sales person). Items of person information relevant to the job (e.g., friendly, persuasive) are connected by short pathways to the occupation node and irrelevant items (e.g., strong, gentle) are more remotely associated. Because decision tasks require explicit activation of these nodes and consideration of these pathways, it is reasonable to posit that such judgment nodes can acquire thematic properties. This supposition was tested and confirmed in our research.

We turn now to the research that has emerged from this analysis of impression organization. The first section examines the effect of themes on memory and the second presents work of how themes can affect judgments.

THE INFLUENCE OF THEMES ON MEMORY

People have a variety of plans and goals when interacting with and acquiring information about others. Sometimes this involves forming a general impression, and sometimes it requires specific judgments or decisions about others. When a judgment is made, it may become a thematic node around which information about the person is organized. For example, a judgment made concerning a graduate school applicant's proficiency as a graduate student may serve as an organizing theme for the cognitive representation of information concerning that applicant. One of the consequences of such a thematic organization is that theme-relevant information should be more readily available in memory than theme-irrelevant information. In the graduate student example, information relevant to the perceiver's judgment (e.g., GPA, GRE scores, research experience, etc.) would be cognitively represented as a thematically organized cluster and hence should be more easily accessed from memory than information irrelevant to the judgment (e.g., hometown, extracurricular activities, physical appearance, etc.).

The series of studies in this section investigated the organizing influence that an initial person judgment can have upon the representation of information about the person in memory. In the first two studies, the influence of an initial person judgment upon subsequent recall and recognition of person information was investigated. In the other three studies, the cognitive processes that are involved in the organization of a person impression were explored in greater detail.

All of the studies reported here utilized a paradigm in which subjects read a list of characteristics describing a hypothetical target person and made a judgment (on a 21-point scale) concerning the target's proficiency at an occupation (e.g., bank teller, pilot, comedian, etc.). After a period of time (ranging over the five studies from immediately to one week), subjects were given a test to determine whether more theme-relevant than theme-irrelevant items were remembered. In all experiments, several stimulus replications were used to provide greater generalizibility.

Relevant Items Are Remembered
Better than Irrelevant Items

In the inital experiment, reported in Lingle, Geva, Ostrom, Leippe, and Baumgardner (1979), subjects were given a list of eight traits describing a target person and were asked to predict the target person's success at a designated occupation. Through pretesting, four of the eight characteristics were chosen to be relevant to the decision and the other four were irrelevant to that occupation. For counterbalancing purposes, other subjects were given an occupational judgment relevant to the latter four traits and irrelevant to the former. On the next page of the booklet, subjects were unexpectedly asked to recall as many of the traits as they could. It was found that subjects were able to recall significantly ($p < .002$) more characteristics that were relevant to their judgment than traits that were irrelevant ($Ms = 2.49$ and 2.09, respectively). Theoretically, judgment-relevant items were more closely linked to the theme node than were the judgment-irrelevant items. The superior recall of judgment or theme-relevant items parallels the findings of Dooling and Lachman (1971) and Sulin and Dooling (1974) concerning the facilitating effects of thematic organization on recall.

In associative network terminology, the occupational judgment or theme constitutes the nodal focus of an organized impression with strong associative pathways extending from it to relevant characteristics. Because the judgment was the dominant goal during information acquisition, the theme node should be easily accessed. The question "What do you remember about the person?" should lead to the theme node being more readily accessed than any informational node.

The second study in this series (also reported in Lingle et al., 1979) had three basic objectives: (1) to extend the findings of the previous study to recognition memory; (2) to examine subject's recall of the theme itself; and (3) to investigate the effects of a thematic judgment over a 1-week period. The interest in investigating the effects of time stems from the possibility that as time passes subjects may gradually forget the exact characteristics that described the person and utilize the recalled theme in an attempt to "reconstruct" the information (Bartlett, 1932). After only a short delay, we may expect subjects whose mental representations of the target person are thematically organized to remember information directly as well as mediated through the theme. As time passes, the ability to directly access information wanes and subjects should come to depend more on the theme as a cue to accessing their memory. Over time, then, overall accuracy should decline because of an inability to remember theme-irrelevant items and the intrusion of theme-relevant errors. Several studies from the cognitive literature on memory document the existence of such memory deficits (e.g., Higgins & Rholes, 1978; Loftus, 1975).

In an initial session, subjects received a photograph and 11 characteristics that described the target person. They were asked to make an occupational judgment concerning the target person (as was done in the first experiment). For half of the subjects, all 11 characteristics were relevant to the judgment, and for the other half, all 11 were irrelevant. Another stimulus replication was conducted in which the occupation was relevant to the latter characteristics and irrelevant to the former. Half of the subjects in each of the two judgment conditions (judgment-relevant information vs. judgment-irrelevant information) returned after 1 day and half returned after a 1-week time lapse.

In the second session, all subjects were asked to recall the occupation that had been the focus of their judgments in the first session and also to indicate the scale rating that they had made concerning the target person's potential success. Subjects were next given a list of 33 characteristics and asked to circle the 11 that had been previously used to describe the target person. Contained in this list were the original 11 characteristics seen in the first session randomly mixed with 22 previously unpresented characteristics. Half of the 22 new characteristics were relevant for the occupation judged and half were irrelevant.

Recall for the occupational judgment and recall for the scale rating were nearly perfect for all subjects and not affected by the time lapse. Ninety-six percent of the subjects were able to recall the occupation and 97% were able to recall their ratings within one point on the 21-point scale.

The mean number of recognition errors for the judgment-relevant and judgment-irrelevant characteristics is presented in Table 2.1. Subjects in the judgment-relevant condition made fewer errors than those in the judgment-irrelevant condition ($p < .002$). This replicated the main finding of the first

TABLE 2.1
Average Number of Recognition Errors

	Stimulus Information	
Time Interval	Judgment Relevant	Judgment Irrelevant
One day	1.50	2.54
One week	2.69	3.15

study. Although the passage of time increased the total number of errors ($p < .001$), it did not have the expected effect of magnifying the relevant-irrelevant difference. One possible explanation is that subjects in the judgment-irrelevant condition spontaneously developed their own theme that was separate from the initial judgment and used this as an aid for recall. This is especially likely when, as in this second study, items of person information were homogeneous in that they all related to a single specific occupation.

Encoding and Retrieval Explanations

There are different ways in which a thematic organization may potentially influence memory for theme-relevant versus theme-irrelevant information. One possibility is that the theme itself may serve as a retrieval cue. From the second study just mentioned, we may infer that the judgment was a highly salient feature of the experimental task. It may be that the recall of the easily accessible theme facilitated recall of the semantically associated theme-relevant characteristics.

Another possibility involves the differential encoding of theme-relevant and theme-irrelevant information. During their initial exposure to the stimulus information, subjects may have attended more closely to those characteristics that were relevant as opposed to irrelevant to their judgments. This may have resulted in subjects either (or both) selectively encoding the theme-relevant items or processing the relevant items more "deeply"(Craik & Lockhart, 1972) and hence showing better retention for them.

These encoding explanations may be contrasted to the retrieval cue explanation in that they emphasize the presence of the judgment theme during the subjects' first encounter with the characteristics. Both the encoding explanations imply that judgments introduced sometime after a subject first encounters the person's characteristics should not have a pronounced effect on recall. A series of studies conducted by Geva (1977) empirically contrasted the retrieval and encoding explanations through the use of a sequential-judgment task. In this task, subjects made two occupational ratings instead of just one. Usually the second judgment was unexpected and made without direct access to the stimulus information.

In the first experiment in this series, subjects were given a list of 10 characteristics describing the target person and asked to judge how successful the target person would be at an occupation. Half of these characteristics were relevant for the initial judgment and half were irrelevant. Immediately following the judgment, subjects were given a 5-minute distractor task (reading a statement concerning discrimination in employment practices). The purpose of the distractor was to temporally separate the exposure of the characteristics from the second judgment task to eliminate the effects of short-term memory.

Following the distractor, one third of the subjects were directly asked to recall as many of the characteristics as they could (this replicates the recall study described earlier and so is termed the replication condition). Another third were asked to make a second occupational judgment concerning the person (without looking back at the characteristics). The characteristics in the original list that were irrelevant for the first occupational judgment were relevant for this second judgment (related second judgment condition). Immediately following the second judgment, subjects were asked to recall the original list of characteristics. The final third of the subjects were also asked to make a second occupational judgment prior to recall; however, none of the original traits were relevant for this judgment (unrelated second judgment condition).

If the retrieval explanation accounts for the original recall findings, then the inclusion of a second judgment that is relevant to half the information (as in the related second judgment condition) just before the recall task should facilitate recall for that information (i.e., the information that was irrelevant for the first judgment). Because the second judgment should be more salient than the first at the time of recall, the retrieval model predicts a reversal of the original finding in this condition. The encoding explanation, of course, would predict no difference between the recall patterns in these two conditions.

In the third condition, the most salient (i.e., the second) judgment was not related to any of the characteristics. In this situation, the retrieval cue explanation would predict a general decline in total recall, whereas the encoding explanation would predict no differences between the recall pattern here and those of the other two conditions.

Table 2.2 presents the recall means across the three conditions for characteristics that were relevant and irrelevant to subjects' first occupational judgments. Note that those characteristics irrelevant for the first judgment were relevant for the second judgment in the related (second judgment) condition. Analyses of these data revealed only a main effect ($p < .001$) for relevancy to the first judgment. In all three conditions, subjects remembered items that were relevant to their initial judgment better than the irrelevant items. Thus, these results favor the encoding over the retrieval explanation.

TABLE 2.2
Recall Means from the First Sequential Judgment Study

	No Second Judgment	Related Second Judgment	Unrelated Second Judgment
Characteristics relevant to first judgment	3.00	3.24	3.06
Characteristics irrelevant to first judgment	2.48	2.37	2.58

If one assumes an encoding explanation of the recall patterns described previously, then several additional predictions follow. If subjects are encouraged to encode information around two theme nodes, each relevant to a different half of the information set, then (1) overall recall should improve; and (2) the relative superiority of recall for items relevant to the first (as opposed to the second) judgment should be eliminated. The last two studies in this section pursued these implications.

The first of the two studies tested these predictions using the sequential judgments paradigm. One condition was a replication of the "related second judgment" condition in the last experiment. The second condition was identical except that subjects were reexposed to the original list of characteristics at the time they were asked to make the second judgment. This "reminder" gave subjects an opportunity to selectively encode the characteristics relevant for the second judgment as well as those relevant to the first judgment.

The recall means for the reminder and no reminder conditions are presented in Table 2.3. Not surprisingly, more characteristics were recalled in the reminder than in the no-reminder condition ($p < .001$). Also, there was an interaction between the two experimental variables ($p < .05$). The previously obtained superiority of recall for items relevant to the first judgment was found in the no-reminder condition but not in the reminder condition. The

TABLE 2.3
Recall Means from the Second Sequential Judgment Study

	No Reminder	Reminder
Characteristics relevant to the first judgment (and irrelevant to the second judgment)	2.69	3.62
Characteristics irrelevant to the first judgment (and relevant to the second judgment)	2.07	3.67

no-reminder condition replicated the results of the preceding experiment, but these recall differences were eliminated when subjects were given the opportunity to reencode on the second judgmental dimension. Although these results are conguent with the encoding model, there exists an alternative explanation of the results. It is possible that the absence of recall differences in the reminder condition was the result of a "ceiling effect" on the recall measure, because reexposure improved memory in all conditions. This alternative explanation was tested in the next study.

A second way to eliminate differential encoding of items relevant to the first judgment would be to make both judgments salient at the time the information was originally presented. One condition of this experiment (Geva, Pryor, & Ostrom, 1978) provided a replication of the "related second judgment, no-reminder" conditions in the last two experiments described. In a second condition, subjects received both judgment dimensions simultaneously in conjunction with their initial exposure to the list of person characteristics. Thus, although the judgments were ordered on the page in the same sequence as in the other condition, subjects were aware of both judgment dimensions during encoding. It was expected that this simultaneous encoding on both dimensions would eliminate any recall differences by encouraging subjects to develop two themes during encoding.

The pattern of recall means was similar to that of the preceding study (see Table 2.4); however, the level of significance was marginal. Overall recall was better in the simultaneous condition than in the sequential condition ($p < .05$, one tail). As in the previous studies, items relevant to the first judgment were recalled better than those relevant to the second judgment ($p < .05$, two tail). This relevance effect was weaker in the simultaneous condition than in the sequential condition ($p < .10$, one tail). Table 2.4 shows that the improvement restulting from providing a second theme at the time of encoding was primarily due to the recall of items that were irrelevant to the first theme. Memory for items relevant to the first theme was not substantially improved.

TABLE 2.4
Recall Means for the Third Sequential Judgment Study

	Sequential Judgments	Simultaneous Judgments
Characteristics relevant to the first judgment (and irrelevant to the second judgment)	2.17	2.25
Characteristics irrelevant to the first judgment (and relevant to the second judgment)	1.69	2.13

Summary and Discussion of Memory Findings

Several basic points emerge from the five studies reported in this section. Theme nodes can be activated in first impression settings by assigning the perceiver the responsibility of making a judgment or decision about the target person. Presumably this is but one of a class of goals the perceiver may have in interpersonal settings. It may be, then, that most any dominant plan or goal a perceiver has at the time he or she is acquiring information about another person could become a thematic node for organizing the information.

The second major point is that theme-relevant information is recalled (and recognized) better than theme-irrelevant information. Relevant information is more readily accessed up to at least a week after acquisition. In the absence of reexposure to the old information (or encountering new information), the thematic organization that originally structured the impression carries forward with little alteration. Even the subsequent imposition of judgments related to different portions of the information set does not lead to a revision of the original thematic structure.

In the tasks employed in the present studies, it appears that the memory findings are due to encoding processes. It is possible that the theme can serve as a retrieval cue for theme-relevant information. However, that could not explain the obtained findings. Selective encoding of the theme-relevant information definitely contributed to the effects of a theme on selective recall. Judgments that were made subsequent to subjects' initial thematic encoding of the information failed to affect recall. Therefore, any retrieval-cue process that may have influenced the reported recall differences was necessarily mediated by selective encoding. There are no doubt other task settings in the person perception domain in which selective retrieval may operate alone to affect the availability from memory of information about others (e.g., Snyder & Uranowitz, 1978).

THE INFLUENCE OF THEMES ON JUDGMENTS

In the studies discussed thus far, first impression judgments were shown to thematically organize impressions by influencing the kinds of person information that are available in memory. This section considers the question of how people draw upon that available information while in the process of making judgments about people.

When making judgments and decisions about friends and acquaintances, we are able to draw upon a large array of past information and thoughts we have had about the person. We needn't rely solely on the information available from our environment at the time the judgment is made. For example, you might be asked to judge how attractive a friend's girlfriend is. If she is physically present at the time of judgment (or if a photo is available), your response could rely exclusively on a direct appraisal of her physical features. However, we can also make such judgments even if she is not present. We do this by drawing on our memory of past encounters with her. This distinction between judgments made with stimulus information directly available (stimulus-based judgments) and judgments that rely on our memory about the person (memory-based judgments) is important when considering past person perception research. Nearly all this work has been restricted to stimulus-based judgments made of hypothetical persons. Yet it would seem that most day-to-day judgments are made in regard to familiar persons about whom we have a fairly rich set of facts and thoughts in our memory.

In the past, there has been little or no work on the difference between judgments that are memory based and information based. The last three studies of the preceding section provide some data relevant to this difference.

In the "related second judgment" conditions of these studies, subjects made two sequential judgments, both of which were relevant to the information that was initially provided. The first judgment was made while the stimulus information was available for review (stimulus based) and the second judgment was made after the stimulus items had been removed (memory based). Because order of the two rating scales was counterbalanced, any differences in the two ratings would be due exclusively to their placement in the experimental booklet. In comparing the two occupational ratings for each of the three sequential judgment studies (see Table 2.5), the memory-based rating was always less polarized than the stimulus-based rating. The stimulus-based rating was more extreme (on a 21-point scale) by 1.1 points in the first study ($p < .06$), 2.7 points in the second ($p < .01$), and 2.2 points in the third ($p < .01$).

This finding is provocative in that it implies that the thematic nature of an initial person impression has direct consequences for subsequent judgments.

TABLE 2.5
Effects of Sequence on Occupation Judgments

	Sequential Judgment Studies		
	First	Second	Third
First judgment (stimulus-based)	6.48	7.10	7.69
Second judgment (memory-based)	5.39	4.36	5.50

[a]All ratings were made on a scale from +10 (very successful in this occupation) to –10 (very unsuccessful in this occupation).

Apparently, the process that people use to make decisions differs according to whether information is directly available as opposed to depending on their memory.

The thematic organization of an impression could affect subsequent memory-based decisions in at least two ways, either of which may account for the judgment polarity differences presented in Table 2.5. First, it might be that people search their memory for previously acquired factual information about the person. It is clear from the studies in the previous section that if such a "memory-for-facts" decision process were employed, a person would be more likely to recall facts that were relevant, as opposed to irrelevant, to an earlier thematic judgment. When a second judgment was similar to a first judgment, these facts would also be relevant for making the new decision. However, when the second judgment was dissimilar to the first (as was the case in the reported studies), remembered facts would not be relevant to the second judgment. Such a memory bias might easily make subjects less certain about a memory-based second decision as compared to a stimulus-based initial judgment. This uncertainty, in turn, could result in subjects making less polarized judgments.

Simply because subjects are capable of remembering facts about a person (as demonstrated in the memory experiments) does not necessarily mean that these facts will be actively recalled and considered whenever a memory-based decision is made. An alternative decision-making procedure would be to rely on memory for the general theme around which subjects organize their impressions. For example, once a subject has decided someone is the kind of person who would make a good lawyer, he or she might then decide that the person would also make a good doctor (based upon some type of stereotypical notion of what a good lawyer is like). A subject might think as follows: "This person would make a good lawyer; traits associated with good lawyers include articulate, well-educated, intelligent, and analytic; such qualities are likely to also result in a person being a good doctor." Such a "memory-for-theme" judgment process would not require recalling the initial facts upon which the first decision (i.e., good lawyer) had been based.

If subjects tended to base their judgments on memory for their initial occupational decision and its associated characteristics, their memory-based ratings could again be expected to be less polarized. This is because the more dissimilar a first judgment was to a second, the less relevant the first occupation and its associated thoughts would be for making the second decision. As with the memory-for-facts judgment model, increased irrelevance of remembered cognitions to the judgment being made could be expected to result in subjects making less extreme ratings.

Both the memory-for-facts and memory-for-theme judgment models are capable of accounting for the depolarization effects found in the first set of experiments. The studies reported in this section allow us to differentiate between the two models and determine which one best describes how subjects draw on their memory when they make memory-based person judgments.

The Effect of Thematic Judgments on the Speed of Decision Making

A series of studies conducted by Lingle and Ostrom (1979) investigated the degree to which people rely on memory for an initial impression judgment, rather than memory for stimulus information when they make memory-based person judgments. In a first study, Lingle and Ostrom determined whether an initial judgment influenced the ease (i.e., speed) with which subjects made a later judgment. They reasoned that if in making a second decision, subjects merely reviewed in memory an unselective set of stimulus traits, the amount of time required to make a decision should not be affected by a previous judgment. However, if an initial judgment in some way influences the set of cognitions subjects remember as the basis of a subsequent judgment, the speed of a second decision should be influenced by its relevance to earlier judgments made about the same person.

To test this, Lingle and Ostrom first had subjects judge the suitability of a described stimulus person for a designated occupation. This judgment was stimulus based, being made while the descriptive traits were continuously in view. After this initial judgment, the traits were removed and subjects were asked to make a second, memory-based judgment about the person's suitability for a second occupation. The dependent variable was the amount of time subjects took to make this second judgment. The independent variable was the similarity of the two judged occupations. On some trials, the first and second occupations involved similar attributes (e.g., doctor–dentist); on other trials the two occupations required dissimilar attributes (e.g., fisherman–dentist). The results indicated that subjects took over a second longer to make a dissimilar second judgment than a similar one ($p < .05$).

This first study by Lingle and Ostrom established that an initial thematic judgment can influence the speed with which a subsequent decision is made. However, it did not determine if the time difference in subjects' second judgments was the consequence of their relying on memory for facts or memory for theme. That is, the decision time differences may have resulted from subjects relying on either memory for stimulus traits relevant to their first judgment or memory for the first judgment itself and its associated characteristics. In both cases, the cognitions that subjects remembered would have been more relevant for making their second decision in the similar, as opposed to dissimilar, condition.

To examine what subjects were recalling during their second judgments, Lingle and Ostrom conducted several additional decision time studies that added a manipulation of the number of traits (set size) used to describe the stimulus persons. They reasoned that subjects' second judgments would be influenced differently by occupation similarity and set size, depending on the set of cognitions subjects were using as the basis of their decisions. In Fig. 2.1, three possible patterns of second decision times, as a function of set size and occupation similarity, are displayed. Note that in each case subjects are predicted to take longer to make a second dissimilar, as compared to similar, occupational judgment when the stimulus person is described by four traits (as was the case in the first decision-time study).

The Memory-for-Facts Model. It has been shown in a variety of decision tasks (e.g., Kintsch, 1974; Posner & Snyder, 1975; Sternberg, 1969), that the

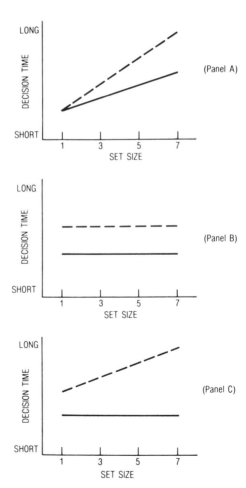

FIG. 2.1. Predicted effects of set size and similarity on decision time for the memory-for-facts model (Panel A), the memory-for-theme model (Panel B), and the mixed model (Panel C). Solid lines represent the similar and dashed lines the dissimilar second judgments, respectively.

amount of time people take to review a set of stimulus items in memory increases as the number of items in the set increases. If it is true that (1) search time increases as set size increases; and (2) subjects base their second judgment on a review of the stimulus traits, decision time should increase with set size in both the similar and dissimilar conditions. This is shown in Panel *a* by the increase in decision time across set size for both similar and dissimilar second judgments.

If it is assumed that subjects review the descriptive stimulus items in memory until they feel they have considered a representative proportion of the judgment-relevant traits in the set, the memory-for-facts model also predicts that increases in decision time across set size should be greater for dissimilar, as opposed to similar, second judgments. The earlier reported research suggests that it is easier to recall traits relevant to a first judgment. In the similar decision conditions, these traits will also be relevant to the second judgment. Consequently, subjects will not have to spend time recalling additional traits in the set to make a decision. In the dissimilar condition, however, the set of first-judgment relevant traits that subjects recall should not be relevant to their second judgment. In this case, they will have to spend additional time recalling traits in the set that were irrelevant to their first judgment but might be relevant to their second. Because the number of these remaining traits will also increase as set size increases, subjects will have to spend more time reviewing them as set size increases. As a result, the difference in decision time for similar and dissimilar memory-based judgments should increase over set size as shown in Panel *a*.

In their experimental design, Lingle and Ostrom were careful to make certain that the relevance of the descriptive traits to subjects' second judgments did not vary across the experimental conditions. Consequently one further implication of the memory-for-facts model is that no difference in decision time should result between the similar and dissimilar conditions when a stimulus person is described by only one item of information. This too is shown in Panel *a*.

The Memory-for-Theme Model.   Panel *b* depicts the expected results if subjects base their second judgment on memory for theme rather than on memory for facts. This assumes that subjects do not retreive the stimulus items but rather use their memory of their first judgment as a basis for their second. Knowing they regard the person as a "good doctor," for example, would allow them to estimate whether the assumed characteristics of a good doctor would lead to good or bad performance in the second occupation. Because there is no reason to expect that theme retrieval time should be affected by set size, subjects' second judgment times should not increase with set size. However, for all set sizes (including set size 1) they should be able to make second similar judgments more quickly than second dissimilar judgments. This is because when the two occupations are very similar, the attributes associated with success or failure in the first occupation will be relevant for making a decision about the second; when the two occupations are dissimilar, the two sets of attributes are not likely to be related and a subject would have to spend additional time generating an inferential chain between the two decisions.

The Mixed Model.   People are flexible information processors. Subjects may sometimes base a decision on memory for an early judgment, whereas at other times they may recall stimulus traits. In the present judgment context, subjects may first recall the initial judgment to see whether it can serve as a basis for the second judgment. If the two are very similar (e.g., doctor–dentist), a decision may be reached quickly. However, if a comparison shows the two occupations to be very dissimilar, subjects may undertake a review of their memory for the original stimulus items in order to obtain a more relevant foundation for their second judgment. Because subjects would only spend time recalling the stimulus traits when the second judgment was dissimilar to the first, decision time would only increase with set size in the dissimilar conditions. For similar pairs of judgments, second decision times would be independent of set size as subjects would not review the stimulus traits. This prediction is displayed in Fig. 2.1c.

Experimental Tests.   Three separate replications were conducted (Lingle & Ostrom, 1979) in which both set size and judgment similarity were manipulated. The results are summarized in Fig. 2.2. Set sizes ranged from one to seven traits; also, both homogeneous trait sets (containing all positive or negative traits) and heterogeneous trait sets (both containing positive and negative traits) were used. For each replication, the results most closely matched the pattern depicted in Fig. 2.1b, the "memory-for-theme" explanation. Subjects' second judgment times were consistently affected by the similarity of the first judgment (all p's < .001) but not by the number of traits used to describe the stimulus person. Even when only one trait was presented, subjects took longer to make a second dissimilar, as compared to similar, judgment. Homogeneity of the trait sets did not affect the results.

The Effect of a Thematic Judgment on Subsequent Attribute Ratings

Decision time as a dependent measure has several advantages. It is relatively unobtrusive and can provide data concerning how subjects are accessing information without interrupting their normal judgment processes. However, our confidence in the conclusion of the previous studies would be strengthened if it were possible to verify them using alternative methods. In

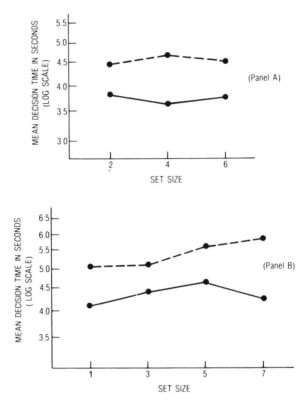

FIG. 2.2.   Obtained effects of set size and similarity on decision time for three experimental replications, all of which support the memory-for-theme model. Panel A gives the average results combining over the first two stimulus replications (one used homogeneous and one used heterogeneous stimulus sets) and Panel B provides the findings for the third stimulus replication (in which homogeneity of the stimulus sets was manipulated). Similar second judgment responses are solid lines and dissimilar second judgment responses are dashed lines.

this section, we examined the implications for the memory-for-facts model and the memory-for-theme model for predicting the scale location of the judgment itself.

A study reported by Lingle et al. (1979) structured a situation in which subjects were expected to exhibit different attribute ratings of a stimulus person depending on whether they were relying on memory for the set of descriptive traits or a judgment they themselves had earlier made about the person. This was done by describing stimulus persons with all negative, all positive, or all neutral traits and then asking subjects to make memory-based ratings of each person's intelligence and friendliness. Before making these two attribute ratings, however, and while the traits were still available, the subjects were asked to make an occupational judgment about each person. Each occupational judgment was relevant to one of the attributes but not to the other (e.g., research physicist for intelligence but not friendliness, and waiter for friendliness but not intelligence). Lingle et al. reasoned that the interaction between descriptive valence (i.e., the positive, negative, or neutral traits used to describe the stimulus person) and occupational relevance on subjects' attribute judgments would be different depending on whether subjects relied on memory for the stimulus traits as opposed to memory for the occupational judgment.

To see why this is so, consider first the pattern of attribute ratings that might be expected if subjects relied on memory for the stimulus traits when making their memory-based attribute judgments. From the previously described research, it is clear that subjects would tend to recall traits relevant to their initial occupational judgment. Such a memory bias should have the effect of polarizing their subsequent attribute ratings when the occupation is relevant, as opposed to irrelevant, to the attribute being judged. To illustrate this reasoning, consider the situation in which a subject judges a stimulus person described by all negative traits. Subjects would typically conclude that the person would be unsuccessful at the occupation. However, that occupational judgment would affect whether or not the subject tended to remember traits relevant to friendliness or intelligence. From the earlier studies, we can expect that when a subject judged the person on an intelligence-relevant occupation as opposed to a friendliness-relevant occupation, the subject would tend to later remember more intelligent-relevant traits. The more intelligence-relevant negative traits a subject can remember, the less intelligent the stimulus person is likely to seem (see Hamilton & Fallot, 1974, for a demonstration of this effect when subjects make stimulus-based judgments). Just the opposite would be expected when a stimulus person described by all positive traits was considered. The increased number of intelligence-relevant traits remembered following an intelligence-relevant occupational judgment would all be positive, thus making the person seem more intelligent (see the upper line in Fig. 2.3a). A similar process would of course also be expected following friendliness-relevant occupational judgments when subjects judge the friendliness attribute. This interaction between person description valence and occupational judgment relevance that would be expected if subjects rely on memory for the stimulus traits (the memory-for-facts model) is graphically depicted in Fig. 2.3a.

A different pattern of attribute ratings would be expected if subjects based their intelligence and friendliness ratings on memory for their initial occupational judgment, rather than memory for the stimulus traits. In this case, subjects' attribute ratings should reflect the degree to which the rated attribute is stereotypically associated with the judged occupation. When

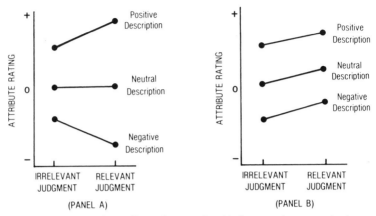

FIG. 2.3. Predicted effects of occupational judgment relevance and valence of the descriptive traits on attribute ratings for the memory-for-facts model (Panel A) and the memory-for-theme model (Panel B).

relying on memory for a previous thematic judgment, subjects would be more likely to judge a person as intelligent who had first been judged as a good physicist (as compared to a good waiter) because a good physicist is generally viewed as more intelligent than a good waiter. A bad physicist is also likely to be more intelligent than a bad waiter. So regardless of the valence of the stimulus traits and the resulting initial occupational judgment, an attribute rating would always be expected to be more positive following a relevant, as opposed to irrelevant, occupational judgment. The memory-for-theme model, then, would predict the pattern of attribute ratings displayed in Fig. 2.3*b*.

To test between the two judgment models, Lingle et al. (1979) used a within-subjects design in which subjects judged negatively, positively, and neutrally described stimulus persons on both intelligence and friendliness. On half of these judgments subjects first made an intelligence-relevant occupational judgment whereas for the other half they first made a friendliness-relevant occupational judgment. The initial occupational judgments were stimulus based, but the subsequent attribute ratings of intelligence and friendliness were memory based. Subjects' ratings of intelligence and friendliness, as a function of person description valence and occupation relevance, are displayed in Fig. 2.4. The most striking aspect of these results is that in every instance subjects rated the stimulus person more positively (i.e., stereotypically congruent wtih the occupation judged) when they had first made a relevant occupational judgment ($p < .001$). These findings, then, are consistent with the decision time experiments in indicating that subjects rely on memory for an earlier thematic judgment, rather than descriptive stimulus traits when making memory-based impression judgments.

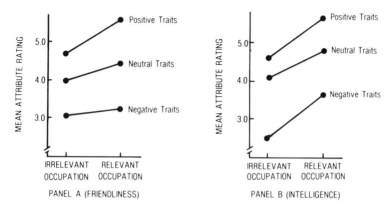

FIG. 2.4.   Obtained effects of occupational judgment relevance and valence of the descriptive traits on attribute ratings. Both attribute replications (friendliness for Panel A and intelligence for Panel B) support the memory-for-theme model. Higher numbers correspond to more positive attribute ratings.

People May Access Both Facts and Themes When Making a Judgment

Earlier, it was argued that people are flexible information processors. We know subjects are capable of recalling many of the items used to describe a stimulus person. It seems likely that in some judgment contexts subjects will rely more heavily on memory for the stimulus items than they apparently did in the studies discussed thus far (see Chapter 3 by Carlston). For example, if subjects had been asked to explain or justify their memory-based decisions, they may have spent more effort in attempting to recall the stimulus traits. To explore this possibility, Lingle (1978) examined the degree to which subjects accessed both relevant and irrelevant stimulus information, as well as an initial thematic judgment, in a memory-based decision task that periodically required them to justify their judgments. Before discussing the experiment, we provide a brief description of the dependent measure Lingle used to assess the thoughts subjects activated in memory when making decisions.

As noted, Lingle was interested in the degree to which subjects might activate relevant and irrelevant descriptive traits, in addition to an earlier judgment, when they knew they might be asked to justify their decision. To investigate this, Lingle had subjects make pairs of judgments about each stimulus person. The stimulus person was described by two stimulus traits. Subjects were first asked to decide the degree to which they thought the stimulus person would be characterized by the third trait. The two traits used to describe the person in each case were selected so that one was relevant and one was irrelevant for making the required trait judgment. For example, a subject might first be asked, "Would this person be friendly?" and then be presented with a person description that contained the traits "outgoing" (relevant) and "smart" (irrelevant). After their initial trait judgment, subjects engaged in a 50-second distractor task; then they were asked to make a memory-based occupational judgment about the same person. The experimental design employed by Lingle was counterbalanced so that across subjects (1) the same set of probe words appeared as relevant, irrelevant, judgment, and control traits; and (2) the occupational judgments were of equal relevance to all the presented traits.

Either early or late during the time subjects were contemplating the occupational judgment, they were interrupted by a probe word that was either (1) the judgment trait they had previously responded to for that stimulus person; (2) the descriptive stimulus trait that was relevant to the judgment trait; (3) the descriptive trait that was irrelevant to the judgment trait; or (4) a matched control trait that had not been associated with the stimulus person. The probe word was written in hard-to-read letters to make the identification task more difficult. The speed with which subjects identified each type of probe was used as an index of the degree to which subjects activated that type of information while making their memory-based occupational judgments. The validity of the probe procedure for making this kind of inference regarding concept activation had been established in a series of earlier studies (Lingle, 1978).

The decision context was structured to encourage subjects to recall the stimulus traits during the decision interval. This was done by unpredictably interrupting subjects on 20% of the experimental trials and asking them to explain the judgment they had just made. Under these conditions, Lingle expected subjects' probe recognition scores to show that they activated in memory both the traits used to describe the stimulus person, as well as their initial trait judgment about the person. In accordance with the earlier reported memory research, Lingle also expected that probe recognition speeds would show that subjects more readily accessed theme relevant, as compared to theme irrelevant, information items.

Subject's probe recognition speeds are pictured in Fig. 2.5. The pattern of obtained probe recognition speeds indicates that subjects accessed both the descriptive traits and their thematic trait judgments when making the memory-based occupational judgments. Both the relevant and irrelevant descriptive stimulus traits were identified faster than a control trait unassociated with the stimulus person ($p < .001$). In addition, the probe recognition times indicated that during the judgment interval subjects more readily accessed stimulus traits that were relevant, as opposed to irrelevant, to their initial thematic judgment ($p < .06$). It should be emphasized that these two traits were not differentially relevant to the occupational judgment,

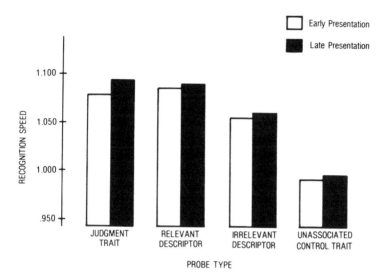

FIG. 2.5. Mean recognition speed for four types of probe words presented early or late in the decision interval. Speed scores equal 1000/response time in milliseconds.

which was the judgment being considered at the time the probe was introduced. Finally, the results indicated that when making their occupational judgments subjects accessed their initial trait judgment, in addition to the two descriptive traits. The speed with which subjects identified the initial judgment trait was equal to the speed with which they identified the most relevant trait descriptor. This overall pattern of results held true regardless of whether the probe was presented early or late in the decision interval.

Researchers in the area of social perception have long aspired to know what thoughts are passing through a person's mind while that person is in the midst of making a judgment. The present findings move us a long way toward that goal. In this study, people were apparently activating both the theme and the theme-relevant descriptive information while making an occupational judgment. To a lesser extent, they were also reviewing the theme-irrelevant information item. People do, then, draw upon their memory for facts when making a judgment, even facts that are irrelevant to the theme.

Some caution is required in interpreting Lingle's results. Studies (c.f. Warren, 1972, 1974; Meyer & Schvaneveldt, 1976) indicate that when a concept is activated in memory, it increases the speed with which subjects can recognize closely associated words (although this association effect is not generally as strong as facilitation for recognition of the world itself). Lingle's traits were selected in a way that resulted in a relevant descriptor trait sometimes being a close associate of the judgment trait. Consequently, it is not clear whether the high recognition speed for the judgment trait and the relevant descriptor resulted from one or both being accessed in memory when subjects made their occupational judgments. Lingle's results, nevertheless, do provide an additional demonstration of the ways in which the thematic organization imposed on an impression by an early judgment is reflected in subsequent responses that are based upon that impression.

Summary and Discussion of Judgment Findings

The studies discussed in this section employed several divergent methods for identifying how people draw on memory when making memory-based decisions. Despite this diversity, the results are strongly convergent in demonstrating the importance of an early organizing impression judgment on subsequent judgments made about a person. Most striking is the persistent evidence that an initial judgment, rather than factual stimulus information, is remembered and used as the basis for subsequent judgments. In the decision time studies, this was demonstrated by the fact that subjects' judgment times were affected by the earlier decision they had made but not by variations in the amount of descriptive information provided about each person. In the attribute rating study, it was shown that the extremity of subjects' attribute ratings reflected the stereotypical characteristics of a previously judged occupation rather than memory for occupation-relevant facts. Finally, in the last study (in which subjects were asked to justify some of their judgments), probe recognition speed showed that an earlier thematic judgment was accessed as readily as any of the traits initially used to describe the stimulus person. Consistent with the recall studies, this last study also indicated that traits irrelevant to an earlier judgment were not accessed as easily as the judgment-relevant traits during a subsequent memory-based decision.

GENERAL DISCUSSION

One of the primary objectives of this chapter is to describe the similarities that exist between past social psychological research on impression organization and contemporary research on memory and cognition. Indeed, it is difficult to find dissimilarities in their fundamental objectives. Both aspire to understand how and why one thought follows another, neither assume people are necessarily aware of all their cognitive activity, and both agree upon the need to posit the existence of cognitive elements (concepts or nodes), interelement associations (units or pathways), and thematic clusters of elements (categories or schemas).

It could be argued that people are a unique and complex category of stimulus objects, and that theories of impression organization cannot be borrowed from memory and cognition research that deals with simpler stimulus units. Of course, this issue cannot be resolved until the dimensions of difference are specified and research is undertaken to establish whether such differences qualitatively alter the character of the cognitive processes. In the meantime, the research reported in this chapter (as well as other chapters in this volume) support the value of establishing the regions of empirical and conceptual comparability between the two areas.

One serious limitation to the breadth and utility of past impression oganization research is illuminated when comparing the two areas of study. Most previous work on impression organization was restricted to studying subjects' subjective reports of elements and associations. However, it is reasonable to expect that the effects of impression organization should be detectable in a variety of other overt responses. Studying the effects of organization on memory and on decision making, as was done in the experiments reported in this chapter, broadens our understanding of organizational processes in at least three ways.

It compels theoretical elaboration because of the new questions that must be answered when a different response domain is explored. For example, the question of whether impression organization operates at the encoding or retrieval (or both) phases of processing had never been raised by earlier researchers in this area. The different accessing strategies used in memory-based versus information-based judgments had also not received previous attention.

The second advantage also has the potential of advancing our conceptual understanding of organizational processes. By having several kinds of organization-related responses available for study, we can avoid the tendency to regard our dependent measure as an error-free index of the underlying construct. Most previous researchers in impression organization treated their subjects' subjective reports of elements and associations as though those reports were unadulterated and that the reports provided accurate indices of their theoretical counterparts. Yet it seems reasonable to expect that organization can, under some circumstances, have different effects on memory, subjective reports, and interpersonal decisions. For example, people may recall a particular fact about a person and report that it had an important bearing on their judgment, and yet no effects on judgment can be detected. Conversely, background information about the target person that is not recalled and/or is not subjectively accorded much importance may have a substantial effect on judgment. Expanding the number of organization-related responses available for study encourages theoretical development into the problem of when and why such differences will emerge.

The third advantage to this approach is of special interest to social psychologists. Much of social interaction involves communicating information that has been learned earlier and must now be retrieved from memory. It would appear that to understand this process, we must first know how that information was originally stored (and organized) in memory. Of course other phases of this communication process (such as the decision to report or withhold a specific recalled item) must also be explored. An adequate understanding of organizational processes should help refine our analysis of interpersonal communication. Many other important social behaviors, such as conformity, aggression, and attitude change, may ultimately be found to be dependent on impression organization.

ACKNOWLEDGMENTS

The authors extend their warmest thanks to D. Carlston, J. Olson, and R. Wyer for their helpful comments on an earlier draft of this chapter. Preparation of this chapter was facilitated by funding from the Office of Naval Research (N00014-79-C-0027).

REFERENCES

Anderson, J. R., & Bower, G. H. *Human associative memory.* Washington, D.C.: Winston, 1973.

Asch, S. E. Forming impressions of personality. *Journal of Abnormal and Social Psychology,* 1946, *41,* 258-290.

Bartlett, F. C. *Remembering: A study in experimental and social psychology.* Cambridge, England: Cambridge University Press, 1932.

Bruner, J. S. On perceptual readiness. *Psychological Review,* 1957, *64,* 123-152.

Bruner, J. S., & Tagiuri, R. The perception of people. In G. Lindzey (Ed.), *Handbook of social psychology* (Vol. 2). Cambridge, Mass.: Addison-Wesley, 1954.

Collins, A. M., & Loftus, E. F. A spreading-activation theory of semantic processing. *Psychological Review,* 1975, *82,* 407-428.

Craik, F. I. M., & Lockhart, R. S. Levels of processing: A framework for memory research. *Journal of Verbal Learning and Verbal Behavior,* 1972, *11,* 671-684.

Dooling, D. J., & Lachman, R. Effects of comprehension on retention of prose. *Journal of Experimental Psychology,* 1971, *88,* 216-222.

Erdelyi, M. H. A new look at the new look: Perceptual defense and vigilance. *Psychological Review,* 1974, *81,* 1-25.

Geva, H. *The role of memory in person perception.* Unpublished doctoral dissertation, Ohio State University, 1977.

Geva, N., Pryor, J. B., & Ostrom, T. M. *Simultaneous verses sequential judgments in the development of thematic organization in recall.* Unpublished study, Ohio State University, 1978.

Hamilton, D. L., & Fallot, R. D. Information salience as a weighting factor in impression formation. *Journal of Personality and Social Psychology,* 1974, *30,* 444-448.

Harvey, O. J., Hunt, D. E., & Schroder, H. M. *Conceptual systems and personality organization.* New York: Wiley, 1961.

Heider, F. Social perception and phenomenal causality. *Psychological Review,* 1944, *51,* 358-374.

Heider, F. Attitudes and cognitive organization. *Journal of Psychology,* 1946, *21,* 107-112.

Heider, F. *The psychology of interpersonal relations.* New York: Wiley, 1958.

Higgins, E. T., & Rholes, W. S. "Saying is believing": Effects of message modification on memory and liking for the person described. *Journal of Experimental Social Psychology* 1978, *14*, 363–378.

Katz, D., & Braly, K. W. Racial stereotypes of 100 college students. *Journal of Abnormal and Social Psychology*, 1933, *29*, 280–290.

Kelly, G. A. *A theory of personality: The psychology of personal constructs.* New York: Norton, 1955.

Kintsch, W. *The representation of meaning in memory.* Hillsdale, N.J.: Lawrence Erlbaum Associates, 1974.

Koffka, K. *Principles of Gestalt psychology,* New York: Harcourt, Brace, 1935.

Köhler, W. *Gestalt psychology.* New York: Boni & Liveright, 1929.

Kretch, D., & Crutchfield, R. S. *Theory and problems of social psychology.* New York: McGraw-Hill, 1948.

Kuethe, J. L. Social schemas. *Journal of Abnormal and Social Psychology.* 1962, *64*, 31–38.

Lewin, K. *Field theory in the social sciences.* New York: Harper, 1951.

Lingle, J. H. *Probe recognition speed as a measure of thought activation during memory-based impression judgments.* Unpublished doctoral dissertation, Ohio State University, 1978.

Lingle, J. H., Geva, H., Ostrom, T. M., Leippe, M. R., & Baumgardner, M. H. Thematic effects of person judgments on impression organization. *Journal of Personality and Social Psychology,* 1979, *37*, 674–687.

Lingle, J. H., & Ostrom, T. M. Retrieval selectivity in memory-based impression judgments. *Journal of Personality and Social Psychology,* 1979, *37*, 180–194.

Lingle, J. H., & Ostrom, T. M. Principles of memory and cognition in attitude formation. In R. Petty, T. Ostrom, & T. Brock (Eds.), *Cognitive responses in persuasion.* Hillsdale, N.J.: Lawrence Erlbaum Associates, in press.

Loftus, E. F. Leading questions and eyewitness report. *Cognitive Psychology,* 1975, *7*, 560–572.

Meyer, D. E., & Schvaneveldt, R. W. Meaning, memory structure, and mental processes. *Science,* 1976, *192*, 27–33.

Osgood, C. E., Suci, G. J., & Tannenbaum, P. H. *The measurement of meaning.* Urbana, Ill.: University of Illinois Press, 1957.

Ostrom, T. M. Theoretical perspectives in the analysis of cognitive responses. In R. Petty, T. Ostrom, & T. Brock (Eds.), *Cognitive responses in persuasion.* Hillsdale, N.J.: Lawrence Erlbaum Associates, in press.

Ostrom, T. M., & Essex, D. W. *Meaning shift in impression formation.* Psychonomic Society, St. Louis, Missouri, 1972.

Posner, M. I., & Snyder, C. R. R. Attention and cognitive control. In R. Solso (Ed.), *Information processing and cognition: The Loyola Symposium.* Hillsdale, N.J.: Lawrence Erlbaum Associates, 1975.

Roediger, H. L. Recall as a self-limiting process. *Memory and Cognition,* 1978, *6*, 54–63.

Rosenberg, S., Nelson, C., & Vivekananthan, P. S. A multidimensional approach to the structure of personality impression. *Journal of Personality and Social Psychology,* 1968, *9*, 283–294.

Rosenberg, S., & Sedlak, A. Structural representations of implicit personality theory. In L. Berkowitz (Ed.), *Advances in experimental social psychology* (Vol. 6). New York: Academic Press, 1972.

Scott, W. A. Conceptualizing and measuring structural properties of cognition. In O. J. Harvey (Ed.), *Motivation and Social Interaction.* New York: Ronald Press, 1963.

Snyder, M. & Uranowitz, S. W. Reconstructing the past: Some cognitive consequences of person perception. *Journal of Personality and Social Psychology,* 1978, *36*, 941–950.

Sperling, G. The information available in brief visual presentations. *Psychological Monographs,* 1960, *74*, 1–29.

Sternberg, S. Memory-scanning: Mental processes revealed by reaction-time experiments. *American Scientist,* 1969, *57*, 421–457.

Sulin, R. A., & Dooling, D. J. Intrusion of thematic ideas in retention of prose. *Journal of Experimental Psychology,* 1974, *103,* 255-262.

Warren, R. E. Stimulus encoding and memory. *Journal of Experimental Psychology,* 1972, *94,* 90-100.

Warren, R. E. Association, directionality, and stimulus encoding. *Journal of Experimental Psychology,* 1974, *102,* 151-158.

Whitten, W. B., & Bjork, R. A. Learning from tests: Effects of spacing. *Journal of Verbal Learning and Verbal Behavior,* 1977, *16,* 465-478.

Wyer, R. S., Jr., *Cognitive organization and change: An information processing approach.* Potomac, Md.: Lawrence Erlbaum Associates, 1974. (a)

Wyer, R. S., Jr. Changes in meaning and halo effects in personality impression formation. *Journal of Personality and Social Psychology,* 1974, *29,* 829-835. (b)

Wyer, R. S., Jr., & Carlston, D. E. *Social inference and attribution.* Hillsdale, N.J.: Lawrence Erlbaum Associates, 1979.

Zajonc, R. B. The process of cognitive tuning in communication. *Journal of Abnormal and Social Psychology,* 1960, *61,* 159-167.

Zajonc, R. B. Cognitive theories in social psychology. In G. Lindzey & E. Aronson (Eds.), *The handbook of social psychology* (2nd ed.). Reading, Mass.: Addison-Wesley, 1968.

Zanna, M. P., & Hamilton, D. L. Further evidence for meaning change in impression formation. *Journal of Experimental Social Psychology,* 1977, *13,* 224-238.

3

Events, Inferences, and Impression Formation

Donal E. Carlston
University of Iowa

Most recent research on attribution and impression phenomena implicitly assumes that a person's judgments of another person are the product of two processes. First, the person making the judgment (the "judge") recalls specific behaviors or events involving a target person, and then the judge determines the implications of these recalled events for the judgment to be made. The latter process, by which people determine the implications of events, has traditionally been the primary focus of research in the attribution area.

The former process, by which people recall the events on which they base their judgments, has not been as widely investigated (an early exception is Anderson & Hubert, 1963). As a consequence, several potentially important aspects of the impression process have been largely overlooked. First, the recall and analysis of specific events may not be the only process underlying impression formation. Some impression judgments may not be based on recalled events at all but may instead be based on other sources, such as internal reactions or thoughts precipitated by these events. Second, even when recalled events are the primary basis for later impressions, these events may bear little resemblance to the objective events originally observed. Event recall may be considerably affected by various inference and memory processes occurring between the original observation of an event and the making of judgments. When this occurs, it may be necessary to examine the effects of event memory processes in order to adequately understand this basis for person judgments.

These possibilities suggest that impression researchers need to examine the bases of impression judgments more carefully. This chapter attempts to do so, focusing both on event memories, and on internal reactions and thoughts that might affect the impression process. Specifically, we shall consider the impact of an observer's initial inferences about an actor on later memories and judgments of that actor. We will suggest that people can recall their own inferences, that these inferences affect event memories, and that the information provided by these inferences may be used to make person judgments instead of, or in an addition to, the information provided by event memories. These possibilities raise a number of important new issues concerning the nature and importance of spontaneous inference processes.

Some Alternative Models

Figure 3.1 illustrates the traditional approach to impression judgments (3.1a) and some of the more complicated possibilities that emerge from the considerations just discussed (3.1b, 3.1c, and 3.1d). The three latter models highlight the possible roles that spontaneous inference making may play in

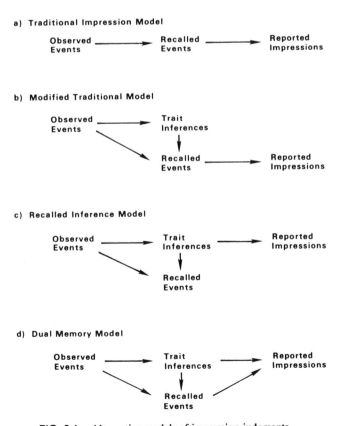

FIG. 3.1. Alternative models of impression judgments.

the impression process. Figure 3.1b combines the assumption that reported impressions are based on recalled events with the assumption that these events may be biased by inference processes. Figure 3.1c assumes that reported impressions are based directly on prior inferences, whereas event memories are largely tangential to the process. And Fig. 3.1d is based on the assumption that both observed events and prior inferences may contribute to impression judgments. All three of these models (3.1b, 3.1c, and 3.1d) recognize that impressions are not simply based on the objective details of observed events and suggest some sort of influence from implicit inference processes. Much of this chapter is devoted to explaining and testing the model represented in 3.1d, which assumes that both inferences and events contribute to impression judgments. However, some attention is devoted to distinguishing this model from the other alternatives.

General Orientation

The general orientation of this chapter differs little from that of other chapters in this volume. For example, the argument that impression researchers need to attend more closely to the nature of event memories is reported in virtually every chapter. Chapters 2 and 7 also discuss the possibility that certain kinds of initial inferences affect subsequent judgment processes.

However, this chapter does differ in terms of theoretical emphasis, factors of interest, and experimental procedures used in reported research. In general, we focus here directly on the contents of event and trait inference memories, on the ways these contents interact and change, and on the ways they contribute to later judgments. Moreover, we consider impression processes as they ordinarily occur, with subjects first observing events, and later making inferences and reporting impressions. The factors of experimental interest help illuminate these processes and are relevant to the circumstances that may often characterize "real-world" impression formation. For example, we examine not only stimulus episodes that imply one particular trait (the kind most often used in experimental research) but also more complex episodes that have multiple implications (and which are probably representative of many actual interpersonal events). The different kinds of inferences people make are also of interest, as are the effects of time delays between stimulus observation and impression report. Finally, the "impressions" discussed in this chapter are generally made along trait dimensions such as those traditionally emphasized in impression research and assumed to be important in spontaneous person judgment processes (cf. Schneider, 1973). Examining these facets of impression making will help to clarify a number of important theoretical issues to be raised in the following sections.

Two Forms of Memory

At the heart of the present approach is the assumption that a person may store in memory both a record of external events that he observes and a record of his accompanying, internal cognitive reactions to those events. Hence, if we observe a student, Brad, turning in his best friend for petty theft, we might store this observation in memory, and we might also make a mental note that Brad is an honest sort of fellow, and store that conclusion in memory. We refer to these two different entries in memory as "event memory" and "trait inference memory," respectively.

There are parallels between this distinction and Tulving's (1972) original distinction between "episodic" and "semantic" memory stores. Event memory, like episodic memory, is essentially an historical record of observed facts that includes behavioral and situational details and preserves the temporal ordering of activity within an event. Event memories may be somewhat organized when individual episodes are linked to superordinate concepts such as the person (cf. Hastie & Kumar, 1979), an abstract theme (cf. Ostrom et al., this volume) or a basic behavioral dimension (cf. Triandis, 1964). Nonetheless, event memories are relatively raw representations of what an observer thinks transpired in a particular episode.

Memory for trait inferences, like semantic memory, involves a greater level of cognitive and semantic involvement than event memory and is organized around a multidimensional framework of concepts and their inter-relationships. For trait inferences this multidimensional framework would be provided by the individual's implicit personality theory (cf. Rosenberg & Sedlak, 1972). Trait inferences are thus relatively processed representations of what an observer thinks characterizes a particular person.

We suggest that trait inferences may be stored in memory, like the behavioral events that precipitated them. In later sections, we consider the implications of this possibility for both memory for the originally observed events and for later judgments of the observed person. But first let us describe the basic experimental paradigm used to investigate these implications and the evidence this paradigm provides concerning memory for trait inferences.

INFERENCE RECALL AND ITS EFFECTS

Basic Paradigm

A complex experiment was conducted to examine the effects of inference making on various recall and impression measures (Carlston, 1977). The basic strategy was to present naive subjects with stimulus episodes describing the behavior of a stimulus person, John, and then to induce subjects to make different kinds of inferences immediately after stimulus presentation. Later, subjects attempted to recall these inferences and the original episodes and judged John on a number of different trait dimensions. Hypotheses concerning these latter variables are discussed in later sections.

Two hundred and eighty-nine subjects took part in the experiment, participating in one of a number of different replications of the following basic procedures. Subjects first received six stimulus episodes, which were selected on the basis of pretesting so that each set implied that John possessed two different, evaluatively incongruent traits (for example, that he was unkind and honest). After reading the set of these episodes, subjects were given an *interpolated judgment* task pertaining to either the positive or the negative trait implied by these episodes. In this way, they were induced to make either a positive or a negative inference.

Because we presently know very little about the kinds of inferences that people ordinarily make (cf. Schneider, 1973), the interpolated judgment task was varied to induce two different kinds of inferences. In *explicit judgment* conditions, the task consisted of several response scales labeled with one of the critical traits or a synonym (e.g., honesty or truthfulness). This task was intended to prompt clearly articulated trait inferences. In *implicit judgment* conditions, the task asked subjects to judge John's suitability for an occupation requiring either one critical trait or the other. The inferences prompted by this task were expected to embody the same trait dimensions as the explicit judgments but not necessarily in the same clearly articulated form. This judgment-explicitness variable thus allows the importance of the precise form of subjects' initial inference to be investigated.

After responding to the interpolated judgment task, subjects took a break of either several minutes or an entire week before attempting the various recall tasks and reporting their impressions. This delay variable was expected to primarily affect event recall but might logically affect inference recall as well. Other experimental factors are discussed in later sections, in conjunction with the hypotheses to which they relate.

Empirical Evidence: Recall for Inferences

At the end of the experiment, subjects were asked to recall their responses on the interpolated judgment task and to indicate their confidence in the accuracy of their recall. It was expected that subjects would be able to recall these judgments accurately and confidently, even after a delay of 1 week. Subjects were able to recall both implicit and explicit interpolated judgments quite accurately. On seven point scales, the average error for either kind of judgment was less than one-sixth of a scale point in brief delay conditions and less than one-half of a scale point after a week's delay.

Recall confidence also remained uniformly high, athough there were small differences among conditions. Confidence was slightly higher among subjects who made explicit interpolated judgments (mean = 6.5 out of 7) than among subjects who made implicit interpolated judgments (mean = 6.2), and it was higher in brief delay conditions (mean = 6.8) than in 1-week delay conditions (mean = 5.9). Thus, although confidence was affected by delay and type of judgment, subjects in all conditions were confident of their ability to reproduce their initial interpolated judgments.

An unexpected negativity bias in the confidence ratings is also of some interest. The decline in confidence from no delay to 1-week delay conditions was greater for subjects who made positive interpolated judgments than for subjects who made negative interpolated judgments. This result is consistent with negativity biases noted in other contexts (cf. Kanouse & Hanson, 1972).

A great deal more needs to be learned about the recall of various kinds of inferences. Differences in recall for inferences pertaining to different traits or made under different circumstances could have implications for other aspects of the impression process. The effects of cognitive elaboration and verbal articulation on inference recall may be similarly important. However, these various factors are beyond the scope of this chapter, and we turn our attention instead toward the implications of inference making and recall on other processes of interest.

Implications of Inference Processes for Event Memory

The making, storage, and retrieval of inferences about an actor may affect the recall of events involving that actor, as represented in Figs. 3.1b, 3.1c, and 3.1d by arrows from *Trait Inferences* to *Recalled Events*. Such effects might come about due to the operation of memory processes such as rehearsal, retrieval, and reconstruction. Interestingly, consideration of all three processes leads to the same conclusion: Memories for events will be shaped so that they eventually become more congruent with the implications of previously reached trait inferences.

Rehearsal. During initial inference-making processes, a person may selectively recall and consider aspects of an observed event that are pertinent to the inference at hand. Both the retrieval of this information and the process of thinking it over, which experimentalists call "elaborative rehearsal," may facilitate subsequent memory for this material. Researchers have demonstrated that prior retrieval (Loftus & Loftus, 1974) and elaborative rehearsal (Loftus & Loftus, 1976) improve long-term memory for some kinds of stimuli. Hence, information that is retreived and considered in the course of inference making may subsequently be better recalled than other pieces of information that were not considered.

Consider a situation where an observer views Marie on four different occasions: twice when she is behaving kindly and twice when she is behaving dishonestly. Suppose that the observer is then asked to infer Marie's kindness. In reaching such an inference, the observer would presumably concentrate on the first two episodes, which pertain to her kindness, retrieving these from memory and evaluating them to reach a conclusion. Subsequently, the observer should be able to recall these episodes, which contributed to the inference, better than the remaining two, which were not considered.

Hence, the *process* of making inferences may strengthen subsequent recall for episodes retrieved and considered during that process. Ordinarily, these episodes will be congruent with the inferences made, because the latter are based on the former. Episodes that do not contribute to an inference because they are less relevant (and possibly evaluatively incongruent, as in the preceding example) should be relatively more difficult to recall.

In addition to the effects of the *process* of inference making, the resultant inferences themselves may have effects on event memory. Two such effects are suggested in the next two sections.

Retrieval. Psychologists have long believed that learned material may be organized in memory around abstract categories or "themes," and that such themes may then affect the recall of this material (Bartlett, 1932; Bransford & Johnson, 1972; Sulin & Dooling, 1974). For example, Tulving and Pearlstone (1966) have shown that providing subjects with category cues facilitates the retrieval of items from a learned list. In the same way, the recall of prior trait inferences may cue the recall of observed events that imply those same traits. Trait inferences might logically serve such a cue function because (1) they become associated with particular episodes during the elaborative rehearsal processes considered earlier; and (2) they may correspond to the attributes spontaneously used to organize information about people in memory. The notion that traits serve as organizing themes for information about people is elaborated in several other chapters in this volume (see especially Chapter 2 by Ostrom et al., and Chapter 5 by Hastie.)

If traits do serve such a cuing function, then people should ordinarily recall best those behavioral events that are congruent with traits they previously inferred the actor to possess. For example, in the preceding illustration, people who infer Marie to be kind should be better able to recall her past kind behaviors than her past dishonest behaviors. Although this is the same prediction made on the basis of rehearsal processes, there may be ways to distinguish the two hypothesized bases for this effect. The rehearsal of particular episodes should improve the overall "strength" of these memories, thus enhancing the accuracy and confidence of their recall as well as their accessibility. Retrieval cues, on the other hand, may increase the accessibility of episode memories without affecting the strength of these memories or the accuracy or confidence of their recall.

Reconstruction. When people attempt to recall a past event, they may actually "reconstruct" the event by integrating all the informational pieces they can remember into a meaningful scenario (Loftus & Palmer, 1974). Several researchers have demonstrated that in such reconstruction processes people may mistakenly incorporate information that was not present in the original event but was learned or inferred later (Johnson, Bransford, & Solomon, 1973; Loftus & Palmer, 1974; Loftus & Zanni, 1975). In the Johnson et al. study, for example, subjects who read that a person pounded a nail into the wall inferred that the person had a hammer, and later incorrectly remembered that a hammer was mentioned in the original episode.

If people recall their own prior inferences and treat these as pieces of information to be combined with other recalled episodic details, the "reconstructed" episode may become distorted in predictable ways. Specifically, people's descriptions of an event should tend to be consistent with prior inferences they have made about the actors. This consistency might be achieved through selective attention to various aspects of the original episode, through interpretations of intent, motive, or other nonobservables, or even through the fabrication of situational details that were not actually present. For example, suppose that an observer viewed a student, Arthur, helping his friend complete a take-home examination for some University course. If this observer inferred that Arthur was helpful, he might later recall that the students were collaborating openly, that Arthur provided hints but not answers, and that the project was more of a learning exercise than a graded exam. On the other hand, if the observer inferred instead that Arthur was dishonest, he might later recall that the students were huddled secretively, that Arthur provided explicit answers, and that the project was an important course examination. Such distortions are hypotheiszed to occur because the observer's own prior inference is one piece of information that must be reconciled with other recalled details in order to create a satisfactory reconstruction of the event. Like rehearsal and retrieval processes, reconstruction processes will tend to increase the similarity between recalled inferences and recalled events.

Empirical Evidence: Trait Inferences Affect Event Recall. In the Carlston (1977) study outlined earlier, two different kinds of stimulus sets were given to subjects at the beginning of the experiment. Some subjects received six *multiple implication* episodes, each of which implied both a positive and a negative trait. For example, one episode involved John making an accurate but unflattering remark to a friend, a behavior implying both honesty and unkindness. Other subjects received sets of six *single implication* episodes, three of which implied the positive trait, and three of which implied the negative trait. These sets were designed to allow selective recall of episodes pertaining to one or the other trait.

After perusing the stimulus sets, subjects were induced to make particular kinds of inferences, as described earlier. Then, at the end of the experiment, they attempted to describe as many of the original stimulus episodes as they could. They also rated their confidence in the recall of each episode, and each episode was graded for accuracy by blind judges.

For some subjects, the recall tasks occurred shortly after the initial stimulus presentation and inference making, while for others, these tasks occurred a week later. As expected, there were considerable declines in the number of episodes recalled and in the accuracy and confidence of their recall, from the brief to 1-week delay conditions. However, the delay factor did not interact with the various recall biases reported later in this section.

Rehearsal and retrieval processes were expected to cause selective recall for events pertaining to a prior inference. Hence, it was predicted that in single-implication conditions subjects would be able to recall more episodes pertaining to the same trait as their interpolated judgment than episodes pertaining to the noninterpolated trait. This prediction was supported. However, although more episodes pertaining to the interpolated trait were recalled, they were recalled no more accurately (as rated by judges) or confidently (as rated by subjects) than were recalled episodes pertaining to the noninterpolated trait. Thus it appears that access to inference-related episodes is facilitated, but that once accessed, such episodes can be described no better than unrelated episodes. This is more consistent with the presumed effects of cuing processes than with the effects of rehearsal, which should strengthen the memory trace, and thus augment accuracy and confidence. The possibility that trait inferences might cue recall for related events has been suggested elsewhere but has been difficult to demonstrate (cf. Hastie's Chapter 5 in this volume).

A second, unanticipated selective memory effect also deserves mention. The number of positive episodes recalled declined much more over time than the number of negative episodes recalled. Consistent with this result, positive episodes were also recalled less confidently and less accurately than were negative episodes. As in the recall of interpolated judgments, there appears to be a negativity bias in the recall of stimulus episodes. Either or both of these phenomena could underlie the negativity biases previously observed in the impression formation literature (cf. Kanouse & Hanson, 1972).

The prediction that event memories would be distorted due to "reconstructive" processes was tested by having judges rate the kindness and honesty of each recalled episode description. Although reconstructive biases could theoretically occur on either single- or multiple-implication episodes, reliable biases were found only on single-implication episodes. In single-implication conditions, episodes were described more positively by subjects who made positive interpolated judgments than by subjects who made negative interpolated judgments. Furthermore, a follow-up analysis indicated that this bias occurred on both positive and negative episodes, considered separately, and thus was not a function of the relative numbers of each kind of episode recalled.

In summary, then, the memory data clearly indicated that in single-implication conditions, inferential processes do affect event memories in several predicted ways. First, the trait inferences people make seem to cue recall for episodes relating to those traits. Second, these trait inferences seem to affect subjects' attempts to reconstruct events from memory. These memory effects influence the kinds of event memories that are available about a person, biasing such memories toward the implications of preceding inferences. The lack of evidence for reconstructive biases on the multiple-implication episodes is addressed in a later section.

Implications of Inference Processes for Impression Judgments

When one needs to make a judgment of another person, one will presumably recall information from memory that pertains to that judgment. If he or she has previously made inferences about the other, those inferences may be included in the information recalled and thus may contribute to judgments. If prior trait inferences comprise the only retrievable information about the other, then these inferences should completely determine later judgments of that person.

For example, suppose we inferred that Mark was an honest person because he reported a friend who was cheating on a test. If we are asked several months later to assess Mark's truthfulness, kindness, or other characteristics, we might recall and use our inference that Mark was honest as a basis for these judgments, without recalling or considering the particular event that precipitated that inference. In doing so, our implicit personality theories would probably lead us to ascribe to Mark other positive characteristics that we associate with honesty. For example, we would judge Mark to be truthful, a judgment that could as easily follow from reconsideration of Mark's original behavior. However, we might also attribute kindness to Mark, based on our perception that honest people are generally also kind. This kindness judgment would actually be inconsistent with implications of the originally observed episode, because turning in a friend is not a particularly kind thing to do.

Of course, if the original event were *also* recalled and considered in making the kindness judgment, we would be unlikely to rate Mark too positively on kindness and might in fact recognize that he was somewhat unkind. However, to the extent that the honesty inference is used in determining Mark's kindness, we should evaluate him more positively than we would if we relied on the recalled event alone. This suggests that the particular inferences that people initially make about others may influence their later judgments of those others. Had we initially concluded that Mark was cold, and had we stored this inference in memory instead of the inference that he was honest, we might ultimately have reached altogether different judgments about his truthfulness and kindness. To the extent that we relied on this earlier, negative inference in making the later judgments, we might have ascribed generally negative traits to Mark in contrast to the positive ones that followed from the honesty inference. In essence then, it is predicted that later judgments will be biased toward the evaluative implications of earlier inferences, with the extent of this bias depending upon the degree to which people rely on their inferences in making a judgment.

It thus becomes important to consider the extent to which people do rely on prior inferences in making a judgment. One factor that might logically affect such reliance is the length of time elapsing between the observation of an event and the reporting of impression judgments. Within a short time of observing an event, the details and implications of that event should be relatively salient, and people seem unlikely to make judgments that contradict these implications. Thus in the preceding example, we might view Mark a little more positively by virtue of our initial inference that he is honest, but we are unlikely to believe that he is actually kind, warm, or thoughtful, conclusions that run counter to an event we can readily recall.

With the passage of additional time, however, the event will become more and more difficult to recall, so that its implications may have less and less influence on judgments. Of course, prior inferences may also become more difficult to recall as they become more remote in time, but inferences may be more readily recalled than events. Thus, for example, we might be able to recall thinking that Mark was honest even after we have forgotten the events leading us to that conclusion. There are several reasons that this superior recall for inferences might occur. Trait inference memories might be more readily activated during memory searches, because the multidimensional implicit personality structure in which they are embedded provides numerous alternative routes of access (cf. Tulving, 1972, for an elaboration of this argument with respect to semantic memories). Additionally, the deeper processing associated with reflective thought might facilitate the retrieval of prior inferences (cf. Craik & Lockhart's 1972 discussion of depth of processing). More extensive consideration of these possibilities is provided by Wyer and Carlston (1979).

If trait inferences are more readily recalled than event memories, then these inferences may be increasingly relied upon in judgment making as event memories begin to fade. Eventually, recalled inferences may provide the entire basis for impression judgments, leading to conclusions that could contradict the implications of no-longer-remembered events. Hence, after sufficient time, people in the preceding example who initially inferred that

Mark was honest might come to believe that he was also kind, warm, and thoughtful.

However, the retrievability of inferences and events probably does not completely determine the extent to which each is relied on in making judgments. Even when both inferences and events are retrievable, the extent to which they are used may differ. We have characterized inferences and events as different forms of memory, which potentially have different attributes and organization, possibly making one easier to use in judgment making than the other. Although there is some evidence that event memories are organized in terms of salient themes (cf. other chapters in this volume), such organization might not be very useful unless the observer is making judgments along those same thematic dimensions. As a consequence, searching event memories for new information may often be a fairly cumbersome process.

On the other hand, trait inferences are linked to a multidimensional trait structure (the observer's implicit personality theory), which could expedite retrieval of information pertinent to a required dispositional judgment. For example, an observer who needs to assess a person's kindness can readily do so from previously inferred traits associated with kindness in his implicit personality structure. Hence, even when *both* events and inferred traits can be recalled, the inferred traits may be more easily used in making dispositional judgments.

It is also possible that people use different memory search strategies, depending on the nature of judgments to be made. Dispositional judgments may stimulate retrieval of dispositional information, such as prior trait inferences, whereas behavior predictions may cue recall for pertinent past behaviors. If the most readily available memories fail to provide information pertinent to the judgment, the memory search may continue, progressing from trait inferences to event memories, or vice versa. Ebbesen's Chapter 6 in this volume provides an elaboration of the kinds of information search strategies that might underlie impression judgment processes.

Empirical Evidence: Trait Inferences Affect Impression Judgments. In the Carlston (1977) study described earlier, subjects received stimulus episodes implying both a positive and a negative attribute, and then were directed to make inferences about one or the other. Then, after either a brief or a 1-week delay, subjects evaluated the stimulus person on a number of trait rating scales. If subjects do use alternative memory search strategies, as suggested previously, this task should cue the use of trait inferences. The impression scales were also administered *prior* to the event memory task discussed earlier, in order to avoid prompting recall and use of event memories.

Subjects who initially made positive inferences were expected to subsequently report more positive impressions than those who initially made negative inferences. This prediction was supported for those subjects who originally received single-implication episodes but not for those who originally received multiple-implication episodes. More specifically, in single-implication conditions, subjects given the positive interpolated judgment task later rated the stimulus person more positively than subjects who were given the negative interpolated judgment task.

Further analyses of the impression ratings in single-implication conditions revealed no significant interactions involving delay, type of interpolated judgment, or impression rating scale. Hence, the observed bias occurred both immediately and after a 1-week delay, for both implicit and explicit interpolated judgments, and on impression scales pertaining to both the positive and the negative traits. There were marginally significant tendencies for the implicit interpolated judgments to produce less bias with time, and for explicit interpolated judgments to produce more bias with time, but only additional research will determine whether these tendencies are reliable.

Although impression judgments in single-implication conditions were partially assimilated toward earlier inferences, these judgments still reflected the implications of the original stimulus episodes. For example, subjects who received unkind and honest episodes rated John negatively on kindness and positively on honesty, regardless of their interpolated inference. However, they rated him less negatively on kindness and more positively on honesty after making positive inferences than after making negative inferences. Thus both interpolated inferences and recalled events contributed to later impression judgments, as outlined in Fig. 3.1d.

We suggested earlier that subjects were unlikely to disregard the implications of previously observed events until those events could no longer be readily recalled. In the present experiment, an average of three and a half of the six stimulus events could still be recalled after a week, suggesting that the events were still quite salient. It is not surprising, therefore, that subjects' impression judgments failed to contradict the implications of these events, despite some effects of the prior inferences on the impression judgments. With longer time delays and more complete forgetting of stimulus events, complete disregard of event implications might occur.

Further Evidence on the Bases of Impression Judgments. We have interpreted the data described earlier as evidence that people recall and use their own inferences as one basis for making impression judgments, consistent with the model outlined in Fig. 3.1d. An alternative interpretation is that prior inferences merely distort event recall, biasing impression judgments based on those recalled events. For example, people who make positive inferences recall more positive episodes, and thus might make relatively positive judgments by basing their judgments entirely on these recalled episodes. This interpretation is more consistent with the model in Fig. 3.1b.

However, there is evidence in the Carlston study that biases in event recall cannot completely account for the biases observed on impression ratings. For example, those biases in event memories that were *not* paralleled by inference effects had no impact on the impression ratings. Thus, although the proportion of recalled single-implication events that were negative increased with time, there was no tendency for impression ratings in single-implication conditions to become increasingly negative with time. In fact, the relative numbers of negative and positive events recalled had *no* apparent effect on impression judgments. Subjects who could recall more negative than positive episodes rated the stimulus person essentially the same as those who could recall more positive than negative episodes and those who could recall equal numbers of each.

Another analysis indicated that there was essentially no difference between the ratings made by subjects who could recall events pertaining to a particular attribute and those who could recall no events pertaining to that attribute. For example, five subjects who received honest and unkind single-implication episodes were unable to recall any episodes pertaining to honesty on the episode memory test. Still, their ratings of John's honesty were equivalent to those made by subjects who could recall at least one honest episode. The honesty ratings made by these five subjects could not logically have been derived from the episodes they could recall—episodes that pertained only to kindness and thus had considerably different evaluative implications than the forgotten honest episodes. The honesty ratings must have been based instead on honesty inferences that could be recalled even when the precipitating episodes could not be.

This evidence seems to rule out the theory that impression ratings are based only on recalled events (as represented in Fig. 3.1b) but supports the idea that they are at least partially based on recalled inferences (as represented in Fig. 3.1d). It appears most reasonable to conclude that events as well as prior inferences were recalled and used as a basis for the impression judgments.

THE EFFECTS OF EPISODE TYPE
ON INFERENCE FORMATION

Another Look at Multiple-Implication Conditions

Two different kinds of stimulus episodes were used in the Carlston (1977) study. The episodes used in single-implication conditions each individually implied only one trait, with positive and negative episodes combined in the stimulus set given to subjects. The episodes used in multiple-implication conditions each individually implied both a positive and a negative trait, so that all episodes in the stimulus set possessed the same implications. Subjects in each condition received a total of six episodes.

Hypotheses concerning the effects of the interpolated judgment manipulation on event recall and impression judgments were supported in single-implication conditions but not in multiple-implication conditions. In fact, the impression data in the multiple-implication conditions actually contradicted the hypothesis. Subjects given the positive interpolated judgment task ended up making more negative impression ratings than those given the negative interpolated judgment task. This raises questions about the differences between these two kinds of stimulus sets that might explain the peculiar behavior of multiple-implication subjects.

One clue may lie in the ambiguous nature of the multiple-implication stimuli: Each multiple implication episode can appropriately be interpreted as an indication of either a positive or a negative attribute. When people receive such episodes, they may spontaneously interpret them in terms of only one of the implied attributes, while totally ignoring the other. Some people may focus on only the positive implications of the event, whereas others focus on only the negative implications. If such focusing occurs *prior* to the interpolated judgment manipulation, the manipulation may prove ineffective, and subjects may store in memory their spontaneous initial encoding rather than the inference manipulated experimentally.

How might a subject who has already encoded the stimulus episodes respond when given the interpolated judgment manipulation? If the interpolated judgment pertains to the same trait dimension as the subject's spontaneous encoding, he or she should respond by making the positive or negative ratings that the judgment task was expected to induce. On the other hand, if the interpolated judgment pertains to the other trait dimension, which the subject ignored in encoding the stimuli, he or she is likely to respond with a neutral rating on the task, and perhaps simultaneously to store in memory an inference along the trait dimension on which he or she originally focused.

If this reasoning is correct, then those subjects who spontaneously attend to the interpolated trait should make the expected extreme interpolated judgments and should produce the same positive impression biases that were predicted and obtained in single-implication conditions. Those subjects who do not prematurely focus on either trait, and who withhold judgment until the interpolated judgment tasks, should similarly make the expected judgments and produce the predicted impression biases. But those subjects who attend to the noninterpolated trait should make relatively neutral interpolated judgments and should produce impression biases in the opposite direction to those predicted. These reverse biases would reflect their spontaneous encoding rather than the intended effects of the interpolated judgment.

To test this possibility, subjects in the multiple-implication condition were divided by a median split within each cell into those who made the expected ratings on the interpolated judgment task and those who made relatively neutral ratings instead. As anticipated, those subjects who made the expected interpolated judgment ratings produced the expected assimilative biases, whereas those who made relatively moderate judgment ratings produced even larger biases in the opposite direction. The same analysis in single-implication conditions revealed that, here, subjects making expected judgment ratings also produced assimilative biases, whereas those who made relatively moderate judgment ratings produced no biases at all. As a consequence, the overall condition means were in the expected direction in single-implication conditions but in the opposite direction in multiple-implication conditions.

It appears then, that the various hypotheses were not supported in multiple-implication conditions because many subjects in these conditions failed to respond as expected to the interpolated judgment manipulation. Possibly, as we have suggested, this occurred because subjects prematurely focused on one implication of the multiple-implication episodes. This focusing phenomena has important implications for impression formation and is discussed at more length in the following section.

The Interpretation of Events

There may be a general tendency for people to interpret events in terms of their single, most prominent implication. Thus, upon learning that an actor helped a friend cheat, an observer may infer that the actor is helpful or that he is dishonest, but is less likely to infer that the actor is both helpful and dishonest. Such a tendency might facilitate processing and understanding of events too complex to be handled in other ways. Consider an episode where an employee compliments his boss for a bad decision. This could imply that the employee is kind, polite, manipulative, ambitious, dishonest, and/or unintelligent. But as Jones and Davis (1965) note, when there are a large number of potential reasons for a behavior, confidence that any single reason is correct diminishes. If observers are to learn anything very useful from this episode, they must narrow their interpretation, possibly by focusing on the single implication they find most convincing: perhaps that the employee is manipulative. Having reached this conclusion, they may then discount other plausible interpretations of the event (cf. Kelley, 1967). The inference that the employee is manipulative is sufficient to explain the behavior, and thus little may be concluded about the actor's kindness, ambition, or intelligence.

Precisely which of an event's multiple implications an observer will focus on may be a function of a number of different variables. Particular implications of an observed behavior may be more unique, more informative, or less expected, so that people tend to attend to these more carefully. Particular implications may also be emphasized in the scripts (Abelson, 1976) society provides for interpreting events. Hence, theft is more commonly interpreted in terms of honesty than in terms of kindness, although it may have implications for the latter attribute as well as the former.

In addition to these stimulus differences, there are undoubtedly individual differences in the implications people focus on in making inferences from events. Researchers have suggested that individuals' needs (Cantor, 1976; Secord, Backman, & Meredith, 1962), self-schemata (Markus, 1977) and stereotypes (Cohen, 1976) affect such inference making. The nature of anticipated future interaction might also affect the dimensions on which other people are evaluated (Jones & deCharms, 1957). For example, someone who is considering whether to loan another person money would be more likely to focus on his honesty than on other traits implied by his behavior. Different traits might also be salient to different individuals because of immediately preceding events in which those trait dimensions were salient or important (Higgins, Rholes, & Jones, 1977). Further research into such factors seems desirable.

If people do tend to draw only one conclusion from one event, then it may require two different episodes to convey two different attributes. That is, to convince you that an actor is both helpful and dishonest, I may need to describe one episode implying helpfulness and a different episode implying dishonesty. A single episode implying both would only lead you to infer one or the other. In fact, several episodes implying both might still lead to only one conclusion if your interpretation of these epiosdes is consistently the same.

Empirical Evidence: Episode Type and Inference Formation

A study was done by Carlston, Groff, Shovar, and Dallas (1979) to examine the inferences people spontaneously make from single- and multiple-implication episodes. In this study, subjects' inferences were not manipulated as they were in the Carlston (1977) study, but they were assessed immediately after stimulus presentation. Other procedures parallel those in the earlier study. Three hundred and twenty subjects took part in the study and were instructed to form an impression of a target (John) who was described to them by four tape-recorded behavioral episodes. The episodes comprised either single- or multiple-implication sets and implied either kindness and dishonesty or unkindness and honesty. The subjects were then asked to report their impressions on several kinds of items, including one that asked for the two trait terms that best described John. (Subjects returned 1, 2, or 4 weeks later to respond to impression rating scales and recall tasks, data discussed in later sections.)

Subjects' two responses to the initial impression question were coded by two "blind" judges. These codings indicated that subjects who received multiple-implication stimuli were far less likely to refer to both John's positive and negative traits in their two responses than were subjects who received single-implication stimuli. Only 36% of the multiple-implication subjects used both positive and negative terms to describe John, whereas 56% of single-implication subjects did so. On the other hand, 63% of the multiple-implication subjects focused on only one trait, compared to 42% of the single-implication subjects who did so. (The remaining 1% to 2% of subjects in each condition referred to neither the positive nor negative traits.) These results are consistent with the hypothesis that subjects receiving multiple-implication stimuli are likely to focus spontaneously on only one of the attributes implied by the presented episodes, even though the episodes have other implications as well. Interestingly, the vast majority of those subjects who did focus on a single attribute focused on the *negative* attribute (70% of the focusers in multiple-implication conditions, 79% in single-implication conditions). This is yet another example of a negativity bias.

FURTHER EVIDENCE ON
THE EFFECTS OF INFERENCES

This study provides a conceptual replication of the Carlston (1977) study discussed earlier. However, instead of manipulating inferences, as done in the earlier study, subjects' spontaneous inferences were simply assessed immediately after stimulus presentation. This procedure eliminates ambiguity about whether subjects actually make particular inferences, though it substitutes a correlational for an experimental methodology. Nonetheless, subjects' spontaneous inferences should have the same assimilative effects on event recall and impression judgments as hypothesized earlier. Hence, recall and impression measures were administered to subjects 1, 2, or 4 weeks after stimulus presentation. Analyses on these measures are discussed in the next two sections.

Empirical Evidence: Spontaneous Inferences
and Event Recall

As in the earlier Carlston (1977) study, the number of episodes recalled, judges' ratings of episode accuracy, and subjects' ratings of recall confidence all declined progressively with longer delays after stimulus presentation. And, as in the earlier study, the delay factor did not interact with the other factors of interest.

The number of positive and negative episodes recalled in single-implication conditions was analyzed as a function of delay, stimulus implications (kind–dishonest or unkind–honest), and initial inference. A trichotomization was obtained on this last variable (subjects who focused primarily on one trait, on the other, or equally on both), based on several questions assessing initial inferences. This composite measure was correlated .77 with the simple two-response open-ended question reported earlier.

This analysis provides no support for an initial inference effect or for any of the other recall biases (e.g., a negativity effect) obtained in the Carlston (1977) study. The smaller number of stimulus episodes used in the present study (two instead of three pertaining to each trait) may have restricted the range of scores too much to allow reliable differences to occur between conditions. Even the effect of delay on the number of episodes recalled was considerably smaller, F (1, 145) = 10.6, than in the original Carlston study, F (1, 115) = 113.9, although delays were up to four times longer in the present study.

This experiment does provide additional evidence of reconstructive biases in the description of recalled episodes. Judges rated these descriptions on implied kindness and implied honesty, and these ratings were used as a repeated measure in an analysis with delay, stimulus implications (kind–dishonest or unkind–honest), stimulus type (multiple or single implications), and initial inference as between-subject factors. As expected, subjects who made positive initial inferences subsequently described the episodes they could recall more positively than subjects who made negative initial inferences, and those who made inferences pertaining to both the positive and negative dimensions gave intermediate descriptions of the episodes. This effect did not interact with any other factors. Thus, this evidence suggests that the attribute to which subjects initially attend colors their descriptions of the stimulus episodes, even when those descriptions are made a month later.

Empirical Evidence: Spontaneous Inferences and Impression Ratings

Impression judgments made along both critical trait dimensions (kindness and honesty) were analyzed as a function of the various experimental factors, including initial inference. Figure 3.2 illustrates subjects' final impression ratings on both the positive and negative attribute dimensions for those who made different initial inferences. As predicted, subjects who made primarily positive initial inferences reported more positive impressions on both rating scales than did subjects who made primarily negative initial inferences. Subjects whose inferences incorporated both positive and negative attributes made intermediate ratings on both scales. These results are entirely consistent with those obtained in the original Carlston (1977) study.

It is also noteworthy that subjects made fairly neutral ratings on the trait dimension that was not represented in their initial impression. Those subjects whose initial inferences did not incorporate the negative attribute rated John at 3.3 (on a 7-point scale) on that attribute in their later impression ratings,

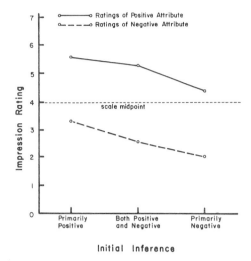

FIG. 3.2. Final impression judgments as a function of spontaneous initial inferences (Carlston, Groff, Shovar, & Dallas, 1979).

and those whose initial inferences did not incorporate the positive attribute rated John at 4.3 on that attribute. Hence, if subjects did not form an inference pertaining to a particular attribute, they made fairly neutral ratings on that attribute at a later time.

These results did not differ between subjects receiving single- and multiple-implication stimulus episodes. As noted earlier, these conditions did differ in the *kinds* of inferences that subjects characteristically made, with single-implication subjects focusing on both traits more frequently than multiple-implication subjects. But such differences affect only the numbers of subjects making positive or negative inferences rather than both and should not affect the magnitude of biases produced by these inferences. Furthermore, since actual rather than manipulated inferences were compared in this study, spontaneous focusing on particular implications prior to the inference task is not a problem here as it was in the multiple-implication conditions of the Carlston (1977) study. The present results suggest that the inferences subjects actually make predictably influence their impression judgments in both single- and multiple-implication conditions.

In the present study and in the original Carlston (1977) study, the means suggested increases in impression biases with time. However, these differences did not achieve acceptable levels of significance. Other researchers have found reliable indications that such impression biases do increase with time, as predicted earlier (e.g., Higgins et al., 1977; Wyer & Srull, in press). Therefore, although the present study provides no support for the proposition, it appears probable that prior inferences do play a larger role in impression formation with longer delays after stimulus presentation.

INFERENCE FORMATION AND
INFERENCE TESTING

A key feature of the Carlston (1977) and Carlston et al. (1979) studies is that subjects made inferences *after* receiving the stimulus episodes. The event memory and impression biases obtained were thus consequences of the formation of inferences during and following the receipt of stimulus information. Under these circumstances, these biases are uniformly assimilative in nature; that is, episode recall, episode descriptions, and impression reports tend to be assimilated toward the evaluative implications of the prior inferences.

After an inference has been formed, an observer may encounter additional information about the object of his inference, and the inference may affect processing of this information as well. However, the biases that occur in event recall and impression reports when stimulus events are perceived subsequent to an inference are likely to differ from the biases obtained when these events are perceived prior to the inference. This is because the observer is no longer concerned with forming an inference but is instead interested in testing the inference already formed.

While inference-formation processes lead to superior recall for inference-congruent, single-implication episodes, inference-testing processes may lead to superior recall for inference-*in*congruent episodes. Incongruent episodes encountered after an inference is made will be more surprising and more difficult to accommodate with implications of the inference. These episodes may thus require more attention and processing, leading to easier retrieval in the future (cf. Berlyne, 1960). As a consequence, the effects of an inference on recall for events observed afterward may be exactly the opposite of its effects on recall for events observed beforehand.

To illustrate these phenomena, consider an observer who infers from a set of previously observed episodes that Judy is kind and who then encounters four more episodes, three of which imply kindness and one of which implies dishonesty. The "kind" episodes provide no information not already embodied in the inference, and thus they would require little attention. However, the "dishonest" episode may receive a great deal of attention, because its implications are new and evaluatively incongruent with the inference. The observer may devote considerable cognitive work to accommodating this episode with his or her prior inferences, thereby facilitating the future recall of this episode. Of the four episodes then, the observer may better recall the dishonest one than the three kind ones.

If such an effect occurred, it could reflect either of two factors confounded in this example. First, it could reflect the evaluative incongruence of the kind inference and the dishonest episode. Information contradicting the evaluative implications of a prior inference is likely to be particularly surprising. Hence, positive inferences might facilitate recall for subsequently encountered negative episodes, and negative inferences might facilitate recall for subsequently encountered positive episodes. Second, the effect could reflect the difference in the trait dimensions involved in the inference and the episode. The inference pertains to kindness, whereas the episode pertains to another dimension, honesty. It may be that people especially attend to *any* new, potentially informative information about other people. Hence, the kind inference might facilitate recall for episodes pertaining to any trait dimensions other than kindness.

Empirical Evidence: Inference Testing and Event Recall

To examine the effects of inferences on memory for subsequently observed events, Groff and Carlston (unpublished study) borrowed an experimental paradigm developed by Hastie where subjects are provided with trait descriptions of an actor *prior* to the presentation of stimulus episodes (cf. Hastie's Chapter 5 in this volume). Providing the traits, rather than allowing subjects to infer them from events, eliminates the effects of inference formation and allows direct examination of the effects of inference testing. Of course, in naturalistic impression-formation situations, events may be observed both before and after inference making, so that both inference formation and inference testing contribute to event recall and impression formation. Such complexities will be considered later.

After subjects were given the trait descriptions, they received four different kinds of behavioral episodes in various counterbalanced orders. Included were six behaviors implying the same trait as the expectancy ("denotatively related" and "evaluatively congruent" behaviors), and three behaviors pertaining to the same trait dimension but differing in evaluative loading ("denotatively related" and "evaluatively *in*congruent" behaviors). For example, when subjects were initially told that the stimulus person was kind, behaviors of the first type implied kindness whereas those of the second type implied unkindness. Also included were six behaviors implying a trait denotatively *un*related to the expectancy but with the same evaluative implications, and three behaviors differing both in denotative relatedness and evaluation. For example, with a kind expectancy, these behaviors implied intelligence and unintelligence, respectively. The study incorporated two complete replications, using either kindness or intelligence as the initial trait expectancy.

Twice as many evaluatively congruent as incongruent behaviors were presented to each subject so that the information as a whole supported the trait originally described to subjects. This was intended to discourage subjects from revising or discounting the trait descriptions they were given upon receiving the stimulus information. This procedure introduces a potential confound, because episodes in the smaller set (the incongruent behaviors) may ordinarily be easier to recall than episodes in the larger set (the congruent behaviors). In the present study, however, no such effect was observed on the denotatively unrelated traits; the ratios of congruent and incongruent behaviors recalled were equal even though the first set was twice as large as the second.

After receiving the stimulus episodes, subjects engaged in a 20-minute interpolated activity unrelated to the present task. They then attempted to recall as many of the episodes as they could, and finally, they reported their impression of the stimulus actor.

The proportions of various kinds of events recalled are shown in Table 3.1. It is evident that recall was poorest for those episodes that were most redundant with trait information already known (the denotatively related, evaluatively congruent episodes). Recall was best for those episodes that directly contradicted the known trait information (the denotatively related, evaluatively *in*congruent episodes) and that were therefore probably most unexpected, surprising, and attention grabbing. Episodes pertaining to a new trait dimension also possessed a recall advantage, although it was not as large. It made little difference whether denotatively unrelated episodes were evaluatively congruent or incongruent.

These data thus suggest that inference-testing processes lead to superior recall for episodes that contradict the inference or that provide new, unrelated information. The former result is consistent with results obtained by Hastie (Hastie & Kumar, 1979). However, the latter result is inconsistent with Hastie's finding that irrelevant episodes are less well recalled than relevant ones. This inconsistency probably reflects the different instructions given to subjects in the two experiments. In Hastie's research, subjects were told to "integrate [the] behavioral information into their initial impression to yield a

TABLE 3.1
Proportions of Various Episodes Recalled[a]

| | | Denotative Relatedness to Expectancy Trait | |
		Related	Unrelated
Evaluative congruence with expectancy	Congruent	.44	.51
	Incongruent	.58	.52

[a]From Groff and Carlston (unpublished study).

single coherent impression of the individual [p. 156]." This instruction obviously encourages attention to information that can be integrated with the trait (that is, relevant information) and discourages attention to new information, which might lead to a second inference rather than a single, coherent impression. The instruction thus encourages processing more similar to inference-formation than inference-testing processes. In the Groff and Carlston unpublished study, subjects were initially instructed simply to form an impression of the actor, which they presumably did when given the trait descriptions, and which they may then have tested when given the stimulus episodes. This suggests that the exact motivation of subjects may influence the manner in which post-inference events are processed.

Empirical Evidence: Inference Testing and Impression Judgments

The implications of inference-testing processes for later impression judgments are unclear. It appears that the recalled inference and the recalled events may have opposing effects on an impression so that the overall effect may be neutral or unreliable. For example, consider two individuals who have made trait inferences along dimensions that we will call A and B, and who subsequently encounter behavioral episodes pertaining to both dimensions. To the extent that these individuals base their impressions on recalled trait inferences, the one who initially inferred A should hold an impression more congruent with that inference, whereas the one who initially inferred B should hold an impression more congruent with that inference. However, the individual who initially inferred A will be able to recall more of the subsequently observed behavioral episodes pertaining to B, whereas the one who initially inferred B will be able to recall more of the episodes pertaining to A. Hence, to the extent that impressions are based on recalled episodes, the one who initially inferred A should hold an impression more congruent with B and the one who initially inferred B should hold an impression more congruent with A. The opposing effects of the inferences and event memories might well offset each other, so that no overall impression biases occur. It is also possible that each individual would revise his or her trait inferences in light of the new event information, producing an intermediate inference congruent with both A and B. In any case, no reliable impression biases would be expected to occur. In fact, no impression biases were observed in the Groff and Carlston study; subjects originally receiving kind trait descriptions and those originally receiving intelligent trait descriptions reported equivalent impressions after encountering the stimulus episodes described earlier.

The Effects of Episode Type on Inference Testing

The discussion in the preceding sections focused on the processing of single-implication episodes. The implications of such episodes are relatively unambiguous so that subjects recognize and attend to the incongruence of certain episodes with their trait preconceptions. People may well prefer *not* to recognize such incongruences as long as their prior trait inference provides an adequate account for information received later. But when the inference is clearly not adequate, they pay special attention to the incongruent information and recall it more readily thereafter. The impressions they then report are not much influenced by their original trait preconceptions.

However, suppose that the event information did not necessarily contradict the individual's trait inferences. Then persons engaged in inference testing might interpret the events as supporting their inference so that later impressions *would be* biased by the original inference. Hence, with multiple-implication stimuli, initial trait preconceptions might well have an effect on later impressions, even though this did not occur with single-implication stimuli.

To test this notion, Groff and Carlston repeated the basic procedures outlined previously but used multiple-implication episodes, each of which implied kindness and intelligence. Only impression measures were taken in this study, because selective memory effects are not a factor when all episodes have the same implications. As hypothesized, subjects who expected the actor to have a given trait rated him as having more of that trait after receiving multiple-implication episodes than did subjects who expected him to have a different trait. Hence, when intervening events could be interpreted as supporting the trait expectancy, the initial trait expectancies did tend to assimilate later impression ratings.

Together, the results involving single- and multiple-implication stimuli present a clearer picture of hypothesis-testing effects. It appears that people interpret events in terms of prior inferences, when possible, but best recall events that cannot be interpreted in terms of those inferences. As a consequence, initial inferences may influence later impressions only when there are no unambiguously disconfirming or nonconfirming events learned after the inference is made.

Conclusions

The evidence suggests that trait inferences have different effects on the retrieval of subsequently observed events than they do on previously observed events. Such inferences facilitate recall for those previously observed events that are congruent with the inferences but facilitate recall for those subsequently observed events that are *not* congruent with the inferences. We have suggested that the processes underlying these results are different, reflecting inference formation in the former instance and inference testing in the latter. During inference formation, particular events become associated with the inference formed so that the inference cues recall of these events. The more closely related an event's implications are to the trait inference, the more the inference should cue recall for that event. However, during inference testing, the inference leads to increased attention to surprising or unexpected events. Here, the more closely related an event's implications are to the trait inference, the *less* the inferences should facilitate recall for that event.

Both inference formation and inference-testing processes appear to lead to assimilative biases on impression judgments, although the latter process may do so only when subsequently perceived events can be interpreted as congruent with the inference. When some subsequent events are clearly not congruent, the special attention paid to these events appears to counteract the effects of the initial inference.

Natural impression formation may ordinarily involve both inference formation and inference-testing processes. An observer often observes some events, makes inferences, and then observes additional events. Thus inference formation is followed by inference testing, and the observer's final impression may be a function of both processes. If the later events are not congruent with the initial inferences, the observer may resume inference formation processes, revising his or her inferences or making new ones altogether. The combined effects of these processes may depend upon the numbers and kinds of episodes observed before and after the inferences, the nature of the inferences made, the time intervals between the various activities, and so on. While precise explication of these effects is beyond the scope of this chapter, the model provided in Fig. 3.1d provides a useful starting point, suggesting that the final impression will be a function of the particular events and inferences recalled. These events and inferences will themselves be functions of inference formation and inference-testing processes such as those described in this chapter. Hence, even more complex impression situations may ultimately be understood in terms of the basic processes and effects we have described.

SUMMARY AND CONCLUSIONS

At the beginning of this chapter, it was suggested that people form inferences about other people they observe, and that these inferences, like the observed events themselves, may be stored in memory. This premise has implications both for the subsequent recall of observed events and for the subsequent impressions that people report. Specifically, several processes (rehearsal, retrieval cues, and reconstruction) could lead episodic memories to be distorted in a manner increasing their consistency with prior trait inferences. Additionally, if people base their impression judgments at least partially on recalled trait inferences, then these judgments should tend to become assimilated toward the implications of those inferences. These predictions are embodied in the model illustrated in Fig. 3.1d.

Several experiments were reported that provide substantial support for these possibilities. The Carlston (1977) study demonstrated that episode retrieval, episode descriptions, and impression ratings are all predictably influenced by subjects' earlier inferences but only when the original stimuli have single implications. The Carlston et al. (1979) study provides additional evidence of these effects, with both single- and multiple-implication stimuli, using a correlational methodology. This study also suggests that people react to single- and multiple-implication episodes differently, possibly explaining the different results obtained in the earlier Carlston (1977) experiment.

Overall, the data are quite consistent with the model represented in Fig. 3.1d. People's initial inferences, whether induced (Carlston, 1977) or simply assessed (Carlston et al., 1979) appear to play an important role in the impression process. Because inferences produce similar assimilative biases in event recall and in later impression judgments, it is difficult to determine the precise basis for impression biases. It is conceivable, for example, that inference effects are mediated by biases in event recall, as represented in Fig. 3.1b. However, there are considerable data suggesting that event recall and impressions are not completely interdependent. For example, a number of instances are described in this chapter where differences in event recall were not manifested in differences in impression judgments. The Carlston (1977) study also showed the persistence of stimulus-appropriate impressions in the absence of recall for pertinent events, suggesting influence from other sources of information, such as prior inferences. The lack of interdependence between event recall and impressions has also been noted elsewhere (Anderson & Hubert, 1963; Higgins et al., 1977; Ross, Lepper, & Hubbard, 1975). The evidence thus seems to suggest that event memories do not provide the entire basis for later impression judgments. Whether event memories contribute at all is less clear. In the Carlston (1977) study, impression judgments were generally consistent with the original events, even though biased to an extent by prior inferences. This seems to suggest that event recall had some effect on impressions, but other interpretations are possible. For example, some subjects may have formed inferences about both the interpolated and the noninterpolated trait, so that these inferences produced impressions accurately reflecting both stimulus implications. In the Carlston et al. (1979) study, only subjects whose inferences incorporated both the positive and negative aspects of the stimulus produced nonneutral ratings of both positive and negative attributes. The remaining subjects made "accurate" ratings of the trait to which their inference pertained and neutral ratings of the noninferred trait. These results could suggest that events do not affect impression judgments except insofar as they affect people's initial inferences. On the other hand, they may simply suggest that people's inferences affect the way in which they interpret events when making impression judgments.

Additional research is clearly needed to determine which of the alternative models represented in Figs. 3.1b, 3.1c, and 3.1d best characterizes impression formation processes. However, it seems likely that all three provide adequate accounts of impression formation under some circumstances. For example, recalled events may principally determine impressions when the events are very salient or when people withhold initial judgments for some reason. Recalled inferences might play a larger role when events can be recalled only with difficulty or when salient inferences appear sufficient for the task at hand. Hence, the important question may not be *which* information contributes to judgments, but *when* each kind of information contributes.

We hypothesized that recalled inferences might play a larger role in impression formation with longer time delays between the observation of an event and the reporting of an impression. The research discussed in this chapter provides little support for this possibility, although condition means were generally in the predicted direction. It appears that subjects in these experiments were influenced equally by their initial inferences, regardless of time delay. Some other researchers (e.g., Higgins et al., 1977) have found time delay effects on impression reports, but these effects may simply reflect procedures that differ from those we have used. Specifically, Higgins et al. may have encouraged subjects to use event information in the impression judgments reported initially but not in the judgments reported after longer delays. Subjects in their study were initially instructed to "take into account all the information contained in the paragraph" describing the event. They also responded to eight factual questions about that paragraph immediately before reporting their impression judgments, a procedure that could increase the salience of event details and encourage the use of this information in making judgments. By fostering the use of event information, these procedures may have diminished the contributions of subjects' inferences, eliminating short-term effects of their inference priming manipulation. However, when the same subjects returned 10 to 14 days later and responded to the impression scale without being encouraged to use event information, the primed inferences substantially influenced their judgments. The accumulated evidence thus suggests that people may initially use either recalled events (as in the Higgins et al. study), or trait inferences, or both (as in the Carlston, 1977, study) in making their impression judgments. The two studies agree, however, that after some time delay, inferences will come to have at least some effect on impressions.

The existence of inference effects on both event recall and impression formation emphasizes the need for research on the processes underlying spontaneous inference making. Only by understanding these processes will researchers obtain a clear picture of the impressions people ultimately form from observed events. Research discussed here has focused on stimulus complexity as one factor that might affect people's initial inferences. This research suggests that people tend to make inferences about only one of an event's implications even when the event has multiple implications (Carlston, et al., 1979). If this principle has generality, it could have important implications for impression formation; it implies, for example, that people learn far less from complex events than they should and that they tend to disregard some (generally positive) personal attributes that are manifested only in the presence of other (generally negative) personal attributes.

A number of important questions remain about spontaneous inference making that have not been addressed in this chapter. When will people make inferences about other people, and when will they withhold judgment? Do the inferences people make pertain to others' traits, and are they articulated using trait labels (cf. Schneider, 1973)? Data reported earlier suggest that explicitly labeled trait inferences may be slightly better recalled than implicit, nonlabeled trait inferences, although this difference did not substantially alter the effects of these inferences on event recall or impressions (Carlston, 1977). Does the articulation of inferences increase their retrievability or their impact on event recall and impressions? Does the amount of time people spend thinking about an event and making inferential judgments affect the subsequent influence of the event or inferences on their impression? As Schneider (1973) notes, we really know very little about the kinds of inferences people make spontaneously. However, the research in this chapter begins to explicate the effects that those inferences may have.

Finally, we have noted that the retroactive effects of inferences are not the same as the proactive effects. The unpublished Groff and Carlston study particularly emphasizes differences in the kinds of events that can be recalled before and after an inference. The inference-formation processes that precede the inference facilitate the recall of previously observed events that are congruent with the inference, whereas the inference-testing processes that succeed the inference facilitate the recall of subsequently observed events that are *not* congruent with the inference. In this research, however, these different event recall effects were not exactly paralleled by differences in reported impressions. The impression judgments seemed to reflect subjects' desire to support their initial inference when possible (as in multiple-implication conditions) but to abandon or revise this inference when exclusive support was not possible (as in the single-implication conditions). Inference-formation processes and inference testing appear to be different parts of overall impression formation processes that deserve additional attention and delineation.

This chapter raises issues concerning the exact basis for the impressions people form. It proposes that people's spontaneous inferences probably play an important role in impression formation processes, both by influencing event recall and by contributing directly to later impressions. Several experiments discussed provide evidence that inferences have such effects. This raises a number of additional issues about the kinds of inferences people make spontaneously, the factors that affect the making and use of such inferences, and the precise reasons that inferences have the effects they do. Although the research discussed here only scratches the surface of these issues, it does suggest the potential utility of examining impression formation processes from this perspective.

REFERENCES

Abelson, R. Script processing in attitude formation and decision making. In J. Carrol & J. Payne (Eds.), *Cognition and social behavior.* Hillsdale, N.J.: Lawrence Erlbaum Associates, 1976.

Anderson, N. H., & Hubert, S. Effects of concomitant verbal recall on order effects in personality impression formation. *Journal of Verbal Learning and Verbal Behavior,* 1963, *2,* 379-391.

Bartlett, F. C. *Remembering: A study in experimental and social psychology.* Cambridge: Cambridge University Press, 1932.

Berlyne, D. E. *Conflict, arousal and curiosity.* New York: McGraw-Hill, 1960.

Bransford, J. D., & Johnson, M. K. Contextual prerequisites for understanding: Some investigations of comprehension and recall. *Journal of Verbal Learning and Verbal Behavior,* 1972, *11,* 717-726.

Cantor, J. H. Individual needs and salient constructs in interpersonal perception. *Journal of Personality and Social Psychology,* 1976, *34,* 519-525.

Carlston, D. E. *The recall and use of observed behaviors and inferred traits in social inference processes.* Unpublished doctoral dissertation, University of Illinois, Champaign, 1977.

Carlston, D. E., Groff, B., Shovar, M., & Dallas, M. *The effects of dominant impressions on recall for behavioral stimuli.* Unpublished manuscript, University of Iowa, Iowa City, Iowa, 1979.

Cohen, C. E. *An information processing approach to social perception: The influence of a stereotype upon what an observer remembered.* Unpublished doctoral dissertation, University of California, San Diego, 1976.

Craik, F. I. M., & Lockhart, R. S. Levels of processing: A framework for memory research. *Journal of Verbal Learning and Verbal Behavior,* 1972, *11,* 671-684.

Hastie, R., & Kumar, P. A. Person memory: Personality traits as organizing principles in memory for behaviors. *Journal of Personality and Social Psychology,* 1979, *37,* 25-38.

Higgins, E. T., Rholes, W. S., & Jones, C. R. Category accessibility and impression formation. *Journal of Experimental Social Psychology,* 1977, *13,* 141-154.

Johnson, M. K., Bransford, J. D., & Solomon, S. K. Memory for tacit implications of sentences. *Journal of Experimental Psychology,* 1973, *98,* 203-205.

Jones, E. E., & Davis, K. E. From acts to dispositions: The attribution process in person perception. In L. Berkowitz (Ed.), *Advances in experimental social psychology* (Vol. 2). New York: Academic Press, 1965.

Jones, E. E., & deCharms, K. Changes in social perception as a function of the personal relevance of behavior. *Sociometry/Social Psychology,* 1957, *20,* 75-85.

Kanouse, D. E., & Hanson, L. R., Jr. Negativity in evaluations. In E. E. Jones, D. E. Kanouse, H. H. Kelley, R. E. Nisbett, S. Valins, & B. Weiner (Eds.), *Attribution: Perceiving the causes of behavior.* Morristown, N.J.: General Learning Press, 1972.

Kelley, H. Attribution theory in social psychology. In D. Levine (Ed.), *Nebraska Symposium on Motivation* (Vol. 15). Lincoln: University of Nebraska Press, 1967.

Loftus, G. R., & Loftus, E. F. The influence of one memory retrieval on a subsequent memory retrieval. *Memory & Cognition, 1974, 2,* 467–471.

Loftus, G. R., & Loftus, E. F. *Human memory: The processing of information.* Hillsdale, N.J.: Lawrence Erlbaum Associates, 1976.

Loftus, E. F., & Palmer, J. C. Reconstruction of automobile destruction: An example of interaction between language and memory. *Journal of Verbal Learning and Verbal Behavior,* 1974, *13,* 585–589.

Loftus, E. F., & Zanni, G. Eyewitness testimony: The influence of the wording of a question. *Bulletin of the Psychonomic Society,* 1975, *5,* 86–88.

Markus, H. Self-schemeta and processing information about the self. *Journal of Personality and Social Psychology,* 1977, *35,* 63–78.

Rosenberg, S., & Sedlak, A. Structural representations of implicit personality theory. In L. Berkowitz (Ed.), *Advances in experimental social psychology* (Vol. 6). New York: Academic Press, 1972.

Ross, L., Lepper, M., R., & Hubbard, M. Perserverance in self-perception and social perception: Biased attributional processes in the debriefing paradigm. *Journal of Personality and Social Psychology,* 1975, *32,* 880–892.

Secord, P. F., Backman, C. W., & Meredith, H. E. Cue dominance in person perception as a function of strength of perceiver need. *Journal of Social Psychology,* 1962, *58,* 305–313.

Schneider, D. Implicit personality theory: A review. *Psychological Bulletin,* 1973, *79,* 294–319.

Sulin, R. A., & Dooling, D. J. Intrusion of a thematic idea in retention of prose. *Journal of Experimental Psychology,* 1974, *103,* 255–262.

Triandis, H. C. Exploratory factor analyses of the behavioral component of social attitudes. *Journal of Abnormal and Social Psychology,* 1964, *68,* 420–430.

Tulving, E. Episodic and semantic memory. In E. Tulving & W. Donaldson (Eds.), *Organization of memory.* New York: Academic Press, 1972.

Tulving, E., & Pearlstone, Z. Availability versus accessibility of information in memory for words. *Journal of Verbal Learning and Verbal Behavior,* 1966, *5,* 381–391.

Wyer, R., & Carlston, D. E. *Social cognition, inference, and attribution.* Hillsdale, N.J.: Lawrence Erlbaum Associates, 1979.

Wyer, R. S., Jr., & Srull, T. K. Category accessibility: Some theoretical and empirical issues concerning the processing of social stimulus information. In E. T .Higgins, C. P. Herman, & M. P. Zanna (Eds.), *Social cognition: The Ontario Symposium.* Hillsdale, N.J.: Lawrence Erlbaum Associates, in press.

4 Organizational Processes in Impression Formation

David L. Hamilton
University of California, Santa Barbara

Lawrence B. Katz
Yale University

Von O. Leirer
University of California, Santa Barbara

Experimental research on first impression formation has been a rich and active area of investigation for over 30 years. Viewed from a historical perspective, there have been two distinct periods in the development of this research area. The first began with Solomon Asch's (1946) classic paper and continued into the mid-1950s. Asch's Gestalt theorizing set the tone for early work in this field, and virtually all of the papers published during this period were replications and/or extensions of, or reactions to, one or another of the 12 experiments reported in that seminal article. Thus, there were reports of experiments concerned with the "warm–cold effect" (e.g., Kelley, 1950; Mensh & Wishner, 1947), the effect of the order in which information is presented (e.g., Luchins, 1957a, 1957b), and how inconsistent information is incorporated into the emerging impression (e.g., Haire & Grunes, 1950; Pepitone & Hayden, 1955). Asch was primarily interested in understanding the cognitive processes perceivers engaged in when developing an overall conception of another person's personality. By having subjects write paragraph descriptions of their impressions of the stimulus persons and having them make inferences about these persons with regard to a variety of trait adjectives, Asch hoped to measure the complexities of developing impressions and to study the "dynamic interaction" among stimulus elements that he argued was central to this process. These methodologies, however, proved to be limited, and by the mid 1950s this line of research had dropped off considerably.

The second period of impression formation research, which began in the early 1960s and continued into the mid-1970s, grew out of Anderson's (e.g., 1962, 1968a, 1971, 1974) research on algebraic models of information integration. Consequently, much of the research activity during this period focused on testing the virtues and vices of various combinatory rules. This work was primarily directed at investigating how persons integrate several items of stimulus information in making a judgment about a person. As such, subjects in the typical study were presented with several trait-descriptive adjectives and were asked to make a judgment about a person so described, usually a rating of their liking for that person. These judgments were then used to determine the goodness of fit between the data and the integration model(s) of interest.

It is important to note that the primary interest of theory and research during this second period was in evaluating models of information integration, and only secondarily in the nature of impressions and their development. The impression formation task first used by Asch provided a simple and useful methodology for testing such models. The use of a single judgment, such as a liking rating, as the dependent variable was certainly appropriate for testing these models, but such a judgment could in no way capture the overall conception of another person's personality that is usually implied by the notion of an impression and that was of central interest to Asch. Thus, whereas discussions of the impression formation literature often emphasize the conflicting approaches of Asch and Anderson, the research that characterized these two periods actually focused on somewhat different questions.

The present authors believe that a third period of research on impression formation has now developed, with a somewhat different orientation than is represented in the work to date. We believe this approach is well represented in the chapters comprising this volume. This orientation reflects a movement away from models of information integration and a return to investigating the cognitive processes that underlie the development of an overall impression of another person. This is basically the same question that intrigued Asch. However, instead of being based on Gestalt principles of perception and relying on intuitive analyses of subjects' paragraph descriptions of their impression, the current approach to impression formation research is based more on recent developments in cognitive psychology. Hence, methods such as reaction time and the analysis of free-recall protocols are more commonly found in studies reflecting this orientation.

WHAT IS AN "IMPRESSION"?

The recent literature on impression formation has emphasized, almost exclusively, the evaluative component of first impressions.[1] That is, the great majority of the studies conducted during the last 15 years have used a rating of one's liking for the stimulus person as the primary dependent variable. Our first impressions clearly include a strong evaluative component, but it is also clear that a first impression includes more than an initial evaluative reaction to a person. It may be instructive, therefore, to consider more explicitly what we mean by the term "impression" and the variety of issues and processes that may be regarded as relevant to the study of impressions.

In our use of the term *impression,* we are referring to *a perceiver's organized cognitive representation of another person.* This definition is intentionally broad, and as such includes a number of processes that potentially could contribute to such a cognitive representation. In what follows we offer some speculations regarding some of these processes, although this should not be considered an exhaustive listing of them.

Acquisition of Information About the Person. The information we learn about a person can be obtained by any of several means—through direct interaction, observation, hearsay, etc. Regardless of how the perceiver comes upon it, some, but not all, of the information available about a person will be processed by the perceiver. Any properties of the information that influence the likelihood of its being encoded—for example, its distinctiveness or salience—would have an effect on the resulting cognitive representation. Thus some items of information about the person would be more likely to be retained than others.

Organization of Information. The information available to the perceiver is not processed into a vacuum. The perceiver brings with him some kind of "knowledge structure" or "schema structure" in terms of which the information is encoded, in this case a knowledge structure based on past

---

[1]Given the pervasiveness of the evaluative component in many kinds of data (Osgood, Suci, & Tannenbaum, 1957), this emphasis is perhaps not surprising. Nevertheless, it seems to have developed inadvertently and does not appear to be based on any theoretical statement regarding the role of evaluation in impression formation. Asch's (1946) conceptualizations were not focused only on evaluative properties, and the information integration models certainly are not limited to this dimension of judgment. It is possible that the availability of normative ratings of likableness for an extensive list of trait words (Anderson, 1968b), which facilitated research using this dependent variable, may have contributed to this characteristic of this research literature.

experiences with person-related information. Person perception researchers have for many years referred to such a cognitive structure as one's implicit personality theory and have invested a good deal of effort into the task of determining the basic dimensions underlying one's implicit personality theory (cf. Rosenberg & Sedlak, 1972; Schneider, 1973). Rather than conceiving of this structure in dimensional terms, we regard an implicit personality theory as a set of cognitive categories or schemas that the perceiver uses in selecting and encoding information about another person. The nature of the perceiver's schemas, then, would influence what information about the other is processed.

In addition, the information will be organized in terms of these schematic categories. As a result of this process, the cognitive representation or impression that emerges as one learns more and more about a person should have coherence and organization to it, and connections between various items of descriptive information should be established in the cognitive representation of the person. This point of view suggests that the nature of that organization and how it is achieved should be an important question for research on impression formation.

Inference Processes. Another consequence of the perceiver's schema structure or implicit personality theory is that it is the basis for inferences made about the target person from the information known about him. We assume that perceivers have a tendency to go beyond the specific information available and to use their schemas as a basis for filling in the gaps in developing an impression (cf. Taylor & Crocker, in press). Thus the cognitive representation of the person becomes developed and expanded beyond the actual information at hand. It is assumed that these inferences are influenced by consistency biases so that the resulting impression would be coherent. Once the cognitive representation has developed, any future reference to the target person by the perceiver would be to that impression rather than to the specific information acquired. One implication of this view is that as time passes the distinction between what is *known* to be true and what is *believed* to be true will become increasingly fuzzy, with the result that errors in recall and judgment may occur. Evidence supporting this proposition is reviewed elsewhere in this volume (Wyer & Srull, Chapter 7).

Imagery. Another potentially important component of first impressions, it seems to us, is imagery. The nature of imagery and its relation to other cognitive processes is currently a rather controversial topic in cognitive psychology. To our knowledge, there has not been any research on the role of imagery in impression formation. It is included in the present discussion simply because of our intuition that imagery seems to be almost inherent in the impression formation process. Certainly when we meet someone for the first time, a visual image of the person is one of the primary ingredients of the cognitive representation of the person we take away with us. More interesting, perhaps, is the case in which the person's physical appearance is not known to the perceiver. If one of your friends were to describe his brother to you, and if that description dealt with the nature of his personality, interests, and values but included no information regarding his physical characteristics, you may nevertheless develop some hunches about what he looks like. This seems almost automatic and suggests that there are visual components of our schematic structures from which such images can be developed. What role, if any, these images might play in the organizational processes discussed in the preceding paragraphs is another question worthy of investigation. If these intuitions are plausible and have merit, then current and future work on imagery should have implications for understanding impression formation.

Evaluation. Evaluation is clearly an important component of impressions. From our very first interactions with another person, we immediately develop a sense of whether or not we like the person, whether we want the relationship to develop or to end. From the recent literature on information integration, we know a good bit about how people make judgments of this type. Among the things we still need to know are how this evaluative component is incorporated into the cognitive representation of the person, how it relates to the more descriptive aspects of the impression, and how, as part of the impression, it influences the processing of subsequent information about the person.

These, then, are some speculations about the nature of impressions as cognitive representations of other persons. They are not presented as a foundation for a theoretical framework, although theory development is badly needed in this domain. Rather, our purpose in this section has been to argue that recent research on impression formation has been unnecessarily narrow in its scope, focusing on only one component of the impression formation process, and to suggest a number of other components and issues that need to be investigated.

CONCEPTUAL ORIENTATION

During the last few years, we have conducted a series of studies concerned with two of the topics noted earlier, namely, processes involved in the acquisition and organization of information in the course of forming a first impression. We began with some simple intuitions about the impression formation process and devised some experiments to test these notions. The results of those first studies were sufficiently interesting and encouraging to lead us on to additional experiments, testing new hypotheses. In this section, we describe the notions about cognitive processes in impression formation that we started with. Subsequent sections describe the experimental paradigm used in our research and present a summary of our research program to date. In a final section, we return to conceptual issues and attempt to evaluate our current understanding of the processes we have studied.

Our initial assumptions about the impression formation process focused on how the perceiver acquires and incorporates information into an emerging impression. In forming an impression of another person, we typically obtain information sequentially over time. The time period may be fairly brief, as during the course of a single occasion when we might interact with or learn about a person, or it may be rather extended, as when we have repeated interactions with the person. In either case, information is acquired over time, and new bits of knowledge about the person are incorporated into a cognitive representation that begins to develop with the first available information. Thus, it seemed to us that, even in our watered-down laboratory representation of this process, sequential presentation of information would be an important feature to build into our research paradigm.

An impression is a cognitive representation of a person. Following Asch (1946), we assume that in forming an impression perceivers tend to develop as coherent a representation of the person as possible. Because each item of information describes the same object—namely, the target person—the perceiver will attempt to incorporate each one into the impression in a way that "makes sense" in view of what else is known or assumed to be true of the person. To a large extent, it is this process of "making sense" that we seek to understand, for it is through this process that a collection of isolated descriptive facts becomes integrated into an overall impression of a person. Several assumptions underlying our view of this process can be specified. First, if the impression is to be a coherent cognitive representation of the person, it seems plausible that biases toward evaluative consistency will influence this process. We will not deal with those biases further here except to note that the widespread evidence of halo effects in person perception provides support for this assumption.

Second, the tendency toward developing an organized impression suggests that during acquisition each item of information will be related to the other items of information known about the person. One implication of this view is that the functional meaning of any given item, and its role in the overall cognitive representation, will be determined by how it "fits into" the emerging impression. Evidence that the connotative meaning of an item of stimulus information is influenced by what else is known about the person has been reported in a number of studies (e.g., Hamilton & Zanna, 1974; Wyer, 1974; Zanna & Hamilton, 1977).

A third assumption concerns the nature of the resulting cognitive representation. If the perceiver relates each new item to other, already acquired items of information during the acquisition process, then it would seem inherent in the impression formation process that the perceiver develops an interlocking network of associative relationships among the various items of information known about the person. The existence of such interitem associations should facilitate later recall of the information one has acquired about the target person. Thus, one implication of this organizing component of the impression formation process is that, in comparison to some task condition that does not include such organizational characteristics, subjects who are instructed to form an impression of a person on the basis of a series of information items should evidence greater amounts of recall. This hypothesis was the starting point of our research program and has been tested in a number of studies to be reported later.

What would constitute a task condition that does not include the organizational activity assumed to be inherent in the impression formation process? For such a comparison condition, we chose the standard memory task in which subjects are instructed to try to remember as many of the stimulus items as possible. This is also a task in which the subject is actively acquiring information for a specific purpose, but in this case the task demands presumably do not require that the subjects organize the separate items of information into a coherent structure. It therefore seems to be a useful comparison for evaluating our notions about cognitive activities characteristic of the impression formation process.

Other aspects of our initial thinking concerned the nature of this organizing process. Presumably the formation of interitem associations can be facilitated or inhibited by various characteristics of the stimulus information. One variable that seemed of potential importance was the presence of a highly distinctive item in the stimulus information. Distinctiveness can be defined in several different ways, as is reflected in previous impression formation research using evaluative judgment tasks. For example, an item of information that is *evaluatively inconsistent* with other information about a person (e.g., negative item in an otherwise favorable description) is distinctive and has been shown to receive differential weight in judgment tasks (e.g., Hamilton & Zanna, 1972; Hodges, 1974). Alternatively, an item which is *incongruent* in denotative meaning with another item can be considered distinctive, and how this type of inconsistency is dealt with by the perceiver has long been a topic of interest to impression formation researchers (e.g., Anderson & Jacobson, 1965; Asch, 1946; Haire & Grunes, 1950; Pepitone & Hayden, 1955). Also, an item that conveys *nonredundant* (though not contradictory) information can be regarded as distinctive (Wyer, 1970), and Asch's (1946) famous "warm–cold" effect is probably best understood as being due to the influence of distinctive (in the sense of unique) information (Rosenberg, Nelson, & Vivekananthan, 1968; Zanna & Hamilton, 1972). These three definitions of distinctiveness are all context based; that is, an item's distinctiveness is based on its relationship to some other item(s) in the stimulus set. Stimulus information can also be distinctive in its own right— for example, as in the case of highly infrequent or bizarre behavior. Such information is known to have an impact on the perceiver's perception of and judgments about the stimulus person (e.g., Newtson, 1973). Given this evidence of the important influence of distinctive information (defined in various ways) in traditional impression formation tasks, it seemed plausible to consider how such information is acquired and represented within the overall impression.

What role might we expect distinctive information to play in the development of an organized cognitive representation of a person? Our assumption was that the presence of a highly distinctive item of information in the stimulus descriptions might serve as a focal point around which an impression could be organized. If this were the case, then we might expect that the perceiver would be likely to develop associative connections between the distinctive item and other items in the stimulus list. Because a distinctive item is highly likely to be recalled, a large number of associative links with this item should facilitate recall of other items as well. Thus, in an impression formation task, recall of stimulus items should be greater when the descriptive information contains a distinctive item than when it does not.

The memory literature, however, suggests that the presence of a distinctive item in a stimulus list may have other consequences. Although the probability that the distinctive item itself will be recalled is quite high, a phenomenon known as the von Restorff effect (Wallace, 1965; see also Hastie, Chapter 5, this volume), it is unclear what effect this item has on recall of other items in the stimulus sequence. There is some evidence that recall of items near it in the stimulus list is suppressed, resulting in the poorer overall recall performance (e.g., Jenkins & Postman, 1948), but the findings on this issue have not been consistent (Wallace, 1965). In any event, there is little basis in this literature for expecting that a distinctive item will result in improved recall of the other items, as was predicted previously for an impression formation task. Thus, the second hypothesis tested in this research was that the difference between impression formation and memory condition subjects in their recall performance would be greater when the stimulus information contained a highly distinctive item.

As noted in our introductory comments, a considerable amount of research has demonstrated that perceivers have cognitive structures or implicit personality theories that, it is assumed, they employ in processing information about others (Schneider, 1973). It seems plausible that, in addition to stimulus characteristics, these structures would influence the organization of information in the impression formation process. One's implicit personality theory presumably provides a schematic structure within which information acquired about another person can be processed and organized. Recognition of this point suggested a means of evaluating more directly the hypothesis that the impression formation task inherently involves information organization and permitted an investigation of how that information was organized in memory. Specifically, the third hypothesis investigated in this research was that in forming an impression the perceiver organizes the stimulus information in terms of meaningful schematic categories concerned with personality content.

EXPERIMENTAL PARADIGM

All of the studies we have conducted thus far have employed the same basic paradigm, and hence an overview of the methodology can be given at the outset. Subjects in these experiments, who in all cases have been college students, are presented with a series of sentence predicates, usually 15 or so in number, although this varies somewhat from study to study. Half of the subjects are told that the study is concerned with impression formation and that they are to form an impression of the person described in the sentences. The other half of the subjects are told that the study is concerned with memory for descriptions of behavior and that they are to try to remember as many of the sentences as they can; there is no mention of the possibility that all of the sentences describe the same person. This instructional manipulation, Impression Formation Set versus Memory Set, was employed in each of the experiments to be described later. After subjects have read the stimulus sentences, a brief filler task (usually 3–5 minutes duration) is administered to eliminate short-term memory effects. They are then given a blank sheet of paper and asked to write down as many of the stimulus sentences as they can remember. This free-recall task constitutes the primary dependent variable throughout this series of studies. In some studies, other dependent measures (which will be described in the context of the individual experiments) were given following completion of the free-recall task.

RESEARCH FINDINGS

Effects of Impression Versus Memory Instructions and Item Distinctiveness

The first experiments we conducted (Hamilton, Katz, & Leirer, 1979, Experiments 1 and 2) were concerned with the first two hypotheses noted earlier, concerning the effects of the Impression Formation versus Memory instructional manipulation and of a distinctive item on recall. The first two studies provided parallel tests of these hypotheses and hence will be presented simultaneously. The stimulus materials for each of these studies consisted of a series of 15 sentence predicates, each one describing a single behavioral act. These statements described common, everyday behaviors that were evaluatively neutral or mildly desirable (e.g., "read the evening paper after dinner," "rented an apartment near where he works," "played ball with his dog in the park.") Half of the subjects were given the Impression Formation instructions described previously, whereas the other half were given the Memory instructions. The second manipulation was contained within the stimulus sentences. For half of the subjects within each of the groups, the middle item in the series of 15 stimulus sentences was a highly distinctive behavior (e.g., "lost his temper and hit a neighbor he was arguing with"), whereas for the remaining subjects the middle item was another common, nondistinctive behavior. Each item was presented for 8 seconds.

We noted earlier that item distinctiveness can be operationalized in several different ways. The distinctive items used in these studies reflect two of the definitions of distinctiveness cited earlier. The behaviors described in these sentences (e.g., hitting a neighbor) occur relatively infrequently and hence were probably salient for that reason. In addition, the distinctive behaviors were undesirable acts that occurred in the context of neutral or mildly desirable behaviors. Because behaviors which are undesirable are usually infrequent in a person's behavior patterns, these two properties are often correlated in everyday behavior.

After the 15 sentences had been presented and a filler task completed, the dependent measures were administered. The first of these was the aforementioned free-recall measure. Our hypothesis was that subjects given the Impression Formation instructions would show better recall of the stimulus items than would subjects in the Memory condition. The number of items (other than the middle item[2]) recalled by each subject was determined, and the resulting group means are shown in Fig. 4.1. In both experiments, subjects in the Impression Formation condition recalled significantly more items than did Memory condition subjects. Thus, the first hypothesis received strong support.

Our second hypothesis—that the difference between Impression and Memory conditions would be greater when the stimulus information contained a distinctive item—fared less well. It received no support at all in Experiment 1 and, although the pattern of means for Experiment 2 conforms

---

[2]Not surprisingly, the middle item was much more likely to be recalled if it was distinctive than nondistinctive. Because the present hypothesis concerns the effect of this manipulation on recall of the other items, the middle item was omitted from the recall score to avoid bias due to the von Restorff effect.

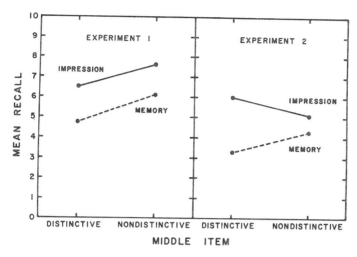

FIG. 4.1. Mean recall as a function of instructional set and item distinctiveness. (From Hamilton, Katz, & Leirer, 1979.)

exactly to our predictions, the interaction depicted in the right half of Fig. 4.1 was not statistically significant.

In addition to free recall, one other dependent measure of interest was obtained. If information is integrated and organized to a greater extent in forming an impression than in learning a series of items, then subjects in the former condition should be more aware of where the distinctive item had occurred in relation to other items in the stimulus sequence. To determine whether or not this was true, subjects were given a sheet that presented, at the top of the page, the item (distinctive or nondistinctive) that had appeared in the middle position in the sequence of stimulus items they had read. Listed below that item, in a scrambled order, were the other 14 sentence predicates, and for each one subjects were instructed to indicate whether it had come before or after the middle item shown at the top of the page. We refer to this measure as the "before–after discrimination task," and it was administered immediately following free recall. Our prediction was that subjects given the Impression Formation instructions *and* the stimulus set with the distinctive item would make the fewest errors on this before–after discrimination task. Because this hypothesis specifies that one group will differ significantly from the other three, it was evaluated by an a priori contrast. The group means, shown in Fig. 4.2, indicate that in both experiments Impression Formation subjects in the distinctive item condition made the fewest errors. The a priori contrast was statistically significant only in the second experiment, however.

We regarded the results of these first two experiments as encouraging. In both of them, we obtained strong support for the hypothesis that Impression

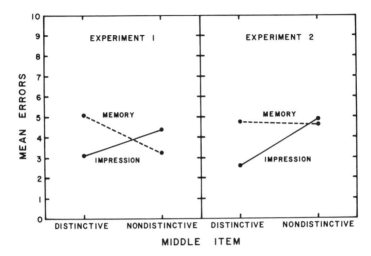

FIG. 4.2.   Mean number of before–after discrimination errors as a function of instructional set and item distinctiveness. (From Hamilton, Katz, & Leirer, 1979.)

Formation subjects would recall more items than would subjects in the Memory condition. We viewed this as due to a higher degree of information organization inherent in the impression formation process. This integrative activity would result in a more extensive pattern of interitem associations, which would subsequently facilitate recall of the stimulus sentences.

The results regarding the role of the distinctive item were less clear. The manipulation of the distinctiveness of the middle item had little consistent effect on recall of other items in the list. On the other hand, scores on the before–after discrimination task indicated that the position of the distinctive item in the stimulus sequence was more salient to subjects in the Impression Formation condition than in the Memory condition.

Varying the Position of the Distinctive Item

Given this ambiguity, a third study (Hamilton, Katz, & Leirer, 1979, Experiment 3) was conducted to examine further the effect of a highly distinctive item in processing information about another person. Whereas in the preceding experiments the manipulation of item distinctiveness occurred in the middle of the stimulus sequence, in this study the position of that manipulation was systematically varied to determine its differential impact when it occurred early, in the middle, or late in the series of stimulus sentences. We have argued that, in forming an impression, a perceiver will attempt to "make sense" of a highly distinctive piece of information in terms of the emerging impression and will try to integrate it into the organized cognitive representation of the person. We have suggested that this process would result in a large number of interitem associations for that item facilitating overall recall. This should occur regardless of when the distinctive item occurs in the temporal sequence, suggesting that variation of the position of the distinctive item in the stimulus sequence should not have a dramatic effect. If, however, this manipulation does have an effect, it should be to improve recall when the distinctive item occurs early in the list, because that might facilitate the formation of associative connections of other items with the distinctive item.

In a memory condition, on the other hand, a somewhat different outcome might be anticipated. If a distinctive item has an interfering effect on the rehearsal of other items in the stimulus list, one might expect that this effect would be greater if that item occurs early, rather than late, in the list. If the distinctive item does not appear until late in the stimulus series, the preceding items would have been rehearsed without the disruptive effect of this item. Its appearance early in the list, in contrast, would presumably interfere with rehearsal of subsequent items.

Based on these considerations, the following predictions were made:

1. Subjects given Impression Formation instructions should manifest better free-recall performance than Memory-condition subjects, replicating the findings of the first two experiments.
2. Overall, the presence of a distinctive item in the stimulus list should, if anything, facilitate performance for Impression Formation subjects, whereas it should interfere with recall in the Memory condition. This hypothesis was also tested in the previous experiments but failed to receive support.
3. In the Impression Formation condition, the position of the distinctive item should not have a noticeable impact on recall performance, or if it does, recall should be better when the distinctive item occurs early, as opposed to late, in the list.
4. In the Memory condition, recall performance should be poorer when the distinctive item occurs early, as opposed to late, in the sequence of stimulus sentences.

To test these hypotheses, we presented subjects with an 11-item series of sentence predicates, similar to those used in the previous experiments. Again, half of the subjects received Impression Formation instructions and half were given Memory instructions. Within each of those groups, half of the subjects were presented a stimulus sequence that contained one distinctive item, whereas the stimulus set for the other half consisted entirely of common, everyday behaviors. Finally, the position of the key item (distinctive or nondistinctive) was varied to occur early (second position), in the middle (sixth position), or late (tenth position) in the 11-item series.

The free-recall performance of the resulting 12 groups of subjects in this experiment is shown in Fig. 4.3. Comparison of the left and right panels of this figure clearly reveals that subjects in the Impression Formation condition again recalled more items than did Memory condition subjects, replicating the results of the first two experiments. (The main effect for this instructional set manipulation was highly significant.) Thus, the first hypothesis received strong support. The second hypothesis—that a distinctive item would facilitate recall in the Impression Formation condition but have an interfering effect for subjects in the Memory condition—again failed to receive support, as it had in the earlier studies. The position in which the distinctive item appeared also had little effect. It clearly had no influence on recall performance in the Impression Formation condition, consistent with Hypothesis 3. However, despite the trends shown in the right panel of Fig. 4.3, the position of the distinctive item did not significantly affect recall in the Memory group, either. In sum, the results of this experiment again demonstrated the superior recall of subjects who formed an impression of a person described by the stimulus sentences over subjects given memory instructions, and neither the presence nor the position of a distinctive item interacted with this effect.

The failure of the distinctive item to have any meaningful impact on subjects' recall performance across three experiments is surprising, especially in view of the fact that similar manipulations are known to have considerable influence on evaluative ratings in impression formation studies (e.g., Anderson, 1965; Hamilton & Zanna, 1972). One possible reason would be that the items we used were not sufficiently "distinctive" to have an effect.

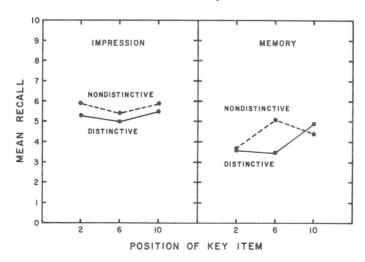

FIG. 4.3.   Mean recall as a function of instructional set and position of key item. (From Hamilton, Katz, & Leirer, 1979.)

However, this explanation does not appear to be justified. In the first two experiments, the proportion of subjects who recalled the middle item was much higher if that item was distinctive than for the nondistinctive case, and although this was less true in the third experiment, an internal analysis comparing subjects who did and did not recall the key item indicated little difference in their recall of the other items. Moreover, in this last experiment subjects made significantly less desirable trait ratings of the stimulus person when the descriptive sentences included the (undesirable) distinctive behavior, indicating that the nature of this item did not go unnoticed. Although any interpretation at this point would be tentative, these findings would be consistent with the viewpoint that evaluative and descriptive components of impressions are stored separately, a possibility which has been suggested previously (Anderson & Hubert, 1963).

Why, then, did the presence of a distinctive item in the stimulus information have so little impact on the recall of other items in the list? As is usually the case for nonsignificant findings, the answer to that question remains unclear. We can only offer some speculations on possible interpretations of this finding. One possibility is that the lack of effect is due to the particular operationalization of distinctiveness employed in these studies. As we noted earlier, there are several factors which can contribute to an item's distinctiveness. Our means of making an item distinctive also made that item to some degree evaluatively inconsistent with the other information describing the target person. We assumed at the outset that perceivers tend to seek coherence and consistency in developing impressions of others. If so, then perhaps a single item that is inconsistent with the coherence of an emerging representation (based on the other items) will not be easily integrated into that representation but will be stored separately. If this is so, then we would not expect this item to have many associative connections with the other items, and hence recall of this item would *not* facilitate recall of the other items. Perhaps stronger suppport for the hypothesis would have been obtained if we had employed a definition of distinctiveness that did not at the same time detract from the evaluative coherence of the developing impression. A second possibility is simply that our hypothesis was wrong; that although a distinctive item may have some special properties, it does *not* become a focal point in the organization of information learned about a person; extensive interitem associations with it do not develop; and hence its presence in a stimulus list will not facilitate recall of the nondistinctive items. Additional research will be needed to further evaluate this issue.

We have found little evidence that a distinctive item will facilitate recall of other items in the impression condition, but it is clear that distinctive information has other effects that have implications for impression formation. First, in Experiments 1 and 2 the probability of recall of the distinctive item was much higher than that for the nondistinctive items. This is not surprising, and similar findings have been reported elsewhere (Hastie, Chapter 5, this volume; Hastie & Kumar, 1979). Nevertheless, this result does indicate that distinctive information about a person is more likely to be retained and represented in the perceiver's impression. Second, Impression Formation condition subjects for whom the stimulus information contained a distinctive item were more aware of where in the stimulus sequence that item had occurred than were subjects in the other conditions (see Fig. 4.2). One might speculate from this finding that, to the extent that information acquired about a person over time is somehow temporally "marked," highly distinctive events might serve as "milestones" along that time period so that other events and acquired information are clearly recognized as having either preceded or followed these milestones. We know of no evidence bearing on this possibility, but its congruence with our intuitive experiences would seem to make it worthy of investigation.

Schematic Organization of Impressions in Memory

Up to this point, we have assumed that impression formation subjects organized the descriptive information in memory to a greater extent than subjects given memory instructions, and we have relied on their superior recall to justify that interpretation. Because it is known that organizing information will facilitate its later recall, this interpretation seems at least plausible. Nevertheless, we have reported no actual evidence that this is the process that has produced the superior performance observed in the Impression Formation condition. It would obviously be desirable to be able to examine more directly the extent to which, and how, the stimulus information is being organized. Our more recent research (Hamilton, Leirer, & Katz, 1979; Hamilton & Lim, 1979) has been concerned with exactly that question.

In order to investigate the organizational process more directly, we have employed a technique known as the analysis of clustering in free recall. The analysis of clustering concerns the extent to which items in a subject's recall list are organized according to certain a priori categories, in ways the items were not organized in the stimulus list. In the typical memory study concerned with clustering, the stimulus list might be composed of nouns representing certain clearly specifiable categories, e.g., birds (robin, sparrow, canary, etc.), fruits (apple, orange, lemon, etc.), and musical instruments (violin, trumpet, piano, etc.). Several instances of each category would be presented in a scrambled order. The subject's free-recall list would then be examined to determine the extent to which the items are grouped into the a priori categories. To the extent that such grouping is evident, the subject has imposed an organization on the stimulus items according to the cognitive schemas that were salient to him. Several indices are available for measuring the extent to which clustering has occurred.

What would constitute the relevant a priori categories that a perceiver might use in forming an impression of another person? We assumed that a perceiver would employ the categories of his implicit personality theory or other personality-relevant schematic categories in organizing information while forming an impression. In our first study to investigate clustering (Hamilton, Leirer, & Katz, 1979), we included items representing four such categories in our stimulus list of behavior descriptions. Two of the categories reflected personality dimensions, one concerning social or interpersonal characteristics (e.g., "had a party for some friends last week," "helped a woman fix her bicycle") and one reflecting intellectual characteristics (e.g., "checked some books out of the library," "wrote an articulate letter to his congressman"). Rosenberg, Nelson, and Vivekananthan (1968) found these to be important dimensions underlying first impressions, and a number of subsequent studies have shown that subjects differentiate between these two content categories on a variety of person-perception tasks (Friendly & Glucksberg, 1970; Hamilton & Fallot, 1974; Hamilton, Fallot, & Hautaluoma, 1978; Zanna & Hamilton, 1972). Two additional categories of stimulus content were also included. One of these consisted of items indicating the person's interest in athletics (e.g., "subscribes to sports magazines," "jogs every morning before going to work"). The final category consisted of items concerned with involvement in religious activities (e.g., "volunteered to teach a Sunday school class at his church"). Four items in each category were prepared, resulting in a total of 16 stimulus sentences. Because the content of each of the items reflected one or another of these categories, the behaviors described in these sentence predicates tended to have considerably greater relevance to and implications for personality than did the rather uninformative neutral behaviors used in the previous studies. The 16 items were presented in a scrambled order so that no two items from the same content category occurred in adjacent positions in the stimulus sequence.

There were two independent variables in this study. First, half of the subjects were given each of the two instructional sets used throughout this series of studies. We predicted that subjects in the Impression Formation condition would evidence greater clustering than would subjects given Memory instructions. Second, within each of those groups, half of the subjects were shown the series of stimulus sentences once, and for half it was shown twice, before the dependent measures were administered. The reason for this manipulation was as follows. We have seen in several studies that subjects given Impression Formation instructions are able to recall more items than subjects in the Memory group. It is also known that clustering values are somewhat correlated with the length of the recall list. From the present point of view, this relationship between amount of material recalled and amount of clustering makes good sense. Organizing information in memory should both facilitate recall of the information and be reflected in the clustering of that information in the recall protocol. Nevertheless, we felt that it would be desirable to be able to evaluate clustering unconfounded by differences in recall. Our assumption, then, was that giving subjects two exposures to the stimulus information before asking for recall might eliminate, or at least reduce, the difference in recall performance by the two groups. We hypothesized that the predicted difference in clustering between Impression and Memory groups would be observed even if the difference in recall were eliminated in the two-presentation condition.

Following stimulus presentation and a brief filler task, subjects completed the free-recall task. The number of items recalled and the amount of clustering in the recall list were determined for each subject, using the Bousfield and Bousfield (1966) measure.[3] The recall performance of the four groups is shown in Fig. 4.4. It can be seen that when the stimulus series was presented only once, the Impression Formation group recalled significantly more items than the Memory group, as had been true in each of the preceding studies. Not surprisingly, presenting the stimulus items twice before recall resulted in better recall for both groups. As anticipated, however, Memory condition subjects evidenced more gain as a result of this second exposure, and although the Impression group still recalled more items than the Memory group, the difference between the two groups in this case was not significant. In the statistical analysis of these data, the interaction term was highly significant.

Mean values of the clustering index are shown in Fig. 4.5. In contrast to the recall data, there is no interaction in these data but two highly significant main effects. Impression Formation subjects organized the stimulus items according to the a priori categories to a considerably greater extent than did Memory-condition subjects. Moreover, although both groups evidenced more clustering after two presentations, the difference between the two groups did not decrease. Because the two groups did not differ in recall performance when they had had two exposures to the stimulus information,

---

[3]Several indices have been proposed for the measurement of clustering, and there is considerable lack of agreement regarding which measure is preferable. In this study, analyses were performed using three different indices, the Bousfield and Bousfield (1966) measure, the D index due to Dalrymple-Alford (1970), and the ARC measure of Roenker, Thompson, and Brown (1971). Because these measures were intercorrelated in excess of .90, it isn't surprising that the results were highly similar for all three indices. The results reported here are based on the Bousfield and Bousfield index. The pattern of means for the other two measures is identical. Statistical analyses yielded the same findings for the D measure, although using the ARC measure, only borderline statistical significance was obtained.

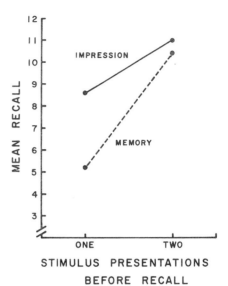

FIG. 4.4.   Mean recall as a function of instructional set and number
of stimulus presentations. (From
Hamilton, Leirer, & Katz, 1979.)

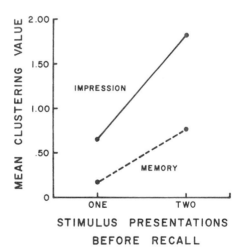

FIG. 4.5.   Mean category clustering as a function of instructional set
and number of stimulus presentations. (From Hamilton, Leirer, &
Katz, 1979.)

the difference in clustering in this case cannot be due simply to a difference in
the length of their recall lists.

The results of this experiment provide strong support for our hypotheses
and offer more direct evidence concerning the nature of the impression
formation process than was previously available. Clearly, subjects instructed
to form an impression organized the information into the personality-
relevant schematic categories to a greater extent than did subjects given
memory instructions. These findings, then, support our interpretation of our

earlier results indicating superior recall on the part of subjects in the Impression Formation condition.

Differences in the Amount or the Nature of Organization?

There is, however, an interpretive problem that remains. With the clustering procedure employed in the preceding study, in order for a subject to achieve a high clustering value he not only must organize the stimulus information but also must use the experimenter's a priori categories in doing so. When a high clustering value is observed, it is clear that this has been done. The problem concerns interpreting the meaning of a *low* clustering score. Such a score could be due to either of two processes: the subject did not not organize the stimulus items, or he organized them in terms of schemas different from those the experimenter had in mind. In the typical memory study on clustering, this has not been a serious problem. When one uses, say, noun categories such as those cited in the example given previously (e.g., birds, fruits, muscial instruments, etc.), the stimulus categories are obvious, and plausible alternative groupings are unlikely. Hence, researchers have felt safe in interpreting a low clustering score as an indication that little organizational activity has transpired. In contrast, the behavior descriptions used in the present research are open to any number of quite reasonable groupings, and subjects may have employed organizing schemas equally plausible to those on which the analyses were based. It therefore becomes important to examine further the nature and extent of organization achieved by our subjects. Specifically, does the impression task result in a greater *amount* of organization, or does it result in a different *type* of organization of the stimulus information? Our next study (Hamilton & Lim, 1979) sought to answer this question.

Another approach to studying organizational processes in memory has been the analysis of "subjective organization" in multitrial free recall (Tulving, 1962). In this procedure, a series of stimulus items is presented to the subject several times, in a different order on each trial. Following each presentation, the subject is asked to recall as many of the items as possible. Similarities between trials in the ordering of items on recall protocols are determined. Because the order of items in stimulus presentation differs with each successive trial, any such intertrial similarities in order of recall presumably would reflect an organization imposed by the subject. In contrast to the clustering technique used in the foregoing experiment, the analysis of subjective organization does not require specification of a priori categories of stimulus items by the experimenter; any organization on the part of the subject will be reflected in the subjective organization measure. On the other hand, although this technique permits one to determine the *extent* of organization imposed on the stimulus items, one cannot determine the bases of that organization (i.e., the categories or schemas used by the subject). To deal with these problems, we have integrated these two paradigms. That is, we employed a multitrial free-recall procedure, which permitted the analysis of subjective organization measures based on intertrial recall similarities, but in addition we used a stimulus set consisting of four items from each of four content areas, as in the previous study, which permitted the analysis of the degree of clustering on each trial. The four content categories provided information about the Social, Intellectual, Athletic, and Religious domains. The 16 stimulus items were presented in a different order on each trial. Following each presentation, a brief filler task and the free-recall task were administered. This procedure was repeated for eight trials.[4] As in the previous studies, half of the subjects were given Impression Formation instructions and half were given the Memory instructions, and the present discussion will focus on comparing the performance of these two groups.[5]

The recall performance observed in this study is shown in Fig. 4.6. Obviously, recall improved substantially during the first few trials, approaching asymptote by around the fourth or fifth trial. The Impression versus Memory main effect was again highly significant. This effect is moderated, however, by the significant interaction of this instructional set manipulation with trials: After the third trial, the difference between the Impression and Memory conditions was nonsignificant. Thus, after several exposures to the stimulus information, the performance of Memory

---

[4]Two minor differences in the procedure in this study from that used in the previous experiments should be mentioned. The first concerned the length of the filler task, which in the other studies was of several minutes' duration. In the present experiment, the stimulus presentation-filler task–free-recall sequence was to occur eight times in the experimental hour, so the filler task was necessarily shortened to 20 seconds. Second, a pilot study had shown that after the first two or three trials the impression formation instructions had lost their impact and subjects believed they were in a memory experiment, making them comparable to the Memory condition. Some means of maintaining the impression formation "set" was necessary. Therefore, subjects in this condition were told that after the last trial they would be asked to write a paragraph description of their impression. In addition, after each recall trial they were asked to make a rating of the extent to which they had formed a well-developed impression of the stimulus person as of that point in the experiment. To give subjects in the Memory condition a comparable judgment task following each recall trial, they were asked to estimate how many items they would recall on the next trial.

[5]In addition to the instructional set manipulation, the nature of the stimulus items was systematically varied in this experiment. Three stimulus conditions were included. The stimuli in one condition were sentence predicates, similar to those used previously, whereas in a second condition the stimulus items were trait terms. In the third condition, two trait terms and two behavior descriptions from each of the four content categories were presented. At the time of this writing, the analyses of these data have not been completed. Therefore, only the major results regarding the effect of instructional set are considered here.

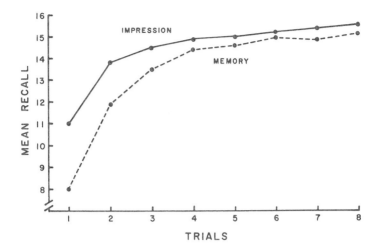

FIG. 4.6. Mean recall as a function of instructional set and trials. (From Hamilton & Lim, 1979.)

condition subjects had improved to the point that it was almost indistinguishable from that of subjects in the Impression Formation condition.

The analysis of the extent to which subjects organized the stimulus items into the four areas of personality content is shown in Fig. 4.7. Clustering

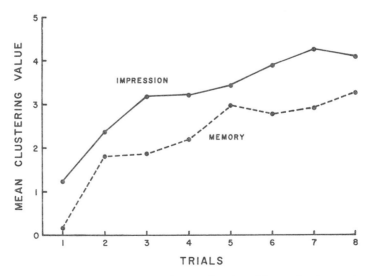

FIG. 4.7. Mean category clustering as a function of instructional set and trials. (From Hamilton & Lim, 1979.)

increased significantly over trials, indicating that our a priori structure became increasingly apparent to subjects with repeated exposures to the stimulus information. Of primary interest is the finding that Impression Formation subjects had significantly higher clustering scores than did subjects in the Memory condition and that the interaction of this instructional manipulation with trials was *not* significant in this analysis. It should be noted that the fact that the Impression Formation and Memory groups converged on their recall performance (Fig. 4.6) but not on the clustering measure (Fig. 4.7) is entirely consistent with the results of the Hamilton, Leirer, and Katz (1979) experiment.

To analyze the extent to which subjects imposed some organization on the stimulus information, irrespective of the a priori categories, the bidirectional pair frequency (PF) measure recommended by Sternberg and Tulving (1977) was used. In this index one determines, for each pair of successive recall trials, the number of times two stimulus items occurred in adjacent positions in the recall protocols from those two trials. Because the order of presentation of the stimulus items differs on each trial, such consistencies in the ordering of recall across trials indicate that the items are stored together in memory and hence reflect organization imposed by the subject. The mean values for the PF index are shown in Fig. 4.8. It is clear from this figure that the amount of organization increased considerably across trials, a finding confirmed by the highly significant main effect for trials. This, however, was the only

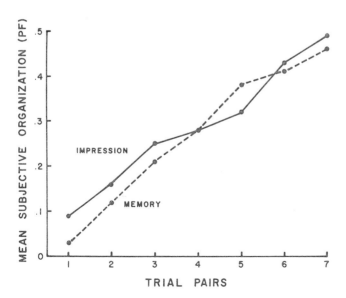

FIG. 4.8. Mean subjective organization as a function of instructional set and trials. (From Hamilton & Lim, 1979.)

significant effect obtained in the analysis of the PF values. Of particular importance for the issues discussed earlier is the fact that the Impression versus Memory instructions had no significant impact on these data. In other words, as reflected in the PF values, subjects in the Memory condition were imposing some kind of organization on the stimulus information as much as were subjects who were forming an impression.

What, then, can we conclude from the findings of this experiment? First, from the PF data it would appear that both Impression Formation and Memory subjects were organizing the stimulus information to an equal extent. This analysis, however, provides no information about the basis or nature of that organization. Storing, and hence recalling, two items together because they begin with the same letter or word contributes equally to a PF score as does storing two items together because they refer to the same aspect of personality content. Thus, the analysis of PF values indicates that all subjects were employing *some* organizational scheme in attempting to recall the series of stimulus items, but it tells us nothing about the nature or meaningfulness of that process.

Second, the analysis of clustering in terms of the four categories of personality content indicates that, although both groups increased in their use of these categories across trials, the Impression Formation group consistently used this organizational framework to a greater extent than did Memory condition subjects. This difference was apparent on the first trial and was maintained throughout the remaining trials. This finding suggests that the Impression Formation instructions served to activate certain schemas for processing person-related information, namely, schemas pertaining to personality structure. Given the nature of the items, these schematic categories proved to be quite useful for organizing the stimulus information. Taken together, the results of the PF and the clustering analyses indicate that the Impression and Memory groups differed more in the *nature* of the organization imposed on the stimulus information than in the amount or *extent* to which that information was organized.

A third conclusion to be drawn from this study concerns the relationship between how information is organized and one's subsequent recall performance. Subjective organization of information is presumably performed to facilitate retention of the information obtained. However, not all organizational schemes are equally effective, a point well demonstrated in the present findings. For despite the fact that the Impression Formation and Memory groups were comparable in the *amount* of subjective organization (Fig. 4.8), there were—at least through several trials—clear differences between these groups in their ability to recall the stimulus items (Fig. 4.6). Thus, the schemas activated by the impression formation instructions appear to have provided a more effective framework for organizing the stimulus information than whatever organizational rules were employed by subjects in the Memory condition.

Organization of Information About Self and Others

In the preceding two experiments, we have investigated the organization of person information according to categories reflecting aspects of personality content. It seems plausible that person information would not always be organized in terms of such themes and that the organization imposed by the perceiver would depend on a number of factors, including the nature of the stimulus information, the task demands under which the information is processed, and the perceiver's cognitive structure. Early work on "cognitive tuning" (Cohen, 1961; Zajonc, 1960) as well as more recent studies of the organization of social information (Ostrom, Pryor, & Simpson, in press) are consistent with this point of view.

In two recent papers (Markus, 1977; Rogers, Kuiper, & Kirker, 1977), it has been suggested that self-schemas may be important cognitive structures in the organization and storage of self-relevant information. This research was not designed to examine the organization process as it has been investigated here but rather has focused on dependent measures (such as recallability and reaction time) which reflect the ease with which various kinds of information are retrievable. However, the authors of both papers discuss the encoding and/or storage of information in terms of self-schemas that would differentiate between (and presumably store separately) information considered by the subject to be self-descriptive and information considered either unrelated to or definitely not characteristic of oneself. If this viewpoint is correct, then we would expect that information processed in relation to the self (e.g., considering the extent to which it is self-descriptive) would be organized in this way in memory and that such organization would be reflected in the subject's free-recall protocol.

There is, however, an alternative argument one can make regarding this point. If perceivers develop cognitive schemas that are useful in processing, organizing, and storing person information, then it would seem to be cognitively economical to use those same categories in dealing with information pertaining to all persons—the self as well as others. In Kelly's (1955) terms, we may employ the same construct system in construing both other persons and ourselves. If this viewpoint is correct, then we might expect self-relevant, as well as other-relevant, person information to be organized in terms of the same personality content themes and not according to its degree of self-descriptiveness. This organizational consistency might exist despite the fact that information characteristic of the self is more accessible and more easily retrieved than information one considers not to be true of oneself (Markus, 1977; Rogers et al., 1977).

In a recent experiment (Hamilton & Leirer, 1979), we have investigated these two ways of organizing person information. Subjects in this experiment were shown a series of 24 sentence predicates, six items representing each of four personality content categories. Because the primary focus of interest was in how information would be organized, the stimulus sequence was shown twice prior to free recall in order to reduce differences between groups in their overall recall performance (Hamilton, Leirer, & Katz, 1979). Prior to stimulus presentation, subjects were given one of four sets of instructions. Two of these instruction conditions were the same ones used throughout this series of studies—the Memory and the Impression Formation instructions. A third group was given instructions highly similar to the Self-Referenced processing set used by Rogers et al. (1977). Subjects in this condition were told that the experiment concerned "the way in which we evaluate information that may or may not be descriptive of ourselves" and were told to consider the extent to which each of the behavior descriptions was characteristic of themselves. The fourth group received what we call Impression and Self-Comparison instructions. These subjects were told to form an impression of a person described by the stimulus sentences *and* to compare that person to themselves. After reading the behavior descriptions, subjects completed several dependent measures, two of which are of interest here. The first was the standard free-recall task. The other measure consisted of having subjects rate, on a 9-point scale, each of the 24 stimulus items in terms of how descriptive they thought the item was of themselves.

Each subject's free-recall protocol was then analyzed twice, examining the extent of clustering in terms of two possible bases of organization. First, clustering values based on the four a priori categories of personality content were determined, as was done in previous studies. Second, each subject's ratings of the self-descriptiveness of the 24 stimulus items were used to establish three new categories—those items rated as high, moderate, or low in the extent to which they are characteristic of the subject. These categories were then used to determine the extent to which each subject's free recall protocol was clustered according to self-descriptiveness. Mean values of these clustering indices for each of the four groups are shown in Table 4.1. For subjects in the Memory condition, there is little evidence of clustering

TABLE 4.1
Mean Clustering Values for Two Possible Bases of Organization[a]

| Instruction Set | Organization Based On: | |
	Personality Content	Self-Descriptiveness
Memory	0.75	–0.18
Impression	2.55	0.55
Impression and Self-Comparison	2.25	0.36
Self-Referenced	1.96	0.48

[a]From Hamilton and Leirer (1979).

according to either of these organizational frameworks. In contrast, subjects in the other three instructional conditions organized the items to a significant degree in terms of the four personality content categories and to a much greater extent than they did in terms of self-descriptiveness. Because chance level of clustering is reflected in a value of zero, it is clear that none of these groups—even those subjects given Self-Referenced processing instructions—organized the stimulus items according to self-schematic categories.

These findings are consistent with the view that perceivers have a cognitive structure for organizing and storing information about persons, and that the schemas comprising that structure are applied to information both about others and oneself. This viewpoint makes great sense in terms of cognitive economics—it is certainly simpler to employ one cognitive structure with regard to all person-objects rather than to have one set of schemas for organizing information about others and another set for the self. As noted earlier, this interpretation is quite compatible with Kelly's (1955) theoretical statements regarding the nature and use of personal construct systems.

What, then, are the implications of these findings for recent research and theorizing on self-schemas? It seems to us that there are at least two possible interpretations worthy of further investigation. The first begins with the recognition that schemas can perform a number of functions within the overall cognitive processing system. For example, they might be influential in encoding stimulus information, in organizing and storing the information acquired, in drawing inferences from that information, and in retrieving information from memory (Taylor & Crocker, in press). Most of the findings reported in recent studies of self-schemas (Markus, 1977; Rogers et al., 1977) have provided evidence that information descriptive of the self is more accessible and more easily retrieved from memory, whereas the present evidence concerns the manner in which information is organized and stored in memory. It may be that certain types of schemas perform some, but not all, of the functions cited by Taylor and Crocker (in preparation). Perhaps self-schemas have their primary influence in making certain kinds of information about oneself easily retrievable but do not play a role in the encoding and organization of such information.

A second possible interpretation questions the notion of self-schema more directly. This view would hold that the organizational process is a major function of a schema, and given the present lack of evidence for a self-schematic basis of organization, the usefulness of this concept is open to question. One could further argue that the findings indicating greater facility in retrieving self-descriptive rather than noncharacteristic information is not compelling evidence for a self-schema structure. Ease in retrievability of self-descriptive items, for example, might simply reflect the fact that we are extremely familiar with ourselves; such familiarity would make response to an item we know to be true of ourselves a much easier task than response to an item that may or may not be characteristic. Thus, a plausible argument could be made that any conclusions about the nature of self-schemas are premature.

CURRENT STATUS AND PERSPECTIVE

In his classic 1946 paper, Solomon Asch made the following observation:

> The impression of a person grows quickly and easily. Yet our minds falter when we face the far simpler task of mastering a series of disconnected numbers or words. We have apparently no need to commit to memory by repeated drill the various characteristics we observe in a person, nor do some of his traits exert an observable retroactive inhibition upon our grasp of the others. Indeed, they seem to support each other. And it is quite hard to forget our view of a person once it has formed. Similarly, we do not easily confuse the half of one person with the half of another. It should be of interest to the psychologist that the far more complex task of grasping the nature of a person is so much less difficult [p. 258].

The program of research we have described, although largely exploratory, has produced a number of findings pertinent to Asch's comments. We have tried to investigate some questions about the impression formation process that have not been addressed in the recent literature and to see where the findings would lead us. In this final section, we attempt to summarize what we have learned, to assess our understanding of the issues we have raised, and to indicate some questions that will need to be examined in the future.

Certainly the most consistent finding from this research is that, given the tasks and procedures we have employed, subjects instructed to form an impression of a person described by a series of descriptive items will be able to remember more of those items than will subjects given memory instructions. This task set manipulation has had a pronounced effect in virtually every test of the hypothesis. We have interpreted this finding as being due to the process by which information becomes organized in memory. The fact that information organization should facilitate recall was the original basis for the prediction, and our analyses of clustering in free recall have provided more direct support for this viewpoint. Thus we are encouraged by these findings.

It may be, of course, that organizational processes are not the only, or even the most important, processes underlying the observed differences in recall. Other interpretations of this finding are possible. One could argue that the instructional sets produced differences in the encoding process—for example, that they resulted in different "levels of processing" of the stimulus information and hence differences in the durability of the memory trace. Although we don't find such an interpretation compelling (cf. Baddeley,

1978), others may consider this a convenient framework for thinking about our results. Similarly, we cannot at this point evaluate the extent to which our findings are due to encoding effects and retrieval effects. These and other issues will need to be investigated before a definitive interpretation is possible. At this point, we simply argue that our findings are quite consistent with the process as we have conceived of it.

It should also be emphasized that we are *not* stating that impression formation instructions will always produce better recall than memory instructions. In fact, we have shown that with repeated presentations of the stimulus list, the difference between groups virtually disappears (Hamilton & Lim, 1979). In addition, one could easily alter the memory instructions in a way that would improve their recall. For example, if subjects in this group were told to "make up a story" based on the items, subsequent recall would in all likelihood be higher. Such an instruction, of course, would have the effect of inducing subjects to organize the information in a meaningful way—the very process we believe mediates the performance of subjects in the impression formation condition. The important point we seek to make is that such organizational activity is an *inherent* aspect of this impression formation process.

A second consistent finding, obtained in all three studies that examined clustering, was that Impression Formation subjects organized the stimulus items according to the a priori personality content categories to a greater extent than did subjects in the Memory condition. These results indicate an important difference between these groups in the organization of information. And as we reported previously, the results of Hamilton and Lim's study suggested that this difference had to do more with the nature than with the amount of organization—*how*, but not *how much*, the items were organized in memory. We consider this latter conclusion to be tentative and believe that a fuller understanding of this issue will require further investigation, for several reasons. First, the indices typically used to study both clustering and subjective organization are fairly limited in that they are based on highly restricted aspects of the recall protocol.[6] It may be that more sophisticated measures would detect differences in the amount, as well as the nature, of organization. Second, the only means of determining the nature of the organization imposed by the subject is to rely on experimenter-defined categories, as in our analyses of clustering. The limitations imposed by this

---

[6]A detailed analysis of these indices would be inappropriate here, but we will simply note that all of them are based on the frequency of occurrence of certain items in *adjacent* positions in the subject's recall protocol. For example, the clustering indices are based on the frequency with which items from the same a priori category are recalled successively. Similarly, the PF measure of subjective organization rests on the frequency with which two items are recalled in adjacent positions on successive trials. Thus, both types of measures can be criticized for failing to consider the overall structure of the recall list.

state of affairs were pointed out in our discussion of Hamilton and Lim's (1979) findings. Recently, Friendly (1977) has proposed several more sophisticated methods of examining the structure of organization in free recall. Perhaps these techniques will provide a means of dealing with both of the problems noted earlier.

Although we feel we have made a useful beginning toward studying cognitive representations of persons, a number of important issues have not yet been examined. Three of them are briefly mentioned here. The first question concerns how inconsistent information is represented in one's impression of another. Except for the distinctive item condition in our first few studies, we have carefully avoided inconsistency in the stimulus items we have used so that it would not influence the other issues on which we were focusing. The presence of stimulus inconsistency would presumably make the organization of information about a person more difficult and would reduce the "coherence" of the resulting impression. Thus, we would expect some influence of this variable on how information is organized and subsequently on recall performance. It is interesting to speculate about how inconsistent information would be represented and stored in memory. One possibility is that all of the items consistent with one theme (e.g., suggesting a friendly, outgoing person) are stored together and that contradictory information (that he is irritable, hostile) is stored separately. Hastie (Chapter 5, this volume), however, found little evidence in support of this view. Alternatively, all information relevant to a particular content domain or theme (e.g., both positive and negative instances of sociability) would be organized and stored together, but would be stored separately from information regarding other types of personality content (e.g., abilities, interests, etc.). This type of organization might facilitate retrieval of all information relevant to a particular personality characteristic, as when the perceiver is asked for information of judgments about the target person's sociability. Other means of organization are possible and conceivably could vary according to the degree of inconsistency present in the information available.

A similar question concerns the organization of person information of differing levels of abstractness. To consider a simple case, suppose some items of information were behavior descriptions and some were trait adjectives. It is usually assumed that trait information is more abstract than, and probably inferred from, more concrete behavioral information. This suggests a hierarchical structure of the cognitive representation, yet little is known about its nature. One interesting question, for example, concerns how the different content themes we have discussed would be represented within such a hierarchical structure.

A third issue concerns how the evaluative component of an impression is incorporated in one's cognitive representation of a person. It is often assumed that evaluative judgments of a person are based on the descriptive information known or inferred about that person, although evidence substantiating this assumption is scarce. Our analyses suggest that this descriptive information is organized around certain content schemas. It may be that each of these organizational units acquires some kind of evaluative "tag" based on the material stored in it. On the other hand, impressions commonly seem to contain an overall evaluative component, rather than several evaluations based on different domains of content. The latter view suggests the possibility that the evaluative aspects of the impression may be represented and stored quite separately from the descriptive material on which our research has focused, with less interplay between the two domains than has frequently been assumed.

The foregoing discussion has focused on issues which have been of interest to impression formation researchers for a long time. We believe that the approach developed in this chapter provides an avenue for investigating these and other issues that may increase our understanding of how impressions are cognitively represented.

ACKNOWLEDGMENTS

Preparation of this manuscript was facilitated by NIMH Grant 29418. The chapter was written in part while the first author was a Visiting Research Associate at Harvard University. The authors are grateful to the following persons who assisted us in conducting the experiments reported in this chapter: Julie Cho-Polizzi, Lydia Deems, Sherri Matteo, and Terry Rose. We also appreciate the helpful comments of Susan Fiske, Shelley Taylor, and Bob Wyer on an earlier version of this chapter.

REFERENCES

Anderson, N. H. Application of an additive model to impression formation. *Science*, 1962, *58*, 305–316.

Anderson, N. H. Averaging versus adding as a stimulus-combination rule in impression formation. *Journal of Experimental Psychology*, 1965, *70*, 394–400.

Anderson, N. H. A simple model for information integration. In R. P. Abelson, E. Aronson, W. J. McGuire, T. M. Newcomb, M. J. Rosenberg, & P. H. Tannenbaum (Eds.), *Theories of cognitive consistency: A sourcebook*. Chicago: Rand McNally, 1968. (a)

Anderson, N. H. Likableness ratings of 555 personality trait words. *Journal of Personality and Social Psychology*, 1968, *10*, 354–362. (b)

Anderson, N. H. Integration theory and attitude change. *Psychological Review*, 1971, *78*, 171–206.

Anderson, N. H. Information integration theory: A brief survey. In D. H. Krantz, R. C. Atkinson, R. D. Luce, & P. Suppes (Eds.), *Contemporary developments in mathematical psychology*. San Francisco: Freeman, 1974.

Anderson, N. H., & Hubert, S. Effects of concomitant verbal recall on order effects in personality impression formation. *Journal of Verbal Learning and Verbal Behavior*, 1963, *2*, 379–391.

Anderson, N. H., & Jacobson, A. Effect of stimulus inconsistency and discounting instructions in personality impression formation. *Journal of Personality and Social Psychology*, 1965, *2*, 531–539.

Asch, S. E. Forming impressions of personality. *Journal of Abnormal and Social Psychology*, 1946, *41*, 258–290.

Baddeley, A. D. The trouble with levels: A reexamination of Craik and Lockhart's framework for memory research. *Psychological Review*, 1978, *85*, 139–152.

Bousfield, A. K., & Bousfield, W. A. Measurement of clustering and of sequential constancies in repeated free recall. *Psychological Reports*, 1966, *19*, 935–942.

Cohen, A. R. Cognitive tuning as a factor affecting impression formation. *Journal of Personality*, 1961, *29*, 235–245.

Dalrymple-Alford, E. C. Measurement of clustering in free recall. *Psychological Bulletin*, 1970, *74*, 32–34.

Friendly, M. L. In search of the M-Gram: The structure of organization in free recall. *Cognitive Psychology*, 1977, *9*, 188–249.

Friendly, M. L., & Glucksberg, S. On the description of subcultural lexicons: A multidimensional approach. *Journal of Personality and Social Psychology*, 1970, *14*, 55–65.

Haire, M., & Grunes, W. F. Perceptual defenses: Processes protecting an organized perception of another personality. *Human Relations*, 1950, *3*, 403–412.

Hamilton, D. L., & Fallot, R. D. Information salience as a weighting factor in impression formation. *Journal of Personality and Social Psychology*, 1974, *30*, 444–448.

Hamilton, D. L., Fallot, R. D., & Hautaluoma, J. Information salience and order effects in impression formation. *Personality and Social Psychology Bulletin*, 1978, *4*, 44–47.

Hamilton, D. L., Katz, L. B., & Leirer, V. O. *Cognitive representation of personality impressions: Organizational processes in first impression formation.* Unpublished manuscript, University of California, Santa Barbara, 1979.

Hamilton, D. L., & Leirer, V. O. *Organization of information about self and others.* Unpublished manuscript, University of California, Santa Barbara, 1979.

Hamilton, D. L., Leirer, V. O., & Katz, L. B. *A clustering analysis of organizational processes in impression formation.* Unpublished manuscript, University of California, Santa Barbara, 1979.

Hamilton, D. L., & Lim, C. *Organizational processes in person impressions and memory: Differences in the amount or the nature of organization?* Unpublished manuscript, University of California, Santa Barbara, 1979.

Hamilton, D. L., & Zanna, M. P. Differential weighting of favorable and unfavorable attributes in impressions of personality. *Journal of Experimental Research in Personality*, 1972, *6*, 204–212.

Hamilton, D. L., & Zanna, M. P. Context effects in impression formation: Changes in connotative meaning. *Journal of Personality and Social Psychology*, 1974, *29*, 649–654.

Hastie, R., & Kumar, P. A. Person memory: Personality traits as organizing principles in memory for behaviors. *Journal of Personality and Social Psychology*, 1979, *37*, 25–38.

Hodges, B. H. Effect of valence on relative weighting in impression formation. *Journal of Personality and Social Psychology*, 1974, *30*, 378–381.

Jenkins, W. O., & Postman, L. Isolation and spread of effect in serial learning. *American Journal of Psychology*, 1948, *61*, 214–221.

Kelley, H. H. The warm-cold variable in first impressions of persons. *Journal of Personality*, 1950, *18*, 431–439.

Kelly, G. A. *The psychology of personal constructs.* New York: Norton, 1955.

Luchins, A. S. Primacy-recency in impression formation. In C. Hovland (Ed.), *The order of presentation in persuasion.* New Haven, Conn.: Yale University Press, 1957. (a)

Luchins, A. S. Experimental attempts to minimize the impact of first impressions. In C. Hovland (Ed.), *The order of presentation in persuasion.* New Haven, Conn.: Yale University Press, 1957. (b)

Markus, H. Self-schemata and processing information about the self. *Journal of Personality and Social Psychology*, 1977, *35*, 63–78.

Mensh, I. N., & Wishner, J. Asch on "Forming impressions of personality": Further evidence. *Journal of Personality*, 1947, *16*, 188–191.

Newtson, D. Attribution and the unit of perception of ongoing behavior. *Journal of Personality and Social Psychology*, 1973, *28*, 28–38.

Osgood, C., Suci, G. J., & Tannenbaum, P. H. *The measurement of meaning*. Urbana, Ill.: University of Illinois Press, 1957.

Ostrom, T. M., Pryor, J. B., & Simpson, D. D. The organization of social information. In E. T. Higgins, C. P. Herman, & M. P. Zanna (Eds.), *Social cognition: The Ontario Symposium*. Hillsdale, N.J.: Lawrence Erlbaum Associates, in press.

Pepitone, A., & Hayden, R. Some evidence for conflict resolution in impression formation. *Journal of Abnormal and Social Psychology*, 1955, *51*, 302–307.

Roenker, D. L., Thompson, C. P., & Brown, S. C. Comparison of measures for the estimation of clustering in free recall. *Psychological Bulletin*, 1971, *76*, 45–58.

Rogers, T. B., Kuiper, N. A., & Kirker, W. S. Self-reference and the encoding of personal information. *Journal of Personality and Social Psychology*, 1977, *35*, 677–688.

Rosenberg, S., Nelson, C., & Vivekananthan, P. S. A multidimensional approach to the structure of personality impressions. *Journal of Personality and Social Psychology*, 1968, *9*, 283–294.

Rosenberg, S. & Sedlak, A. Structural representations of implicit personality theory. In L. Berkowitz (Ed.), *Advances in experimental social psychology* (Vol. 6). New York: Academic Press, 1972.

Schneider, D. J. Implicit personality theory: A review. *Psychological Bulletin*, 1973, *79*, 294–309.

Sternberg, R. J., & Tulving, E. The measurement of subjective organization in free recall. *Psychological Bulletin*, 1977, *84*, 539–556.

Taylor, S. E., & Crocker, J. Schematic bases of social information processing. In E. T. Higgins, C. P. Herman, & M. P. Zanna (Eds.), *Social cognition: The Ontario Symposium*. Hillsdale, N.J.: Lawrence Erlbaum Associates, in press.

Tulving, E. Subjective organization in free recall of "unrelated" words. *Psychological Review*, 1962, *60*, 344–354.

Wallace, W. P. Review of the historical, empirical, and theoretical status of the von Restorff phenomenon. *Psychological Bulletin*, 1965, *63*, 410–424.

Wyer, R. S., Jr. Information redundancy, inconsistency, and novelty and their role in impression formation. *Journal of Experimental Social Psychology*, 1970, *6*, 111–127.

Wyer, R. S., Jr. Changes in meaning and halo effects in personality impression formation. *Journal of Personality and Social Psychology*, 1974, *29*, 829–835.

Zajonc, R. The process of cognitive tuning in communication. *Journal of Abnormal and Social Psychology*, 1960, *61*, 159–167.

Zanna, M. P., & Hamilton, D. L. Attribute dimensions and patterns of trait inferences. *Psychonomic Science*, 1972, *27*, 353–354.

Zanna, M. P., & Hamilton, D. L. Further evidence for meaning change in impression formation. *Journal of Experimental Social Psychology*, 1977, *13*, 224–238.

5

Memory for Behavioral Information that Confirms or Contradicts a Personality Impression

Reid Hastie
Harvard University

This chapter is an outline of a program of empirical research on person memory. Subjects in the research viewed information, in sentence or film formats, that described individual characters. Following the information about each character, the subjects were required to make impression judgments evaluating the individual on several personality dimensions. Finally, subjects were asked to recall as much information about each character as possible.

We think that the conclusions from this research generalize to acquaintance situations where people learn about one another in natural settings. The strongest support for this assertion comes from the stability of our results across several sets of personal information materials, across a wide range of subjects, and in written or film format presentations. We also believe that the research is an important beginning to the experimental analysis of memory in decision-making situations. The focus of all the experiments we describe is on the differential recall of information that confirms one conclusion and information that contradicts that conclusion. A clear understanding of the relationships between memory and judgment is an important preliminary to any theory of decision making (Anderson, 1977; Fischhoff, 1976; Tversky & Kahneman, 1973).

For example, we might form an initial impression of a person as a friendly, extraverted individual. The questions addressed in the present research concern the effects of that initial impression on our perception and memory of additional information about that person. Will our initial impression lead us to treat unexpected events, behaviors that are incongruent with our impression, differently from impression-congruent events, as we perceive them? Will attention and encoding process focus on incongruent events or

155

avoid them? What will happen when we attempt to retrieve impression-congruent and impression-incongruent events from memory? Will memory favor impression-confirming information or will informative, impression-incongruent events be better remembered?

Our preliminary hypothesis is that in the context of an impression formation task, in which subjects are encouraged to *integrate* all available information into a unitary impression, events that are incongruent with an initial impression will be perceived as highly informative about the person's character and will receive extensive consideration during encoding. Thus, we would predict higher recall of information that is incongruent with the impression than information that is congruent with it.

EMPIRICAL FINDINGS

All of the research presented in this chapter utilizes a single experimental paradigm. The paradigm was selected to maximize the impact of a trait impression on perception and recall of behaviors, to allow the independent manipulation of trait and behavioral information, and to permit us to counterbalance the occurrence of specific behaviors so that our conclusions would generalize beyond item-specific effects. From the subject's point of view, the procedure included the following events.

First, an ensemble of between five and seven traits (depending on the experiment) was presented with the instruction to integrate this information into a coherent impression of a person. The traits were selected from the Rosenberg and Sedlak (1972) multidimensional scaling analysis of implicit personality theory. Traits in each ensemble were selected from one narrow sub-area of the implicit personality space to induce a simple, unitary initial impression. For example, a "friendly" character might be initially described as, "Friendly, sociable, gregarious, outgoing, and extraverted." Central traits in these ensembles for different characters included intelligent, unintelligent, friendly, hostile, honest, liar, sentimental, cynical, conscientious, irresponsible, aggressive, and shy. These traits were selected to span the multidimensional space.

Second, immediately following the trait ensemble, a series of sentences or film clips was presented, each item depicting a character engaged in a single behavioral episode. One central actor appeared in each episode and subjects were instructed to combine this behavioral information with their initial trait-based impression to yield a single coherent impression of that individual.

The manner in which these lists of episodes were constructed is a critical feature of the method. The episodes were generated in pretest studies in which subjects were given the central traits, used in the initial trait ensembles, as cues and told to write down behaviors which would be typical of a person who was extreme on the cued trait. These behavior descriptions were edited to a uniform length and given to additional subjects to be rated on a variety of judgment dimensions. The friendly character might be depicted as:

Telling a joke at a party.
Visiting a sick friend in the hospital.
Playing with two children in the kitchen.
Giving directions to a foreign tourist on the street.
Introducing himself to strangers in the cafeteria.

Finally, the pool of descriptions was reduced to yield approximately 20 behaviors that were judged relevant to each trait and neutral or uninformative on other trait dimensions. The usual experimental list included about 15 of these descriptions. When an experiment required a mix of descriptions, some of which were congruent and some incongruent with the initial trait impression, acts were selected from the set generated for the central trait (e.g., friendly) and for the opposite-meaning trait (e.g., hostile). Care was always taken that all descriptions appeared as congruent and incongruent items for different trait ensembles presented to different subjects. This counter-balancing technique always allowed us to be confident that effects of the impression-behavior relationship (i.e., degree of congruence effects) are not solely attributable to specific item effects. Furthermore, the entire procedure, generating behavior descriptions from traits and defining congruence with reference to the implicit personality theory formulation, makes our conclusion, that trait (-like) relationships are critical in memory for concrete behaviors, difficult to impugn.

Third, the subject would evaluate the target character, described by the traits and behaviors, on a series of personality rating scales. Typically there were six scales labeled with personality trait adjectives from the original Rosenberg and Sedlak (1972) space.

Fourth, the subject would be asked to recall as much of the information presented in the episode descriptions as possible. The instructions emphasized that the subject was free to order the output of information (free recall) and that all relevant detail should be included. In most experiments, the subject was instructed not to report trait information at recall and to concentrate on recalling the behavior descriptions. In some experiments, the ordering of these last two steps, rating and recall, was reversed.

Subjects repeated this four-phase sequence as many as six times for different characters in a single experimental session.

Four types of experiments were conducted to explore the effects of trait schemata on memory for behavioral information. First, experiments in which the relative number of trait impression-congruent and trait incongruent behaviors were varied. The primary goal of these experiments was to establish the existence, magnitude, and generality of trait schemata effects. Second, experiments in which the nature or degree of incongruence was varied. Again, subjects evaluated and recalled characters depicted as performing trait congruent and incongruent behaviors. The relationship between the traits representing congruent and incongruent aspects of the character was varied systematically. These experiments were designed to evaluate a "judgment-informativeness" explanation for the schematic effects observed in the initial experiments. Third, experiments in which the subject's cognitive reaction to each behavior at the time of presentation was measured. The analysis of these experiments concentrated on attributional processes at the time of initial comprehension of the behaviors and on the relationship between attribution and memory. Fourth, experiments were conducted in which the retention interval between the initial presentation of behavior descriptions and the request to recall the behaviors was varied. These experiments were designed to evaluate suggestions from the traditional literature on memory schemata (Bartlett, 1932) that schematic effects would increase with the passage of time.

Set Size Experiments

The first three experiments in the research program studied the effects of variations in congruent and incongruent behavior set sizes. The incongruents were always high-incongruence behaviors in the sense that they were behaviors that had been generated as congruent to a trait opposite in meaning to the trait represented in the initial trait ensemble. These experiments yielded virtually identical results, and so we will review only one of them here. In this experiment (Hastie & Kumar, 1979, Experiment Three), the list always included 14 behaviors with the mixture of congruent and incongruent items varying across four levels: 13 congruents, 1 incongruent; 11 and 3; 9 and 5; and equal set sizes 7 and 7.

The major results of the experiment are presented in Fig. 5.1. Three features of the data should be noted. First, recall of congruent behaviors does

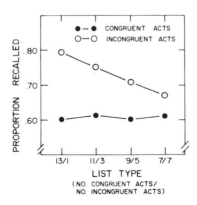

FIG. 5.1. Mean proportions of behavior descriptions recalled (from Hastie & Kumar, 1979).

not depend on set size (7 to 13 items per set). Second, recall of congruent acts is dependent on set size with higher probabilities of recall associated with smaller set sizes. Third, in the equal set size condition (7 vs. 7), recall of incongruent behaviors is slightly, but reliably, higher than for congruent behaviors.

This last result can be interpreted as a "pure" trait ensemble effect. The only factor that distinguishes congruent and incongruent acts in the equal set size list is the content of the trait ensemble. In addition, the set size effects are also trait effects in that the "sets" of behaviors are defined by pretest subjects with reference to personality trait adjectives.

Incongruence Level Experiments

In a subsequent experiment (Hastie & Mazur, 1978), the set size variable was varied in conjunction with the level of incongruence variable described previously. In this experiment, 108 college women viewed films of four actors each performing 10 to-be-remembered acts, and recall for all materials was delayed until the end of the experimental session. The set size factor occurred at three levels: 9 congruent behaviors and 1 incongruent, 7 congruent and 3 incongruent, 5 congruent and 5 incongruent (equal-size sets). The incongruence factor appeared at three levels: high incongruence (as in previous research), medium incongruence, and low incongruence. This second factor was conceptualized as variation in the degree of incongruence. For example, if we consider a character who is described as essentially "friendly" in an initial trait ensemble, three types of incongruent behaviors could be presented: (a) "hostile," *high*-incongruence behaviors; (b) "stupid," *medium*-incongruence behaviors; or (c) "intelligent," *low*-incongruence behaviors. The ordering of these degrees of incongruence reflects the distances between the congruent trait (friendly) and the incongruent traits (hostile, stupid, and intelligent) in the Rosenberg and Sedlak (1972) scaling solution.

Pretest subjects' ratings also supported this ordering of incongruent behavior sets. For the example of the friendly character, hostile acts were rated as most incongruent or least likely to be performed by such a character, followed by medium-incongruent stupid acts, and lastly by low-incongruent intelligent acts, which were rated as fairly likely to be performed by a friendly person.

The major results from this nine-cell design are plotted in Fig. 5.2. Recall of incongruent behaviors is an orderly function of the set size and level of incongruence variables. Figure 5.2 presents the results from each level of the degree of incongruence variable separately. First, the results from the high degree of incongruence lists (rightmost panel) essentially repeat the results of the first experiment described earlier. Variations in set size do not affect the

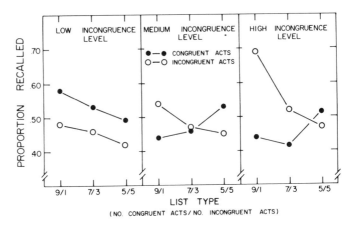

FIG. 5.2. Mean proportions of behaviors recalled (from Hastie & Mazur, 1978).

recall of congruent behaviors, but there is a dramatic effect of set size on incongruent item recall. This result is an indication that the phenomena observed in the initial experiments are quite robust. This last experiment utilized a new set of behavior descriptions, presented the materials in a realistic filmed format, inserted a retention interval delay between presentation and recall, and studied a new population of subjects. However, the major features of the set size effect are clearly replicated.

One difference from the first experiment occurs for the relative recall of congruent and incongruent items from equal sets. In this experiment, congruent items are slightly better recalled than incongruent items, but the difference in recall is no longer statistically reliable. Our experience with numerous variations on the experimental task suggests that with written materials and short (less than 5 minutes) delays between study and recall, the recall of high-incongruent acts will be superior to the recall of congruent acts. The results of the first experiment reported are typical; a 5–10% superiority for incongruent acts when congruent and incongruent set sizes are equal. This difference does not reliably appear under conditions such as those in the present experiment. However, in no case has a statistically significant reversal been obtained, where congruent acts were *better* recalled than incongruent under equal set size conditions.

Shifting to the center panel, medium-incongruence lists, the pattern of results changes. Congruent item recall again shows no notable effects of the set size variable. Incongruent items also show little if any influence of set size. (The interaction between the list type [set size] and item [congruent–incongruent] factors is significant at the .05 level.)

Finally in the leftmost, low-incongruence panel, the pattern changes again to yield a simple main effect of the congruence–incongruence item type factor.

The results for low-incongruence lists, unlike the medium and high-incongruence cases, appear quite consistent with a traditional schemata theory of the sort proposed by Bartlett (1932). Under the low-incongruence conditions, information that is incongruent or irrelevant to the initial impression of a person is not as well recalled as information that is congruent with the impression. The data from the low-incongruence lists also exhibit a main effect for the set size variable with recall dropping for both congruent and incongruent items as the respective set sizes become equal. In a moment, we argue that the results from these three panels are consistent with a model that assumes that information is recalled to the extent that it was relevant and important in the decision-making task that is performed at encoding.

The results of this experiment confirm our expectations about set size effects from earlier experiments. This is important because this last experiment used realistic, perceptually rich films as stimulus materials rather than the simple sentence descriptions from the first three experiments. The suggestion is that results from this research will generalize to more natural settings where person information is embedded in an active multimodal perceptual field. Furthermore, the stability of the results across the variations in procedure, timing, and subject samples in these experiments assures us that the results are empirically reliable.

Our preliminary theoretical analysis was an attempt to develop an information-processing model along the lines suggested in the introduction to this chapter (see also Wyer & Srull, Chapter 7, this volume, and Hastie & Carlston, Chapter 1, this volume). We supposed that the initial trait ensemble in the context of the impression formation task common to the first four experiments would produce a certain perceptual set of expectancy for our subjects. Behavioral information that was incongruent with the initial ensemble would appear surprising, striking, and especially informative with reference to the nascent impression. Our hypothesis was that incoming events would elicit attention and encoding elaboration to the extent that they were informative about the character's personality impression. Two principles were invoked to establish "event informativeness": set size and degree of congruence. Infrequent types of events were deemed to be more informative than frequent events, and highly incongruent events were predicted to be more informative than less incongruent events.

Elaboration of an event at encoding was hypothesized to yield a richly connected representation of that event in long-term memory. The event's memory trace would be associatively linked to many other events and access routes in the long-term store. Thus, at the time of retrieval, highly elaborated events (e.g., highly informative events) would be relatively available to a search of long-term memory.

This preliminary theoretical analysis accounts for the general features of the data we have described thus far. The analysis also suggests further data analysis and several additional experimental tactics. For example, the emphasis on informativeness of incongruent events, at least of high-incongruent behaviors, implies that events that occur early in the sequence of behaviors attributed to a character will receive especially thorough elaboration as compared to events that occur later in the sequence. This follows from the assumption that, at least with reference to the personality impression, additional events of a particular type (e.g., friendly, hostile, intelligent, or stupid) will be redundant with preceding events and thus be less informative. An analysis of input serial position effects in the first three experiments showed that early-occurring events of all types were relatively well recalled and that recall was enhanced even further if the events were incongruent (Hastie & Kumar, 1979).

At this point in the research, we were confident that trait impressions (or trait-related mental schemata) are important in the recall of behaviors. The next experiments explore the effects of the congruence–incongruence difference on subjects' processing of information during the comprehension or encoding stage of the task and during the retention interval between presentation and the memory test. Our preliminary theoretical analysis suggested that differences in processing should occur during encoding with incongruent events receiving more elaboration than congruent. However, this analysis did not suggest that differential effects should appear during the retention interval. The aim of the next two types of experiments is to isolate critical differences in the encoding processes or in the forgetting rates for congruent and incongruent information.

Encoding Process Experiments

In the experiments on encoding processes, the experimental procedure was varied to allow us to measure subjects' "cognitive responses" or encoding strategies during the initial presentation of behaviors. First, the trait ensembles were dropped from the procedure and only unbalanced set sizes were used: 6 congruents and 3 incongruents, 4 and 2, 2 and 1. The behaviors attributed to a single character were presented in written form and the subject read through the entire list of nine, six, or three descriptions once with the instruction to form an impression of the character. Our assumption was that the smaller set of behaviors would be perceived as incongruent with the overall impression of the character given that these acts comprised one-third of the total set. (All incongruents were "high" incongruents in the terminology presented earlier.) On a second, experimenter-paced pass through the list of behaviors, subjects were instructed to write a short phrase after each sentence describing a behavior. For example, if the behavior description read, "James Bartlett cheated in the poker game," the subject might add the phrase, " . . . by looking at another player's cards." Subjects were told that this task was employed to study grammatical constructions in extemporaneous writing.

They were told to attempt to form a clear impression of each character and then spontaneously to generate a sentence continuation for each behavior description. Twenty-four subjects were paced through the task and, after writing continuations for six characters, they were asked to recall all of the experimenter-presented behaviors that they could remember.

The results of the recall test, displayed in Fig. 5.3a fit our expectations from earlier experiments. Incongruent items are recalled at a higher level than congruent items with the set size effect serving as a summary for the overall pattern.

A detailed analysis was performed on the sentence continuation data. Judges were given the sentences and continuations and asked to classify each continuation into one of three categories: (a) Explanation—the continuation provided an explanation, rationale, or cause for the act described by the sentence (e.g., "James Bartlett cheated in the poker game...because he needed the money to make car payments."); (b) Elaboration—the subject's phrase provided detailed elaboration of the setting, characters, or actions described in the behavior episode (e.g., "James Bartlett cheated in the poker game...by looking at another player's cards."); and (c) Other—continuations not clearly either explanations or elaborations. Most of these phrases mentioned the consequences of events in the behavior descriptions (e.g., "James Bartlett cheated in the poker game...and was never invited to play again."). The results of these analyses are summarized in Fig. 5.3b, where the probability of continuing a description with an explanation is plotted.

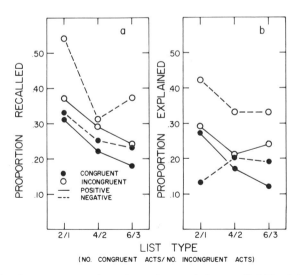

FIG. 5.3. Mean proportions of behavior descriptions recalled (Panel A) and explained (Panel B).

(Almost all of the remaining continuations were classified as elaborations; only 7% of the total fell into the Other category.) First, the rate of Explanations in each condition reflects the probability of recall plotted in Fig. 5.3a. Second, a new variable affects Explanation rates; the evaluative valence of the behavior described. Acts that are morally negative or unattractive are more likely to elicit an Explanation than positive, attractive acts. Evaluation did not have a statistically significant effect on recall, although the pattern of results suggests that negative behaviors are better recalled than positive behaviors.

It is clear that there is a substantial correlation between continuation type and recall in the data in Fig. 5.3. A correlation coefficient calculated on the 12 pairs of recall–Explanation mean proportions equals +.83. However, we sould also examine the correlation between recall and Explanation at a finer level within conditions. A separate index of correlation (phi-coefficient, Siegel, 1956) was calculated for each character studied by each subject. The two dichotomous variables were defined across behavior descriptions categorized in a 2 × 2 table as recalled or not recalled by Explained or Not Explained. An analysis of variance was performed using the phi-coefficients as a dependent variable. The average phi-coefficient across all subjects and characters (grand mean of the dependent variable) was significantly greater than zero indicating that the recall–Explanation correlation held at the level of individual subjects' performance for single characters.

These results, the correlations between Explanation, recall, and incongruence, are consistent with our preliminary theoretical analysis. First, congruent and incongruent events did receive differential treatment during comprehension and encoding. Second, if we assume that Explanation requires more extensive processing than Elaboration, then we can conclude that incongruent events are more likely to receive Explanatory continuations and therefore receive richer, deeper encoding than congruent events. This assumption is quite plausible if we consider the requirements of a subject's explanatory causal analysis. Such processing would almost certainly include a review of information observed and inferred about a character in an effort to find factors that would cause the character to exhibit the to-be-explained behavior.

The results of this analysis are also interesting because they have implications for the conditions under which causal attribution (Explanation) will occur spontaneously. Although no current attribution theories predict the circumstances under which causal attribution is likely to occur, these results are consistent with formulations such as those proposed by Kelley (1973), Jones and Davis (1968), and Ajzen and Fishbein (1975). Attribution occurs when events are incongruent or unexpected and attribution occurs when events are negative or unpleasant.

Retention Interval Effects

In a final series of experiments (Anderson & Hastie, 1978), we explored the relative forgetting rates of congruent and incongruent behavior descriptions. In these studies, we returned to the experimental method employed in the first experiments described earlier. These experiments used both filmed and sentence materials with each subject viewing 16 behavior descriptions attributed to a single character. Each list of behaviors was preceded by a trait ensemble and followed by a retention interval delay before the recall test. These intervals, the major independent variable in the studies, ranged from 5 minutes to 2 weeks in length. The experimental materials differed from previous experiments in two respects. First, the trait ensemble preceding each character's behavior descriptions was comprised of four (congruent) adjectives selected to represent a single personality type (e.g., friendly, extraverted, sociable, gregarious) and three diverse adjectives, one from each of three different personality types (e.g., hostile, stupid, intelligent). Second, the set of 16 behaviors attributed to the character included 10 behaviors from the congruent trait category (friendly behaviors in the present example) and two behaviors each, from each of the three noncongruent categories. Note that this plan puts two low, two medium, and two high incongruent items in every experimental list along with the larger set of 10 congruent items. The second experiment reported in this chapter studied level of incongruence effects and found that medium- and low-incongruent items did not show the high levels of recall apparent for high-incongruent items (in small sets). Recall of low- and medium-incongruent items exhibited the same pattern in the experiments on retention interval effects, although these results were extremely unstable. The present section concentrates on the recall of congruent and high-incongruent items.

A summary of performance in the film and sentence conditions is presented in Fig. 5.4. It is clear that there is no differential forgetting of congruent and high-incongruent information. Initial differences in recall are preserved almost perfectly at all delays. Furthermore, in these experiments subjects were asked to recall both the abstract trait adjectives from the ensemble preceding the list and the behavior episodes. The pattern of recall for the trait material exactly paralleled the results for the behavior episodes. Recall declined with increasing retention intervals, and the separation between congruent and incongruent item recall curves remained nearly constant.

Note on Organization at Retrieval

Before we attempt to develop a final theoretical account for these findings, one more important empirical result must be added. In all of these

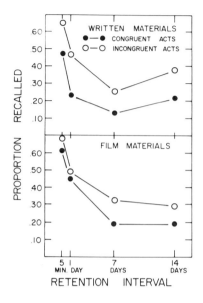

FIG. 5.4. Mean proportions of behaviors recalled (from Anderson & Hastie, 1978).

experiments, we used a recall format memory test. It is conventional to study the order of output in free-recall memory data to draw conclusions about the structure of information in long-term memory (Bower, 1970; Friendly, 1977; Sternberg & Tulving, 1977). Indices of organization to measure clustering by trait category (Bousfield & Bousfield, 1966) have been calculated for every experiment conducted in this research program. Clustering was assessed when each distinct trait category was considered separately, when congruent items were contrasted with all types of incongruent items, and when evaluatively positive items were contrasted with negative items. In only one case did the mean of this index reliably exceed zero (chance) levels of clustering. A careful examination of the pattern of clustering scores across experiments did not reveal any apparent system such that scores consistently differed from chance levels in any subset of conditions. Of course, any conclusions about degree of organization at output must be qualified by acknowledging that none of the available clustering measures is perfectly sensitive to the patterns we hoped to detect. Nonetheless, the Bousfield and Bousfield (1966) index is as sensitive as any measure in current use (Sternberg & Tulving, 1977), and conceptually it is designed to summarize exactly the kind of categorical organization of theoretical interest. Finally, we certainly do not intend to suggest that retrieval processes are disorganized or unsystematic. Surely, an ideal scientific theory of person memory would include a characterization of regularities in retrieval processes. However, for the present we conclude that there is no discernible structuring of behavior recall at output, with reference to trait categories.

THEORETICAL DISCUSSION

Now we are ready to outline a theoretical account for the catalog of results presented earlier. In this discussion, we will describe one elaborate model to characterize the experimental subject's performance. We do not mean to imply that there is only one possible model for our results; in fact, we are confident that there are countless workable models. For the moment, we think that it will be an important advance if we can construct one coherent model that is complete enough to account for the present results and that is embedded in current theoretical traditions in cognitive psychology.

This model is closely related to John Anderson's computer program models of memory, FRAN (Anderson, 1972) and HAM (Anderson & Bower, 1973), and it incorporates several insights from Craik and Lockhart's "levels of processing" framework (1972). Our exposition follows the stages of events during the experimental procedure: (a) The subject comprehends or recognizes the behaviors described by sentences or films. (b) The subject reviews the behavior and integrates or encodes it into a memory structure representing the character being studied. (c) The subject retains information about the character during the interval between presentation and the memory test. (d) At a signal from the experimenter, the subject attempts to retrieve information from memory.

During the presentation of each behavior description, the subject attempts to understand or evaluate each act by classifying it in relation to information stored in a long-term conceptual memory store. Just as words are comprehended and sentences parsed, the behavior stream is segmented and the segments classified. We assume by analogy to lexical memory models (Smith, 1978), that there exists a long-term memory structure that serves these functions. Social psychologists have studied this structure under the label *Implicit Personality Theory,* but until recently almost no research has been conducted on its functions to guide perception and comprehension of on-going behavior (see Ebbesen, Chapter 6, this volume). One function of the comprehension stage is to identify unexpected or surprising events. We anticipate that comprehension involves an interaction of contextual, top-down, expectancy-guided subprocesses and featural, bottom-up, stimulus-driven subprocesses (Neisser, 1976; Rumelhart, 1977). Disconfirmation of an expectancy, such as the trait impression expectancies in the present research, would be noted early in perception.

Encoding Processes

Following and overlapping with the comprehension process, information about the behavior episode is being transformed and encoded in memory. We assume that the final representation of the behavioral information takes the form of an abstract propositional network. Currently the most thoroughly grounded system of propositional networks is the HAM structure model proposed by Anderson and Bower (1973). Applications of a simplified version of this model to person memory are available in Anderson and Hastie (1974), Anderson (1977), and Hastie and Kumar (1979).

Information summarizing the events in a behavioral episode would be stored in a HAM network of the form depicted in Fig. 5.5. The subject of the sentence or film clip, an idea node in the HAM structure, would be linked to node locations in memory representing information about the act, (verb and object) and its context (location, co-actors, and so forth). In the present rendition of the HAM model, each of the episode structures may be linked to other episode structures as well as to individual entry-point node (labeled "Jim Bartlett" in Fig. 5.5.)

The overall memory structure for an individual, following the presentation of an experimental list, would be a large network of episodes linked with one another and with the entry-point node by many associative paths. The critical feature of the representation is that some episodes will be linked to many other episodes whereas some episodes will be linked to only a few or to no other episodes. In a moment we will show how the differential linkage patterns will produce different rates of recall on a subsequent memory test. First we must discuss the conditions that influence the formation of interepisode links.

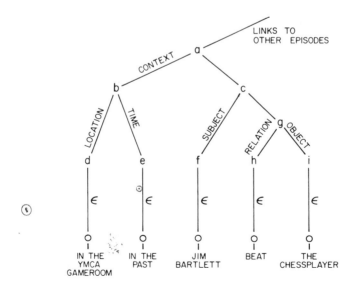

FIG. 5.5. Example propositional network to represent a single behavioral episode.

Interepisode links are formed when information from two episodes is simultaneously considered, transformed, or compared in Short-Term store or in an intermediate-term Working Memory store. A considerable amount of linguistic and propositional-encoding is assumed to occur in a limited-capacity short-term store of the sort postulated by Atkinson and Shiffrin (1968), Waugh and Norman (1965), Broadbent (1958), and others (see Hastie & Carlston, Chapter 1, this volume). For example, HAM network structures are produced as information accumulates in Short-Term Memory, and linguistic and perceptual concept classification occurs as physical information from the environment is recoded as conceptual information with reference to knowledge stored in a long-term Conceptual Memory. The Short-Term store is a sharply limited processing area that is associated with conscious awareness. Its primary functions involve maintaining and recoding information flowing from the environment or from long-term memory stores. Information processes that involve more than simple retention, restructuring, recoding, or comparison of a limited set of information are carried out elsewhere in the cognitive system.

A major locus of more elaborate processing is the intermediate-term Working Memory. The two dominant functions of the hypothesized Working Memory are to generate and adjust a mental model of the subject's immediate physical and social environment and to house and execute inference-making information processing subroutines. In the context of the present experiments, two classes of inferences, impression formation and causal reasoning, would be hypotheiszed to occur in Working Memory. The impression formation process would lead to the formation of links between some behavioral episodes as well as generating and maintaining a current impression of the experimental character. This impression, part of the subject's model social world, is the basis of judgments of informativeness or surprisingness that lead to differential processing of congruent and incongruent behaviors. Causal reasoning processes would be especially likely to be invoked by the appearance of incongruent, unexpected events and would lead to a review of information previously stored in memory about the character. (Note that some information stored in memory will be the products of inferences. For example, once an impression process is terminated, the resulting impression will be stored in the long-term memory network of episodes and events relevant to an individual character.) This review of information, in search of explanatory factors, would result in the formation of numerous links between the representation of the to-be-explained event and the other relevant events. Furthermore, making an event the focus of causal reasoning maintains the event representation in active memory for additional units of time, thus increasing the likelihood of link formation to subsequent events.

To some extent this additional processing of highly informative events occurs automatically, but it is also under the subject's deliberate control. For example, the subject may elect to retain an episode in working memory until old information is found in long-term memory or until the experimenter presents new information that will explain why the episode occurred. Of course, there are other conditions that will cause an episode in one of these experimental lists to be retained in working memory and lead to extensive linkages to other episodes. Episodes that are striking, vivid, or motivationally important to the subject might also be expected to receive extra processing. Episodes that are perceived as quintessentially characteristic of a character will doubtless also receive extensive processing under the impression formation instructions in these experiments. In fact, any of the factors that have been hypothesized to affect rehearsal processes can be expected to affect the episode linkage process we have postulated (Shiffrin & Schneider, 1977).

It is important to note the relationship between our linkage process and Craik's levels-of-processing framework (Craik & Lockhart, 1972; Craik & Tulving, 1975). The linkage process occurs whenever two episodes make *contact* in Working Memory or in Short-Term Memory. We follow conventional approaches in supposing that both of these stores are limited in the amount of episode information that can be present or activated in them (Baddeley & Hitch, 1974; Bower, 1975; Shiffrin & Schneider, 1977). We assume that the operation of automatic or control processes that maintain or return an episode to an active state increase the chances it will contact other episodes. This would happen because: (a) new information moves into Short-Term and Working Memories through the perception of additional, experimenter presented, episodes; (b) the subject continually reviews old episode information to perform the task of forming an impression; and (c) special tasks will be undertaken by the subject to comprehend or make sense of incoming information that require the review of information already stored in long-term memory. (The prime example of such a task is causal attribution to explain inconsistent or unexpected behavior by the character being observed.) The emphasis on residence time in limited memory stores makes this analysis similar to a "rehearsal process" approach (Atkinson & Shiffrin, 1968; Rundus & Atkinson, 1970). But the emphasis on particular conditions for interepisode link formation in Working Memory distinguishes our analysis from the traditional research approach. The linkage analysis is in the spirit of the Craik and Lockhart (1972) framework. Mere residence in Short-Term Memory does not lead to maximum link formation and later increases in recall. We think that extensive formation of links corresponds to Craik and Lockhart's elaborative processing at a deep level. Craik and Lockhart have hypothesized that variations in elaborative processing will affect performance on subsequent memory tests (see Anderson, 1976, for a similar analysis).

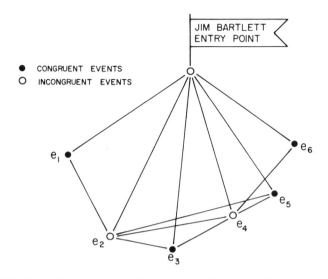

FIG. 5.6. Example interepisode associative network to represent information about a single individual.

An example of a network structure that might result from study of a six-behavior list containing two incongruent episodes and four congruent episodes is depicted in Fig. 5.6. Each of the nodes labeled e_i corresponds to an episode structure such as the one presented in Fig. 5.5. The two incongruent episodes (e_2, e_4) each have five links emanating from them, twice as many as the average for the congruent nodes.

In summary, we hypothesize that as behavior episodes are presented in our experiments, the subject comprehends each episode and establishes long-term memory associative networks to encode the information about each character. For present purposes, the critical feature of these networks is that information about unexpected, incongruent behaviors will be linked to more other episodes than information about expected, congruent behaviors. We have argued that the process that establishes these links shares features with both rehearsal and levels-of-processing analyses of acquisition.

Retention and Retrieval Processes

In our research, increasing the interval between study and test produced an overall decrement in recall but no differential effects on congruent and incongruent behavior recall. Consequently, we have little to say about memory processes during the retention interval. We would account for forgetting by supposing that links become less accessible in long-term memory as additional network structures are encoded during the retention interval (Anderson & Bower, 1973).

Finally, at some point in our experimental session each subject is instructed to recall as much information as possible about each character. We hypotheisze that the retrieval process underlying recall performance follows the conventions discussed in Anderson's papers on the FRAN and HAM models (Anderson, 1972; Anderson & Bower, 1973).

1. A search process starts at the entrypoint node and traverses associative links until it reaches a terminal-behavior-episode node.

2. Upon reaching a behavior episode, the subject reviews it to see if the item has been recalled previously.

3. If the episode has not yet been recalled, the subject writes it down on the recall form. If the act has already been recalled, the subject does not write it down.

4. After the behavior has been reported (or not reported), the search process continues traversing additional links in the network until another behavior episode is reached.

5. The probability that the search process chooses a particular link as it passes through a node is determined by the number of links emanating from the node. The search process has a blind, random character, and the likelihood of reaching any single node is a function of the pattern of paths in the network and, in particular, a function of the number of links connected to the node. (Note this is a departure from Anderson's usual assumption that recent links are searched before older links (Anderson & Bower, 1973; Anderson & Hastie, 1974)).

6. This process continues until the subject becomes "exhausted" and stops. We suspect that the stopping point is chiefly determined by the number of times the subject repeats nodes; that is, the number of times the process encounters previously retrieved episodes. Subjectively, this "clogging effect" is quite frustrating and is a signal to the subject that additional retrieval will be difficult or impossible. At any point in the retrieval process, the subject may return to the entry point (proper name) node and begin the search "from the top."

It should be clear how the differential linkage variable that we discussed with reference to encoding predicts the recall of episodes, given this summary of the retrieval process. The more paths there are to a node, the likelier it is that the retrieval search process will reach the node and report it. Of course, there are alternate models of the retrieval process that could be proposed to operate on our network structures that would mimic the behavior of our simple serial-link traversal process (Townsend, 1974). For example, Anderson (1977) and Collins and Loftus (1975) have hypothesized the existence of a parallel "spreading activation" search process that could doubtless be applied to the networks we have postulated. However, the serial search process we have outlined is preferred at present on the grounds that it is conceptually simpler than the parallel search models. In any case, almost all plausible search processes would predict that richly connected nodes will be accessed before sparsely connected nodes.

Evaluation of the Model

The present analysis provides a sketch of a complete model to account for the results of our experiments on person memory. The model can be represented as a simple computer program in which three parameters vary to account for variations in performance across experiments. First, the structure of the interepisode networks will vary to produce different levels of incongruent and congruent episode linkages. This could be summarized in two parameters, average congruent linkage and average incongruent linkage, but this is not completely sufficient as the exact pattern of links will exert some influence on recall. Second, the subject's motivation to traverse links to search for new episodes during retrieval will also vary across experiments, individuals, and characters. We summarize this in one parameter, the average number of links traversed. Of course, in future research we would like to go beyond the measure of mean number of items recalled and account for output sequence patterns and the shapes of the distributions of number of items recalled. Further research would also elaborate the model to account for recognition memory test statistics and verification reaction-time results.

At present, the limited amounts and types of data available in our research do not justify such analyses. However, we believe that the empirical and theoretical foundations outlined in this paper will support development in these directions.

The major findings of the first experiments on set size effects are easily accommodated within the proposed theoretical framework. The basic set size effects, establishing the primacy of trait impressions in the perception of behavioral events are accounted for by the postulation of differential processing at encoding of congruent and incongruent events. The special advantage for early incongruent events, paralleling the von Restorff effects obtained with traditional word list materials (Wallace, 1965), can be explained if we suppose that these items receive extensive processing in Working Memory inference routines.

The results of the second experiment reported in this chapter, which studied variations in type of incongruence as well as set size, are considerably more difficult to account for. The central pattern of results, relative superiority of recall of incongruent events decreasing as set size increases and decreasing as degree of incongruence decreases, is easily modeled with the principles from an account for the first experiments. Informativeness, or unexpectedness, is an inverse function of set size and a direct function of degree of incongruence. When informativeness is high, more elaborate encoding is likely to result and higher recall will follow. One less prominent but apparently reliable result is more problematic. The crossover interaction pattern holding between the set size and congruent–incongruent variables at medium levels of incongruence does not fit any straightforward account in terms of event informativeness.

If the results from incongruent conditions are considered in their own right, the pattern of recall is quite sensible in the context of the informativeness principle. First, each type of incongruent condition exhibits a straightforward set size effect, such that membership in smaller sets results in higher probabilities of recall. Second, the incongruence type factor modifies the set size factor effects, producing a fan-shaped array of curves with lower probabilities of recall and flatter slopes appearing with less extreme incongruent sets. Thus, it is possible to summarize incongruence effects by supposing that the set size and type of incongruence variables combine multiplicatively to produce informativeness, that informativeness determines quantity and quality of processing, and that associative linkages generated during initial processing affect recall.

The pattern of recall of congruent items, considered in isolation, is more problematic. (The major puzzle is lack of consistent set size effects for these items.) Of course, because congruent item set sizes are larger than incongruent set sizes, the magnitudes of set size effects should be smaller for congruents. But the absence of any systematic effects is unexpected and unaccounted for in the present theoretical analysis.

The results of the third experiment reported, studying encoding processes, are quite consistent with the present theoretical framework. The suggestion that extensive or elaborative processing is especially likely to occur for incongruent events is confirmed by the clear main effect of congruence on the measure of probability of generating an explanatory sentence continuation. Furthermore, the pattern of probability of explanatory continuation results across experimental conditions fits the assumption that items in small sets, hypothetically highly informative items, will receive extensive processing. Finally, the correlation between probability of explanation and probability of recall is a strong suggestion that extensive processing increases recallability.

The results from the final class of experiments on retention interval effects are the least relevant to our theoretical analysis. Forgetting, indexed by the falling probability of recall with increases in retention interval, occurred at the same rate for congruent and incongruent items, presented in written or filmed formats. These results relieve us from the necessity of developing a complex account of retention interval processes. For the present, we will assume that a cue-dependent, retrieval interference account such as those developed by Anderson and Bower (1973) and Tulving (1974) is applicable. Future research to explore the adequacy of this preliminary hypothesis is underway.

It is interesting to contrast the present social psychological research with current research using nonsocial materials and encoding tasks. First, the experimental method used in our research closely resembles the word list and prose memory paradigms in cognitive research. The method departs from standard paradigms in that the to-be-remembered materials describe people, the list structure is defined with reference to implicit social categories, and the subject's task requires a decision to be made on the basis of the to-be-remembered material. We have suggested that these changes are not radical departures from traditional memory research. We have argued that general conceptual social knowledge is similar to, perhaps even part of, the general lexical memory for semantic information. We have treated list organization in our experiments in much the same way cognitive psychologists have described categorized lists (Tulving, 1968), paragraphs (Kintsch, 1974), and stories (Mandler & Johnson, 1977; Thorndyke, 1977). Probably the most distinctive aspect of our person memory research is the use of a decision-making impression formation task in combination with the memory task. There are three clear changes from the typical word list memorization task; the experimental materials were descriptions of attributes and behaviors of a person; the to-be-remembered list was preceded by a trait ensemble that established expectations about the nature of the events to appear in the list; and the primary task for the subject during list presentation was to study the materials as the basis for a decision.

This task motivated our analysis of encoding processes and the focus on causal attribution responses by the subject when exceptional, incongruent episodes were encountered. We believe that these are the greatest empirical contributions of the present experiments: an introduction to research on memory in decision-making tasks and an explication of the conditions under which a subject will initiate causal attribution responses.

Our theoretical analyses depend heavily on cognitive psychology. We borrowed extensively from Anderson and Bower's (1973) HAM model; the Atkinson and Shiffrin (1968) and Rundus and Atkinson (1970) discussion of rehearsal; and Craik and Lockhart's (1972) levels-of-processing framework. Our combination of the three approaches and the discussion of differential acquisition and retrieval of congruent and incongruent episodes is original, but hardly theory shaking. We think that the thoroughness of our analysis surpasses most social psychological discussions of person memory, and we look forward to the extension of our model to account for output sequencing and recognition test data.

We must be clear that the present analysis is a loose framework for a theory and not a specific information-processing model. The analysis is a sketch of the sorts of processes and structures that could be combined to yield a precise, sufficient cognitive model. However, only subparts of the analysis have been represented as an operating computer program, and we are a long way from writing a single program that incorporates all of the necessary subroutines to actually perform the subject's impression formation and memory tasks. However, we believe that it is useful to outline the full extent of our speculations without claiming that they provide a complete model or that the present research strongly tests such a model.

ACKNOWLEDGMENTS

The author is grateful to Thomas Ostrom and Robert S. Wyer, Jr. for their useful comments on earlier versions of this chapter. This research was supported in part by a research grant to the author from N.I.M.H. (MH 28928).

REFERENCES

Ajzen, I., & Fishbein, M. A Bayesian analysis of attribution processes. *Psychological Bulletin,* 1975, *82,* 261–277.
Anderson, C., & Hastie, R. *Effects of retention interval on recall of information about people.* Unpublished manuscript, Harvard University, 1978.
Anderson, J. R. FRAN: A simulation model of free recall. In G. H. Bower (Ed.), *The psychology of learning and motivation* (Vol. 5). New York: Academic Press, 1972.
Anderson, J. R. Memory for information about individuals. *Memory and Cognition, 1977, 5,* 430–442.
Anderson, J. R., & Bower, G. H. *Human associative memory.* Washington, D. C.: Winston, 1973.
Anderson, J. R., & Hastie, R. Individuation and reference in memory: Proper names and definite descriptions. *Cognitive Psychology,* 1974, *6,* 495–515.
Anderson, N. H. *Integration theory applied to cognitive responses and attitudes.* CHIP Technical Report #68, University of California, San Diego, 1976.
Atkinson, R. C., & Shiffrin, R. M. Human memory: A proposed system and its control processes. In K. Spence (Ed.), *The psychology of learning and motivation* (Vol. 2). New York: Academic Press, 1968.
Bartlett, F. C. *Remembering: A study in experimental and social psychology.* London and New York: Cambridge University Press, 1932.
Baddeley, A. D., & Hitch, G. Working memory. In G. H. Bower (Ed.), *The psychology of learning and motivation* (Vol. 8). New York: Academic Press, 1974.
Broadbent, D. E. *Perception and communication.* New York: Pergamon, 1958.
Bousfield, A. K., & Bousfield, W. A. Measurement of clustering and of sequential constancies in repeated free recall. *Psychological Reports,* 1966, *19,* 935–942.
Bower, G. H. Cognitive psychology: An introduction. In W. K. Estes (Ed.), *Handbook of learning and cognitive processes* (Vol. 1). Hillsdale, N.J.: Lawrence Erlbaum Associates, 1975.

Collins, A. M., & Loftus, E. F. A spreading-activation theory of semantic processing. *Psychological Review*, 1975, *82*, 407-428.

Craik, F. I. M., & Lockhart, R. S. Levels of processing: A framework for memory research. *Journal of Verbal Learning and Verbal Behavior*, 1972, *11*, 671-684.

Craik, F. I. M., & Tulving, E. Depth of processing and the retention of words in episodic memory. *Journal of Experimental Psychology: General*, 1975, *104*, 268-294.

Fischhoff, B. Attribution theory and judgment under uncertainty. In J. H. Harvey, W. J. Ickes, & R. F. Kidd (Eds.), *New directions in attribution research*. Hillsdale, N.J.: Lawrence Erlbaum Associates, 1976.

Friendly, M. L. In search of the M-Gram: The structure of organization in free recall. *Cognitive Psychology*, 1977, *9*, 188-249.

Hastie, R., & Kumar, A. P. Person memory: Personality traits as organizing principles in memory for behaviors. *Journal of Personality and Social Psychology*, 1979, *37*, 25-38.

Hastie, R., & Mazur, J. *Memory for information about people presented on film*. Unpublished manuscript, Harvard University, 1978.

Jones, E. E., & Davis, K. E. From acts to dispositions; The attribution process in person perception. In L. Berkowitz (Ed.), *Advances in experimental social psychology* (Vol. 2). New York: Academic Press, 1968.

Kelley, H. H. The processes of attribution. *American Psychologist*, 1973, *28*, 107-128.

Kintsch, W. *The representation of meaning in memory*. Hillsdale, N.J.: Lawrence Erlbaum Associates, 1974.

Mandler, J. M., & Johnson, N. S. Remembrance of things parsed: Story structure and recall. *Cognitive Psychology*, 1977, *9*, 111-151.

Neisser, U. *Cognition and Reality*. San Francisco: Freeman, 1976.

Rosenberg, S., & Sedlak, A. Structural representations of implicit personality theory. In L. Berkowitz (Ed.), *Advances in experimental social psychology* (Vol. 6). New York: Academic Press, 1972.

Rumelhart, David E. *Introduction to human information processing*. University of California at San Diego: John Wiley & Sons, 1977.

Rundus, D., & Atkinson, R. C. Rehearsal processes in free recall: A procedure for direct observation. *Journal of Verbal Learning and Verbal Behavior*, 1970, *9*, 99-105.

Shiffrin, R. M., & Schneider, W. Controlled and automatic human information processing: II. Perceptual learning, automatic attending, and a general theory. *Psychological Review*, 1977, *84*, 127-190.

Siegel, S. *Nonparametric statistics for the behavioral sciences*. New York: McGraw-Hill, 1956.

Smith, E. E. Theories of semantic memory. In W. K. Estes (Ed.), *Handbook of learning and cognitive processes* (Vol. 5). Hillsdale, N.J.: Lawrence Erlbaum Associates, 1978.

Sternberg, R. J., & Tulving, E. The measurement of subjective organization in free recall. *Psychological Bulletin*, 1977, *84*, 539-556.

Thorndyke, P. W. Cognitive structures in comprehension and memory of narrative discourse. *Cognitive Psychology*, 1977, *9*, 77-110.

Townsend, J. Issues and models concerning the processing of a finite number of inputs. In B. Kantowitz (Ed.), *Human information processing: Tutorials in performance and cognition*. Hillsdale, N.J.: Lawrence Erlbaum Associates, 1974.

Tulving, E. Theoretical issues in free recall. In T. R. Dixon & D. L. Horton (Eds.), *Verbal behavior and general behavior theory*. Englewood Cliffs, N.J.: Prentice-Hall, Inc., 1968.

Tulving, E. Cue-dependent forgetting. *American Scientist*, 1974, *62*, 74-82.

Tversky, A., & Kahneman, D. Availability: A heuristic for judging frequency and probabiity. *Cognitive Psychology*, 1973, *5*, 207-232.

Wallace, W. P. Review of the historical, empirical and theoretical status of the von Restorff phenomenon. *Psychological Bulletin*, 1965, *63*, 410-424.

Waugh, N. C., & Norman, D. A. Primary memory. *Psychological Review*, 1965, *72*, 89-104.

6

Cognitive Processes in Understanding Ongoing Behavior

Ebbe B. Ebbesen
University of California, San Diego

Most forms of social influence begin with or include a rather common event: one person observing the stream of another person's behavior. Conformity, imitation, group pressure, persuasion by communication, impression formation, and so on, generally involve one or more people (the observers) being exposed to the ongoing behavior of other people (the actors). Investigations of these social influence situations have focused primarily on "context" variables that moderate the impact of an actor's behavior on an observer. Only peripheral attention has been given to the processes that determine: (1) how the observer extracts information from the ongoing behavior of the actor; (2) how that information is represented in the observer's memory; and (3) how the information that is in memory affects the behavior of the observer (but see Bandura, 1969).

One way to analyze these issues is with concepts that are more common in cognitive than social psychology (see Hastie & Carlston, Chapter 1, this volume). Specifically, the observer can be thought of as an information-processing system that consists of several stages. In the first stage, ongoing behavior is *encoded* into a cognitive representation. This representation or code forms the input to a second stage that *stores* the information in memory. The representation of the behavior segment in memory then serves as material that is *retrieved* at some later time and from which responses are constructed in measurement situations. Although it is clearly possible to conceive of the entire system as involving more than these three stages (see Crowder, 1976; Hastie & Carlston, Chapter 1, this volume; Kintsch, 1974; Taylor, 1976; Wyer & Srull, Chapter 7, this volume), in this chapter I concentrate on models that emphasize processes in these three stages. The purpose of this chapter, then, is to discuss alternative conceptions of the way in which people encode, retain, and retrieve information contained in the stream of behavior.

ENCODING THE STREAM OF BEHAVIOR

Although there is relatively clear agreement that people must encode the stream of ongoing behavior prior to engaging in other social psychological processes of interest, (such as forming attributions about the causes of that behavior; Harvey, Ickes, & Kidd, 1976; Jones & Davis, 1965; Jones, Kanouse, Kelley, Nisbett, Valins & Weiner, 1972), until recently little research has been designed to study, in a direct way, the encoding process. In a series of highly original and thought-provoking experiments, Newtson and his associates (e.g., Newtson, 1973; Newtson & Engquist, 1976; Newtson, Engquist & Bois, 1977) have provided an interesting exception. Newtson (1973) began by reviving Heider's (1958) claim that information is extracted from the continuous stream of another person's behavior by first breaking the continuous stream into chunks—each chunk consisting of a meaningful action.

The perceptual process being suggested seems similar to that usually invoked to explain speech perception. In particular, the continuous stream of sound energy (which often does not contain physical breaks) is thought to be perceptually divided into meaningful units, such as words. These basic units are then combined to form still higher level meanings by stringing them together into hierarchically organized lists (as phrases, and then as sentences, and then as paragraphs, etc.). In speech perception, the word is a more or less basic unit in the sense that people do not generally break speech into new nonword units, i.e., by combining the last phoneme of one word with the first of the next word.

Newtson and his colleagues have amassed a rather impressive array of data that suggests that nonverbal behavior is perceived more or less in the same fashion as speech. However, the evidence for their model rests almost exclusively on a particular technique for measuring, on-line, the behavior perception process. This technique requires that observers press a button while watching the actor's behavior to indicate where they perceive one meaningful action to end and another to begin. The resulting button presses thereby define the boundaries of the basic action-units assumed to underlie behavior perception.

Based on a series of experiments using this measure, Newtson and his associates have refined their model of the behavior-encoding process. Three assumptions seem to characterize their current views. First, the perceptual or encoding process is seen as actively constructive and selective, rather than receptive. Specifically, events early in a segment or even before a segment (e.g., expectancies, intentions, sets, prior knowledge, and so on) can control the type of information that is perceptually selected from the segment. Second, observers are assumed to perceive behavior by breaking the continuous stream into actions. That is, the information that is encoded from behavior is assumed to have a particular *form*. Specifically, the form of the code is a list of discrete, temporally nonoverlapping chunks in which the end of one action-chunk is the beginning of another. The size of the chunks that observers report (via the button-pressing task) will depend upon the observers' set and the content of the behavioral stream. However, each higher level (larger) chunk will generally consist of a connected string of lower level action-chunks and most of the boundaries of the larger action-units should coincide with the boundaries of some of the smaller units. Thus, even though the encoding process is selective and active, the units that are constructed under one set or expectation condition should be hierarchically related to those constructed in other conditions. Third, the boundary between two actions (the dividing line where one action ends and another begins—called a breakpoint) is assumed to be the point in the stream that provides the defining information for the prior action. The observer does not know what the content of an action is until that action ends and the next one begins. Thus, the *transition* from one action to another tells the observer what the nature of the prior action was. Stated differently, breakpoints contain most of the information that an observer would need to reconstruct and interpret the intervals between the breakpoints (Newtson, Rindner, Miller, & LaCross, 1978).[1]

The results of several different experiments have been used to support these three assumptions. First, Newtson (1973) found that observers who were instructed to divide a segment of behavior into the smallest possible meaningful actions simply divided into smaller units those actions that had been constructed by another group that was told to divide the same segment into the largest possible meaningful actions. Such a hierarchical organization is similar to that between words (small units) and phrases or sentences (large units) and suggests a consistency in the structure of the units being measured. Newtson (1973) also found a correlation between the number of units into which a segment was divided and the confidence subjects had in various attributional inferences they made about the observed actor (but see Deaux & Major, 1977, for a partial failure to replicate this result). This correlational evidence has been used to suggest that the button press is a sensitive indicator

---

[1]Because Newtson and his associates have not specified the assumptions that their model makes in the same detail as that provided here, it is conceivable that my representaton of their position is inaccurate in certain respects. Nevertheless, the model, as I have described it, is of sufficient intrinsic interest to warrant further examination whether or not my description accurately reflects the subtleties of Newtson's views.

of when information is being extracted from the behavior. That is, the press signifies the point in a segment when an action is defined as having occurred. Therefore, more presses imply that more information about the behavioral stream is being extracted and encoded.

In another set of studies, Newtson and Engquist (1976) found that observers were more likely to notice that a small part of a segment was missing if it came from a point in the segment that most observers had marked as a breakpoint between actions (i.e., pressed the button) than if it came at a nonbreakpoint between actions (a place in the segment where almost no one pressed the button). Breakpoints seem to command greater attention than nonbreakpoints. In addition, after viewing either the first or second half of a segment, subjects were better able to recognize slides taken from the half they had seen if the slides were taken from proportions of the segment defined as breakpoints than if the slides were constructed from nonbreakpoints. Apparently, the observers pay more attention to, and therefore remember better, those parts of the sequence that are marked as breakpoints. Finally, sequences of slides constructed from breakpoints were rated as more intelligible than sequences constructed from nonbreakpoint slides. Thus, breakpoints also seem to be more informative. In short, observers seem to press the button at those points that are most attended to and are most informative.

Critique of the Unitizing Task

Two issues are of major concern. First, does the button-pressing task tap a basic encoding process—one that underlies behavior perception? Second, whatever the answer to this question, which of Newtson's assumptions about the encoding process are useful?

With regard to the former question, there is little doubt that the button-pressing task is responsive to features of the behavioral stream being observed (e.g., Newtson et al., 1978). Nevertheless, there are several reasons to question the claim that the task taps a basic *encoding* process. Certainly, the task seems quite reasonable in the context of the Newtson et al. (1977) view of behavior perception. If behavior is perceived as a list of actions and the important or defining information regarding the content of each action occurs at the boundaries between actions, then a button press indicating where those boundary locations are would provide a useful representation of the observer's perceptual process. On the other hand, if observers encode the information in a stream of behavior in a form other than (or in addition to) a list of action-chunks, the use of the button-pressing task would almost certainly be quite insensitive to such processes. The response will necessarily produced a record of perception that consists of a list of chunks. Neither multiple and simultaneous encodings nor a more continuous single encoding can be detected with a one-button task. For example, if observers perceive behavior by simultaneously extracting several different levels of information and each level has its own series of actions with nonoverlapping boundaries, a string of button presses will not reflect such a structure. Alternatively, it might be possible for observers to extract (at least some types of) information from behavior without chunking the behavior into actions. Information might be in the form of features (e.g., direction of gaze, facial expression, body position, limb position, orientation of hands relative to arms, speed of movement, verbal content, and so on) or of continuously changing images rather than in the form of a list of actions. Although these general criticisms may seem reasonable, they do not explain the relatively consistent pattern of results that has been obtained with the button-pressing measure.

Two quite different interpretations of the button-pressing results are possible. One assumes that the task taps a basic encoding-process—a process that operates whether or not observers are told to press a button to define action boundaries. Alternatively, the button-pressing results may reflect a *secondary* process added to the "normal" encoding process. Specifically, each button press may be part of a process that is *created* by the instructions to press the button whenever one action ends and another begins rather than tapping the already existing process by which behavioral information is encoded and stored in memory.

Figure 6.1 shows schematic representations of these two alternative views. In the top primary-process model, the button-pressing task taps the encoding process that provides the input to later stages of the system. In this view (consistent with Newtson's interpretation), the procedure does not create apparent perceptual units of behavior; it measures them. In the bottom secondary-process model, the task and associated instructions are assumed to create a novel process. This new process is a secondary one in that it does not provide the input to later information-processing stages. Instead, another process encodes the information in behavior and provides the input to later stages.

With these alternatives in mind, let us reconsider some of the evidence used in support of the primary-process model. First, it is important to note that in many of the behavioral segments used in Newtson's research, the actor assumes similar body positions several times throughout the segment. For example, one sequence shows a person leafing through the pages of a magazine, another shows a person pacing back and forth, and in another the actor is collating pages of a booklet. Often, less frequently occurring behavioral events are interspersed among the repetitive ones. For example, after pacing back and forth several times, the actor might pick up a nearby telephone, put it down, and then begin pacing again. Assume that in attempting to follow the instructions to press a button whenever one action ends and another begins, subjects look for places in the behavioral stream

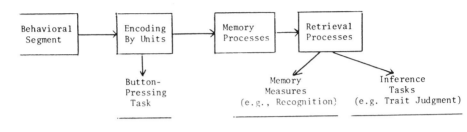

FIG. 6.1. The model in the top half of the figure assumes that the button-pressing task taps an encoding process, the output of which forms the primary input to later stages. The model in the bottom half of the figure assumes that the button-pressing task taps a process of secondary importance because its output does not form the input to later processing stages.

where major *changes* in behavior are occurring—that is, places where new body positions are displayed or where the actor starts or stops manipulating an object. Such places would, after all, represent those locations where one action ended and another began. In segments with repetitive events, those body positions and/or object manipulations that occur frequently may be somewhat less likely to be marked as significant changes in action than those events that occur infrequently. Results from Newtson et al. (1978) lend tentative support to this idea. After being shown videotapes of an actor collating 20 booklets of 5 pages each, observers were significantly more likely to press the button when the actor stacked each completed booklet (the less frequent event) than when the actor picked up each page of the booklet (the more frequent event). This difference in button pressing remained even after the stack of completed booklets was hidden from the observers' view.

Additional support for the idea that the instructions focus the observers' attention on change and on infrequently occurring events comes from the fact that breakpoints seem to share fewer features in common with each other than do nonbreakpoints. Newtson et al. (1977) found that a greater number of body parts were in different positions when one breakpoint was compared to another than when one nonbreakpoint was compared to another. That is, nonbreakpoints were more similar to each other than were breakpoints.

The fact that the breakpoints from a behavioral segment consist of a series of events that share fewer common characteristics with each other than do nonbreakpoints from the same segment provides a foundation for an alternative view of Newtson's button-pressing results. Consider the fact that subjects were better able to recognize, in a memory test, slides of stop-actions taken from the half of a segment that had been seen before when the slides coincided with a breakpoint than when they coincided with a nonbreakpoint. One interpretation of this result that is consistent with Newtson's view is that subjects attend to breakpoints more than to nonbreakpoints and that behavioral information is encoded and stored as a list of breakpoints. In contrast to this primary-process explanation, it is likely that the nonbreakpoint slides from the two halves of the segment—observers saw one half and then were tested with slides from both halves—were more similar to each other (shared more common features) than the breakpoint slides from each half. If so, the subjects may have found it more difficult to discriminate one nonbreakpoint slide from another than one breakpoint slide from another, whether they had seen one half of the segment or not. In short, the superior recognition of breakpoints than nonbreakpoints might reflect a property of the slides used in the test rather than the kinds of behavioral information subjects *remembered*.

A similar explanation applies to the result that observers were more likely to notice missing breakpoints than missing nonbreakpoints. If nonbreakpoints are more likely to mark those places where novel changes in body position occur, then removing those points is equivalent to removing the transition from one position to another. One would expect that the actor would appear to "jump" from one position to another in such films. Removing a part of the segment where few changes in body position are occurring should be less noticeable, however. Because little change is taking place, removing a few frames from the film should have little effect.

If slides of breakpoints obtained from sequences with repetitive actions are less similar to one another than are slides of nonbreakpoints, then the result that a series of breakpoint slides were rated as more informative than a series of nonbreakpoint slides (from the same segment) is easily explained. The latter tend to look alike; the former do not. Not surprisingly, a series of dissimilar slides should be rated as more informative than a series of slides showing the actor in similar positions.

To summarize, by assuming that subjects follow the task instructions and search for *changes* in behavior, it is possible to explain much of the button-pressing results without assuming that the task taps the process by which people usually encode behavior. For the behavioral sequences typical in

Newtson's work, breakpoints seem to represent infrequently occurring changes in behavior whereas nonbreakpoints seem to represent more frequent and possibly more static body positions. The latter are, therefore, merely more difficult to discriminate from each other than the former.[2]

Although the previous discussion provides an alternative explanation for a major portion of the button-pressing evidence that has been taken as support for the action-unit model of behavior encoding, Newtson's view of encoding may be correct. Even if the secondary-process model of the button-pressing task is correct, all or part of the action-unit model of encoding may still be a useful one. The remainder of this chapter discusses implications of the research that Robert Allen, Claudia Cohen, and I have done to explore the utility of the button-pressing task and to examine the way in which observers encode, retain, and retrieve behavioral information.

Unitizing: Does it Tap a Primary or a Secondary Process?

An adequate test of the primary-versus secondary-process models of the button-pressing task requires that the covariation between properties of action-units and measures of later processing stages (e.g., memory for behavioral details) be studied. However, it is unclear which property of the units should be examined. Although Newtson has argued in several places (e.g., Newtson, 1973; Newtson et al., 1977) that the total number of units generated reflects the amount of information about behavior that observers have extracted, it is reasonable to assume that the behavioral stream can contain many different *types* of information. This raises the possibility that not all action-units are equally informative about all types of information. For example, some action-units might provide useful information about an actor's personality (e.g., a brief facial expression) but be relatively uninformative about the details of the actor's gross motor behavior and vice versa. If this latter view of action-units is accepted, then we might expect the total number of units to covary with some measures of the amount of information that has been extracted and not with others. To make more detailed predictions would require that we know which units reflect which type of information, and Newtson's task does not do this.

One's confidence in the primary-process model would be enhanced if Newtson's (1973) findings about the hierarchical nature of the button-press-

---

[2]This interpretation of Newtson's results does not imply that the button-pressing task will always yield results indicating that breakpoints are more easily discriminated than nonbreakpoints. Recall that the secondary-process model assumes that the instructions create the strategy that subjects use in deciding when to press the button. Therefore, it should be possible to change the features of behavior that elicit presses merely by changing the task instructions given to subjects.

defined units generalize. Although observers who watch a segment of behavior for one reason may unitize the segment differently than observers who watch the same segment for different reasons, if the units produced by the two sets of observers were hierarchically related, then it would lend support to the claim that the button-press was tapping an important encoding process.

A recent experiment that Claudia Cohen and I (Cohen & Ebbesen, 1979) conducted provided data relevant to the primary- versus secondary-process interpretations of the button-pressing task. In this experiment observers watched, with one of two different observational sets, four brief behavioral segments (each less than 2 minutes long) of an actress engaging in various activities. In one set condition, the observers were told to form a detailed impression of the actress' personality. In the other set condition, observers were told to remember what the actress did. To motivate adherence to these instructions, observers were also told that they would be tested for the accuracy of their impressions (or knowledge of what the actress did).

All subjects were told to unitize the segments while watching them. In addition, half of the subjects in each instruction condition were given a recognition-like memory test to determine how much of the detailed behavioral information contained in the segments they could remember. The other half of the subjects were given a series of personality trait scales to determine their impressions of the actress. Confidence ratings for each response were also obtained from all of the subjects.

If behavior perception is selective, as the first assumption of the action-unit model implies, then the observers who viewed the actress' behavior in order to form an impression might be expected to encode different kinds of information than the observers who were trying to memorize the actress' behavior. Such differences in encoding should produce differences in performance on tests of the content of the behavioral information that the observers have retained. Furthermore, if the unitizing task does reflect the encoding process that produces these differences in remembered content, the pattern of button-pressing should differ across the conditions as well.

When the accuracy of the observers' memory for behavioral details was examined, we found that the observers who were trying to form an impression correctly identified fewer details (56% correct) than those who were trying to remember the actress's behavior (70% correct). If breakpoints represent the only information that observers extract from a segment and each breakpoint supplies information that is equivalently useful in answering questions about all aspects of a behavioral segment, then the foregoing differences in memory should be associated with a difference, across conditions, in the total number of breakpoints. This is exactly what we found. The observers with a behavior-memory set not only remembered more details, they also constructed approximately twice as many breakpoints as those observers who were trying to form an impression.

The same assumptions predict that the observers who constructed more units should also have more extreme personality ratings (Deaux & Major, 1977) or, at least, be more confident in their ratings of the actress. This follows from the assumptions that breakpoints provide the only information about a segment that an observer has and that more behavioral information about an actress should produce more extreme personality inferences or at least greater confidence in those ratings. Contrary to these predictions from the action-unit model, neither result was obtained. Observers in the two conditions were, on the average, equally confident and equally extreme in their personality ratings of the actress.

It is possible to account for these findings with the action-unit model by giving up the assumption that all breakpoints supply the same kinds of information about the segment. For example, assume that the breakpoints in the impression formation condition supplied some information about the actress' personality and some about the details of her behavior. Assume further that these same breakpoints were also constructed in the behavior memory condition; that is, these breakpoints coincided across the two set conditions. Finally, suppose that the additional breakpoints in the behavior-memory condition largely provided information about the details of the actress's behavior. In such a case, we would expect the observers in the behavior-memory condition to have acquired more information about behavioral details but not about personality—exactly as was found.

This explanation assumes that action-units are hierarchically structured. However, when we measured whether the boundaries of the units (breakpoints) generated by subjects who were trying to form impressions coincided with the boundaries of the behavior-memory units, we found that they did not. Less than 25% of the impression formation breakpoints were within one second of breakpoints defined by observers in the behavior-memory condition. If breakpoints can supply different types of information about a segment, the breakpoints do not appear to be hierarchically structured, as Newtson (1973) suggested.

The failure to find differences in the average extremity of the personality ratings might be explained by assuming that the traits we used were unrelated to the personality information contained in the segments. Observers in both conditions may have been forced to generate their inferences on the basis of little or no *actress-specific* information. If this were the case, then we might expect the pattern of ratings (as well as the average extremity) in the two conditions to be very similar to each other. If the observers based their answers on the same *normative* information (e.g., females tend to be generous, emotional, etc.), then not only should the pattern of ratings be similar but they should also reflect the structure inherent in such *implicit* personality trait inferences.

We assessed these predictions by computing correlations, separately in each instruction condition, between all pairs of traits. Contrary to what one would expect if both groups of subjects were basing their inferences on the same normative information, the patterns of correlations in the two intertrait correlation matrices were completely different ($r = .08$). Furthermore, when the patterns in these two matrices were compared to a perceived co-occurrence matrix (obtained from a different group of subjects), the intertrait correlation matrix produced by the impression-set observers was more similar to this normative co-occurrence matrix than was the intertrait correlation matrix produced by observers in the behavior-memory condition.[3] That is, not only were the associational patterns among the trait ratings different in the two conditions but the pattern in the impression condition had a more normative structure—and therefore by inference was less dependent upon actress-specific information—than that in the behavior-memory condition.

Although these results are inconsistent with the view that the personality traits we used were equally irrelevant to the information in the behavior segments, they are consistent with Newtson's claim that the amount of *segment-specific* information that is extracted increases as the number of breakpoints that observers identify increases. Observers in the behavior-memory condition constructed more action-units, correctly remembered more behavioral details, and seemed to rely less on previously acquired normative information (implicit personality associations) and therefore presumably relied more on segment/actress-specific information when generating their trait inferences than did observers in the impression condition. The failure to find differences in the average extremity of the ratings and in confidence might have been due to the fact that different observers encoded very different actress-specific personality information and therefore different subjects may have rated the actress as extreme on different trait dimensions.

Although the results described thus far can be made quite consistent with the primary-process view of the button-pressing task, other findings are inconsistent with this view. In particular, the primary-process model assumes that each new breakpoint supplies additional information about the content of the behavioral segment—although different subjects may encode different things by constructing different breakpoints. Even though the unitizing patterns might differ from one subject to another within a condition, the primary-process model therefore predicts that subjects who construct more breakpoints should extract more segment-specific information. Further-

---

[3]The perceived co-occurrence matrix was generated by asking a group of female undergraduates, who had not seen the behavioral segments, to rate the likelihood that a person who had one of the traits also had another. The average ratings over subjects for each pair of traits were used as the observations in the co-occurrence matrix. Comparison of this matrix with the intertrait correlation matrices was accomplished by treating a given pair of traits as a "subject" and computing correlations between the matrices (see Ebbesen & Allen, 1977).

more, even if we assume that different breakpoints relate to different information contents, the within-condition correlations between number of units and (1) recognition memory for behavioral details, (2) extremity of the personality ratings, and (3) confidence should be significant.[4] In fact, however, none of these correlations, nor any others with the number of units, even approached being significant. In short, these correlational results provide relatively strong evidence *against* the primary-process model of the button-pressing task. Each press does *not* seem to provide a subject with more information about the content of the behavioral segment.

Of course, it would be possible to account for the entire pattern of results from the Cohen and Ebbesen (1979) experiment by arguing that different subjects within a set condition generated different proportions of personality and behavior units. That is, some subjects may have generated mostly behavioral units whereas others may have constructed mostly personality units. If such were the case, correlations based on the *total* number of units would be severely attenuated. Unfortunately, although capable of explaining the findings, this view lacks real empirical content until a method is developed for determining which units are which. In any case, such reasoning seems far removed from the idea that the button presses represent basic units of behavior perception. It seems more reasonable simply to question the utility of the primary-process model of the button-pressing task.

Behavior Encoding Without Action-Units

If one concludes, from the results of the Cohen and Ebbesen (1979) study, that button presses do not reflect—in a simple way—the information that is extracted from behavior, the assumption that the form of the code consists of action-units may still be correct. Observers may extract information in bursts of cognitive activity even if button presses do not signal when these bursts occur. By giving up the primary-process model of the button-pressing task, the failure to find within-cell correlations between the number of presses and post-exposure performance measures can easily be explained. After all, if the button press did not signal when an encoding burst was taking place, the

---

[4]It might be argued that all (or most) of the units in the impression-set condition conveyed completely different kinds of information about the segment than the units in the behavior-memory condition. For example, units in one condition might reflect changes in features of the face while units in the other condition might reflect changes in gross body movements (Cohen & Ebbesen, 1979). This view predicts that the correlation between the number of units and recognition memory should be significant in the behavior-memory condition (because subjects who constructed more behavior units should know more about behavioral details), whereas the correlation between number of units and extremity and/or confidence in the personality inferences should be significant in the impression condition (because subjects who extract more personality information should be more confident in their impressions).

between-subject variation in number of presses could well have been unrelated to the between-subject variation in the number of real action-units that were constructed. Furthermore, the effects of the set instructions on the performance measures can also be easily explained in a manner consistent with Newtson's model merely by assuming that more *real*, but unmeasured, action-units were created in the behavior-memory condition than in the impression condition.

The notion that encoding of behavior proceeds in terms of action-units may have empirical consequences even if it is not possible to measure the units directly. If the content of each action-unit is defined, more or less, at the end of the action, and the information at the boundaries between actions is sufficient to reconstruct events in between these boundaries, then one might expect the encoding process to utilize the observers' limited cognitive resources (Norman & Bobrow, 1975) in cycles or bursts. Some level of analysis must be operating more or less continuously, but the major strain on the available resources should occur at the end of each action-unit—at breakpoints—when the meaning of the action is being defined and encoded.

Of course, there are other conceptualizations of the form of the code(s) by which behavioral information might be cognitively represented. Only some of these—of which the notion of action-units is one—assume that information is extracted from the behavioral stream in bursts or cycles of cognitive activity. Other models assume that the information is extracted in a more continuous fashion. In such models, a more or less constant amount of the available cognitive resources would be used by the encoding process as the behavioral stream unfolds. Analogies for such a process are the making of a videotape recording and a continuous visual image.[5]

An experiment that Robert Allen and I (Ebbesen & Allen, 1979b) conducted was designed, in part, to provide evidence relevant to these two contrasting views—bursts versus more continuous activity—of the encoding process. We reasoned that if encoding did proceed by bursts of relatively highly demanding cognitive activity separated by longer periods of relatively undemanding activity, then an increase in the *rate* at which the behavioral segment is presented should have a detrimental effect on the amount of behavioral information that can be encoded. The size of this detrimental

---

[5]It is, of course, possible to transform all (or almost all) of the information in a continuous visual image into a list of chunks if the sampling rate is high enough. In fact, this is precisely what a video system (or film) does. For this reason, the distinction between the burst conception of encoding and a more continuous process might be best thought of in terms of initial sampling rate. The rate would be much slower in the burst conception than in the other model. The videotape analogy also offers a reasonable explanation for the effects of set on memory. We need merely assume that the sets alter the features of the behavioral stream to which the subjects attend in much the same way that we might alter the depth of focus, orientation, and/or zoom of a videocamera.

effect should depend on the amount of nonencoding time that exists prior to the increase in rate. If the average time between encoding bursts is large to begin with, then only a relatively large increase in the rate of exposure should produce detrimental effects because there is a sufficient amount of "downtime" to absorb the increase. On the other hand, when the time between encoding bursts is short initially, a moderate increase in the rate of exposure should have a large detrimental effect on the amount of information that can be encoded because the bursts will be more likely to interfere with each other. That is, a point in the segment that would otherwise have put a large demand on the available cognitive resources will arrive at a time when a prior event is already placing great demands on the system. In short, a moderate increase in the rate of exposure should be more detrimental to observers who are constructing very frequent action units than observers who are constructing infrequent ones. A sufficiently large increase in rate should be equally detrimental to both types of observers because the processing of even the infrequent chunks would tend to overlap with each other under such conditions.

If the set effects in the Cohen and Ebbesen study were due to differences in the number of action-units constructed, observers who are set to form an impression should construct fewer real action-units (at normal exposure rates) than observers who are set to memorize the behavior. Therefore a moderate increase in the rate of exposure should have a *less* detrimental effect on the amount of information encoded in the impression condition than in the memory condition. On the other hand, if the differences in recognition memory and in the structure of the personality ratings were not due to a difference in the number of action-units that were constructed in the two set conditions but rather were caused by other processes—yet to be described—and if encoding places more or less continuous demands on an observer's cognitive resources, then an increase in the rate of exposure should produce detrimental effects of approximately equal magnitude in the two conditions.[6]

The foregoing predictions were examined in a 3 (rate of exposure) × 2 (instructional set) between-subjects factorial design. Observers viewed a videotape at normal, twice normal, or seven times normal playback speed. Half of the subjects in each of these conditions were given the behavioral

---

[6]This expectation is based on two assumptions. The first is that the differences in recognition memory performance and in reliance on normative information as a function of the observers' set were not due to differences in the total *amount* of information that was encoded but rather were due to differences in the *type* or content of the information that was encoded and/ or retrieved. The second assumption asserts that an increase in rate of exposure should not cause differential interference with the encoding of some as opposed to other types of behavioral information. It is possible, of course, to devise a model that assumes that information is continuously encoded and that predicts differential effects on performance measures. Nevertheless, the model outlined in the text seems reasonable in the present context.

memory set instructions and the other half were told to form a detailed impression. Two different videotapes depicting common social interactions between a male and a female (e.g., cooperatively preparing and eating a meal) were used in each condition to increase the generality of the results. Immediately following exposure to the videotape, the observers were given a recognition memory test (for behavioral details) and a trait impression test, counterbalanced for order. The recognition memory test consisted of 50 sentences describing behavioral events, half of which actually occurred in the tape that the observers had seen. The trait-impression test also consisted of a list of 50 sentences of the same form. "He (she) was_____." The blank was filled with a trait or emotion adjective (e.g., annoyed, generous, anxious, excited, outgoing).

We attempted to measure the accuracy with which subjects could remember the personality information in the videotapes by constructing a pool of trait items; half of these actually described the personality information in the videotapes and half did not. To obtain these traits items we generated, on an intuitive basis, a large list of terms half of which we believed would conceivably apply to the actors in the videotapes. Then, an independent group of subjects was shown each videotape three times, with instructions to watch closely. After viewing the tapes, these subjects then indicated which of the characteristics they felt applied to the actors and which did not. The items were then ordered in terms of the percent of subjects who believed an item applied to one or the other. The top 25 and the bottom 25 items were selected (separately for each videotape) and used as the true and false, respectively, items in the test.

Both memory performance tests were presented on a videoteletype that was connected to a PDP-8A computer. The actual procedure was controlled by FOEP software (Allen, 1978). Subjects pressed a true or false key on the teletype keyboard to indicate whether a sentence presented on the videoscreen described an event or an attribute of the actor that they had observed in the videotape. Reaction times and confidence estimates were also obtained for all responses.[7]

Of primary concern is whether the increase in the rate of exposure from normal to twice normal speed caused a greater reduction in the quality of the observers' performance in the behavior-memory (frequent action-units) than the impression (infrequent action-units) condition. Table 6.1 presents the mean recognition-accuracy scores for the behavioral details in the six conditions.[8] As can be seen, an increase in the rate of exposure produced a

---

[7]Ebbesen and Allen (1979b) provide a more detailed description of these procedures.

[8]These memory scores were computed using the confidence data as described in Mischel, Ebbesen, and Zeiss (1976). The same pattern of results was also obtained when a more conventional, but less sensitive, percent-correct measure was employed.

TABLE 6.1
Average Accuracy Score for Behavioral Details as a Function of
the Observer's Set and the Rate of Exposure to Ongoing Behavior[a]

Instructional Set	Rate of Exposure		
	Normal Speed	Twice Normal	Seven Times Normal
Remember what was done	1.71	1.09	.71
Form impressions	1.40	.51	.30

[a]Higher scores mean greater accuracy.

reduction in the accuracy of recognition memory for behavioral details, $F(2, 72) = 16.60$, $p < .001$. Equally important, the Cohen and Ebbesen (1979) finding of greater accuracy in the behavior-memory condition than in the impression condition was replicated with completely different videotapes, test items, and experimental procedures, $F(1, 72) = 8.38$, $p < .01$. Most important, however, the detrimental effect of the increase in rate of exposure was virtually identical in the two set conditions. Both the overall interaction and a planned contrast that ignored the seven-times normal speed were not significant ($Fs < 1.0$).

The results for the personality memory test were quite unexpected. *Neither* the rate of exposure *nor* the set instructions had significant effects on this measure. Furthermore, the interaction between these two factors was also not significant. In short, to our surprise, observers seemed to remember the personality information in the tapes equally well in all conditions.

Focusing on memory for behavioral details, the results from this study were inconsistent with the predictions we had derived from the action-units model—an increase in the rate of exposure to the behavioral stream did *not* interfere, to a greater extent, with observers who were assumed to be constructing more action-units than with observers who were assumed to be constructing fewer units.

As always, it is possible to devise an explanation for these results that retains features of the action-units model. For example, the claim that units differ in the *type* of information that they encode could be resurrected. Assume further that the different types of units place different demands on the observers' cognitive resources and therefore that the time taken to encode the different types of units varies. Finally, if a proportionally greater number of longer duration units were constructed in the impression condition even though there were fewer total units in this condition, it is conceivable that the timing characteristics of these different types of cognitive events might have compensative effects such that the average "downtime" between encoding bursts would be similar in the two set conditions. Under such circumstances, a moderate increase in the rate of exposure might have equivalent effects in the two set conditions.

An alternative view assumes that encoding does not necessarily proceed in terms of action-units in which bursts of cognitive activity are separated by periods of no activity. As discussed earlier, it is possible to conceive of the information contained in behavior as being coded in many forms other than a list of actions. If information is being more or less continuously encoded and the set instructions primarily affect the content of the code, then an increase in rate would not be expected to affect memory more in one set condition than in another. On the other hand, the fact that rate had a deleterious effect in both conditions supports the claim that the encoding process involves cognitive work and that encoding is an active rather than a passive process.

Selectivity in Encoding

One feature of the results from both the Cohen and Ebbesen (1979) and Ebbesen and Allen (1979b) experiments that has yet to be discussed is the effect of the set instructions on the observers' memory for behavioral details and on their personality inferences. In both studies, observers who were trying to form an impression correctly recognized fewer behavioral details than observers who were trying to remember the actors' behavior. In addition, the Cohen and Ebbesen study suggested that the observers' impressions of the actress were more normative and, therefore, were apparently less dependent on actress-specific information when the observers were trying to form an impression of the actress than when they were trying to remember her behavior.

Both of these findings could have been explained by an action-units model of encoding if the predicted effects of rate of exposure had been obtained. We would merely have assumed that a greater number of action-units (and therefore more segment-specific information of all types) had been encoded in the behavior-memory condition. It is possible, of course, to retain the "amount-of-information" explanation and give up action-units. One form of this view argues that the set instructions simply caused some observers to attend more carefully to or to allocate more resources to encoding the behavioral stream, thereby extracting more segment-specific information. An alternative view—one that emphasizes the selective as well as the constructive aspects of encoding—assumes that the set instructions caused the observers to attend *differentially* or *selectively* to various features of the behavioral segment (Cohen, 1977; Cohen & Ebbesen, 1979; Mischel, Ebbesen, & Zeiss, 1976).

A reasonable implication of the amount-of-information hypothesis that is not as strong a consequence of the differential attention model is that different measures of the amount of segment-specific information acquired by observers should covary—both across conditions and across subjects within conditions. Some of the results from the post-exposure performance measures in the Cohen and Ebbesen experiment were consistent with this covariation prediction, whereas all of the findings from Ebbesen and Allen (1979b) were inconsistent with this prediction. In the latter study, although subjects in the behavior memory condition and in the normal rate of exposure condition remembered more behavioral details, they did *not* perform better on the trait-inference task.

After the fact, several explanations of these inconsistent results can easily be constructed. One is a methodological critique of our attempts to establish which attributes of the actors might be correctly inferred from our videotapes. It is conceivable that the procedures we used created *different* impressions of the actor rather than tapped what might be considered the correct impressions. Viewing someone's behavior three times may substantially alter the interpretations given to various behavioral events. In short, the baseline may have been inadequate.

Another explanation is suggested by the nature of the information that might lead a group of people to agree that a particular trait applies to a given individual. Suppose that the total amount of information the subjects had extracted did differ across the set conditions but that the trait items we used were such that all (or most) of them could be easily inferred from even a meager amount of segment-specific information. Recall that the trait items used in this study were selected because the majority of an independent group of subjects agreed that they applied (or not) to the actors in the videotapes. Agreement between observers may occur only when the relevant behavioral information is highly redundant, lasts for a long period of time in the segment, and/or is based on highly sterotypic information. If any of these is correct, then neither the set nor, for that matter, the rate manipulation would be expected to have a substantial effect on the encoding of such obvious information, even though the same manipulations might well affect measures of the amount of less easily extracted information that was encoded (e.g., nonredundant, brief, and/or nontypical behavioral details). If any of these post-hoc explanations for the failure of the two memory measures to covary is accepted, the results presented thus far seem largely consistent with a model that assumes that the behavior memory set caused subjects to encode more segment-specific information than did the impression formation set. On the other hand, the data are consistent with other models as well.

THE ROLE OF STORAGE PROCESSES

The discussion, thus far, has centered on the idea that the set-induced post-exposure performance differences were a result of the different observational goals causing subjects to encode behavioral information in different ways.

Several very different classes of explanations can be generated for these performance results, however, by focusing on the fact that storage and retrieval processes intervened between exposure to the behavioral segments and our performance tests. The sets may have affected retention and/or retrieval processes rather than (or in addition to) encoding. For example, the set instructions may have caused the observers to employ different rehearsal strategies rather than to encode the information differently.

Selectivity in Storage Processes

One method for examining the role of storage processes is to manipulate the length of time that intervenes between exposure to the segment and the performance tests. An experiment that Claudia Cohen, Robert Allen, and I (Ebbesen, Cohen, & Allen, 1979) conducted was designed with this in mind. We reasoned that if the set effects were due to processes occurring during the retention interval, then an increase in the length of the retention interval should enhance these effects. If, for example, some observers were differentially rehearsing behavioral details, then the difference in memory for these details should increase with the amount of such rehearsal.

The experiment had several additional purposes. First, we hoped to replicate the major results of the Cohen and Ebbesen (1979) study using more sensitive measurement procedures. Second, we wanted to determine whether the decay in performance produced by lengthening the retention intervals would have equivalent effects on different measures of the amount of segment-specific information that subjects could retrieve. It might be argued that if all of the information about a behavioral segment is in a similar form (whether action-units or not), not only would different measures of that information be expected to covary but their decay rates should be similar as well.[9]

A third reason for conducting this experiment was to examine, in greater depth, the role that normative information was playing in the performance tests. In particular, it seemed counterintuitive that subjects who were actively trying to form an impression of the actress constructed impressions whose structure could be predicted, at least in part, from the co-occurrence ratings of observers who had never seen this actress. One might have expected observers who were trying to form an impression to have extracted *more* rather than less

---

[9]This prediction may seem too strong. After all, it seems very likely that different types of behavioral information will decay at different rates. On the other hand, the action-units model does not have a formally specified notion of *type* of information. Unless a method of distinguishing among the different types of action-units is specified, the model lacks empirical content. In any case, it is heuristically useful to note that the common decay-rate prediction is a reasonable consequence of a model that does not allow for the storage of different types of information.

actress-specific personality information. An obvious explanation for this result is that our methods were at fault. These observers may have indeed encoded more actress-specific personality information but our small sample (eight) of trait terms may have been completely irrelevant to the extracted information. The observers may have been forced to infer these traits from implicit personality information and from the highly detailed, but largely irrelevant, information that they encoded. Therefore, in this study we utilized many more trait terms from a larger variety of dimensions.

A rather different explanation for the effects of the set instructions on the pattern of trait inferences was proposed by Cohen and Ebbesen (1979). On the basis of a schema-activation model, we suggested that when trying to form an impression, subjects associate and interpret incoming information in light of previously acquired implicit personality information. That is, we proposed that an impression is formed by linking specific behavioral events to already known properties of personality—a person who smiles is happy, happy people are generous, generous people are kind, and so on. Then, *both* the specific information and the implicit personality inferences are stored as features of the observed behavioral segment (see Carlston, Chapter 3, this volume). Thus, when asked to rate the actress on various trait dimensions, the subjects would be basing their ratings, at least in part, on implicit personality information that had been activated and then stored as a result of trying to form an impression. We also argued that subjects in the behavior-memory condition should associate the input with schema-activated information; however, the schema that these subjects activate should be one that is useful in memorizing behavior (e.g., a script; see Schank & Abelson, 1977) rather than one that is directly related to implicit personality. In short, in this view, the pursuit of observational goals consists, in part, of relating the incoming behavioral information to previous acquired and goal-specific information about people and then storing both the old and the new (or only the normatively consistent new) information in memory.

Several features of the schema-activation model are of interest. First, the extent to which the observers' performance will reflect the structure of normative information depends on: (1) the extent to which the content of the behavioral segment deviates from the content of the norms that are activated by the set instructions; and (2) the extent to which the questions we ask tap the normative versus nonnormative features of the segment. A second feature of this view is that it seems reasonable to expect the influence of normative information to increase as the retention interval increases. This could occur either because nonnormative information is not closely linked to already acquired information (Hamilton, Katz, Leirer, Chapter 4, this volume) or because as segment-specific information is forgotten, it is replaced with normative information. A third feature of this approach is that the influence of normative information on memory for behavioral details should be as detectable as its influence on trait ratings.

The basic experiment involved a 2 (instructional set) × 2 (length of retention interval) factorial design. Eighty subjects watched a 7-minute videotape of a continuous interaction between a male and a female. The actors were graduate drama students who wrote and performed an involving domestic scene. The scene began with the female preparing a meal. The male actor entered the room, greeted the female, and sat down. They discussed the cost of both food and the female's graduate education. The male complained about not having enough money. The female told of an accident she had with their car that day in a supermarket parking lot. The male became furious and shouted about the female's carelessness and lack of concern about money. Finally, he told her he had been laid off his job that day and did not know when he would be rehired. After additional discussion, the two calmed down, kissed, and made up. Throughout these incidents, the female engaged in a series of domestic chores around the kitchen. The male helped with some of them. At one point, obviously very angry, the male threw paper plates on the floor and jumped up from the kitchen table. At another point, he helped set the table. Both actors sat down at the table briefly and ate some of the food. In short, a two-person interaction, involving a considerable amount of verbal and nonverbal behavior, was shown to the subjects.

Prior to observing this scene, half of the subjects were told to form impressions of both actors and half were told to remember what the actors did. After observing the videotapes, half of the subjects in each set condition were immediately given both a recognition test for behavioral details and a personality-inference questionnaire, counterbalanced for order over subjects. The remaining subjects were given the same tests after a 4 to 5 day delay.

The memory test consisted of 76 sentences describing specific behaviors (half about each actor). The impression test consisted of 39 personality trait items on which the subjects were asked to rate both the male actor and the female actress. The items were selected from several different sources and included items found on the extremes of various common personality dimensions, such as socially good–bad, intellectually good–bad, dominant–submissive, introvert–extravert, and angry–happy.

Three additional groups, of 20 subjects each, were run in order to obtain normative baselines for our test items. Two of these groups supplied information about the strength of the intertrait associations. One of these groups rated the likelihood of the co-occurrence of all of the trait pairs (Ebbesen & Allen, 1977, 1979a; Rosenberg & Sedlack, 1972). The other group rated the *semantic* similarity of the pairs.[10] The third group not only provided additional normative information about the traits, they also provided normative information about the behavioral detail test items. Briefly, subjects in this group were told that a male and a female had had an argument and that

---

[10]Ebbesen and Allen (1979a) argued that co-occurrence inferences may be based on semantic inference processes.

on the basis of this information the subjects were to guess, as well as they could, the answers to both the recognition-memory and the personality test items. Thus, without having seen the videotapes, these subjects were to guess which traits and behaviors the two actors displayed, knowing only the sex of the actors, that there had been an argument, and whatever could be inferred from the test items themselves.

Several different measures of the amount of segment-specific information that subjects retained were constructed: the overall accuracy of memory for behavioral details, the extremity of and the confidence in trait inferences, the similarity of the pattern of responses on the behavioral detail test to the normative baseline pattern, and the similarity of the structure of the trait ratings to that of implicit personality (measured in three different ways). A comparison of the effects that the set instructions and the length of the retention interval had on these various indicators suggested that, contrary to the amount-of-information model, the segment-specific information was *not* in a single form. The pattern of effects depended on the measure being examined.

Table 6.2 presents the average accuracy scores for the behavioral detail test items.[11] The mean accuracy score for the normative-guessing control group was not different from chance responding. This implies that the segment contained some nonnormative behavioral features and that some of our test items tapped those features. Equally important in this regard, the performance of subjects who saw the videotape was far superior ($p < .001$) to those who did not (the normative-guessing control).

Both the instructional sets and the length of the retention interval produced significant effects on memory for behavioral details. Observers who were trying to form impressions of the actors did less well than observers who were trying to remember what was done, $F(1,90) = 7.00$, $p < .01$. This result replicated one aspect of the prior studies using very different procedures, stimulus materials, and test items. Not surprisingly, as the length of the retention interval increased, the quality of the observers' performance decreased, $F(1,90) = 102.49$, $p < .001$. Finally, the rate of decay of actor-specific behavioral details seems to have been equivalent in the two set conditions—the F for the interaction was far from significant.

The extent to which the pattern of responses to the behavioral detail test items reflected normative information was assessed by computing the proportion of "true" responses to *each* test sentence in each condition. Then, treating sentences as subjects, these proportions were correlated with the identical string of proportions produced by the normative-guessing control group. Separate correlations were computed for each experimental condition. Table 6.3 presents these correlations. As can be seen, only the

---

[11]An exact description of the method of computing these scores is available in Ebbesen, Cohen, and Allen (1979). Suffice it to say that they reflect the percent of correct responses weighted for confidence and that a score of zero reflects random guessing.

TABLE 6.2
Average Accuracy Score for Behavioral Details as a Function
of Instructional Set, Length of Retention Interval, and a
Minimal Information Control[a]

Instructional Set	Delay Between Exposure and Test	
	Short	Long
Remember what was done	7.10	4.74
Form impressions	6.69	3.77
Normative-guessing control		−.03

[a]The higher the score the more accurate the performance. A score of
zero reflects random guessing.

TABLE 6.3
Effects of Instructional Set and Length of Retention
Interval on the Normativeness of Responses to
Behavioral Detail Questions.[a]

Instructional Set	Length of Retention Interval	
	Short	Long
Remember what was done	.16	.31*
Form impressions	.16	.30*

*$p < .05$
[a]The normativeness of the response patterns was measured by
correlating the proportion of "Yes" responses to the behavioral
detail questions (treating question as the unit of analysis)
obtained in each experimental condition with similar proportions obtained from the normative-guessing condition.

duration of the retention interval affected the extent to which the pattern of
responses matched those obtained from the normative-guessing group. The
pattern became more normative as the delay increased ($p < .05$).[12] Thus, the
effect of the observational goals on overall accuracy was not mirrored by a
similar effect on the normativeness of the response pattern. Apparently, the
process that caused the decay over time in memory for behavioral details is

---

[12]Identical results were obtained when a different response-pattern measure was used. In
particular, the frequency with which the subjects in a given condition gave the same response to
two trait items was computed for all pairs of traits. When these co-occurrence matrices were
compared to the same matrix obtained from the normative-guessing control group, only the
length of the retention interval affected the size of the correlations (min. $p < .05$). The patterns
were more normative in the delayed than the immediate test conditions.

not the same as the process that mediated the effects of set on overall accuracy.

Similar inconsistencies emerged within the trait inference data. The set instructions had no reliable effect on either the extremity of or confidence in the trait ratings (whether examined item by item or as a composite score). However, increasing the retention interval did significantly decrease the confidence that subjects had in five of their 39 trait inferences. On the other hand, the length of the retention interval only affected the extremity of the trait ratings given to three items. Overall, even though there were many significant differences between ratings of the male and those of the female, neither the set nor the delay manipulations seem to have produced large effects on the average extremity of or confidence in the personality inferences.

On the other hand, both set and delay had large effects on the extent to which the structure of the ratings matched that of implicit personality theory. Table 6.4 presents the correlations between the matrix of intertrait correlations produced in each condition and three different normative matrices. With a short retention interval, the structure of the trait inferences was more normative (regardless of the baseline) for observers who were trying to form an impression than for observers who were trying to remember what was done (minimum $p < .01$). After a delay, this difference disappeared and the structure of the ratings became even more normative ($p < .01$).

Because the various indicators of the amount of segment-specific information that subjects retained did not covary across conditions, it seems likely that different information sets were being used to construct answers to these different tests. The idea that behavioral information is contained in a single form (whether a list of action-units or not) again seems untenable.

The results also suggest that the instructional sets did not alter the amount (and/or type) of segment-specific information that was retained (rather than the amount that was encoded or retreived). The pattern of effects produced by alterations in the retention interval was different from the pattern of effects produced by variations in the set instructions. In particular, an increase in the retention interval produced a *general* reduction in segment-specific information. The structure of responses to both the behavioral detail and the personality inference tests became more normative as the delay increased, and the overall accuracy of memory for behavioral details also decreased with time. On the other hand, although a similar difference in overall accuracy was observed across the set conditions, it was not accompanied by a difference in the normativeness of responses to the behavioral detail items. Another indication that the set effects were not due exclusively to retention processes is the fact that the size of the set effects did not increase with time. They either remained constant or decreased.

The pattern of findings also seems inconsistent with the schema-activation model outlined by Cohen and Ebbesen (1979). Recall that we had

TABLE 6.4
Effects of Instructional Set and Length of Retention Interval on the Normativeness of the Pattern of Trait Ratings[a]

Experimental Conditions		Source of Normative Matrix[b]		
Length of Retention Interval	Instructional Set	Semantic Similarities	Co-occurrence Estimates	Normative-Guessing
Short	Remember what was done	.24	.24	.28
Short	Form impressions	.33	.38	.35
Long	Remember what was done	.41	.45	.50
Long	Form impressions	.39	.47	.53

[a]N = 1482 for all correlations

[b]The normativeness of the pattern of trait ratings was measured by computing the correlations among all pairs of traits within each experimental condition and then comparing the pattern of correlations in these matrices with the semantic similarities, the co-occurrence estimates, and the normative-guessing condition correlations. The patterns were compared by treating entries in the matrices as the unit of observation and computing correlations between the matrices.

hypothesized that observational goals activate schema, which, among other things, associate incoming information to already known, schema-relevant information. On the assumption that implicit personality theory serves as the schema for forming impressions, this model explained the effects of set on the structure of the personality ratings.

The same general notion applies to the behavioral memory condition but with a different schema. If the relevant schema for subjects set to remember someone's behavior consists of expected actions and associations among actions, much as implicit personality theory consists of expected traits and associations among them, then the schema-activation model predicts that subjects set to remember actions should produce a *more* normative pattern of responses to the behavioral detail items than subjects trying to form impressions. This prediction was not confirmed. The observers' goals had no effect on the normativeness of the pattern of behavioral-detail responses.

In summary, it appears that the selectivity predicted by Newtson's model and found in the various experiments reported here is not simply due to set-induced differences in the *total amount* of information that is encoded (in a single form) nor to set-induced differences in rehearsal strategies. In addition, the schema-activation model may not be as valuable as we had originally assumed. Finally, the normative information seems to play a different role for behavioral details than for personality information.

ENCODING AND
RETRIEVAL PROCESSES

One explanation for the failure of the various performance measures to covary across conditions assumes that observers can and do construct more than one code to represent the information contained in behavior. Allen and I (Allen & Ebbesen, 1979) therefore proposed that at least two codes might be constructed as the behavior unfolds. We further assumed that one of these codes might consist of a generalized, abstract, and/or impressionistic representation of the information in the segment. One can think of this code in several different specific ways—an evaluative reaction to the segment, a "typical" feature of the segment, a point in multidimensional space, a list of semantic features representing the meaning of the segment, and so on. The most important characteristic of this code, however, is that it provides a global *summary* of the content of the segment. We further suggested that the second code might provide a far more detailed representation of specific events in the segment, e.g., a visual image or mental movie of the observed events.

Two Classes of Retrieval Processes

If the information in a behavioral stream is encoded in a general, as well as a specific form, it is conceivable that some types of questions about a segment might be answered in reference to one code and other types of questions in reference to the other code. Allen and I initially assumed that answers to questions about behavioral details might be more likely to be based on the specific code whereas answers to questions about an actor's traits would be more likely to be based on the general code.

Two rather different retreival processes might guide the construction of answers to these two types of questions if our hypotheses were correct. In the case of questions about behavioral details, it seems reasonable that the subjects would search or scan the specific code for a sufficiently good match between the representation of the behavior described in the test item and aspects of the specific code. In the case of trait inferences, however, the observer might simply compute the overall similarity between the global representation of the segment (or actor in the segment) and a cognitive representation of the trait. A scan or search of all of the specific actions would therefore not be required.

One way to distinguish between a process based on an extended search and one based on a single similarity computation is to vary the amount of information that the observer has in memory and measure the length of time that it takes to answer specific questions about that information. If answers are based on a search of a specific code, then the length of time that it takes to construct an answer should increase with the length of the behavioral segment—because the length of the code should increase as the length of the segment increases. If, on the other hand, answers are based on the similarity of the test item to a global code whose content, but not necessarily *length,* may change as a function of the length of the segment, then the time it takes to construct answers should *not* increase (or should increase at a slower rate) as the length of the behavioral segment increases.

Search Processes

Several specific features of search processes determine the exact pattern of outcomes to be expected in a reaction-time paradigm. One such feature is whether the search is assumed to be a serial one or a parallel one (Kintsch, 1974; Sternberg, 1969; 1975; Townsend, 1974). The former generally assumes that the information is searched in a fixed, serial order whereas the latter assumes different elements of the code are all searched simultaneously. Within the serial model, one can distinguish between self-terminating and exhaustive searches. In the former, the search stops when a sufficient match is found; in the latter, the entire code is scanned even if a match is found early in the search.

Unlike the parallel search and the exhaustive serial model, the self-terminating serial model predicts that the effect of the length of the segment should be greater on false response times than on true response times (Sternberg, 1969). All of the former must result from a complete scan of the code whereas some of the latter should result from only a partial scan of the code—a match will be found and response made before the entire code is scanned. The self-terminating serial model also predicts a serial position effect for true response times—events that occur early in the code should be found sooner than events that occur later in the code (Sternberg, 1969). Unfortunately, elaborate forms of the parallel and exhaustive serial models cannot be easily discriminated with empirical results (Townsend, 1974).

Similarlity-Based Processes

Retrieval models that are based on global similarity estimates have two consequences of interest in the present context. The first concerns the role of time and the second concerns the exact nature of the rules used to compute similarity.

Exact reaction-time predictions for similarity models depend upon the manner in which the similarity estimate is translated into a true or a false response (assuming our questions require a true or false response). Previous work that Allen and I had done (Ebbesen & Allen, 1979a) implied that a dual-cutpoint, two-stage decision process (Atkinson & Juola, 1974; Smith, Shoben, & Rips, 1974) provided a more than satisfactory model for normative trait judgments. In this model, subjects are assumed to respond true, rapidly, if the similarity estimate is above one cutpoint and to respond false, rapidly, if it is below another cutpoint. However, if the similarity estimate is between these two cutpoints, the subject performs additional processing and recomputes the similarity estimate. The subject then responds true if the new estimate is high enough; otherwise a false response is given. This model therefore predicts fast reaction times for very high and very low similarities and longer decision times for moderate similarities (because the latter are more likely to enter the second, and time-consuming, stage). More important for our present concerns, if the second stage merely involves a recomputation of similarity based on the same global code involved in the first stage, then this model predicts that the length of the segment should have little or no effect on true or false reaction times.

The rules used to compute the similarity estimate can take any of many different forms, largely depending on the structure that segment-specific information is assumed to have.

Consider two broad classes of models. In one class, each trait item is thought to be more or less relevant to different parts or elements of a code. For example, if we assume that traits and the representation of the segment/actor are in the form of a list of features, then it is possible to argue that the similarity of different traits to the segment's representation will be based on different subsets of all of the features of the representation. An alternative class of models assumes that each trait item is compared to the entire code in order to compute similarities. No part of the code is irrelevant to any given trait. In the feature-list example, this is equivalent to assuming that all of the features of the segment's representation are used to evaluate each different trait item.

Within the class of models in which the entire code is used for every item, some rules for computing similarity will weight different elements of the code differently depending on the trait being evaluated. Continuing with the feature-list example, features that are shared by the segment and the trait might be differently weighted than those that are not shared. In this way the similarity of different traits will depend, in part, on which elements the traits have in common with the segment. In a slightly different class of similarity rules, elements will not be weighted differently for different trait items. Suppose, for example, that all traits are represented by the same list of features but that each trait has a different set of values for each feature. Suppose further that the similarity of a trait to the segment's representation is based on the sum, across features, of the absolute differences between the trait and the segment values (or alternatively on the number of features on which the two representations have the same values). In this and similar models (based on different assumptions about the form of the representations), similarity would be a *global* relationship between the trait and the segment.

If we assume that different subjects in an observational condition have different abstract representations of the segment, then an interesting property of the last model described earlier emerges. Namely, traits whose representations are similar (that is, are semantically similar or are associated in implicit personality theory) will tend to covary over subjects whereas traits with different representations will tend not to covary. For example, if one observer concludes that the trait, honest, is similar to his/her representation of the segment, then all other traits that are initially similar to honest (e.g., trustworthy) will also tend to be seen as similar to the representation. If the same intertrait similarity pattern is shared by other observers, then a different person who concludes honest is not similar to his/her representation will also conclude that the same additional traits (e.g., trustworthy) are not similar to his/her representation of the segment. In short, this model predicts that the intertrait structure of a group of observers will tend to match that of implicit personality theory, even though the subjects have not directly associated implicit personality information with segment-specific information during encoding or during the retention interval. Stated differently, the normative pattern of trait ratings may result from the facts that the same global representation of the segment is used for each trait (within a subject) and that the similarity evaluation process is a global one.

Length of Segment and Reaction Time

Allen and I showed 74 observers four different lengths of behavior (30, 60, 90, and 180 seconds long) selected from one of two continuous interaction sequences in such a manner that we controlled both for the content of the segment and for the nature of the questions we asked. Each observer was exposed to each length but in different orders across observers. All of the observers answered 24 true/false questions about behavioral events—such as, "Did she hold the spoon in her hand?"—(half of which actually occurred in the segment) and 12 true/false trait questions—such as, "Was she critical?"—immediately after observing each sample of behavior. The observers were all instructed to answer the questions with reference to the behavior segment they had just seen. They were also told to watch the samples closely—no set instructions were given—and knew that they would be asked both behavioral detail and trait questions. All of the test items were presented on a videodisplay. Reaction times were recorded to the nearest millisecond by a PDP-8A laboratory computer under the control of FOEP (Allen, 1978) software.

Figure 6.2 shows the effect of the length of the segment on the time it took subjects to answer both the behavioral-detail and the trait-inference questions. As can be seen in the top panel, observers took more time to decide whether a given behavioral event had occurred in the segment, the longer the segment, $F(3,168) = 8.05$, $p < .001$. True responses took as long as false responses and most important, the interaction between segment length and response direction was far from significant, $F(3,168) = 1.59$.

These results are inconsistent with the self-terminating serial search model but are quite consistent with both the exhaustive serial and the parallel search models. Further evidence against the self-terminating serial model is the fact that serial position effects were not found either for true or for false responses. Apparently, observers do search their memories of the behavioral stream in order to find a match between the behavior described in the test item and parts of the behavioral segment. The search does not appear to be a serial self-terminating one, however.

These results are important for two reasons. First, they show that similar processes may govern the retrieval of behavioral as well as nonbehavioral information (e.g., list of letters, digits, names, and such). Second, because the code that represents behavioral information in memory seems to increase in

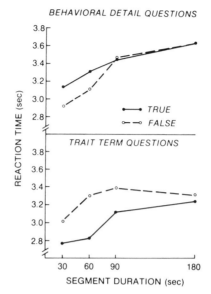

FIG. 6.2. The top panel shows the effect of segment duration on true and false response times to questions about behavioral details. The bottom panel shows the effect of segment duration on true and false response times to trait terms. Of importance is the increase in reaction times (for both types of questions) as the length of the segment increases.

length as the length of the segment increases, it is likely that this code provides a rather detailed representation of the behavioral segment.

The results for the trait questions, in the bottom panel in Fig. 6.2, were not at all what one would expect from a similarity-based retrieval model. Reaction times increased as the length of the segment increased, $F(3, 168) = 6.29$, $p < .001$. The difference between true and false responses was also significant, $F(1,56) = 10.32$, $p < .01$, but the interaction between length and response type was not. In short, it appeared that answers to trait questions were also being constructed by an exhaustive serial or a parallel search of a detailed code. The global similarity-based retrieval process did not seem to apply to traits. Based on these analyses, the hypothesis that two codes are constructed during encoding appears to be incorrect.

Because some aspects of our previous work strongly implied that more than one code was being constructed during encoding, Allen and I reexamined our reasoning behind the global-similarity approach to trait inferences. It soon became obvious that we expected this process to operate because we had assumed that the trait terms were themselves represented in memory in a global manner, e.g., as a list of features or a set of people known to possess the trait. Suppose, however, that at least some traits were represented in memory as very specific behaviors (e.g., a typical action or a brief script). Under these assumptions, it is reasonable that a subject might search a detailed code for a match between elements of the code and the remembered action that defines the meaning of the trait item. Such a search would lead to longer decision times with increasing segment length.

On the other hand, the intuition that some traits are not easily represented in terms of a single behavior or script led us to search for a method to distinguish between traits. We therefore asked another group of college students to rate each of the traits we had used in the reaction-time study in terms of the ease with which they could be inferred from a single sample of behavior versus from many different samples. The average ratings were then used to divide (at the median) the trait terms into two groups: those that were specific or could be inferred from one action and those that were abstract and could only be inferred from many *different* types of actions. We then reanalyzed the reaction-time data separately for each group of traits.

We expected that if our procedure for dividing the traits was a reasonable one, then the effect of segment length on reaction times should be limited to the specific traits. Because the representation of these traits was more likely to be a single action, observers could answer the test item by searching the segment for a sufficiently good match between the action and parts of the segment. In contrast, answers to the more abstract trait items might be more readily based on their similarity to a global representation of the segment, and therefore the effect of the length of the segment on decision time would disappear or be greatly reduced.

Figure 6.3 presents the reaction-time functions for the two types of traits separately. As can be seen, exactly the opposite results to those we had anticipated were found. It was the *abstract* trait items (top panel) that showed increasing reaction times as a function of segment duration. The slope increased, significantly, for both the true, $t(63) = 3.11$, $p < .01$, and the false,

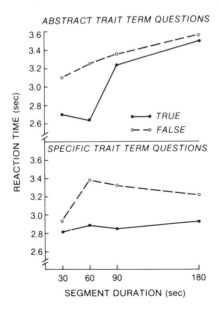

FIG. 6.3. The top panel shows the effect of segment duration on true and false response times to trait items rated as having many behavioral implications (abstract traits). The bottom panel shows the effect (or lack of it) of segment duration on true and false responses to trait items rated as having one (or only a few) behavioral implications (specific traits).

$t(63) = 2.63$, $p < .01$, responses. The slopes were far from significant in the case of the specific trait terms, max. $t(63) = .90$, however.

Although these results were exactly opposite to those we had expected, it is still possible that the reaction-time differences were due to the use of different codes for the two types of items. If the answers to the abstract items resulted from an extended search of a detailed code and the answers to the specific items were generated by a global similarity-based process, then the co-occurrence pattern for the specific traits might be more likely to reflect implicit personality theory than the co-occurrence pattern for the abstract traits. To test this hypothesis, the pattern of co-occurrences among pairs of trait items was derived, separately for each group of traits, by counting the number of times subjects gave the same response to both trait items in a pair. These co-occurrence patterns were then compared to the pattern of semantic similarity ratings obtained from different groups of subjects. If responses to the specific trait items are based on a gobal similarity process and those for the abstract terms are based on a search of a detailed code, then the specific trait co-occurrence pattern should correlate more highly with the semantic similarity pattern than the abstract trait co-occurrence pattern correlates with the semantic similarity pattern.[13] These predictions were supported. The correlation of the co-occurrence and semantic patterns were significant ($rs = .23$ and .16 for the two videotapes, min. $p < .05$) in the case of the specific trait items but not in the case of the abstract items ($rs = .01$ and .02).

In summary, the reaction-time results were consistent with the view that answers to behavioral detail items and abstract traits were constructed after a search of a detailed code, but that answers to the specific trait items were based on a global similarity process. The latter seems to have involved a different code and a similarity rule that does not differentially weight different parts of the code across all trait items.

A Two-Stage Retrieval Process

If one accepts the claims that two codes are constructed as the observed behavior unfolds and that different processes are used to construct answers to questions about the behavior depending on the code being used, then it is of interest to ask how these processes are related to each other, if at all. One view of the system, for example, argues that some trait items (the more abstract ones) and all behavioral detail items are answered with reference to a more

---

[13]This prediction is based on two assumptions. First, it assumes that the similarity rule is a global one, at least for some trait pairs. Second, it assumes that the co-occurrence pattern of relevant remembered actions (over subjects)—put differently, the co-occurrence of elements of the detailed code—does not match that of the semantic similarities (see Shweder, 1978, for support of this point).

detailed code of the segment, whereas the remaining trait terms (the specific ones) are answered with reference to a more global code. In this view, a link between the two processes does not exist.

One justification for this view argues that subjects may have attempted to verify the abstract trait terms by searching the detailed code for several matches rather than one. Because the abstract traits depend on several samples of behavior, subjects may have decided whether to say "true" by determining how many samples reflected the underlying trait. An exhaustive search in which the number of matches was tallied could account for the reaction-time results.

A different view argues that the two processes are organized in time. One such organization that provides a reasonable explanation for various aspects of the reaction-time results is a two-stage model in which the first stage consists of the global similarity process and the second consists of the search process. In particular, assume that all trait items (and even behavioral detail items) are first compared to a global representation of the segment. If the resulting similarity estimate is above a cutpoint, subjects respond true, rapidly, and if it is below another cutpoint, subjects respond false, rapidly. Assume further that the extra processing that is performed when the similarity estimate falls between these two cutpoints is an extended (exhaustive serial or parallel) search of a more detailed code. If a sufficient match is found during this search, a true response is emitted; otherwise a false response is emitted.

To explain the results with this two-stage model, we need merely assume that the similarities of most of the specific trait terms to the global representation of the segment are more extreme than the two cutpoints and therefore exit in the first stage. If the similarities of most of the abstract trait terms fall between the two cutpoints, i.e., are generally moderately similar to the global representation of the segment, then most of these trait items would tend to be answered by the second-stage search-and-match process. The assumption that the specific terms would fall outside, and the abstract terms inside, the cutpoints in the first stage seems intuitively reasonable when it is realized that the specific terms have single implications—they imply one particular action—and the abstract terms have multiple implications—they imply several different actions. It seems likely that single-implication items will, on the average, be either very similar to or very dissimilar from a global representation of the segment, whereas abstract terms will tend to have some but not all of their implications (features, or whatever) in common with those of the global representation and therefore will only be moderately similar to it.

This two-stage model explains one feature of the results that an independent processes model does not;—the fact that the average specific trait (stage 1) reaction time was shorter than the average abstract trait (stage

2) reaction time, $t(63) = 2.80$, $p < .01$. In the two-stage model, this is explained by the fact that most of the abstract trait items must pass through both stage 1 and stage 2, whereas most of the specific items should exit without going through stage 2.

If the same two-stage process is proposed for behavioral-detail items, it is of interest to note that very abstract and highly detailed behavioral questions seem to take the same route. One reasonable explanation for this result assumes that the position of the cutpoints are different for the trait and for the behavioral-detail items. If the cutpoints were wider for behavioral detail than for trait questions, then most of the former would reach the second stage. In short, the criteria determining when an extended search of a detailed code is performed may vary as a function of the question being asked. In support of these ideas, Ebbesen and Allen (1979a) found that the position of the cutpoints in a similarity-based decision does seem to shift with the nature of the question being asked.

GENERAL DISCUSSION

Button-Press Defined Units: Do They Measure a Primary Encoding Process?

Several findings from the research presented here imply that Newtson's unitizing task reflects a secondary rather than a primary encoding process. The number of units into which segments were divided did not correlate with other measures of the amount of information that was encoded. In addition, different patterns of results were obtained for different post-exposure measures of the amount of information that was encoded. Because there does not appear to be a single source of information on which all measures of encoding are based, a model that assumes that unitizing taps the same encoding process that produces variation in other measures (top panel of Fig. 6.1) seems untenable.

Is Behavior Encoded as Action-Units?

Regardless of the nature of the process that the button-pressing task reflects, it is likely that information is not extracted from ongoing behavior in bursts of cognitive activity. The failure to find an interaction between rate of exposure and instructional set contradicted the view that selection occurs by bursts of cognitive activity. Thus, the selective aspect of encoding does not seem to come about because observers are attentive to the behavioral stream (or constructing a code) at some points in time and not at others. A somewhat different view of selection assumes that greater attention is being paid to some (continuously changing) features of behavior than to others. For example, observers who are trying to form an impression might be more likely to attend to an actor's face than observers who are trying to remember the actor's behavior. This latter view of the selective aspects of encoding also assumes that different performances on memory tests do not necessarily reflect differences in the *total* amount of information that has been extracted from behavior but rather may reflect differences in the relative amounts of different *types* of information that have been encoded.[14]

As noted earlier in this chapter, there is some indeterminacy concerning the form or structure of the code or codes that observers construct. The codes might consist, as Newtson suggests, of lists of hierarchically organized action-units—although not those units measured by the button-pressing task and not ones that have been constructed in bursts of cognitive activity—or they might consist of something else. There are sufficient indications from the present work, however, that more than one code of a behavioral segment can, and probably usually is, developed *and* that these different codes are used differently in the construction of answers to questions about the observed behavior. The different effects of instructional set and of delay on the normativeness of trait inferences and on memory for behavioral details and the fact that an increase in the length of a segment affected the time to answer some questions but not others are results that are consistent with this dual-code hypothesis.[15]

Encoding as a Two-Code Process

A dual-code model is congruent with the proposal, made by other researchers both in cognitive and social psychology, that information is not necessarily stored in only one form (e.g., Carlston, Chapter 3, this volume; Craik & Lockhart, 1972; Craik & Tulving, 1975; DeRosa & Tkacz, 1976; Higgins, Rholes, & Jones, 1977; Nelson, Reed, & McEvoy, 1977; Rafnel & Klatsky, 1978; Tulving, 1972). In addition, although the exact form of the two (or more) codes is unclear in the present work, many theorists who propose the existence of two codes often assume that one code is abstract, Gestalt-like, internally organized, and/or semantically based, whereas the other code is highly detailed and faithfully reproduces the exact nature of the stimulus

---

[14]Although the present work was not designed to explore this selectivity issue, Cohen's (1977) dissertation and other work with verbal stimulus materials (e.g., Ebbesen, 1971; Mischel, Ebbesen, & Zeiss, 1976) shows that expectancies can cause *selective* memory effects.

[15]An additional bit of evidence in support of the dual-code hypothesis not reported earlier is the fact that the overall confidence subjects expressed in their responses to the behavior-memory items was uncorrelated with their confidence in their responses to the trait items, Ebbesen et al. (1979), minimum r (18) = –.10, maximum r (18) = .25.

events to which the subject was exposed. A similar view seems appropriate for the present research.

The dual-code hypothesis raises several questions whose answers we can only speculate about. One issue concerns whether the formation of one code will interfere with the formation of the other code. If a limited-processing-capacity model of selective encoding (e.g., Posner, 1975; Townsend, 1974) is adopted, one might expect that whatever cognitive resources are dedicated to the formation of one code will limit the resources available for the formation of the other code. If we assume that the observers in the impression-set conditions were attempting to form two codes (a general one and a specific one), whereas those in the behavior-memory-set conditions were trying to form only one detailed code, then the results from several of our experiments could be taken as support for the limited-capacity model. The inferior memory for behavioral details and the greater normativeness of the trait inferences in the impression-set condition than the memory-set condition may have resulted, in part, from two encoding processes interfering with each other in such a way that fewer behavioral details were encoded in the former condition. Alternatively, these results might reflect differential encoding, across conditions, of those features of the behavior that were sampled by the memory test (e.g., gross motor actions) and the activation of different retrieval strategies (one based on a general code and the other on a more detailed behavioral code).

If two codes are indeed formed, it would be of great interest to know the social conditions that tend to elicit one over the other. Is meeting someone who is a potential date (Berscheid, Graziano, Monson, & Dermer, 1976) more likely to be encoded in a general way than watching a professor give a lecture? If one code is more "impressionistic" than the other, then it might be that any social conditions that intensify the observer's need to form an impression will increase the resources dedicated to this code. A similar issue is raised on the response side. Are some social conditions more likely to cause observers to generate descriptions of known others from one or the other code? It would also be of interest to know which type of code is most likely to be used in certain common evaluative situations, e.g., in letters of recommendation or in psychiatric judgments (Konečni, Mulcahy, & Ebbesen, 1979).

Another interesting aspect of the dual-code model is that it may apply equally well to self-perception (see Salancik & Conway, 1975 for a similar treatment). Bem (1972) argued that people infer their attitudes from their past behavior if prior information about their initial attitude position is weak or nonexistent. In short, observers are assumed to be able to build up two codes for their past actions: One is a detailed code (past behavior in Bem's terms) and the other is a more global one (initial attitude position in Bem's terms). If this analogy is correct, one should be able to duplicate the results of our length-of-segment study in a self-perception rather than an observer paradigm.

Selective Processing of Behavioral Information

Several converging sources of evidence from the present research are consistent with the Newtson et al. (1977) hypothesis that the behavior-encoding process is both an active and a selective one. The content (and possibly the form) of the mental codes that are developed as behavior unfolds seems to vary with the observer's reasons for viewing the behavior. We have seen that the kinds of behavioral details that observers remembered, and the structure of their impressions depended on the goals the observers had while watching the behavior. In addition, an increase in the rate of exposure of the behavior substantially interfered with the number of behavioral details observers were able to remember.

Results from Claudia Cohen's (1977) dissertation suggest that the observers' expectations concerning the specific events that might happen in a given segment of behavior also affect the kind of details that are remembered. She found that prior information about an actress's occupation caused observers to remember occupation-consistent details relatively better than occupation-inconsistent details. In short, behavior perception does *not* appear to rest on a passive process. Observers seem to selectively and actively attend to different features or aspects of the ongoing behavior depending on their reasons for viewing the behavior and their expectations about what will happen.

The powerful effects of observer goals and expectations on the encoding of *nonsocial* stimuli have been well documented (e.g., Bransford & McCarrell, 1974; Neisser, 1967; Palmer, 1975; Snyder & Uranowitz, 1978). It is not surprising that similar effects are observed with social stimuli. The idea that the perception of ongoing behavior is based on a selective process is quite compatible with many different views of the role of attention in information processing (e.g., Broadbent, 1958; Kahneman, 1973; Neisser, 1967; Posner, 1975; Treisman, 1964). Apparently, observers are capable of adjusting attentional effort to different features of ongoing behavior just as they are able to devote differential attention to different aspects of auditory and written stimulus material.

The Role of Normative Information
in Selective Processing

Many different types of models can account for these selective effects. One class argues that the context—sets, expectations, prior information—activates previously stored, usually normative information (e.g., Cohen & Ebbesen, 1979). The models within this class often differ in terms of the form that they assume the previously stored information takes—scripts, schemas, prototypes, visual images are but a few. In general, some process is postulated that links the content of the previously stored information to the content of the incoming information in such a manner that certain elements of the incoming information receive selective treatment during encoding, rehearsal, or both (e.g., Cantor & Mischel, 1977; Cohen & Ebbesen, 1979; Markus, 1977; Rumelhart, 1975; Schank & Abelson, 1977).

There was some evidence in the research described in this chapter that was inconsistent with simple versions of such models. In particular, observational goals produced significant differences in recognition memory performance but *not* in the normativeness of the pattern of the recognition responses— although an increase in the length of the retention interval affected both measures. If the observational goals had activated certain types of previously stored information during encoding (and our normative-guessing control group provided a reasonable estimate of the content of that information), then both measures (accuracy and normativeness) ought to have been equivalently affected. The increase in total errors should have been due to observers remembering that normative events, which were not in the segment, actually occurred and/or that nonnormative events, which were in the segment, did not occur (e.g., Rogers, Rogers, & Kuiper, 1979). Instead, the greater number of set-induced errors did not seem to result from a greater reliance on normative information.

An alternative class of models argues that the set effects (or at least some portion of the effects) originate from processes which occur *after* encoding and rehearsal. One subset of this class focuses on the process by which observers construct answers to questions. In particular, with regard to the behavioral detail questions, the rule that is used to determine whether a sufficient match exists between the test item and elements of the segment might include an *inference* that relies on normative information about behavior.

Several different versions of this kind of model can be distinguished depending on the aspects of the segment that are assumed to be used in the inference. Specifically, when asked whether a given actress dropped a cup of coffee, a subject might respond affirmatively. However, this could be because: (1) a code of the exact event is found in memory; (2) other very specific events that are normally associated or co-occur with the test event are found in memory (e.g., the actress is remembered with a cup in her hand and is also remembered cleaning up a large stain); (3) an attribute of the actress is remembered that implies the test event (e.g., the actress is clumsy or has the "shakes"); and or (4) the remembered baserate of the test event is high (e.g., the subject believes most people generally drop coffee cups). The distinction between these different inference processes is an important one. If the subjects who supplied our normative-guessing baseline data constructed their guesses on the basis of one inference rule and the subjects who saw the segment used a different rule, then the correlation between the two patterns of responses should depend on the extent to which inferences from the different sets of norms were, themselves, correlated. If our test items tapped uncorrelated features of the different norms, we would not expect the observers' pattern to match that of the normative-guessing control group.

This reasoning provides an interesting explanation for the failure of the observational goals to produce differences in the normativeness of responses to the behavior recognition items even though there was a difference in overall accuracy. When tested immediately, subjects in both set conditions may have been equally likely to employ the first two inference rules described earlier because they could retreive many detailed features of the segment. On the other hand, the subjects in the normative-guessing control group (all of whom did not see the segment) may have employed the last two rules because the only information they had about the segment was very general. In short, the norms being used by the control subjects may have been different than those being used by the subjects who saw the segment. If we also assume that subjects who were trying to form an impression initially encoded fewer features of the type sampled by our test questions (our items dealt mostly with gross motor events)—although they may well have encoded more behavioral details of a type not sampled by our test questions (facial expressions, subtle body positions, tone of voice, and such)—then they would be expected to make more recognition errors on our test. Furthermore, if the content of these detailed codes deteriorated with time, we might expect both groups of subjects to rely less on inferences derived from remembered details and more on inferences derived from baserates and global attributes of the actors (e.g., their sex, the fact that the actors argued). Because the global information was also available to subjects in the normative-guessing group, the response pattern of subjects who saw the segment would be expected to become more similar to that of the normative-guessing group as the retention interval increased.

In short, one explanation for the selective effects of the observational goals on memory for behavioral details assumes that the goals alter the kinds of details that are encoded, possibly via selective attention, but not necessarily the role that normative information plays in encoding, rehearsal, or retrieval of behavioral details. That is, the differences in overall accuracy need not be explained by assuming that observational goals cause normative information to have a differential impact on one or more of these stages.[16]

---

[16]It should be noted that the multiple-norms assumption can be used in an activation model to explain our results. Four major assumptions are required: (1) the instructions to remember the actors' behaviors activated specific rather than general norms; (2) the content of these norms increased the memorability of the behavioral events in the videotape; (3) our normative-guessing data reflected general but not specific norms; and (4) the contents of the observers' memories for behavioral details became more normative in a general way (and less normative in a specific way) as the length of the retention interval increased.

A somewhat different explanation may be required to understand the selective effects of observational goals on the trait inferences, however. Although the schema-activation model proposed by Cohen & Ebbesen (1979) provides a satisfactory account of the tendency for observers who were trying to form impressions to construct more normatively structured trait inferences, these results can be equally well explained by a model that allows norms to operate during retrieval rather than during encoding or rehearsal. In particular, as outlined earlier, the structure of implicit personality will dominate the trait ratings of individuals if the similarity rule used in computing the trait inferences is a global one. The set effects can then be explained by assuming that observers who try to form impressions are more likely to use a global similarity rule to construct their inferences than observers who try to memorize the behavior. The increased normativeness of the ratings as the length of the retention interval increased can also be explained in this way. After a period of time, as the detailed code deteriorates, the likelihood of a global similarity rule being employed increases.

Thus, it appears that a case can be made for models that assume that normative information has its effects on performance at the point of retrieval rather than during encoding or during retention. Such models are of interest because they provide a novel explanation for: (1) the apparent role of implicit personality in trait inferences about people whose behavior has been observed; and (2) the tendency for the structure of personality to match the structure of *implicit* personality theory (e.g., D'Andrade, 1974; Ebbesen & Allen, 1977; Shweder, 1978).

In the first case, the extent to which the structure of people's trait ratings matches that of implicit personality theory is explained by the likelihood that the various trait inferences are based on their global similarity to an abstract code of the person's behavior rather than on the extent to which they match specific elements of a more detailed code (or on their nonglobal similarity to the abstract code). A requirement of this model is that similar representations of the trait terms be employed when people make co-occurrence estimates as when they rate a specific person.

The same assumptions offer a cognitive explanation for the highly replicable finding that personality structures (derived from peer, teacher, parent, and/or self-ratings) look remarkably like semantic similarity and co-occurrence structures (e.g., D'Andrade, 1974; Ebbesen & Allen, 1977; Mulaik, 1964; Passini & Norman, 1966; Shweder, 1978). Such ratings (whether of personality traits or some other attributes) need merely be produced by a similarity process of the type outlined in this chapter. The common finding (Mischel, 1968; Shweder, 1978) that the structure of personality ratings does not match the actual co-occurrence structure of those behaviors that serve as indices for the rated attributes is also explained by the retrieval model. In this model, the inferences are assumed to be based on a global representation of the person being evaluated and not on a detailed code—one that would contain behavioral co-occurrence information. If we could force subjects to base more of their ratings on the detailed code, as possibly occurred in the behavior-memory condition, we might find that personality structure will resemble behavioral co-occurrence frequencies and depend less on semantic similarity.[17]

The proposed retrieval models are interesting for other reasons. They provide an approach to attribute inferences, which is somewhat different than that supplied by attribution theory. For example, in the present approach, norms are not conceived of only in terms of baserates. Instead, a norm is any previously acquired information which might be used to answer questions about a person (e.g., associations between actions, associations between attributes and actions, baserates, "features" of attribute representations). Which norms, if any, play a role in the responses that subjects give depends primarily upon the questions we ask and the amount of information available in the detailed code.

The role of motivation to seek causal explanations is also minimized in the present account. The subjects in our studies were not assumed to be seeking causal explanations for the behavior they observed. Instead, they were merely assumed to be constructing answers to questions by retrieving both person-specific and normative information. We do not assume that higher attribute ratings reflect a greater perceived causal influence of the attributes on the actor's behavior but rather the similarity of the attributes to an abstract representation of the actor and/or the degree of their match to elements of a more specific representation of the actor's behavior.

Search Processes

It seems unlikely that an exhaustive search would be made of all behavioral details when an observer is asked a specific question about a longtime friend. In fact, there are indications that the internal structure of the to-be-searched information can be used to limit the portion of the code that is scanned. For example, if a list consists of both letters and digits and a subject is asked whether a particular letter was in the list, the number of digits in the list seems to have no or little effect on the time to decide whether the letter was present in the list (e.g., Naus, 1974). In other words, people may be able to limit a search only to "relevant" parts of the detailed code. If such is indeed possible, future work will have to specify how various parts of the detailed behavioral code are marked and then identified as relevant for later retrieval.

---

[17]Two important secondary consequences of this view are: (1) that the cognitive process underlying self-ratings of personality is potentially no different than that underlying other-person personality inferences; and (2) that (contrary to the claims of Shweder, 1978) the finding of a match between semantic and personality structure provides no direct evidence about whether the obtained ratings reflect personality characteristics (see Ebbesen, in press).

An alternative possibility is that the detailed codes, even for very well-known and frequently seen others, are quite short. *Most* answers to specific behavioral questions about well-known people might be based on the similarity of the item representation to a more general and abstract code. Only a few-remembered details might be available for direct search, even of well-known people. The rate of decay of elements of the detailed code might be much greater than the rate of decay of a more abstract code. Most of us have experienced remembering an impression of or feeling about a person without being about to retrieve the specifics that lead to those global reactions.

A different approach to the problem of extremely long searches would assume a working and a long-term memory. Relevant portions of an extensive detailed code stored in long-term memory might be retrieved, placed in working memory, and then exhaustively searched for a match. This model also requires a "relevancy" indication system to specify how parts of the code in long-term memory are accessed.

SUMMARY

Several tentative conclusions summarize the major points raised in this chapter. First, the information in the stream of behavior may not be encoded as action-units. In contrast, it seems likely that two codes are constructed: one being a detailed representation of the behavior and the other being a more abstract or global representation. Second, the behavior-encoding process seems to be both a selective an an active (or constructive) one; however, the selectivity probably is not accomplished by people encoding behavior at some points in time and not others. Instead, the selectivity may involve differential attention to different aspects or features of the behavioral stream—different types of information may be encoded rather than a different total amount of information. Third, observational goals and expectations may produce selective effects by altering the way in which information is retrieved as well as the way in which it is encoded. Fourth, in contrast to most current models, normative information (whether we think of it as scripts, prototypes, schemata, lists of features, or something else) may influence the retrieval stage rather than the encoding (via activation) or retention (via selective forgetting) stages. Furthermore, to adequately assess the role that normative information does play may require the use of several different types of normative baselines. Fifth, the process by which people answer questions about another person whose behavior they have observed may consist of two-stages in which the first stage is based on a dual-cutpoint, global similarity decision and the second stage is an exhaustive serial or parallel search of parts of a more detailed code.

EPILOGUE

One of the most obvious features of the material in this chapter is the inability to choose, with reasonable certainty, among several quite different cognitive explanations for the findings from our reasearch. I belive this problem is not unique to our work. The indeterminacy may well be a built-in feature of cognitive models. It may always be possible to "save" characteristics of a model of one stage of the information-processing system (e.g., action-units in encoding) by altering other features of that stage (e.g., redefining the nature of an action-unit) or by changing characteristics of other stages in the system (see Townsend, 1974, for further discussion). The utility of a particular model of encoding can only be evaluated, therefore, in the context of specific assumptions about other stages of the system and vice versa. At the very least, the present work has shown how there are a number of plausible explanations for the effects of context on memory for, and inferences about, an actor's behavior and for the role that encoding processes play in the way in which people understand behavior.

ACKNOWLEDGMENTS

This research was supported by NIMH Grant No. 26069. Claudia E. Cohen and Robert B. Allen worked very closely with me on the studies reported here. Their stimulation greatly influenced my thinking about the topics presented in this chapter.

REFERENCES

Allen, R. B. FOEP, a Fortran-based experimental package. *Behavior Research Methods and Instrumentation,* 1978, *10,* 63–64.
Allen, R. B., & Ebbesen, E. B. *Cognitive processes in person perception: Retrieval of personality trait and behavioral information.* Unpublished manuscript, University of California, San Diego, 1979.
Atkinson, R. C., & Juola, J. F. Search and decision processes in recognition memory. In D. H. Krantz, R. C. Atkinson, R. D. Luce, & P. Suppes (Eds.), *Contemporary developments in mathematical psychology,* San Francisco: W. H. Freeman, 1974.
Bandura, A. *Principles of behavior modification.* New York: Holt, Rinehart & Winston, 1969.
Bem, D. J. Self-perception theory. In L. Berkowitz (Ed.), *Advances in experimental social psychology, Vol. 6.* New York: Academic Press, 1972.
Berscheid, E., Graziano, W., Monson, T., & Dermer, M. Outcome dependency: Attention, attribution and attraction. *Journal of Personality and Social Psychology,* 1976, *34,* 978–989.
Bransford, J. D., & McCarrell, N. S. A sketch of a cognitive approach to comprehension: Some thoughts about understanding what it means to comprehend. In W. D. Weimer & D. S. Palermo, *Cognition and the symbolic processes.* Hillsdale, N.J.: Lawrence Erlbaum Associates, 1974.

Broadbent, D. E. *Perception and communication.* London: Pergammon Press, 1958.

Cantor, N., & Mischel, W. Traits as prototypes: Effects on recognition memory. *Journal of Personality and Social Psychology,* 1977, *35,* 38–48.

Cohen, C. E. Cognitive basis of stereotyping: An information processing approach to social perception. (Doctoral dissertation, University of California, San Diego, 1976). *Dissertation Abstracts International,* 1977, *38,* 412B. (University Microfilms No. 77–13681).

Cohen, C. E., & Ebbesen, E. B. Observational goals and schema activation: A theoretical framework for behavior perception. *Journal of Experimental Social Psychology,* 1979, *15,* 305–329.

Craik, F. I. M., & Lockhart, R. S. Levels of processing: A framework for memory research. *Journal of Verbal Learning and Verbal Behavior,* 1972, *11,* 681–684.

Craik, R. I. M., & Tulving, E. Depth of processing and the retention of words in episodic memory. *Journal of Experimental Psychology: General,* 1975, *104,* 268–294.

Crowder, R. G. *Principles of learning and memory.* Hillsdale, N.J.: Lawrence Erlbaum Associates, 1976.

D'Andrade, R. G. Memory in the assessment of behavior. In H. M. Blalock, Jr. (Ed.), *Measurement in the social sciences.* Chicago: Aldine, 1974.

Deaux, K., & Major, B. Sex-related patterns in the unit of perception. *Personality and Social Psychology Bulletin,* 1977, *3,* 297–300.

DeRosa, D. V., & Tkacz, S. Memory scanning of organized visual material. *Journal of Experimental Psychology: Human Learning and Memory,* 1976, *2,* 688–694.

Ebbesen, E. B. *The effects of levels of success–failure on selective memory for and self-adoption of positive and negative information about oneself.* Unpublished doctoral dissertation, Stanford University, 1971.

Ebbesen, E. B. Cognitive processes in inferences about a person's personality. In E. T. Higgins, C. P. Herman, & M. P. Zanna (Eds.), *Social cognition: The Ontario Symposium.* Hillsdale, N.J.: Lawrence Erlbaum Associates, in press.

Ebbesen, E. B., & Allen, R. B. *Further evidence concerning Fiske's question: "Can personality traits ever be empirically validated?".* Technical Memorandum 77-1229-4, Murray Hill, N.J.: Bell Laboratories, 1977.

Ebbesen, E. B., & Allen, R. B. Cognitive processes in implicit personality trait inferences. *Journal of Personality and Social Psychology,* 1979, *37,* 369–486. (a)

Ebbesen, E. B., & Allen, R. B. *Cognitive processes in person perception: Rate of exposure, observational goals, and memory for features of ongoing behavior.* Unpublished manuscript, University of California, San Diego, 1979. (b)

Ebbesen, E. B., Cohen, C. E., & Allen, R. B. *Cognitive processes in person perception: Behavior scanning and semantic memory.* Unpublished manuscript, University of California, San Diego, 1979.

Harvey, J. H., Ickes, W. J., & Kidd, R. F. *New directions in attribution research, Vol. 1.* Hillsdale, N.J.: Lawrence Erlbaum Associates, 1976.

Heider, F. *The psychology of interpersonal relations.* New York: Wiley, 1958.

Higgins, E. T., Rholes, W. S., & Jones, C. R. Category accessibility and impression formation. *Journal of Experimental Social Psychology,* 1977, *13,* 141–154.

Jones, E. E., & Davis, K. E. From acts to dispositions: The attribution process in person perception. In L. Berkowitz, (Ed.), *Advances in experimental social psychology, Vol. 2.* New York: Academic Press, 1965.

Jones, E. E., Kanouse, D. E., Kelley, H. H. Nisbett, R. E., Valins, S., & Weiner, B. *Attribution: Perceiving the causes of behavior.* Morristown, N.J.: General Learning Press, 1972.

Kahneman, D. *Attention in effort.* Englewood Cliffs, N.J.: Prentice-Hall, 1973.

Kintsch, W. *The representation of meaning and memory.* Hillsdale, N.J.: Lawrence Erlbaum Associates, 1974.

Konečni, V. J., Mulcahy, E. M., & Ebbesen, E. B. Prison or mental hospital: Factors effecting the processing of persons expected of being "mentally disordered sex offenders." In P. D. Lipsitt, & B. D. Sales (Eds.), *New directions in psycholegal research.* New York: Van Nostren Reinhold, 1979.

Markus, H. Self-schemata and processing information about the self. *Journal of Personality and Social Psychology,* 1977, *35,* 63–78.

Mischel, W. *Personality and assessment.* New York: Wiley, 1968.

Mischel, W., Ebbesen, E. B., & Zeiss, A. M. Determinants of selective memory about the self. *Journal of Consulting and Clinical Psychology,* 1976, *44,* 92–103.

Mulaik, S. A. Are personality factors raters' conceptual factors? *Journal of Consulting Psychology,* 1964, *28,* 506–511.

Naus, M. J. Memory search of categorized lists: A consideration of alternative self-terminating search strategies. *Journal of Experimental Psychology,* 1974, *102,* 992–1000.

Neisser, U. *Cognitive Psychology.* New York: Appleton-Century-Crofts, 1967.

Nelson, D. L., Reed, V. S., & McEvoy, C. L. Learning to order pictures and words: A model of sensory and semantic encoding. *Journal of Experimental Psychology: Human Learning and Memory,* 1977, *3,* 485–497.

Newtson, D. A. Attribution and the unit of perception of ongoing behavior. *Journal of Personality and Social Psychology,* 1973, *28,* 28–38.

Newtson, D. A., Engquist, G. The perceptual organization of ongoing behavior. *Journal of Experimental Social Psychology,* 1976, *12,* 436–450.

Newtson, D. A., Engquist, G., & Bois, J. The objective basis of behavior units. *Journal of Personality and Social Psychology,* 1977, *35,* 847–862.

Newtson, D., Rindner, R., Miller, R., & LaCross, K. Effects of availability of features changes on behavior segmentation. *Journal of Experimental Social Psychology,* 1978, *14,* 379–388.

Norman, D. A., & Bobrow, D. G. *On the role of active memory processes in perception and cognition.* Technical Report No. 50. San Diego: Center for Human Information Processing, 1975.

Palmer, S. E. In D. A. Norman, D. E. Rumelhart, & the LNR Research Group. *Explorations in cognition.* San Francisco: Freeman, 1975.

Passini, F. T., & Norman, W. T. A universal conception of personality structure? *Journal of Personality and Social Psychology,* 1966, *4,* 44–49.

Posner, M. I. Psychobiology of attention. In M. S. Gazzaniga & C. Blakemore (Eds.), *Handbook of psychobiology.* New York: Academic Press, 1975.

Rafnel, K. J., & Klatzky, R. L. Meaningful-interpretation effects on codes of nonsense pictures. *Journal of Experimental Psychology: Human Learning and Memory,* 1978, *4,* 631–646.

Rogers, T. B., Rogers, P. J., & Kuiper, N. A. Evidence for the self as a cognitive prototype: The "false alarms effect." *Personality and Social Psychology Bulletin,* 1979, *5,* 53–56.

Rosenberg, S., & Sedlak, S. Structural representations of implicit personality. In L. Berkowitz (Ed.), *Advances in experimental social psychology, Vol. 6.* New York: Academic Press, 1972.

Rumelhart, D. E. Notes on schema for stories. In B. Bobrow & A. Collins (Eds.), *Representation and understanding: Studies in cognitive science.* New York: Academic Press, 1975.

Salancik, G. R., & Conway, M. Attitude inferences from salient and relevant cognitive content about behavior. *Journal of Personality and Social Psychology,* 1975, *32,* 829–840.

Schank, R., & Abelson, R. *Scripts, plans, goals, and understanding: An inquiry into human knowledge structures.* Hillsdale, N.J.: Lawrence Erlbaum Associates, 1977.

Shweder, R. A. *Fact and artifact in personality assessment: The influence of conceptual schemata on individual difference judgments.* Paper presented at American Psychology Association Convention, Toronto, Canada, August 1978.

Smith, E. E., Shoben, E. J., & Rips, L. J. Comparison processes in semantic memory. *Psychological Review,* 1974, *81,* 214–241.

Snyder, M., & Uranowitz, S. W. Reconstructing the past: Some cognitive consequences of person perception. *Journal of Personality and Social Psychology,* 1978, *36,* 941-950.

Sternberg, S. Memory-scanning: Mental processes revealed by reaction time experiments. *American Scientist,* 1969, *57,* 421-451.

Sternberg, S. Memory scanning: New findings and current controversies. *Quarterly Journal of Experimental Psychology,* 1975, *27,* 1-32.

Taylor, D. A. Stage analysis of reaction time. *Psychological Bulletin,* 1976, *83,* 161-191.

Townsend, J. T. In B. H. Kantowitz (Ed.) *Human information processing: Tutorials in performance and cognition.* Hillsdale, N.J.: Lawrence Erlbaum Associates, 1974.

Treisman, A. Selective attention in man. *British Medical Bulletin,* 1964, *20,* 12-16.

Tulving, E. Episodic and semantic memory. In E. Tulving & W. Donaldson (Eds.), *Organization of memory.* New York: Academic Press, 1972.

7 The Processing of Social Stimulus Information: A Conceptual Integration

Robert S. Wyer, Jr.
Thomas K. Srull
University of Illinois at Urbana-Champaign

It is clear from the theory and research described in this volume that substantial progress has been made in understanding how information about people is represented and stored in memory, and what the effects of these representations are on social perception. However, it is desirable that we periodically step back from the myriad of specific research findings and attempt both to organize and integrate existing knowledge and to identify presently uncharted areas of investigation that require future research. It is hoped that the present chapter will serve these dual functions by: (1) presenting a comprehensive theoretical framework of social information processing that can be used to conceptualize and integrate many of the phenomena identified by other contributors to this volume; and (2) providing a structure within which new and creative research in social cognition can continue to be performed and evaluated.

A common theme underlying contemporary work in social cognition concerns the manner in which previously acquired information about people is retrieved and used to interpret new information about them. A related concern has been the way in which old and new information about a person is combined in order to make a particular judgment. These matters are closely related to a number of issues concerning memory and encoding processes that are currently the subject of intense investigation within the field of cognitive psychology. However, with few exceptions (e.g., Anderson & Pichert, 1978; Schank & Abelson, 1977; Spiro, 1977), previous efforts have not considered the processing of information nearly as complex and heterogeneous as that one often receives in one's social environment. Information about people consists not only of verbal statements but also of observations of their ongoing behavior and physical appearance and even of one's own emotional reactions to these people experienced during the course of interacting with them. Moreover, although this information may be received simultaneously, it is more likely to be acquired piecemeal over a long period of time.

In addition, cognitive psychologists typically have not been concerned with the interrelations among the diverse types of responses that are made in the course of processing social stimulus information. These responses include the recall of previously acquired material about the people to whom the information refers, the interpretation of new information in terms of abstract concepts or traits, evaluative and nonevaluative judgments of these persons, predictions of future events involving these persons, and decisions about how one should personally behave toward them.

In the first section of this chapter, we propose a preliminary model of information processing that meets many of the requirements of a cognitive system outlined by Hastie and Carlston in Chapter 1 of this volume. As such, it attempts to specify in relatively precise terms the processing of information at each of the major stages described by Crowder (1976): acquisition, retention, and retrieval. The later sections of the chapter are then used to demonstrate how the formulation proposed can be used to organize and interpret existing research in social cognition. Here, we will show how the formulation can potentially account for the major phenomena described in earlier chapters of this volume, as well as those identified in research reported elsewhere. In this context, we address issues of concern in both conceptual social memory and social event memory (see Hastie & Carlston, Chapter 1, this volume). We are specifically concerned with the way in which information about persons or events is represented in memory and the effects of these representations on: (1) the recall of previously acquired information about these people and events; (2) the interpretation of new information about them; and (3) judgments that are subsequently based on this information. Several phenomena identified in earlier chapters will receive particular attention:

1. Once a general impression of a person is formed on the basis of information about him or her, the implications of this impression are most likely to be recalled and used as a basis for future responses to the person, whereas the direct implications of the original information are either forgotten or ignored. Similarly, once a judgment is made of a person, this judgment rather than the information on which it was based is more likely to be recalled and used as a basis for subsequent judgments and decisions involving the person. Finally, once these cognitive representations of a person have been formed, their effects on later responses to the person tend to increase with the passage of time.

2. Concepts that recently have been used to encode information for one purpose are often retrieved from memory and used in processing additional, unrelated information that is acquired in a completely different context. Thus, the interpretation of information and judgments based upon it may be affected substantially by events that lead one or another concept to be easily accessible at the time this information is presented.

3. The ultimate representation of information stored in memory may differ dramatically, depending on the original processing objectives. These objectives may therefore affect both the likelihood that the information is recalled later on and the accuracy with which it is recalled.

4. Once a complex representation of a person has been formed, additional information that is consistent or inconsistent with the implications of this representation will be differentially recalled and interpreted, and its effects on later judgments may also differ.

The last two major sections of this chapter are devoted to a discussion of these and other phenomena in terms of the formulation proposed.

A PRELIMINARY MODEL OF
SOCIAL INFORMATION PROCESSING

The formulation to be proposed distinguishes between two general functions of a cognitive system—storage and processing. This is done metaphorically by postulating different storage and processing units, each with a different function, and then specifying the relations among these units and the conditions under which material is transmitted from one to another. Other metaphors exist (e.g., see Norman, 1970, for examples derived from the cognitive literature, and Wyer & Carlston, 1979, for an example specifically concerned with the domain of social information processing). However, the one considered here is both conceptually economical and comprehensive in its implications. Moreover, it provides a general theoretical model that can be refined and elaborated as empirical and conceptual advances accumulate.

The information-processing system we propose, which incorporates many of the requisite features necessary for a complete cognitive system (Hastie & Carlston, Chapter 1, this volume), is diagramed in Fig. 7.1. The system consists of four primary storage units (denoted by rectangles in the figure): a Sensory Store, a Goal Specification Box, a Work Space, and a Permanent (or long-term memory) Storage Unit. In addition, there are five processing units (denoted by circles or ovals): a Preencoder, an Executive Unit, an

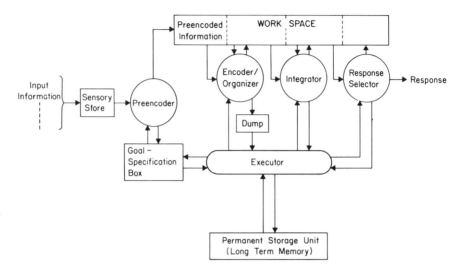

FIG. 7.1. Flow diagram of proposed information-processing model. Processing units are denoted by ovals and storage units by rectangles. Arrows denote direction of information flow. (Only those paths of primary concern in this chapter are presented.)

Encoder/Organizer, an Integrator, and a Response Selector. After some general remarks on the type and sources of information to be considered, we discuss each set of components and their individual functions. Following this, we provide a hypothetical example illustrating the operations of the system as a whole and point out several of its implications. The present conceptual framework is potentially relevant to the processing of information about a variety of objects, but we will restrict our attention to information about persons and events involving them.

Sources of Information

Two general types of information may enter the processing system. One type consists of descriptive stimulus information about a person, object, or event. A second concerns the goals or objectives for which this stimulus material is to be used. We comment on each briefly.

Information About Persons and Events

New information about persons and events may enter the processing system from a variety of sources and in different sensory modalities. For example, it may consist of a written or oral description of a person or behavior. It may also be communicated visually as the result of observing someone engage in a certain behavior, seeing a picture or film of a person or event, etc. This information can vary along numerous dimensions, several of which are worth noting.

Information about a person may consist of specific behaviors manifested in specific situations, general behaviors (e.g., helps others), traits, physical characteristics, social roles, or groups to which the person belongs. Information about an event may describe characteristics of the people involved in it, or characteristics of the action itself and its consequences. Moreover, it may describe either a single action, a series of related actions, or episodes extending over either a short or long period of time. In addition, the information may vary in generality. For example, it may refer either to a specific person or event or to many, and either to a particular behavior in a given situation or to a general behavior manifested in several situations. Moreover, it may either specify the particular situation and point in time to which it is relevant, or be nonspecific as to time and place.

Finally, the information may differ in the completeness with which it describes the event or persons involved. For example, the verbal description "Mary got up from her chair and got a handkerchief from her coat pocket" does not include the information that she walked over to the coat rack. Alternatively, information that "John pounded a nail into the wall" does not include a description of the tool he used to accomplish this feat. In such instances, the missing details may need to be added in order for the information to be completely understood (Bobrow & Norman, 1975; Bower, 1975). The processes involved in adding these details will be considered presently.

The information that enters the processing system may depend on the perspective of the receiver. For example, Mary's representation of herself slapping John at dinner may include the expression on John's face, the feelings of anger that led her to commit the act, and the stinging sensation of her hand hitting John's cheek, whereas John's representation of this event may consist primarily of Mary's facial expression and the pain resulting from being slapped (cf. Taylor & Fiske, 1978). In this regard, much of the new information that enters a person's processing system may be generated by the person himself and may consist of thoughts or nonverbalized feelings that occur in the context of information from external sources. Tulving (1972) notes that the reception of information about a person or episode is itself an event in which the receiver is an active participant. Characteristics of this event (e.g., the activity of receiving the information in one or another modality, thoughts generated or inferences made in the course of receiving it, emotional experiences at the time of its receipt, etc.) are components of the overall configuration of stimulus information. Thus, if I am told or I see that my wife fell over a chair at a New Year's Eve party, I may conclude that she had too much to drink and, moreover, may experience a bit of emotional discomfort or upset. The information transmitted includes my awareness of being told about (or seeing) the act under certain situational conditions, the conclusion I draw, and my emotional reaction. In some instances, the cognitive activity that occurs in the course of processing information will feed back to serve as information input to the system. Although we will not elaborate greatly upon this possibility in the present chapter, it should be recognized and its implications ultimately explored.

Goals of Information Processing

Information is typically processed in order to attain some objective. The goal may be either general (e.g., to form a general impression of the person involved) or specific (e.g., to decide whether to ask the person out to dinner on a particular evening, or to decide whether a defendent on trial is innocent or guilty). Some goals may be preconditions for others; for example, a precondition for attaining most objectives is simply to comprehend the information that is relevant to attaining these objectives and to interpret the information in the context of previous knowledge about the people and events involved. As we see later, the manner in which information is organized and stored in memory may depend on the processing objectives at the time it is first received. For example, the objective of deciding whether a person would be a good graduate student may lead the judge to attend to different aspects of the information, and thus may lead the information to be interpreted much differently than if the objective were to decide whether the person would be a good date, or simply to remember the information as accurately as possible. The possibility that a recipient's processing objectives at the time information is received may influence the manner in which this information is subsequently recalled, and the type of judgments based upon it, is an important consideration that we discuss in some detail throughout this chapter.

Storage Units

The processing system described in Fig. 7.1 includes four main storage units: a Sensory Store, a Work Space, a Permanent Storage Unit, and a Goal Specification Box. In addition, a temporary storage unit (Dump) is associated with the Encoder/Organizer and is discussed in the context of this processor. The Permanent Storage Unit is the most important and therefore is described in most detail.

Sensory Store

All external information, regardless of modality, is assumed to enter the processing system through the Sensory Store. At any given moment, the unit holds all the information impinging on any of the sense organs. Furthermore, it holds this information in veridical form. The Sensory Store holds a large amount of information that decays extremely rapidly, usually within several seconds (Crowder, 1976; Sperling, 1960).

Work Space

The Work Space is a temporary repository for all information that is being operated upon by the processing system in pursuit of its objectives. As shown in Fig. 7.1, it is divided into four compartments. One compartment contains original input material that has been sent to it by the Preencoder.[1] This compartment, unlike the others, has limited capacity, and its contents are continually being displaced by new information. Consequently, any information that is not drawn from it by the Encoder/Organizer is eventually lost.

The other three compartments contain the material (both input and output) involved in processing by the three main processing units (the Encoder/Organizer, the Integrator, and the Response Selector). Although the capacity of these compartments is also limited, it is much greater than that of the first compartment. Therefore, as long as material is likely to be useful for attaining processing objectives in the present or near future, or if no other processing demands require the use of this space, the information may remain in the Work Space for some time. However, when processing objectives have apparently been attained, or if a considerable delay is expected before the material is likely to be used again, the Work Space may be cleared for other purposes. Once this is done, any material that has not been sent to Permanent Storage is lost. The implications of this become clear presently.

Permanent Storage Unit (Long-Term Memory)

The permanent information store, which is analogous to that referred to elsewhere as long-term memory (e.g., Klatzky, 1975; Loftus & Loftus, 1976), is a major source of material to be processed and a repository for the results of this processing. It contains all material that has, at one time or another, been an output of one or more of the processing units. The precise manner in which such information is organized and stored has been the focus of many theorists in both the area of person memory (Ebbesen & Allen, 1979; Hastie, Chapter 5, this volume; Wyer & Carlston, 1979) and elsewhere (Anderson, 1976; Anderson & Bower, 1973; Collins & Loftus, 1975; Meyer & Schvaneveldt,

---

[1]The Preencoder functions as an initial filtering system that is capable of distinguishing between the input material to be processed and information pertaining to processing objectives. Once this is done, the Preencoder directs the various material to different storage units. The specific functions of this unit are described in more detail shortly.

1971; Rumelhart & Ortony, 1977; Schank & Abelson, 1977). Many of these formulations conceptualize the organization of information in memory in terms of a network of interrelated concepts, represented by nodes and interconnected by pathways denoting their association (for a detailed application of a network model of person memory, see Wyer & Carlston, 1979).

A network model of memory is useful in accounting for many phenomena in the area of social cognition, and aspects of such a model may ultimately need to be incorporated into a complete theoretical description of memory and encoding processes. However, an alternative formulation that seems more appropriate for conceptualizing the phenomena of concern in this volume is developed here.

Specifically, we conceptualize long-term memory as consisting of a set of content-addressable storage bins. Each bin is tagged in a way that identifies the particular object or type of object to which its contents refer. The contents of these bins are not mutually exclusive. That is, similar (or identical) information may be deposited in and subsequently drawn from more than one bin. For example, a representation of Mary Smith slapping John at last year's New Year's Eve party could be contained in a bin referring to "Mary Smith," a bin referring to "John," a bin referring to "last year's New Year's Eve party," and/or one pertaining to New Year's Eve parties in general. On the other hand, a piece of information may not necessarily be stored in all bins to which it is potentially relevant. The bins in which it is stored may depend in part on processing objectives. For example, if information about Mary's slapping John at dinner is processed with the objective of forming an impression of Mary, it may be stored in only the bin that is tagged with her name, whereas if the objective is to evaluate John, it may be stored in only a bin about John. Alternatively, if the objective is simply to recall the event for purposes of telling a friend about it later on, it may be stored only in a bin pertaining to the dinner party. Note that to the extent the event is stored in only the bin pertaining to (e.g.) Mary, it may not be retrieved at a later date when information about (e.g.) John is sought.

Information is stored in bins as it is deposited, with more recently deposited material on top. Moreover, when information is drawn from a bin, it is returned to the top of the pile rather than to the position from which it was drawn. One implication of this is that the information stored in any given bin is more likely to be retrieved and used if it recently has been used in the past. Moreover, information that is contained in two bins may sometimes be at the top of one bin but near the bottom of the other. (This could occur either because the information in the first bin has been used more recently than it has in the second, or because additional information has been received and deposited on top of existing information in the second bin but not the first.) Thus, the likelihood that a given piece of information is retrieved and used will often depend on which bin is searched.

A "piece" or unit of information of the sort retrieved from a storage bin may sometimes consist of only a single judgment, or verbal label, that is assigned to the object to which the bin refers. For example, information that Mary is a university professor may be stored as a single phrase, "university professor," in a bin associated with Mary. However, a unit of information may also be configural in nature, consisting of an organized set of features. Thus, for example, Mary slapping John at dinner may be encoded in terms of an interrelated series of events that both led up to and followed the incident, as well as the incident itself. Morever, it may include nonverbal representations of the participants and their behavior. Alternatively, a more abstract representation of Mary may be formed that consists of a hierarchical organization of traits, and behaviors associated with these traits. In either case, such a configural representation may function as a single unit of information and thus may occupy a single location in the bin in which it is contained. As a result, different units of information may vary substantially in both type and complexity. Therefore, although there is no inherent organization of the units of information contained in a bin, the features contained within a given unit may be quite highly organized, with certain features more prominant than others.

Finally, it is important to note that the memory bins do not contain the original input information that initially impinges on the processor but only representations of this information (Tulving & Bower, 1974). That is, stored material has passed through at least the Encoding/Organizing Unit and therefore will often differ in form from the original stimulus material. For example, those aspects of the original stimulus information that have not been encoded never become part of the representation stored in long-term memory. As we see later, it is also possible for certain features that were not part of the original information to be added to the representation (Bower, 1975). In sum, although the stored representation will include many features of the original information, it may also contain additions, distortions, or deletions.

The bins in the Permanent Storage Unit are of several types. One type consists of simple concepts, typically denoted by words or phrases, that are used to label features of social stimuli (e.g., trait terms, descriptions of behavior, etc.) but are not directly connected to specific persons or events. A second type contains information about *particular* social objects (persons, groups, or events). A third type contains goals or objectives and information relevant to attaining them.

Semantic Bins.   Semantic bins function as "mental dictionaries" of concepts that can be used to interpret specific aspects of one's social experience. Each concept has a nominal representation and a definition, each of which may be either verbal or nonverbal. Although it may ultimately be necessary to be more precise, for the present we postulate two bins, an *attribute* bin and a *behavior* bin.

The concepts contained in the attribute bin may refer either to traits (e.g., "honest" or "dull"), emotional states (e.g., "happy" or "afraid"), or physical characteristics (e.g., "short" or "brown-haired"). However, each concept may also be represented in terms of a configuration of both trait terms and behaviors that, in combination, serve to define it. Each such configuration of trait terms and behaviors may be conceptualized as an *attribute schema*. Thus, an "honest" schema may consist of trait terms such as "trustworthy" and "sincere," and may also include prototypical behavioral descriptions such as "tells the truth," "returns lost property," etc. A much more simple schema (e.g., "brown-haired") may consist only of a nonverbal representation of its physical referent.

The concepts contained in the behavior bin refer to general or specific actions that can be used to interpret information about behavioral events. The nominal representations of these concepts are typically words or descriptive phrases (e.g., "tells the truth," "works hard"). These concepts, like those contained in the attribute bin, may be defined in terms of verbal or nonverbal descriptions of behavior at more concrete levels. Moreover, they may include contextual features that are directly or indirectly relevant to the behavioral act. For example, "studying" may be defined in terms of general behavioral concepts pertaining to doing homework problems, reading and taking notes, etc. These behavioral concepts may in turn often be defined in terms of configural representations of the actions to which they refer and the objects associated with them. For example, "reading and taking notes" may be defined in terms of a nonverbal representation of a person hunched over a desk with a book propped in front of him, pencil in hand, and a note pad at his side. In some instances, the representations may be mental images (Kosslyn, 1976; Kosslyn & Pomerantz, 1977; Paivio, 1971). However, these representations are fairly static in character and are not specific in certain details. Thus, whereas the actual behavior of reading and taking notes may in practice consist of a sequence of activities by a specific person, the *concept* may be defined in terms of a prototypic representation of a person that is nonspecific as to appearance, the type of reading and writing materials, and the particular point in the behavioral sequence. This static quality of the material in the behavior bin distinguishes it from that contained in the "event bins" to be described presently.

Person and Event Bins. The semantic bins just described basically function as "dictionaries" for encoding bits and pieces of information about social objects in general. In contrast, person and event bins each contain information about either specific objects or groups of objects (i.e., a particular person, group, or event). Each bin is tagged with a label that denotes the object to which the material refers. Although the material contained in these bins can be of several types, much of it is configural in nature. That is, it includes organized clusters of features, the nature of which is outlined as follows.

Person bins contain material about either a single individual or a category (type) of individual (e.g., "professor" or "feminist"). Individual person bins may contain configural representations of the person's appearance, or several such representations at different times in the person's life or in different situations. They may also contain representations of behaviors the person has manifested in specific situations, or sequences of related behavior involving the person over a period of time. In addition, they may contain trait terms, general behavioral dispositions, groups to which the person belongs, or judgments that have been made of the person in the past. They may also contain configurations of traits and behaviors that have been associated with the person in different general or specific situations. For example, a "Mary Smith" bin may contain a configuration of features associated with her in high school, another configuration associated with her as a lover in graduate school, and a third associated with her as a professor at Northwestern. Moreover, different clusters may exist for Mary in her professional role and in her role as a close personal friend. These configurations of features will be denoted *person schemata.* It is also important to note that the traits and behaviors contained in one schema of a person may differ and may even be semantically inconsistent with those in other schemata of this person. In any case, each judgment, trait, or schema is stored as a separate unit of information about the person and thus occupies a separate location in the bin.

Bins pertaining to prototypic persons or categories contain information very similar to that of individual person bins. In addition, they may contain names of individual persons who exemplify these prototypes or groups. Aside from this, these bins differ from individual person bins primarily in terms of the relative proportions of different types of information included in them. For example, bins of information about prototypic persons may contain a greater proportion of trait terms and a smaller proportion of instances of behavior in specific situations than do individual person bins.

The contents of a person bin and that of the general attribute bin can now be distinguished more clearly. As an example, the attribute bin may contain a "hostile" attribute schema composed of trait terms and behavioral descriptions that are denotatively related to this attribute and serve as bases for encoding new information that contains these features. In addition, a hostile person bin may contain person schemata, or configurations of traits and behaviors associated with a prototypic hostile individual. However, these latter schemata may contain attributes that do *not* imply hostility per se but are simply believed to characterize certain types of hostile people. These traits may comprise one's "implicit personality theory" (Rosenberg & Sedlak, 1972) of what characteristics are typically associated with hostile persons.

Event bins typically contain one or more temporally related sequences of actions involving one or more persons. Our conceptualization of these configural sequences, or *event schemata,* is similar to Schank and Abelson's (1977) concepts of scripts, plans, and goals. These schemata may refer to specific events involving specific persons (e.g., "the party at Mary's house last Friday," "Professor Smith's chewing out Cathy for not doing her homework") or to more general, prototypic sequences of events (e.g., "building a model airplane," "eating at a restaurant," "getting an education"). As implied by these examples, the sequences of actions contained in these schemata may occur in a single situation over a short time span or over an extended period of the person's life. Moreover, the events may be represented at either an abstract level (e.g., "graduating from Yale") or at a specific level (e.g., an image of a farmer picking up a cat who has tipped over a milk pail and throwing the cat against the barn door). To the extent that event bins contain representations of specific action sequences and characteristics of specific individuals, their contents differ from the contents of behavior bins that contain static representations of acts that are not person specific.

An event bin may contain one or more event schemata, each of which functions as a different unit of information. For example, the "party at Mary's house" bin may not necessarily contain a single sequence of events extending from the beginning to the end of the occasion but, rather, may contain several fairly unrelated episodes involving different persons at different times during the course of the evening. Moreover, the "eating at a restaurant" bin may contain several different event schemata, each pertaining to a different prototypic restaurant (e.g., McDonald's, Four Seasons, etc.).

The process of acquiring information is itself an event and may often be stored in memory as a specific event schema involving both the recipient of the information and his reactions to it. For example, my observation of John spilling his drink at a party last Saturday evening involves not only the details of John's behavior but also myself as an observer of the act and the situational context in which the observation is made. Similarly, acquiring this information by listening to another's verbal report of it involves my experience of hearing the information from a particular other in a particular situation. Thus, my representation of the episode may include not only the object of the information but also the conditions under which the information is presented. For example, in the course of learning about John's pratfall, I may infer that he had too much to drink, that he is a clumsy oaf, and that his wife must have been embarrassed. To the extent they are encoded, these inferences will also become part of the total event schema that is stored.

The foregoing conceptualization suggests a highly interrelated memory system. For example, event bins can contain names and features that are used to identify other bins about individual persons or groups. Alternatively, person bins may contain tags used to denote other person or event bins, as well as concepts contained in the two semantic bins. As a result of this interrelatedness, the processing of material contained in one bin may often lead material in others to be accessed as well. For example, the "professor" bin may contain prototypic behaviors and attributes that are defined in terms of concepts in semantic bins. Moreover, it may contain the names of particular persons that denote individual person bins. The latter bins may in turn consist of configurations of features, or specific event schemata, the components of which include names of still other bins. Thus, the attainment of processing objectives (e.g., to describe a college professor) may ultimately involve the accessing of information from a variety of bins in addition to the "professor" bin. Which other bins are accessed and what material is drawn from them will depend in part on the order in which the various pieces of information lie in the bins at the time the processing occurs.

Goal Bin. The goal bin contains *goal schemata* that are used both to identify and interpret processing objectives and to specify the procedures for attaining these objectives. Each goal schema has a label that may be general (e.g., to form an impression of a person, or to remember the information acquired about a person or event) or specific (e.g., to decide whether to ask someone for a date, or to estimate one's liking for a person along a category scale). The schema itself consists of a set of step-by-step instructions for processing information in pursuit of the goal to which it refers. (For a more formal treatment of plans and goals, see Schank & Abelson, 1977.)

Relations Among Bins. Much of the previous discussion has been devoted to an analysis of the organization of information within the various bins. At this initial stage in the development of the model, no explicit organizational scheme has been assumed to govern the relationship between bins in Permanent Storage. That is, all bins are assumed to be equally accessible. In later refinements of the formulation, however, it may be desirable to postulate a higher-order organization of bins. There are many possibilities but the most appealing would appear to be a hierarchical system of bins associated with related individuals and groups. For example, it may eventually prove useful to postulate a higher-order "professional" bin with separate lower-order bins associated with "doctor," "lawyer," etc., each of which contain units of information specific to these professional subgroups. Winograd (1976) has recently outlined a similar organizational scheme that uses many of the same processing assumptions described in the present model and should be considered seriously. In any case, no such higher-order organizational system is necessary to account for the empirical findings of concern in this volume.

Goal Specification Box

The Goal Specification Box contains one or more representations of the immediate processing objectives, which are either transmitted to it by the Preencoder or retrieved from the goal bin in Permanent Storage. In addition, it contains goal schemata that provide directions for the processing of information in pursuit of these objectives. These schemata identify the bins in Permanent Storage from which information should be sought for use in attaining processing objectives, the units to which it should be sent, and the bins to which the results of processing should be returned. The Goal Specification Box can contain information about more than one objective at a time, thus enabling information to be processed in parallel in pursuit of more than one goal simultaneously. However, the capacity of the unit is limited. Therefore, as additional objectives enter the unit, others are removed and therefore cease to affect the manner in which information is processed.

Processing Units

The present model contains five separate processing mechanisms: a Preencoder, an Executive Unit, an Encoder/Organizer, an Integrator, and a Response Selector. The operation of each processor is assumed to be the same, regardless of whether the information being processed is from an external source, retrieved from memory, or both. Whereas the operations of all five units are central to a complete understanding of information processing, the Executive Unit and the Encoder/Organizer are most central to the concerns of this volume and therefore will be described in the greatest detail, with other units discussed more briefly.

Preencoder

The Preencoder is an initial editing and selecting device that is capable of categorizing input material and transmitting it to different storage units (e.g., the Work Space or the Goal Specification Box). It is conceptualized as a series of filters, each of which is designed to permit passage of material of a certain type while prohibiting the passage of other types. One function of these filters is to distinguish between input that concerns stimulus objects and events and input that specifies goals or processing objectives. Input that is identified as goal related is transmitted to the Goal Specification Box of the Executive Unit, as shown in Fig. 7.1. The remaining material is transmitted to the Work Space to await processing by other units.

More generally, the filtering system enables potentially important encodable material to be extracted from the input information and sent on for further processing. In this regard, it may be viewed as separating "signal" from "noise." If the stimulus information is simple and the amount of it is not great, it may be transmitted in nearly its original form. However, if it is complex and the amount of it is large, only a portion of it may be transmitted (cf. Norman & Bobrow, 1975). Thus, for example, input material consisting of a verbal statement containing familiar words may be transmitted intact. However, if the input is a complex verbal passage, the Preencoder may identify and transmit only key sections of the passage that are recognized as meaningful. Alternatively, if the input consists of a sequence of ongoing behavior, only segments of this behavioral sequence may be transmitted.

In addition to "general-purpose" filters that simply separate interesting or important information from uninteresting or irrelevant stimulus information, special-purpose filters may exist that are specific to certain processing objectives. If a processing objective has already been identified at the time the input material to be processed is received, a specific-purpose filter may be activated on the basis of instructions from the Executor, thus allowing only material that is potentially relevant to this objective to be sent to the Work Space. However, these special-purpose filters may not be invoked unless the amount of input material is large. Consequently, under low information load, goal-irrelevant as well as goal-relevant material may be transmitted to the Work Space. In combination, these assumptions allow the formulation to account for the effects of selective attention to input information, the nature of which depends on the purpose for which the information is expected to be used. On the other hand, it also provides for "incidental learning" of goal-irrelevant information under conditions of low information load.

Executor

The Executor's function is similar to that of the Executive subroutine postulated by Hastie and Carlston (Chapter 1, this volume). That is, it directs the flow of information between various storage and processing units in a manner that will attain processing objectives. This is done on the basis of instructions specified in the goal schemata contained in the Goal Specification Box. It accomplishes this is several stages. First, when a new processing objective enters the Goal Specification Box, the Executor identifies a goal schema corresponding to this objective from the goal bin in Permanent Storage and deposits it in the Goal Specification Box at a location associated with this objective. Then, based on procedures specified in this schema, it identifies bins contianing material necessary to attain this objective and sends it to the appropriate processing unit (e.g., the Encoder/Organizer, the Integrator, or the Response Selector). The information is transmitted one unit at a time, with additional material transmitted only on signals from the processing unit involved that the material is either insufficient or inappropriate for performing the task assigned to it.

The material transmitted to processing units may be of several types and may be used for several purposes. Information sent to the Encoder/Organizer and Integrator may consist in part of previously acquired information about a person or event to be reencoded, reorganized, or integrated with new information about the object. The material sent to the Encoder/Organizer may also consist of concepts or prototypic schemata in Permanent Storage that, together with their definitions, provide bases for encoding and organizing the information to be processed. Finally, when an overt response is required, the Executor may send to the Response Selector a set of concepts or labels that are potentially applicable for decoding the output of internal encoding and integration processes into an appropriate language or behavioral alternative.

Thus, for example, suppose the processing objective is to evaluate an acquaintance as a potential graduate student on the basis of information contained in her application folder as well as other previously acquired information about her. Based on the goal schema associated with attaining this objective, the Executor may first identify general attribute schemata in semantic bins that permit the information in the application folder to be interpreted and send it to the Encoder/Organizer (discussed later). Once this preliminary interpretation is made, the Executor may then identify and transmit the contents of a storage bin associated with the acquaintance that may be potentially relevant to the objective (e.g., person schemata pertaining to the candidate in academic situations, prior judgments of her academic ability, etc.) and transmit it to appropriate processing units to be encoded, organized, or integrated along with the new information acquired. Finally, the Executor may identify prototypic "good graduate student" and "bad graduate student" bins and transmit configurations of attributes that are associated with these prototypes (e.g., "hardworking," "interested in research," "high math ability," etc.) for use as bases for deciding whether the features of the acquaintance are sufficient to conclude that she is an instance of one or the other category. In each case, concepts and their definitions are transmitted to appropriate processing units in the order they are identified.

In this regard, the Executor is assumed to send only a limited amount of material to processing units at any give time. Hence, not all potentially relevant material is transmitted. If the processing objectives can be attained on the basis of the material initially transmitted (e.g., if this material can be used to encode or organize the new information presented), no further material is sent. However, if the objectives cannot be attained, additional information is then transmitted.

Once the processing unit has completed its work, the Executor takes material from this unit and returns it to Permanent Storage. Concepts and prototypic schemata that were transmitted to processing units for the purpose of processing other information are returned in their original form to the top of the bins from which they were drawn. However, material that was transmitted to processing units to be *operated on* (i.e., to be reecoded or reorganized along with any new information being processed) is not always returned to Permanent Storage in the form it was taken. Rather, only the output of this processing, which may be a schema containing aspects of both the new information and the information acquired from storage, is returned. The specific bins in which it is deposited are typically those implied by the processing objectives indicated in the Goal Specification Box. Thus, if the objective is to "form an impression of Mary," material is returned to either a previously established bin of information about Mary, or (if Mary was not known before the information was received) to a new bin constructed specifically to hold such information. On the other hand, if the objective is simply to interpret the events in the situation described, the material may be sent to several different bins.

The specific factors that lead information to be stored in one place or another have not been conceptualized in detail at this writing. However, an understanding of this matter has important theoretical implications within the framework we have proposed. If a piece of information is not stored in a person or event bin to which it is potentially relevant, it will not subsequently be retrieved when information about that person or event is sought. Rather, it can be retrieved only by accessing other bins that may not be identified in a way that enables the Executor to know a priori that they are relevant. Thus, if information that Mary slapped John is stored only in the "Mary" bin, it may never be retrieved for use in making judgments of John unless it is fortuitously accessed by searching the "Mary" bin for some other purpose. The dynamics postulated here can account for the fact that in the course of informal conversations, we often stumble on information about persons and events that we had not thought about for some time and would probably never retrieve in the course of actively searching for information about these objects. However, a more precise description of these phenomena is ultimately needed.

Encoder/Organizer

The Encoder/Organizer takes information from the first temporary storage compartment of the Work Space, and encodes and organizes it along with other relevant material acquired from Permanent Storage. It then returns the output of this processing, along with the original input material involved, to the second compartment of the Work Space (see Fig. 7.1).

Encoding and organizational processes are conceptually very similar. However, since it will often be convenient to refer to the two processes separately, we will discuss each in turn.

Encoding. The Encoder interprets new or previously acquired items of information by designating them as exemplars of concepts or schemata that already exist in Permanent Storage and are transmitted to it by the Executor. This encoding, which may be either verbal or nonverbal, is based on the similarity of features of the input information to those contained in the previously formed schema to which it is compared. (For a relatively theoretical analysis of feature comparison processes of the sort that may be involved here, see Smith, Shoben, & Rips, 1974.) This encoding may be at either a higher or lower level of generality than the information itself. Thus, a visual experience of a woman's behavior at a party may be encoded in either concrete behavioral terms, or in terms of more general attributes, such as "seductive." Alternatively, the verbal information that a woman is "seductive" may be encoded in terms of a prototypic configural representation of a woman's amorous behavior when interacting with males.

Information may often be encoded in two stages. For example, suppose that information is presented about one or more behaviors of a person. In the first stage, each behavior considered separately may be encoded in terms of a trait, based on a comparison of its features with those in a schema contained in the attribute bin. Once this is done, the set of traits may be further encoded into a configural representation of the person based on a prototypic schema obtained from a person bin. The bin from which this latter schema is drawn may either be specified in the goal schema used to attain processing objectives, or determined on the basis of labels that have been assigned to various features during the first stage of encoding. (Thus, for example, if one of the behaviors initially presented was encoded as "honest," this may lead the configuration of traits to be encoded in terms of a schema drawn from a prototypic "honest person" bin.)

The features of the material to be encoded are unlikely to match exactly those of the schema used as a basis for encoding it. In such cases, features of the original material that are not contained in the schema do not become part of the representation being formed. On the other hand, features of the schema that are not specified in the original material may be included in the representation. To give an example borrowed from Johnson, Bransford, and Solomon (1973), information that "John pounded the nail into the wall" may be encoded in terms of a behavior schema that contains the implement with which the action was performed (a hammer). This feature may therefore be added to the encoded representation of the event that is returned to Permanent Storage. Similarly, the encoding of a person as a "professor" may carry with it features of a professor that are not explicit in the information about the person being described.

In this regard, there is no fundamental distinction between our conceptualization of encoding processes and that of *inference making*. In many instances, an inference may be considered an integral part of encoding, which occurs when features are added to the representation of a person or event on the basis of the schema used to construct it. These inferences often occur automatically in the course of forming the representation, as in the just cited example of encoding the statement that John pounded a nail into the wall. In other cases, they may occur in the course of attaining specific processing objectives that are imposed after an initial encoding has been made. Thus, a person who has been labeled a college professor may subsequently be inferred to be "out of touch with reality" or "underpaid" by an individual responding to a request to describe the person; this is a result of the presence of these features in a prototypic "college professor" schema used to encode the original information. In each case, however, the underlying processes may be similar; that is, both involve the encoding of features of a person or event in terms of a prototypic schema, and the addition of features of this schema to the characterization of the person or event as a consequence of this encoding.

Organization. Information may be organized in several ways and on the basis of many different criteria. Descriptive information about a person or event may be organized either spatially or temporally. For example, information that a person has brown hair and eyes, has a beard, wears glasses, and plays basketball may be organized into a spatial representation of the person's appearance. Similarly, information that a person went to Europe for a year at the age of 18, was valedictorian of Hannibal High School, had two children, received his Ph.D. at Harvard, married his childhood sweetheart, and got divorced while attending Ohio State may be organized into a sequence of events approximating the order in which the events actually occurred in the person's life. Furthermore, this will be true whether these component pieces are new and presented simultaneously, are retrieved from memory, or both.

In addition, information may be organized on the basis of criteria that are not directly tied to the sensory experience but instead are semantic, logical, or affective in character. We have implicitly recognized the possibility that information may be organized semantically (e.g., in a hierarchy of traits and behaviors) in postulating the existence of attribute schemata such as those contained in the attribute bin. Information about an individual person may be organized in a similar, hierarchical fashion, with specific behaviors nested within attributes ("honest," "kind," etc.), which are in turn nested within still more general attributes (e.g., "good" or "bad") or role categories ("professor," "liberal," etc.) to which the person belongs. (For an elaboration of this type of organization and its implications, see Wyer & Carlston, 1979).

Information may also be organized according to certain general rules of inference. For example, syllogistic rule schemata may exist of the form "A; if A, then B; B," or "A is B; B is C; A is C," where A, B, and C are either attributes of a person, events in which the person was involved, or in some cases, propositions about one's social environment. (For a theoretical analysis of the role of syllogistic inference rules in social cognition, see Wyer & Hartwick, in press.)

More generally, Abelson and Reich (1969) have postulated the existence of implicational molecules (e.g., "A wants Y; X causes Y; A does X," or "A wants X; B has X; A is jealous of B") that are applied in order to understand specific people and events and to make inferences about them. Principles of cognitive balance (Heider, 1958) and congruity (Osgood & Tannenbaum, 1955) have also been postulated to govern the organization of affective relations among objects and events. Which organizational principle is invoked will most likely depend on the type of information to be organized and the processing objectives at the time.

To organize a body of information, one must first identify prior concepts or schemata to use as a basis for the organization. For example, to organize the sequence of events in a person's life, one must invoke a more general event schema, or possibly a set of schemata, to which the specific events can be compared. Thus, an organization that indicated that someone attended Ohio State after becoming Hannibal High's valedictorian but before receiving his Ph.D. from Harvard may be based on a "getting an education" schema in which people attend undergraduate school after graduating from high school but before going to graduate school. This organized sequence of specific events becomes itself an event schema associated with the particular protagonist to which the information refers. The processes underlying the identification and application of prototypic schemata that are used in interpreting and organizing information are surprisingly complex to describe in detail and are beyond the scope of the present chapter (for greater specificity, see Norman & Bobrow, 1976; Rumelhart & Ortony, 1977; Schank & Abelson, 1977).

Two additional aspects of organizational processes should be noted at this time. First, there is obviously a distinction between the order in which information is received and the manner in which it is organized. Moreover, the information being organized may originally come from different sources and may be received at different points in time. Thus, new information about a person or event may be combined with previously acquired information to provide a new schema of the element that includes both (Rumelhart & Norman, 1978).

Second, in attempting to organize information in relation to a preexisting schema, the processor may find that the position of certain aspects is ambiguous. For instance, the event schema use to organize events in the foregoing example may not allow one to determine whether the protagonist got married and had children while in high school, after graduating but before leaving for Europe, or while attending Ohio State. It may be equally unclear whether the person went to Europe before or after high school graduation. In some instances, other schemata may be invoked to resolve these ambiguities. If this cannot be done, however, the events may be arbitrarily positioned in one of the places they could conceivably occur without violating the implications of the existing schemata. Alternatively, the events may be omitted altogether from the schema being constructed.

In still other instances, unspecified features of events may need to be added in order to construct a meaningful interpretation of the information available. For example, the event "graduated from Ohio State University" may be inferred to occur in between getting divorced and receiving a doctorate from Harvard. Alternatively, in constructing a clear representation of a person's appearance from partial information about certain of his characteristics, the processor may add additional, unspecified features of the person. Or, to organize information that a particular person, John, wants a high salary and that John publishes numerous journal articles, one may invoke the general implicational molecule schema "A wants Y; X causes Y; A does X" and add the element "publishing numerous journal articles leads to a high salary." (This latter possibility is also implied by the "completion principle" postulated by Abelson and Reich [1969] in their original conceptualization of implicational molecule theory.) In each case, the added features then become part of the organized configuration along with those specified in the original information.

Dump. As noted previously, the schemata drawn from Permanent Storage to encode or organize material are drawn from a bin beginning at the top and working down. When a schema is determined by the Encoder/Organizer to be applicable for encoding the material, the search is typically terminated. However, to avoid interference with this search and encoding activity, schemata that have been drawn from a bin during the course of the search but are not applicable for performing the encoding are not returned to Permanent Storage immediately but are temporarily deposited in a Dump until the time an encoding has been made. Once the encoding has been successfully performed, the material in the Dump is returned immediately to the bin from which it is drawn, in the order in which it was deposited, followed by the schema that was used for the purpose of performing the encoding.

Thus, suppose that A, B, C, and D are the first four schemata stored on top of the attribute bin, and of these, only D is applicable for encoding a piece of input information. In the course of searching for an applicable schema, A, B, and C are each drawn from the attribute bin in turn, determined to be inapplicable, and deposited in the Dump in the order they are considered. Note that because A was first considered and deposited in the Dump, it is at the bottom, followed by B and then C. If D is applicable for encoding the information, this encoding is performed. The contents of the Dump are then returned to the attribute bin, with C (the schema on top of the Dump) deposited first, followed by B, then A, and finally the schema that was used to perform the encoding *(D)*. Thus, as a result of this processing, the position of the schemata in the attribute bin has been altered, with D now on top, followed by A, B, and C.

Integrator

The Integrator acquires material from the second compartment of the Work Space and, as specified by processing objectives, identifies its implications for a particular judgment of the object to which the material pertains, or a decision to which the material is relevant. It then integrates these implications with those of other previously acquired information transmitted to it by the Executor to arrive at a single judgment or decision. Next, it returns the results of this integration to the third compartment of the Work Space.

In this regard, the organization and encoding of information along the lines described in the previous section can be viewed as information integration in the broad sense of the term. However, we will restrict our use of the term to refer to the manner in which different implications of information, of possibly different types and from different sources, are combined for purposes of making a single judgment or arriving at a decision. For example, suppose that a professor is asked to evaluate a candidate for a position in his department. In doing so, he may take into account a variety of factors bearing on the candidate's teaching ability, the quality of his research, the number of publications he has, his ability to get along well with faculty and students, his administrative skills, etc. Moreover, the implications of some of the information bearing on these characteristics, gleaned from letters of reference as well as from other sources, may be inconsistent. In this case, the evaluator may have to weight the implications of the various separate pieces of information and combine them in some way into a composite judgment.

Several attempts have been made to describe algebraically the processes involved in combining the information about persons and events to arrive at judgments (for reviews, see N. H. Anderson, 1974; Wyer, 1974; Wyer & Carlston, 1979). However, the processes themselves and the conditions in which they are invoked have rarely if ever been investigated empirically. In fact, as Abelson (1976) notes, these conditions may not be nearly as general as some algebraic model enthusiasts (e.g., N. H. Anderson, 1974) tend to assume. (For one attempt to circumscribe the conditions in which these combinatorial processes are used, see Wyer & Carlston, 1979.) Nonetheless, it seems likely that when the implications of information bearing on a judgment or decision are inconsistent, a person will attempt to resolve this inconsistency either by discounting certain aspects of the information, or by arriving at some compromise or "average" of the total set of implications.

Still other integration processes may sometimes be invoked that are not necessarily "algebraic" in nature. Several of these are outlined by Hastie and Carlston in Chapter 1 of this volume. For example, persons may invoke deductive or syllogistic inference processes to arrive at judgments based on a set of information (McGuire, 1960; Wyer, 1974, 1975; Wyer & Carlston, 1979), or invoke principles analogous to those implied by set theory (Wyer & Carlston, 1979; Wyer & Podeschi, 1978). A discussion of these processes and their use is beyond the scope of this chapter. However, their ultimate consideration in an overall conceptualization of human information processing is, of course, imperative.

Response Selector

The fifth processing mechanism presented in Fig. 7.1 is most often employed when the output of the information integration must be communicated publically. Its function is to transform the internally coded judgment formed by the Integrator into a language that is understandable to another. This language may be either verbal or nonverbal. Because many of the processes involved in making this translation have been elaborated elsewhere (Upshaw, 1969, 1978; Wyer, 1974), they are not described here. However, they are important to consider in empirical research (cf. Upshaw, 1978).

An Illustrative Example

The processes implied by the formulation we have proposed depend to some extent on processing objectives, and a detailed consideration of each ramification is beyond the scope of this chapter. However, a step-by-step description of the hypothetical processes underlying judgments made in a prototypic situation may suffice to convey the important features of the formulation and some of its implications.

The example under consideration is suggested by materials constructed by Spiro (1977) for use in a study described later in this chapter. Suppose that a person who wishes to form an impression of the relationship between a man and woman hears about a prior conversation between them in which the man tells the woman that he does not want children, and the woman reacts with intense negative emotion, resulting in a bitter argument. However, the person also learns that the two persons eventually married and were still happily together. Later on, in recounting the original information, the person recalls being told that the woman changed her mind about having children, despite the fact that the information contained nothing to indicate that such was the case. How might the formulation we have proposed account for this error?

To explain this phenomenon and to describe the processing that led up to it, we would assume that the stimulus information enters the processing system through the Sensory Store, with the substantive information about the couple's interaction being transmitted by the Preencoder to the first compartment of the Work Space, and the objective ("to form an impression . . . ") being sent to the Goal Specification Box of the Executive Unit. Upon receipt of this information, the Executor first identifies a goal schema in the goal bin of Permanent Storage that corresponds to the objective and places it in the Goal Specification Box for reference in governing subsequent processing. Based on rules specified in the schema, the Executor then identifies schemata contained in the attribute and behavior bins in Permanent Storage that can be potentially used to encode individual features of the information presented and transmits them to the Encoder/Organizer in the order in which they are found. When the Encoder finds a schema that is appropriate for interpreting a given feature of the information in the Work Space, the encoding is made. If the information can be encoded using more than one schema, the first one identified and transmitted to the Encoder is the one used. Thus, for example, if the description of the couple's argument can be encoded either as "fought about having children" or as "disagreed about having children," whichever encoding is identified first will be applied. When each feature of the input material has been encoded, the encodings are sent to the second compartment of the Work Space.

As a result of this processing, the second compartment of the Work Space now contains both details of the original stimulus material and the attribute and behavioral concepts used to encode them. However, to form an overall understanding of the conversation between the couple and the events following it, further encoding or organization is necessary. To accomplish this, the Executor identifies person and/or event bins that contain event schemata appropriate for interpreting and organizing the set of encoded features as a configuration in a manner that will fulfill processing objectives. When the objectives are fairly specific, the schemata retrieved may be tagged with labels that are explicitly used in describing these objectives. However, when the objectives are more general, as in the present example, bins may be identified on the basis of labels that have been assigned to features of the information presented during the first stage of encoding (e.g., "in disagreement over having children," "lovers' quarrels," "happy marriage," etc.). Which of several alternative bins are selected may depend on the most recent encoding of the material. Thus, the bin selected may be one tagged with a label similar to the encoding of the last piece of information presented, or in this case, "happy marriage."

Once a bin containing information of potential relevance to processing objectives has been identified, the schemata and concepts contained in this bin are transmitted by the Executor to the Encoder/Organizer. This unit identifies an appropriate schema for interpreting the information by comparing its features to those found in the second compartment of the Work space. Once a schema is found with features that match those contained in this information to a sufficient degree, it is selected as "applicable," and the contents of the Work Space are then organized and interpreted in terms of it. In the present example, the result of this processing is presumably an event schema representing the sequence of events involving the two persons being described. However, the representation may not include features of the original material that are irrelevant to the schema used to construct it; at the same time, it may contain other features that were not in the original material but are components of the schema. In our example, the schema selected is apt to contain both a representation of the couple arguing over having children and a representation of the couple being happily married. However, to the extent that being happily married implies agreement on issues of importance, such a schema may also contain the features "changed his/her mind about having children" or "willing to compromise on important issues," thus leading to ultimate agreement among the parties involved. (Other schemata not involving this particular feature might, of course, also be invoked.)

The result of the foregoing processing is therefore an encoded representation of the particular parties to which the original stimulus information referred and the events involving them. This representation is sent back to the Work Space to be available for any further processing by the Integrator or Response Selector, should further processing be necessary for attaining the objectives contained in the Goal Specification Box. In addition, the prototypic schema used to construct this representation is returned to the top of the bin from which it was originally drawn, whereas the representation itself is returned to a bin specified in the instructions contained in the Goal

Specification Box. This latter bin may be either previously formed or newly constructed to hold information about the particular couple to which the information refers.

The event schema formed of the couple, which may include representations of events that occur either before, in between, or after those described in the original material, may be sufficient to form an impression of the interaction. If a simpler representation of the information is required (e.g., a single label or judgment characterizing the relationship, such as "successful," "stormy," "unlikely to last," etc.), or if a judgment based on this information is required, an additional level of processing may occur. These possibilities, however, are not directly relevant to our example, and therefore will not be elaborated.

Subsequent Recall of Stimulus Material and Judgments Based on It. If the processing objectives stated in the Goal Specification Box have been attained, and if no subsequent processing of the stimulus material and its encodings is anticipated in the near future, both the original information and the encoded representations of it are cleared from the Work Space. However, if additional processing of the information is likely (e.g., if later questions about the material are expected), the information will be retained in the Work Space for subsequent use. The length of time it is retained presumably depends on: (1) the subsequent demand for space required by processing information in pursuit of other objectives; and (2) the expected length of time before the information will be used again. In any event, when a subsequent judgment is required on the basis of information, or if the goal of recalling the original information is activated, the Work Space will initially be searched to determine whether information relevant to this processing objective is contained in it. If information that is sufficient to attain the objective is found, it is used without retrieving additional information from Permanent Storage. However, if this information is not found in the Work Space, the Executor retrieves information from relevant bins in Permanent Storage and uses it to attain the objectives specified according to procedures just described.

Thus, suppose in our example that the recipient is unexpectedly asked to recall the original information he received. If this request is made only a short period of time after the original material was processed, the material may still exist in the Work Space and therefore may be recalled fairly accurately. However, if a longer period of time has elapsed, the original material may have been removed from the Work Space, and thus only the encoded representation of it in Permanent Storage may be retrieved. As we have noted, this representation is likely to include features that were not contained in the original stimulus material. One such feature might be "changed his/her mind about having children." To the extent this is true, such a feature will be incorrectly "recalled" as having actually existed in the original information, as noted in our example. Moreover, judgments of the parties involved in the interaction will be based on the implications of this representation and not on the original information.

Additional Considerations

As is soon apparent, the present formulation allows much of the current research in social psychology to be reconceptualized in terms of the way in which information is represented in memory. Moreover, it suggests numerous avenues for future research on issues related to these phenomena. In its present state, however, the formulation presented is admittedly preliminary. and many specific details must be articulated before it can be considered a complete model of social information processing. Space does not allow a detailed consideration of these matters, but several important aspects of the proposed formulation that require refinement and elaboration are worth mentioning.

Determinants of Information Retrieval

The proposed formulation postulates that when information about a person or event is required in order to attain a processing objective, the Work Space is first searched in order to determine whether information relevant to this objective has been retained there. If it has not, information is then retrieved from a bin in Permanent Storage in which material relevant to the objective has been deposited, starting from the top of the bin and working down. Thus, the likelihood of retrieving and using a given piece of information depends in part on whether the information is in the Work Space at the time the information is sought or, if it is not, whether it has been sent to Permanent Storage. It also depends on where it is located in the storage unit being searched. The location of information in the Work Space has not been clearly specified and may be assumed to be random, subject to certain considerations raised later in the chapter. Its location in Permanent Storage depends on the bin to which it was assigned at the time it was first received, and its accessibility depends on how much additional information has been deposited on top of it in this bin.

Given these assumptions, the formulation can potentially account for the effects of several different factors on the likelihood of recall and use of information, although in some cases admittedly ad hoc assumptions are required to do so. At the same time, it suggests some qualifications on the conditions in which these effects will occur. The effect of how information is encoded on its subsequent recall is discussed in detail in the next two sections of this chapter. However, it may be useful to consider some of the more general determinants of information retrieval, and the implications of the proposed formulation for why and when they may have an effect.

Recency. The more recently a piece of information has been received and processed, the more likely it is to be recalled and used again. According to the proposed formulation, there are two possible reasons for this. One reason is that not all of the information received is encoded and transmitted to Permanent Storage. As time goes on, the likelihood that the original information is removed from the Work Space becomes greater. Once this occurs, pieces of the original material that were not sent to Permanent Storage will not be recalled at all, whereas pieces that were encoded at a more general level than the original information may be recalled in less detail. (For example, the information that John picked up the cat with his left hand and hurled it ten feet across the living room may be encoded, and therefore recalled, as "John threw the cat across the room").

The decrease in recall of details over time is of course also predicted by a "copy theory" of the memory trace, which assumes that the stimulus information simply becomes more vague and thus harder to recall as time goes on (see e.g., Tulving & Bower, 1974). In the present formulation, however, the decreased detail with which information is recalled is strictly a function of whether: (1) it was encoded at a less detailed level than it was originally presented; and (2) it is no longer retained in the Work Space. Once the information has been sent to Permanent Storage and the Work Space is cleared, there should be no further decrease in the detail with which it is recalled, given that the person is able to access it at all. The only way in which further details would be lost is if the information were first retrieved from Permanent Storage, encoded at a still less detailed level (e.g., "John hurt a cat") and redeposited in Permanent Storage. In fact, empirical evidence that memory for details of information decreases as a function of time per se is somewhat limited (Anderson & Bower, 1972, 1973; Hinrichs, 1970; Murdock, 1974; Postman, 1961; Wells, 1974).

Although the detail with which information is recalled should not decrease further once information is deposited in Permanent Storage, the *likelihood* of actually recalling and using it also depends on how much additional information has been deposited in the bin to which it has been assigned. That is, the more recently a piece of information has been processed, the more likely it is to be near the top of the bin in which it is stored, and thus the more likely it is to be retrieved and used to attain processing objectives. There is an important distinction between this type of recency effect and the effect described in the preceding paragraph. The earlier considerations bear on whether the information presented is transmitted to Permanent Storage and thus whether it is "available" (Tulving & Pearlstone, 1966) to be recalled at a later time. The latter considerations bear on the likelihood that the information, although it exists in memory, will be recalled at all.

In this regard, the proposed formulation implies that the recall of information is not a function of the time interval between its presentation and attempts to retrieve it *per se*. Rather, it is a function of factors that are likely to covary with time (e.g., the likelihood that the Work Space is cleared, or that additional material is deposited on top of it in Permanent Storage). Information could in principle be recalled quite accurately after a long period of time if the processing objectives have not yet been obtained, or if for other reasons the original material has been retained in the Work Space. Morever, once it is transmitted to Permanent Storage, its likelihood of being recalled should decease over time only insofar as additional information on the same topic has been stored on top of it in the bin to which it has been assigned. It is therefore quite conceivable that information in some instances may be recalled very quickly and accurately after a long period of time, whereas other material will be recalled poorly even after a short time delay (see e.g., Baddeley & Hitch, 1977).

Instructional Set.   As implied, the retrievability of information depends on where it is stored. That is, if information that John beat Bob in three straight sets of tennis is stored in a bin pertaining to John, it may not subsequently be recalled when information about Bob is sought. More generally, the likelihood of retrieving information about a person may depend substantially on the similarity between one's set or perspective at the time the information is received and one's set at the time an attempt is made to recall it (Tulving, 1976).

Primacy.   Although the proposed formulation can easily account for recency effects, the tendency for the initial pieces of information received about an object to be remembered better than subsequent ones is not directly implied by it. In fact, the conditions in which primacy effects actually occur in retrieving social stimulus material are unclear. (Primacy effects on recall have typically been detected in research requiring subjects to learn lists of unrelated material such as nonsense syllables for short periods of time; see e.g., Crowder, 1976; Kintsch, 1977). Data reported by Miller and Campbell (1959) suggest that primacy effects on the *use* of information to make judgments occur only when there is a short delay between the initial and later pieces of information presented; when the interval is long, recency effects are the typical result. Baddeley and Hitch (1977) have also found strong recency effects in long-term memory for meaningful material obtained in naturalistic settings. Under these conditions, there was also a virtual absence of any primacy effect. In terms of the proposed formulation, this suggests that primacy effects are a result of the simultaneous processing of information that exists in the Work Space. When pieces of information are processed and deposited as separate units in Permanent Storage, as is likely when a long delay occurs between the presentation of the first pieces of information and presentation of the later ones, recency effects of the sort previously described are expected to occur.

Primacy effects are predicted by the present formulation only under conditions in which the initial information is more likely than later information to remain part of the overall representation of the object or event to which it is relevant. It is under these conditions that the initial information is more likely to be transmitted to Permanent Storage as part of the encoded representation. For example, people may often consider the first information presented about a person to be more indicative of the person's personality and, therefore, may give it a more central role in the schematic representation formed of this person. Alternatively, if the temporal order in which information is presented is meaningful, as in a story or an observation of ongoing behavior, the initial events may be recalled and used as bases for interpreting subsequent ones, thus being retained as part of the overall representation of the information presented. This possibility raises further questions concerning when and under what conditions primacy effects on recall and judgments will occur. (For a fuller discussion of several of these questions, see Jones & Goethals, 1971.)

In considering these matters, a distinction should be made between primacy effects on the *recall* of information and primacy effects on its *interpretation.* In instances where the information presented may be encoded in different ways, the proposed formulation makes reasonably clear predictions that the initial information presented will affect the manner in which the later information is interpreted. This prediction is based on the assumption that the schemata used to encode early pieces of information in a sequence are returned to the top of the bin from which they are drawn and, therefore, are more likely to be retrieved later on to encode other information to which they are applicable. Thus, suppose a person is described as helping an elderly woman carry out her garbage, giving someone an answer to an examination question, and taking a candy bar from the grocery store without paying for it. The first behavior is apt to be encoded as "kind" and the third as "dishonest," based on schemata in the attribute bin. However, the second behavior may be encoded as either "kind" or "dishonest." Thus, if the behaviors are presented in the order given, encoding the first behavior may lead the "kind" attribute schema to be at the top of the attribute bin at the time the second is encoded, leading the latter also to be interpreted as kind. However, if the behaviors were presented in the reverse order, the "dishonest" trait schema would presumably be at the top of the attribute bin at the time the second behavior is encoded, thus leading the second behavior to be interpreted in this way instead. As a result, the target person may ultimately be judged more favorably in the first case than in the second, suggesting a primacy effect. However, this effect may be independent of the recall of the information originally presented. (For empirical evidence suggesting this possibility, see Anderson & Hubert, 1963.)

Frequency of Exposure. It seems likely that the more often someone is exposed to information about a person's attributes or behavior, the more likely it is that these attributes or behavior will be recalled and used later on. However, this possibility is not directly implied by the proposed formulation, and some ad hoc assumptions are necessary to account for it. When information is presented close together in time and is recalled and used a short time after it is presented, the likelihood of retrieving a given piece of information can be predicted to increase with its frequency of presentation if one assumes a nonexhaustive random search of the Work Space in which this information is temporarily stored. That is, suppose each repetition of a given piece of information occupies a different location in the Work Space. Then, if only a finite sample of the information contained in the Work Space is retrieved, the probability that a given item is contained in this sample increases with the number of times it was repeated but decreases with the number of other pieces of information in the Work Space about the same stimulus object.

The effect of frequency of exposure to information on the likelihood of retrieving it from Permanent Storage is more difficult to account for. When the information is presented within a short time interval, pieces that are repeated frequently may be encoded or organized differently than those that are presented only once. For example, a number of repetitions of the statement "Joe is honest" may be interpreted as an indication that honesty is the most representative characteristic of Joe, and therefore this attribute may occupy a more central role in the representation of Joe. Similarly, an attribute that is mentioned only once is likely to be represented more peripherally. To this extent, a frequently mentioned attribute of Joe is more likely to be transmitted to Permanent Storage as part of the representation, and thus is more likely to be recalled in the future.

Different considerations arise when each repetition of the information about a person comes at a different point in time. Here it is theoretically very important to determine whether the new information is integrated with the previously stored representation of the person. If it is, frequency effects would be expected for reasons similar to those noted earlier. For example, if Harry reports that Joe is "honest" and "intelligent" on Monday and Bruce reports that Joe is "honest" and "kind" on Tuesday, "honesty" is likely to be the most salient characteristic of any integrated impression that is formed of Joe. Thus, the most frequently repeated piece of information about Joe is most likely to be recalled.

However, when each repeated piece of information is not integrated with the previously stored representation of a person but rather is stored as a separate unit, frequency effects are not predicted to occur. To see this, suppose that one recipient over a period of time has received 10 pieces of information about a person, the 1st, 3rd, 7th, and 10th pieces all testifying to the fact that the person is honest, and the recipient stores each piece separately in a bin pertaining to the target person. However, suppose that a second recipient has also received and stored 10 pieces of information, only the last of which asserts that the person is honest. Because "honest" should be on top of the bin in Permanent Storage pertaining to this person in both cases, it should be retrieved with equal likelihood, independently of the number of times it has occurred in the past. To predict the probability of recalling the more frequently stored information, it would be necessary to postulate a probabilistic retrieval process whereby bins are searched from the top down, but there is some probability of "missing" a unit of information contained in it. To this extent, the probability of retrieving a given piece of information would be greater when it occurs more frequently in the bin. Although this ad hoc assumption can account for the effect of frequency in the absence of any integration, it has implications for other phenomena predicted by the model, the nature of which remain to be explored.

Some Theoretical Ambiguities

The proposed formulation is admittedly preliminary in its present state. Space does not permit a detailed consideration of its currently ambiguous features, but certain general problem areas are worth describing.

Storage and Retrieval. Considerable work must be directed toward refining the "storage bin" conceptualization of memory proposed. First, a more rigorous statement must be provided concerning the precise manner in which bins are tagged. Although we have implicitly assumed that each bin is identified with a single name, it seems likely that the "tag" is itself a complex concept that may be referenced by several functionally equivalent labels. The nature of these equivalences and how they are recognized must ultimately be specified.

Encoding and Organization. We have postulated that information is encoded and organized with reference to previously formed concepts or schemata. However, we have been very vague as to the criteria for determining that a concept or schema is in fact appropriate for this purpose. The use of a concept or schema to encode or organize a cluster of information will be determined by the relationship between features of the information and features of the particular schema or concept. However, the number and type of common features required to accept a concept or schema as applicable is unclear, both theoretically and empirically. Work by Smith, Shoben, and Rips (1974), Rosch (1973, 1975), and Tversky (1977; Tversky & Gati, 1978) may help to resolve this matter.

In general, the structure of complex representations contained in any given bin must ultimately be made more precise. We have assumed the existence of person and event "schemata" without stating with any precision the structural characteristics of these schemata. Some preliminary work by the authors suggest that physical attributes of persons, although presented verbally, are recalled more accurately than trait descriptions of these persons. This suggests that person schemata may be organized around representations of a person's physical appearance, with more abstract traits peripheral to these physical representations. Also, as Hamilton, Katz, and Leirer (Chapter 4, this volume) find, behavioral information about a person may be organized into schemata around various traits to which these behaviors are directly relevant. These structural characteristics may affect which aspects of a schema are most apt to be used as a basis for encoding new information to which it is applicable. Similar considerations arise in conceptualizing the structure of event schemata. The script-processing formulations developed by Schank and Abelson (1977) and by Rumelhart and Ortony (1977) provide a major step in the direction of understanding these latter representations.

Processing Objectives. The examples we have provided of how the proposed system operates, and most of those considered in the research described in the next section, concern conditions in which the information-processing objectives are externally imposed and are reasonably well specified (e.g., to recall the information presented, to form an impression of a person, to judge the person's suitability for a particular job, etc.). However, much ongoing cognitive activity is stimulated by internally generated objectives that may in turn become salient as a result of other prior activity. The manner in which these objectives are identified and come to affect the processing of information has not been precisely stated.

A related matter concerns the description of cognitive activity in the absence of specific objectives. According to the bin formulation proposed, a concept or schema contained in one bin may include features that tag other bins, the contents of which contain features that tag other bins, and so on. Moreover, because the order in which material in those bins is stored at any given time is a function of how recently this material has been used in the past, a mechanism is provided for describing the progression of ideas in a fairly continuous flow across different, sometimes remotely connected topics. However, we have not dealt with when and under what conditions this sort of "stream of consciousness" occurs, and we have not specifically indicated how it can be accounted for in terms of the overall processing system outlined in Fig. 7.1.

Despite these and other ambiguities in the model at this state in its development, it is of considerable use in conceptualizing many of the phenomena of concern in this volume and in raising additional empirical issues related to these phenomena. In the next few sections, we consider some of these matters in detail and attempt to demonstrate the utility of the proposed model for considering the dynamics of the underlying psychological processes.

THE COGNITIVE REPRESENTATION
OF SOCIAL STIMULI

To recapitulate, information that enters the processing system and is sent to the Work Space is first encoded in terms of general concepts contained in attribute and behavior bins. Then, the material may be further organized and encoded by comparing its encoded features to characteristics of previously formed person or event schemata that are drawn from the Permanent Storage Unit. The particular schemata selected for this purpose depend on not only their applicability but also on the processing objectives. In any event, once a prototypic schema is used to encode or organize the input material, the result is itself a schema about the specific persons or events to which the input information refers. However, this representation may differ from the original information in any of four ways:

1. Ambiguous features of the original material may be encoded in a manner that is consistent with the implications of the schema used to interpret it.
2. Features of the original material that are not relevant to or interpretable in terms of this schema may be omitted.
3. Certain features that are not explicit in the original information but are components of the schema used to interpret it may be added.
4. The original material may be reorganized in a way that is consistent with the schema but differs from its original organization.

The schematic representation of the persons or events constructed on the basis of information and the prototypic schema used to interpret it is then placed in Permanent Storage on top of bins pertaining to the objects to which they refer. Consequently, these representations rather than the original information are most likely to be recalled in the future for use in making judgments of these objects or in answering questions about them. Note that once the representation is stored in memory, there may be no distinction between the features of the original information and features that were added or reencoded in the course of constructing this representation. Thus, after the original information is removed from the Work Space, subjects who are asked to recall the information may often be unable to distinguish between the original characteristics of the stimulus information and features that were added or relabeled in the course of processing it.

These possibilities, which were first recognized by Bartlett (1932), have been explored both in the area of social cognition (e.g., Cohen, 1976; Higgins & Rholes, 1978; Snyder & Uranowitz, 1978; Spiro, 1977) and in cognitive psychology more generally (e.g., Barclay, Bransford, Franks, McCarrell, & Nitsch, 1974; Bransford & Franks, 1971, 1973; Franks & Bransford, 1974; Loftus, Miller & Burns, 1978; Loftus & Palmer, 1974; Moyer, 1973, Peterson & McIntyre, 1973). A distinction has sometimes been made in this research between constructive processes and reconstructive processes. Specifically, construction is typically used to refer to the encoding and organization of new information at the time this information is received, whereas reconstruction is used to refer either to the reorganization and reencoding of previously acquired information, or to the integration of new and old information (Loftus & Loftus, 1976). From the perspective outlined in this chapter, however, the cognitive processes involved are similar, regardless of whether the information being processed is new, retrieved from memory, or both. To this extent, certain distinctions made between the two phenomena may be more academic than practical (cf. Royer, 1977).

Much of the research reported both in this volume and elsewhere bears on the various aspects of the phenomena described previously. We first consider certain issues associated with the encoding of visual sequences of behavior, relying primarily on the work of Ebbesen (Chapter 6, this volume) and Newtson (1976). Then we turn to research on the manner in which the encoding of verbal material affects its subsequent recall and reproduction.

The Representation of Ongoing Behavior—
The Construction and Use of Event Schemata

The extent to which a cognitive representation differs from the input information on which it is based may depend on how closely this information approximates the content and organization of previously formed schemata that are used to interpret it. For example, if the information is presented visually and is already organized temporally, as in a sequence of ongoing behavior manifested in familiar situations, it may require little reorganization in order to be interpreted in terms of an existing event schema and stored as such in bins pertaining to the persons or events involved. Moreover, when the activity is routine (e.g., compiling a questionnaire) and therefore the sequence of actions involved is easily predictable in terms of a previously formed prototypic event schema, the details of those actions need not be stored in order to reconstruct the behavioral sequence in sufficient detail to understand it and, if necessary, to reconstruct the activity in a manner that closely approximates the original. Rather, only certain key segments of the behavioral sequence, which one might think of as "frames," may be encoded and stored. Thus, the sequence of actions involved in leaving one's desk to get a handkerchief from one's coat pocket may consist of pushing one's chair back, standing up, walking over to the coat rack, etc. Moreover, each of these component behaviors involves still more molecular acts. However, prototypic event schemata may exist for both these component actions and for the behavioral sequence as a whole. When a person observes the sequence of ongoing behavior described previously and the sequence is consistent with an existing event schema, its details may be encoded and stored only to the extent that they are not predictable on the basis of this schema, and thus would be needed in order to reproduce the observed behavior accurately.

Empirical Evidence

The foregoing considerations underlie the work of Newtson and his colleagues on the unitizing of ongoing behavior (for a review, see Newtson, 1976). Newtson argues that the information sufficient to reconstruct a sequence of routine behavior typically occurs at points of transition between successive actions that the observer interprets as meaningful. Consequently, observers typically encode and store the information contained at these successive "breakpoints" without attending carefully to the material in between them. Results reported by Newtson and Engquist (1976) support this contention. Specifically, subjects first viewed a taped sequence of ongoing behavior and then were asked to determine whether single frames came from this or a different taped sequence of similar behavior. Identifications were significantly more accurate for frames that were taken from breakpoint intervals than for those that occurred at nonbreakpoints.

The number and type of frames stored in any given instance may depend on which ones the recipient believes will permit him to reconstruct the observed behavior at a level of detail sufficient to attain his processing objectives. Direct evidence of this is reported by Newtson, Rinder, Miller, and LaCross (1978). Subjects viewed a tape of a target person collating questionnaires with instructions to break the taped sequence into units they considered meaningful. In one condition, subjects were able to see a cue at the end of each collation that distinguished it from the preceding one, whereas in a second condition, this distinguishing feature was absent. Subjects analyzed the tape sequence into finer units in the second condition than in the first. Presumably, the presence of the distinguishing cue permitted subjects to encode the sequence into broader units and still differentiate the collations from one another, whereas without this cue, more detailed units were necessary.

However, even when few frames are stored, the recipient may often be able to reconstruct a behavioral sequence with sufficient accuracy to recall most relevant aspects. In our previous example, one person may encode the sequence of actions involved in getting the handkerchief by selecting frames associated with fairly specific actions (e.g., pushing the chair back, getting up from the desk, walking over to the coat rack, reaching into the coat pocket, pulling out a handkerchief, walking back, sitting down, and redepositing the chair.) Another may select far fewer frames to encode the sequence (e.g., three frames depicting the actor sitting at his desk, standing by the coat rack in the process of extracting a handkerchief from his coat pocket, and sitting back at the desk). Yet, because the sequence of events is likely to be consistent with a prototypic event schema, both persons may be able to reconstruct the sequence with about equal accuracy.

In fact, a decrement often does occur in the recall of information that is broken into larger units. Ebbesen (Chapter 6, this volume) reports that subjects who viewed someone's ongoing behavior broke the behavioral sequence into finer units when they were instructed to remember details of the sequence than when they were told to form an impression of the person involved. Moreover, subjects asked to remember details were subsequently 70% accurate in their recall of the observed sequence, whereas subjects asked to form impressions were only 58% accurate. However, this difference is not necessarily inconsistent with the present formulation. The difference may depend largely on whether the particular details observers are asked to recall are relevant to their processing objectives and also on whether these details are likely to be inferred correctly as a result of reconstructing the sequence from a small number of frames.

We have argued that information that is processed with different objectives will often be interpreted differently and that these different interpretations will affect the subsequent recall and use of the information in making judgments. Differences in interpreting ongoing behavior should be evidenced by differences in the positioning of the breakpoints in the sequence of behavior observed. Two recent studies, by Cohen and Ebbesen (1979; see also Ebbesen, Chapter 6, this volume) and by Massad, Hubbard, and Newtson (1979), both provide evidence of such interpretative differences. For example, Cohen and Ebbesen found that only 25% of the breakpoints identified under impression-set instructions roughly coincided with breakpoints identified under memory-set instructions. In a more extensive investigation of this possibility, Massad et al. first had observers view a videotape describing an interaction between one large and two small geometric figures representing people. They were told in one case to assume that the large figure was a rapist who was attacking the two smaller figures, and in the other case to assume that the large figure was a "guardian of treasure" and that the two small figures were burglars. The breakpoints identified by subjects given the first set of instructions differed substantially from those identified by subjects given the second set.

As Ebbesen (Chapter 6, this volume) points out, it is not entirely clear whether the breakpoints identified using Newtson's procedure are the result of a primary perceptual process or the result of a secondary process that occurs subsequent to information input and accompanies but does not itself affect the storage of information in memory. Despite the fact that both memory for details and the number of breakpoints identified are affected by manipulations designed to alter the size of the units into which behavior is analyzed, the correlation between these variables is low (Ebbesen, this volume). This suggests that unitizing does not itself affect recall. Rather, both unitizing and recall may be independently influenced by some third factor. Ebbesen also suggests that the breakpoints identified using Newtson's procedure may often signify events that observers believe to be important from the standpoint of their processing objectives and do not necessarily indicate the beginning and end of "informational units" per se. However, these concerns do not call into question the basic conceptualization we have proposed. Rather, they pertain only to the experimental procedures developed by Newtson to investigate them.

The Construction of Person Schemata
from Behavioral Information

Both the studies of Cohen and Ebbesen (1979) and Massad et al. (1979) provide evidence that processing objectives affect the manner in which sequences of ongoing behavior are encoded and organized. These objectives may affect not only the particular interpretation placed on the behavioral information but also the nature of the encoding and organizational processes that underlie this interpretation. These effects can be seen with reference to the information-processing formulation considered in this chapter. For example, consider the effect of instructions to form an impression of the actor. In the first case, it seems likely that the series of behaviors will be encoded and stored as an event schema, consisting of a series of breakpoint frames similar to those postulated by Newtson (1976) without being further encoded or interpreted in terms of more abstract concepts or attributes of the persons described. However, suppose that the objective is to form an impression of the actor. In this case, the Encoder-Organizer will draw on information in Permanent Storage to organize relevant aspects of the behavioral sequence into a schematic representation of the actor. In the process, attributes of the actor that are contained in the prototypic schema but are not directly implied by the behavioral information may be added. The constructed schema of the actor that results is presumably then stored in a bin associated with that person, *in addition to but on top of* the previously formed event schema involving this person. Thus, whereas subjects' later judgments of the target person under memory-set conditions are based on a review of the sequence of behavioral information in the event schema (i.e., the series of frames comprising this schema), judgments under "impression-formation" conditions are likely to be based primarily on the more abstract and static schema of traits that is stored on top of the event schema.

Several results reported by Ebbesen (Chapter 6, this volume) are consistent with this general prediction. For example, subjects in one study were asked to infer traits of a target person immediately after observing a sequence of his ongoing behavior under either memory-set or impression-set conditions. The trait inferences of subjects in the memory-set condition were generally unrelated either to one another or to any obvious prototypic conception of the person. Moreover, the time required to make these inferences increased with tape length, suggesting that subjects in this condition actively scanned a stored representation of the behavioral sequence in order to extract information relevant to their judgment. In contrast, the inferences of subjects whose objective was to form an impression of the target person were highly interrelated and, moreover, were predictable from their implicit personality theories of how traits in general are associated. This suggests that impression-set subjects formed a schema of the actor based on a few critical aspects of the behavioral information presented in the tape and used the traits contained in the resulting schema as a basis for their judgments.

In this regard, it is noteworthy that once subjects under the memory-set condition had made trait inferences, their subsequent judgments 1 week later were correlated with their implicit personality theories, much as were judgments by impression-set subjects tested immediately after the original information was presented. Apparently once judges make trait inferences of an actor, they are stimulated to construct a person schema similar to that provoked by initial instructions to "form an impression" of the actor. Further, it is this construction, rather than the original behavioral information, that serves as a basis for their subsequent judgments.

Differential Effects of Prototypic Schemata on Representations of Ongoing Behavior

In the preceding studies, the actor was typically not identified as a member of any particular group. When a person is known on a priori grounds to belong to a group or occupy a particular social role, prototypic schemata specific to this group or role may be used as a basis for organizing and encoding the person's behavior and the events surrounding it. This may also affect the subsequent recall of the information.

This latter possibility is suggested in a study by Cohen (1976). In this study, subjects viewed a videotaped sequence of a woman returning home from work and participating in an informal birthday dinner party prepared by her husband. Before viewing the tape, some subjects were told that the person was a librarian in town, whereas others were told that the person was a waitress in a local restaurant. The tape itself contained some features that, based on normative data, were consistent with the stereotype of a librarian (e.g., has brown hair, eats roast beef, drinks wine, etc.) and others that were consistent with the stereotype of a waitress (e.g., has blond hair, eats hamburgers, drinks beer, etc.). Subjects, either a short time after viewing the tape or several days later, were given a forced-choice recognition task in which they were asked on each item to indicate which of two features (one consistent and one inconsistent with the stereotype) was actually contained in the tape.

The conceptualization proposed here suggests that the initial description of the protagonist's occupation will lead an occupational stereotype, or schema, to be selected for use in organizing and encoding the information on the tape. As a result, information consistent with the stereotypic schema will be encoded as part of a specific schema pertaining to the target person, whereas material inconsistent with or irrelevant to the stereotype will not. The representation of the target person should therefore contain more stereotype-consistent features than stereotype-inconsistent ones. Consequently, the former features should be more accurately recalled than the latter. Moreover, this differential accuracy should be greater after a period of time has elapsed and the original material is no longer contained within the Work Space. Cohen's (1976) results are consistent with both hypotheses.

An ambiguity in interpreting Cohen's data results from the manner in which the recognition data were collected. Specifically, in each case, subjects were required to distinguish between a stereotype-consistent feature and a stereotype-inconsistent feature. It is possible that subjects simply forgot *both* types of features in the original material to an equal degree. However, when they were unable to recall this information, they may simply have guessed the feature that was consistent with the stereotype. Because recall of the original information is apt to decrease over time, thus increasing the frequency of guessing, this analysis could also account for the increase in stereotype-consistent responses over time. Evidence that subjects do in fact tend to rely more on normative behaviors of a prototypic person in making inferences after a period of time has elapsed is reported by Ebbesen (Chapter 6, this volume). This raises the possibility that previously formed schemata may affect both the selective encoding and organization of information at the time it is received and inferences about the objects involved under conditions of uncertainty in which little of the original information is available. These two possible effects of schemata should be isolated, and the conditions that affect their relative contributions should be investigated.

Another implication of our conceptualization is that once information is encoded and stored, the encoding rather than the original information will serve as a basis for subsequent judgments. Thus, if information has been encoded and organized in terms of one schema and this representation is then deposited in Permanent Storage, aspects of the information that are relevant to other schemata may no longer be available once the Work Space is cleared, and thus the effects of the encoding may persist despite new evidence that the encoding was inappropriate.

Intriguing evidence of this possibility was obtained in the previously mentioned study by Massad et al. (1979). Recall that some subjects initially viewed a videotaped sequence of actions involving three geometrical figures under instructions to assume that it was about a person guarding a treasure from two thieves, whereas others viewed it under instructions to assume it was about two people being attacked by a rapist. Presumably in the course of viewing the tape, observers encoded and organized the information with reference to a prototypic schema associated with one or the other of these general types of events. After viewing the tape and making judgments of the protagonists, some subjects were told that there had been a mistake and that the questionnaire they had just completed pertained to a different tape than the one they had viewed. They were then told that the tape they had been shown actually was meant to be interpreted in terms of the other perspective from the one they had first been given. (That is, subjects who were first led to believe that the tape was about guarding a treasure were told it was actually about a rapist, etc.) They were then asked to make new ratings of the figures, either after viewing the tape a second time or without doing so. Subjects who were allowed to see the tape a second time encoded it differently from the way they did at first (as inferred from a comparison of breakpoints identified using Newtson's procedure), and their evaluations of the figures changed accordingly. In contrast, subjects who were *not* given an opportunity to view the tape a second time did *not* alter their evaluations of the figures despite the change in perspective. This finding is consistent with the asumption that once visual information is encoded, only the encoding of it is retained in storage. Thus, subjects who had encoded and stored the visual information from the first perspective were unable to reconstruct it from a different perspective without actually seeing the tape again; thus their final judgments, which were based upon the original encoding, were unaffected by the perspective shift. Similar conclusions may be drawn from research on the processing of verbal information, as we see later in this chapter.

Effects of Schemata on Amount of Verbal Information Recalled

In most respects, the processes underlying the representation of verbal information about a person or event are similar to those involved in representing visual information. Thus, the separation of our discussion of this material from that in the preceding section is somewhat artifical. However, whereas visual information about a person often has a built-in temporal organization that may affect its reconstruction and recall, verbal information is often much less organized. For example, it may pertain to events occurring at different times, and it is not necessarily presented in the true temporal sequence. As a result, the reorganizational processes affecting the recall of verbal information may play a greater role.

The effect of organizing person information on the amount of this information recalled was shown rather strikingly in research reported by Hamilton, Katz, and Leirer (Chapter 4, this volume). Briefly, subjects first read a set of 15 behavioral descriptions under instructions to either learn and remember as many of them as possible or to form an impression of a person who was described by them. It seems reasonable to suppose that memory-set instructions would lead subjects to learn the list of behaviors in roughly the form in which they were received, without attempting to encode or organize them in terms of any semantic or schematic criteria. In contrast, impression formation instructions are likely to lead the information to be organized into an integrated person schema. This organization is presumably made with reference to a prototypic schema of a person who might or might not be likely to manifest the behaviors presented. The resultant representation may then be stored as a single integrated unit.

After receiving the behavioral information, both groups of subjects were asked to recall it. In fact, subjects recalled the behaviors better under impression-set conditions than under conditions in which they had been explicitly told to remember as many of the behaviors as possible. This suggests that the organization of unrelated behaviors into an integrated person schema facilitates their recall in relation to conditions in which such an organization is not demanded. In this regard, it is worth noting that when behavioral information is already organized, as in Ebbesen's (Chapter 6, this volume) research on the processing of ongoing behavior, information is recalled better under a memory set than under an impression formation set. Thus, under conditions in which the information is already sufficiently organized so that a new organization is not required in order to interpret it, objectives that require such an organization may produce little additional effect on the amount of material recalled.

Some evidence that subjects do in fact organize information differently when they are asked to form an impression of a person than when they are asked to remember the information was obtained in a second study by Hamilton et al. (Chapter 4, this volume). This study was similar to the one described previously except that each behavior presented was selected to be representative of one of four different content categories. In this study, like the earlier one, subjects recalled more behaviors under impression-set instructions than under memory-set instructions. Moreover, additional analyses using various clustering techniques (e.g., Bousfield & Bousfield, 1966) indicated that the behaviors recalled under impression-set instructions tended to be clustered in part on the basis of the content categories to which they pertained, whereas those recalled under memory-set instructions were less so. This suggests that in the person schemata formed under the impression set, behaviors were organized according to various general traits of the person involved, and that this organization facilitated the subsequent recall of these behaviors.

One should not conclude from this that the information was not organized at all under memory-set conditions. Rather, it may simply have been organized according to different criteria than those relevant to the formation of impressions of people. Using an index of "subjective organization" that does not require an a priori specification of content categories but rather identifies consistencies in the order of recall of stimulus items over trials, Hamilton et al. (this volume) found that the overall level of organization was not appreciably different under the two instructional sets. However, organization in terms of the four a priori person-relevant categories continued to be greater in the impression-set condition. This supports our assumption that the *type* of organization is affected by processing objectives, although the *degree* of organization may not be.

Effects of Schemata on the Type of Information Recalled

The Recall of Schema-Consistent Information

It seems reasonable to suppose that the organization of information about a person or event with reference to a previously formed schema will affect not only the amount of information recalled but also which particular aspects of this information are remembered. Specifically, features of a person that can be interpreted or organized in terms of a prototypic schema may be more likely to be included in a representation of the person and, therefore, may be recalled better than features that are not contained in this schema. This should be particularly true after a period of time, when the original information has been cleared from the Work Space.

Some evidence supporting this line of reasoning is reported by Snyder and Cantor (1979). In this study, subjects read a description of an ostensibly real person who was applying for a position as either a real estate salesman (i.e., a job requiring extraverted qualities) or a librarian (i.e., a job requiring introverted qualities) and were asked to judge the candidate's suitability for the job in question. The information presented contained descriptions of both introverted and extraverted behaviors. According to the formulation proposed, an evaluation of the candidate's suitability for the job will be based in part on the similarity of the candidate's attributes with those contained in a previously formed schema of a prototypic person who is successful in that vocation (e.g., a prototypic real estate salesman). Because this schema presumably contains only features that characterize the prototypic job considered, the comparison process is likely to involve a biased sample of the candidate's characteristics. Therefore, if these characteristics are then used to form a representation of the individual candidate, they are more likely to be subsequently recalled than those that are included in this representation. Consistent with this hypothesis, Snyder and Cantor found that subjects recalled features of the information that were consistent with the requirements of the job they were asked to consider better than features that were inconsistent with these job requirements. Moreover, they judged the candidate to be more suitable for this job than for jobs requiring other characteristics, despite the fact that characteristics consistent with these latter jobs were also described in the original information about the candidate.

Research with similar implications is reported by both Carlston and Ostrom, Lingle, Pryor, and Geva (Chapters 3 and 2, respectively, in this volume). In Carlston's study, subjects received a set of behaviors and traits, some of which had implications for kindness and others of which had implications for honesty, and they were asked to judge the target with respect to one of these traits. Then, they were asked to recall the original information. Subjects recalled significantly more behaviors that were relevant to the judgment they had made than behaviors that were irrelevant to this judgment. In the study by Ostrom et al., subjects were first presented a series of traits describing a person, half of which were relevant to a given occupation and half of which were not. After receiving the information, they were asked to judge the person's suitability for an occupation, and then to recall as many of the original traits presented as possible. As expected on the basis of the preceding analysis, subjects consistently recalled more occupation-relevant traits than occupation-irrelevant ones.

Further clarification of the reasons for this bias was obtained in a second study reported by Ostrom et al., in which either all trait information was relevant to the interpolated occupational judgment or all information was irrelevant to this judgment. After judging the candidate's suitability for the job, subjects were dismissed but returned 1 day or 1 week later and completed a recognition task concerning the items they had seen in the earlier session. Subjects made fewer recognition errors when the traits had been relevant to the interpolated judgment than when they had not. This finding suggests that the memory bias was not simply due to selective attention to the relevant pieces of information at the time they were first presented. Rather, subjects who were exposed to judgment-relevant information may have been able to organize the information in relation to a schema of the occupation to which the judgment pertained, and thus they were able to remember it better later on. In contrast, when the information was irrelevant to the occupational schema with which it was compared, an organization of it was not possible, and thus it was less well recalled.

The Recall of Schema-Inconsistent Information

In the studies just described, the processing objectives did not require the recipient to form an integrated representation of the person based on all of the information described. Rather, they were allowed to select those aspects of the information that were relevant to the job being sought or the judgment to be made. In other instances, processing objectives may require a consideration of all of the information presented and an attempt to integrate it into an overall impression of the person to whom it pertains. Here again, it seems likely that features of the information that can be incorporated into a schematic representation of the person are more likely to be recalled later on than features that are irrelevant to an impression of the person, or for other reasons are not included in the representation formed. This is particularly true after a long period of time, when the original information is no longer available in the Work Space.

However, some additional considerations arise with respect to the processing of information that is inconsistent with the representation of the person being formed. In some cases, there is reason to believe that such information will actually be remembered *better* than information that is schema-consistent. Craik and Lockhart (1972) note that information is recalled better if it is processed "deeply" than if it is processed less extensively (see also a recent elaboration of this position by Craik, 1977, and a critique of the conceptualization by Baddeley, 1978). It seems reasonable to suppose that information about a person will be processed more extensively if it is difficult to incorporate into a schematic representation of the person than if it is easy to fit into such a schema. It may therefore actually be recalled better than schema-consistent information. Perhaps the only information that is unlikely to receive sufficient processing to be recalled well is information that is totally irrelevant to the schema being constructed of the person and thus is completely ignored.

The series of studies by Hastie and his colleagues (e.g., Hastie & Kumar, 1979; see also Hastie, Chapter 5, this volume) supports this line of reasoning. In an early and representative experiment (Hastie & Kumar, Experiment 1), subjects were told to "form an impression and recall information about" several persons, each described by a set of related traits and behaviors. All traits pertained to a single general characteristic. (For example, in one case the characteristic was intelligence, and the traits were "intelligent," "clever," "smart," "bright," etc.). The behaviors in each set were either congruent with (e.g., "won the chess tournament"), irrelevant to (e.g., "had a cheeseburger for lunch"), or incongruent with (e.g., "was confused by the television show") the trait ensemble. Subjects received the information about a particular person in sequence, with the traits preceding all behaviors, and then were asked to recall the behavior descriptions as accurately as possible.

Presumably the instructions to form an impression of the person led subjects to attempt to organize the behavioral information into an integrated impression, based on the prototypic schema of a person with characteristics implied by the original trait ensemble. This is, of course, easy to do in the case of trait-congruent behaviors but more difficult in the case of incongruent ones. Note that the neutral behaviors used were not only irrelevant to the traits but were also largely irrelevant to the objective of forming an impression of the person described. Consequently, these behaviors are likely to have been ignored in forming an integrated representation of the person. In fact, Hastie and Kumar found that incongruent behaviors were recalled better than congruent ones and that both congruent and incongruent behaviors were recalled better than irrelevant ones. The latter finding is quite consistent with our supposition that if material is irrelevant to processing objectives (in this case, to form an impression of the person described), it is not considered for inclusion in the representation of the stimulus information and is therefore not processed sufficiently to be recalled. However, if information about a person is relevant but inconsistent with the schema being constructed, thus making it difficult to attain processing objectives, it may elicit more attention and therefore may be recalled better than information that is readily assimilated.

Two additional aspects of Hastie's data bear on these notions. First, subjects in a later study (Hastie, Chapter 5, this volume) were asked to write a phrase after each behavior in order to complete a sentence concerning it. "Explanations" were used much more often to complete sentences concerning incongruent behaviors than to complete sentences concerning congruent or irrelevant behaviors. Moreover, the tendency to add "explanations" to sentences was correlated positively with the accuracy of recalling them. This suggests that subjects did in fact attempt to reconcile these behaviors with the representation they were forming and that these attempts led to better recall of the behaviors involved. Second, the proportion of incongruent behaviors recalled decreased as the number of such behaviors presented increased. This could indicate that as the number of incongruent behaviors becomes greater, they become less novel, decreasing the average length of time spent trying to interpret any given one of them and consequently leading them to be recalled less well.

The inferior recall of schema-irrelevant behaviors deserves further comment. As we have noted, behaviors that are irrelevant to the objective of forming an impression of the person being described should induce little cognitive activity and therefore should be recalled poorly, as Hastie and Kumar (1979) found. However, consider the case in which the behaviors are unrelated to the context traits used to define the schema being formed, but yet are related to *other* traits, and thus are relevant to the objective of forming an impression (e.g., behaviors conveying friendliness in the context of traits associated with intelligence). Such behaviors may require *more* cognitive work to be incorporated into the schema than do trait-consistent behaviors. Results bearing on this possibility are equivocal. In a later study reported by Hastie (Chapter 5, this volume), such behaviors (denoted by Hastie as "low-congruent" behaviors) were still recalled less well than behaviors that were implied by the context traits presented. On the other hand, Carlston (Chapter 3, this volume) found that "low-congruent" behaviors were recalled better than highly congruent ones. Although these disparate results are hard to reconcile, they suggest that whether behaviors are regarded as consistent, inconsistent, or irrelevant to the schema being formed, and thus the amount of work involved in processing them may depend not only on the processing objectives but also on idiosyncratic characteristics of the behaviors and traits involved.

Situational Influences on the Recall
of Schema-Related Information

Situational factors such as instructional set may also affect processing objectives and therefore may influence the extent to which incongruent information is recalled better than congruent material. In Hastie and Kumar's (1979) study, subjects were told *both* to form an impression of the person described and to recall the original information, thus introducing two different processing objectives. The formulation we have proposed suggests that if these objectives were separated, better recall of trait-incongruent behaviors than trait-congruent ones would be less apt to occur under a memory set (where processing objectives do not require that the information be organized semantically) than under an impression formation set.

The relative ease of recalling congruent and incongruent behaviors may also vary with the type of schema being constructed from the information presented. In Hastie's research all traits and behaviors presented were associated with the same individual, and therefore the representation formed was of a single person. However, in some instances, a representation may be formed of a group, based on information about individual members of this group. It may be easier to understand the deviant behavior of a member of a group than to comprehend a person's behavior that is inconsistent with his general personality. For example, it is less surprising for a single college professor (a member of a group typically characterized as very intelligent) to behave stupidly than it is for a particular very intelligent individual to behave in a stupid fashion. To this extent, less cognitive work may be required to assimilate the schema-discrepant behavior in the first case, and this behavior may therefore not be recalled as well. Research by Rothbart, Evans, and Fulero (1979) suggests this possibility. Here, subjects received information about the behaviors of individual members of a group they believed either "tend(ed) to be more friendly and sociable than average" or "tend(ed) to be more intellectual than average." The behaviors attributed to some of the individuals were consistent with the trait used to characterize the group, whereas others were inconsistent. Subjects subsequently recalled more behaviors that were consistent with the group stereotype than behaviors that were inconsistent with it. This suggests that subjects did not attempt to reconcile the inconsistent behaviors in order to predict characteristics of the group but simply ignored them, thus leading to decreased recall of these behaviors relative to schema-consistent ones.

In any case, the recall task in Hastie's (Chapter 5, this volume) studies was administered immediately after the stimulus information was presented. Recall may therefore have been attempted before the processing required to form an integrated impression of the person was completed. (In fact, although subjects were ultimately asked to rate the person along several evaluative dimensions, this was not done until *after* the recall task.) Suppose that subjects had not only been given an opportunity to complete their processing of the information but were also led to believe that they would not be required to use the information again for some time. According to the formulation we have proposed, the encoded representation of the person, which might not contain *either* irrelevant or incongruent behaviors, would then be transferred to Permanent Storage, and the Work Space would be cleared for attaining other objectives. If subjects were then (unexpectedly) asked to recall the original material, the results obtained by Hastie and Kumar (1979) might be reversed; that is, subjects might then recall *more* congruent than incongruent behaviors. More generally, the present formulation predicts that the greater recall of inconsistent behaviors relative to congruent ones should decrease over time. Moreover, any incongruent behaviors that are recalled should be those that were reinterpreted to make them consistent with the schema formed on the basis of the traits, and they therefore should be recalled inaccurately. (For example, the behavior "was confused by the television show" in the context of traits implying intelligence might be recalled as "disliked the television show", etc.) Such possible distortions are discussed in more detail in the next section.

Summary

The results described in this section suggest that the invocation of a prototypic schema to organize new information about a person affects the amount of schema-relevant material that can be recalled subsequently. In general, material that is used to form a schema of a person to whom the new information pertains is remembered better than material that is irrelevant to the schema, or for other reasons, is not included in it. However, if the recipient's processing objective is to assimilate the entire information presented into an integrated impression of the person being described, as was the case in Hastie's research, the additional cognitive work required to do this may lead information that is inconsistent with the schema being formed to be recalled better than schema-consistent information, at least within a short period of time after the information is acquired.

Distortions in the Recall of Information

We have discussed evidence bearing on the effect of organizing information with respect to a schema on both the amount of information recalled and the type of information recalled. However, to the extent that information is encoded or interpreted in different ways as a result of these organizational processes, its representation in memory may qualitatively differ from the original material. For example, the information that Bob gave someone an answer on an examination may be encoded as "Bob helped another" in a schematic representation of a kind person but as "Bob cheated on an exam" as a result of interpreting the information with reference to the schema of a dishonest person. To this extent, the original information is much more likely to be recalled inaccurately once the Work Space has been cleared and only the encoding of the information in Permanent Storage is available

Several bodies of research bear on this possibility. Perhaps the most direct indication of the effect of encoding verbal information on recall was reported by Woll and Yopp (1978). Six pairs of sentences were constructed, each pair describing a person's reaction in one of two situational contexts. These contexts were assumed to affect the encoding of the reaction described. For example, one pair consisted of the sentences "Vicky turned red when she heard Howard's flattering remarks about her" and "Vicky turned red when she heard Howard's nasty remarks about her." Vicky's reaction is likely to be interpreted as blushing in the first case but as indicating anger in the second. Subjects then read one sentence of each pair, under instructions that the study was concerned with how judgments of people are made. After an interpolated task, they were presented test sentences in which the key context phrase (e.g., "flattering") was omitted. Some test sentences described the actor's reaction exactly as it was described in the original sentence, others in a way that was consistent with the implications of the context (e.g., "Vicky blushed when she heard Howard's remarks about her"), and still others in a way that was inconsistent with these implications (e.g., "Vicky got angry when she heard Howard's remarks about her"). Then, some subjects were asked to infer whether each test sentence was likely to follow from the stimulus sentences presented earlier, whereas others were asked to indicate the likelihood that the test sentences were identical in wording to the stimulus sentences.

As expected, subjects judged sentences more likely to follow from the original stimulus sentences if they contained context-consistent descriptions of the behavior than if they contained context-inconsistent descriptions. More important, subjects were also relatively more likely to believe that test sentences were *identical in wording* to the stimulus sentences when the concept used to describe the behavior was context-consistent than when it was inconsistent. These beliefs,however, were not as strong as their beliefs that actually identical sentences had the same wording. This suggests that some subjects may not have encoded the ambiguous behavior with a context-related concept at the time it was first processed and thus were able to recognize the test sentence as being different in wording. Alternatively, some subjects may simply have retained the original sentences in their Work Space and therefore were able to make direct comparisons.

Two additional studies, by Carlston (Chapter 3, this volume) and by Higgins and Rholes (1978), go a step further in suggesting that the representation of stimulus information, and thus the manner in which it is subsequently recalled, may depend on more specific objectives of the processor.

In some conditions of Carlston's study, subjects read descriptions of a target person, each of which implied either (1) both kindness and dishonesty or (2) both unkindness and honesty. They were then asked to judge the target along dimensions associated with one of these traits. Finally, either a few minutes or several days later, they were asked to recall the descriptions they had read. These recalled descriptions were then rated for favorableness by independent judges who were blind to experimental conditions. These descriptions were recalled as evaluatively similar to the implications of the judgment they had made. Moreover, such evaluative distortions were more evident when the behaviors were recalled several days after making this judgment than when they were recalled only a few minutes afterwards. This supports the notion that in order to make their initial judgment, subjects encoded the information in a way that was relevant to the judgment, and that this encoding, rather than the original material, was then recalled and used as a basis for making later judgments. Moreover, these effects were more apparent after a period of time, consistent with the assumption that distortions in recall increase once the original material has been cleared from the Work Space and is therefore no longer available.

In the study by Higgins and Rholes (1978), subjects read a description of a target person's general behavior in a series of situations. Their objective was to use this information to prepare a message describing the target person to someone who either liked or disliked the target person. However, half of the subjects actually prepared such a message, whereas the remaining subjects did not. Then, either 20 minutes or 2 weeks later, they were asked to reproduce the original stimulus information as accurately as possible.

As expected, subjects who wrote messages about the target person constructed descriptions using terms that were evaluatively consistent with the intended recipient's attitude. According to the formulation proposed here, these constructions should then be placed in Permanent Storage in a bin pertaining to this person. Recall of the original material should be based at least in part on this representation, and therefore its implications should be similarly distorted in the direction of the recipient's attitude. Moreover, this distortion should be greater after a sufficient period of time has elapsed for the original material to be removed from the Work Space and therefore no longer available.

Results support this line of reasoning. Subjects who expected to write a message but did not actually do so showed little systematic distortion in their reproductions of the original material. This suggests that these subjects did not perform the cognitive activity required to encode the stimulus information in anticipation of writing the message and that the awareness of processing objectives had little effect in the absence of activity required to attain these objectives. In contrast, subjects who did write messages later reproduced the original material in a way that was evaluatively biased in the direction of the recipient's attitude.[2] Moreover, the magnitude of this distortion was greater when the reproduction was written 2 weeks after the message had been prepared than when it was written only a short time afterward. Finally, estimates of the amount of distortion in messages to the recipient and the amount of distortion in reproductions were correlated only .18 when these reproductions were written a short time after preparing the message but were correlated .74 when they were prepared 2 weeks later. These data strongly support the notion that subjects' reproductions after a short delay were based partially on information in the Work Space and thus were partly a function of the original stimulus material but that their reproductions after a 2-week period were primarily a function of the encoded representation of the material stored in Permanent Storage.

Intrusion of New Material into Reproductions of Original Information

The preceding studies provide evidence that the organization of stimulus information into schemata for purposes of attaining particular processing objectives leads subjects to recall this material in a manner that is consistent with these schemata. An additional effect of constructing these schemata may be the addition of new material that is not actually present in the original information (see e.g., Barclay, 1973; Brown, 1935; Harris & Monaco, 1978; Loftus & Palmer, 1974). In the area of social perception, this possibility is perhaps best demonstrated in a study by Spiro (1977). This study is of

---

[2]This was apparent in both independent judges' overall ratings of the reproductions and their ratings of each separate component description.

additional interest because it bears directly on the possibility that information is not reencoded and reorganized in response to new information unless this new information is useful in attaining present processing objectives.

Subjects initially read one of two allegedly true stories about an engaged couple with instructions that the information was being presented either as part of an experiment on memory or an experiment on "reactions to situations involving interpersonal relations." In each story, the man informs the woman that he does not want children. However, in one story the woman ostensibly shares the man's views, whereas in the other she expresses considerable upset at the man's position and enters into a bitter discussion of the matter as the story ends. It seems reasonable to suppose that subjects who read the first story with the objective of reacting to the interpersonal relations described are likely to interpret it with reference to a prototypic event schema of two persons who love one another, share similar views, get married, and live happily ever after. However, those who read the second story with the same set of objectives may interpret it with reference to a schema of a couple who initially love one another but find they cannot agree on matters of personal importance, wind up in personal conflict, and ultimately separate. In contrast, subjects who believe they are involved in a memory experiment may not invoke a prototypic schema at all in interpreting the information and thus may store it with a minimum of encoding or interpretation.

After reading one of the two stories, subjects engaged in several minutes of routine activity unrelated to the experimental task. However, during this period, the experimenter "incidentally" remarked to some subjects that the couple eventually married and were still happily together, while telling others that the couple had eventually broken their engagement and had not seen each other since. Thus, in half of the cases, the additional information was presumably consistent with the prototypic schema used to interpret the original material, whereas in the other cases it was inconsistent with this schema. According to the formulation proposed, the additional information should have little effect on memory-set subjects, whose sole objective is to remember the original material. However, subjects whose objective is to interpret and react to the interpersonal reactions described are likely to attempt to incorporate the new information into their representation of the situation. To accomplish this when the outcome is not consistent with the prototypic schema they originally used to interpret the information, they may need to draw upon other prototypic event schemata applicable to the sort of interaction that might have taken place. This reconstructed representation will then be stored in memory rather than the original construction.

After performing a routine activity unrelated to task objectives, subjects were released. They returned either 2 days, 3 weeks, or 6 weeks later, at which time they were asked to recall the story they had read in the first session. In both conditions they were explicitly told to include only ideas that were present in the story and *not* to include any personal reactions or inferences they may have made. Thus, every precaution was taken to discourage subjects from adding material to their reproductions. In fact, subjects under memory-set conditions recalled the material with reasonable accuracy, and errors in their recall were not systematically affected by the additional information they received about the outcome of the couple's interaction. However, subjects whose original objective was to interpret the interpersonal relationship made frequent errors, which increased in number over time. Although the specific nature of these errors differed in detail, they were typically of the sort one would intuitively expect as a result of attempts to reconcile the ancillary material with the original information. For example, when subjects were first told that neither party wanted children but later were led to believe the couple had broken their engagement, several recalled the original information as stating that the couple had actually disagreed about having children; others recalled it as stating that one party ultimately changed his or her mind about the desirability of having children. In contrast, when subjects were told that the couple disagreed but wound up happily married, they tended to add details that minimized the implications of the disagreement, recalling that "the problem was resolved when they found that (the woman) could not have children anyway," or that although one person thought the matter was important, the other did not (for these and other concrete examples, see Spiro, 1977, pp. 144–145).

These responses are all quite plausible explanations of the outcome of the couple's interaction that one might expect to invoke in an attempt to reconcile the unanticipated outcome with the initial information. What is striking is that these explanations were recalled as actually having existed in the information presented, despite explicit instructions not to include inferences or personal reactions. This is quite consistent with the general notion that if inferences about a person or event are made in order to attain processing objectives, and if these inferences are incorporated into the schematic representation placed in Permanent Storage, they are subsequently not distinguishable from aspects of the original information that are also contained in that representation. The increase in these effects over time is once again consistent with our notion that when the time interval is relatively short and the processing objectives have presumably not yet been accomplished, the original information as well as the encoding of it is likely to be retained in the Work Space, and thus available for recall. When the anticipated delay in using the information is considerable, however, the processor is more likely to transfer the representation of the information to

Permanent Storage and clear the Work Space for the other purposes. Thus, much of the original information is unavailable at the time subjects are asked to reproduce it, and they must rely on their reconstruction of it.

Discussion

The research described in this section supports both the information-processing formulation we have proposed and, more generally, the hypothesized role of previously formed schemata in encoding, organizing, and subsequently recalling information. These effects are quite wide ranging. They include the representation of both visual and verbal information, the deletion of original information, the recall of interpretations rather than the information itself, and the recall of unspecified features or events as having actually been presented as part of the original material. Moreover, there is consistent evidence that these effects increase over time.

The alternative ways in which a person schema may be used to reconstruct and recall original stimulus material must ultimately be identified and isolated. For example, we have typically argued that these schemata affect the interpretation of information and inferences based on it at the time it is first processed and thus the representation of this information that is stored in memory. However, as we noted in our discussion of Cohen's (1976) study, prototypic schemata of persons and events may also affect "guesses" about the content of the original information under conditions in which neither it nor the encoded representation of it is readily available. Moreover, the use of a protoypic schema as a means of *organizing* new material, as suggested by Spiro's study, needs to be separated from its use as a basis for comparison in *evaluating* new material.

With a few recent exceptions (e.g., Markus, 1977; Rogers, 1977; Rogers, Kuiper & Kirker, 1977), the use of self-schemata in encoding and organizing information has generally been ignored in the research we have considered here. As we pointed out earlier, however, the receipt of information is itself an event that may be stored in a "self" bin along with the conditions surrounding it. The role of the perceiver in the representation of events has been emphasized by Schank and Abelson (1977; see also Abelson, 1976). It is conceivable that many of the schemata constructed of persons on the basis of information include oneself as a participant in the interaction with these persons, plus various reactions to these persons during the course of this interaction. Indeed, these reactions may be important aspects of the impressions of persons or events surrounding them. Our judgments of a person as intelligent or warm may often be based more on our recall of having thought that the person made a brilliant observation, or as feeling very good while in the company of the person, without having any recollection at all of the specific behaviors that gave rise to these reactions. However, once the reactions have been encoded into general traits of the person who elicited them and these traits have been stored in memory, the traits may be recalled for use in describing or evaluating the person. Moreover, this may occur independently of the reactions that led these traits to be initially assigned.

We have assumed that the information being processed remains in the Work Space for a period of time after it is received and therefore is available to be recalled and used as a basis for judgments. However, after the Work Space is cleared, only the encoded representation of the information (retrieved from Permanent Storage) is available. A question arises as to whether factors that theoretically affect the length of time that information is retained in the Work Space will affect the duration of its influence. One factor may simply be whether the processing objectives have ostensibly been obtained. A second may be the immediacy with which the information is expected to be used. That is, holding constant the actual time interval between the receipt of stimulus information and the request to recall it, recall may be less accurate (and the encoded representation of it may have less effect) when subjects believe they have completed their use of the information than when they expect to continue to use it. Moreover, it may be more accurate when subjects expect to use the information in the near future than when they do not expect to use it for some time. This possibility may warrant future empirical investigation.

EFFECTS OF ENCODING AND ORGANIZATION OF STIMULUS INFORMATION ON JUDGMENTS

To the extent that stimulus information is encoded differently as a result of different processing objectives (or other reasons), this encoding and its implications may affect judgments of the persons or events to which the information is relevant. Several studies have investigated this possibility. Some have shown the effects of using concepts in one situation on the likelihood that they will be used to encode information in a second unrelated situation. Others have demonstrated that previous judgments of a stimulus object affect subsequent judgments of it independently of the information upon which the first judgment was based. A third area of research provides indirect evidence that complex representations of one event affect inferences about similar events, regardless of the validity of the information that led the initial representations to be constructed. We discuss these bodies of research later in the present section.

Priming Effects on Semantic Encodings

If more than one attribute schema is appropriate for encoding a given piece of information, the schema selected should be the one that has been used most recently and, therefore, is nearest to the top of the general attribute bin from which it is drawn. This attribute may then subsequently be used as a basis for making later encodings of information to which it is relevant. This may be true even when the previous situation in which the schema was used is irrelevant to the information presented and the judgment to be made. For example, suppose that the schema associated with "kind" is retrieved from the attribute bin for some purpose and then is redeposited in the bin on top of the other material contained in it. As a result of its new position in the bin, this schema is more likely to be retrieved for use in interpreting information that a person has helped another out on an examination than would the trait schema associated with "dishonest," even though both schemata are potentially applicable. Moreover, if this encoding leads the actor to be labeled a "kind person," this person is more likely to be evaluated favorably and to be assigned favorable characteristics than would otherwise have been the case. This possibility suggests that judgments of people may often be affected by quite fortuitous events that lead one or another concept to be more accessible at the time the information about these people is first received.

Empirical Demonstrations of the Phenomena

Two studies, each using a somewhat different research paradigm, have demonstrated the effect of priming trait categories on the interpretation of information about persons. In a study by Higgins, Rholes, and Jones (1977) subjects were first required to use four trait names along with six names of inanimate objects as part of a "color-naming" task that was ostensibly irrelevant to the main experiment. These traits were either all favorable or all unfavorable and were either all applicable or all inapplicable for interpreting a particular set of behavioral and attitude descriptions of a target person. (For example, one description was "well aware of his ability to do many things well" and could be encoded either favorably as "self-confident," or unfavorably as "conceited.") After performing the color-naming task, subjects then read a paragraph about a stimulus person that contained these descriptions. Those subjects who had previously been exposed to trait names that were applicable for encoding the target's behavior subsequently used either these terms or (more frequently) synonyms in generating spontaneous descriptions of the target. Moreover, their evaluations of the target were biased in the direction of the evaluative implications of the primed traits. In contrast, the descriptions generated by subjects exposed to trait terms that were inapplicable for encoding the behavior were not systematically related to the evaluative implications of those terms and their subsequent evaluations of the target were unaffected by the favorableness of these terms. These latter findings indicate that the primed trait concepts did not have direct effects on judgments of the target person, but influenced these judgments only insofar as they affected the interpretation of the target's behavior.

As conceptualized in this chapter, the trait schemata contained in the attribute bin consist not only of alternative labels for an attribute (e.g., "honest," "trustworthy," "sincere," etc.) but also of prototypic behaviors that reflect this attribute (e.g., "returns lost property," "tells the truth," etc.). To the extent that this is true, an attribute schema may be made more accessible not only by priming one of its alternative labels but also by priming behaviors that exemplify the attribute. This latter possibility was tested by Srull and Wyer (1979). Specifically, subjects first completed a questionnaire purportedly designed to investigate how people perceive word relationships. Each questionnaire item consisted of four words, and the subject's task was to underline any three words that would make a complete sentence. In one replication of the study, the concept "hostile" was primed and the possible sentences formed from some items (e.g., "leg break arm his") each described an instance of hostile behavior, whereas the sentences formed from the remaining items (e.g., "her found knew I") were each irrelevant to this attribute. A second replication was similar except that the critical items were intended to prime the concept "kind." The number of priming items relevant to the concept was varied over experimental conditions.

Either immediately after performing the task or some time later, subjects took part in an ostensibly unrelated experiment on "impression formation" that was conducted by a different experimenter. In this experiment, subjects read a paragraph about a target person that contained behaviors that were ambiguous with respect to the primed trait concept (that is, they could be interpreted as conveying either a high or low degree of the primed attribute). They then rated the target person along a series of attribute dimensions. As expected, ratings of the target along dimensions that were related directly to the primed attribute increased monotonically with the number of trait-related priming items in the initial questionnaire.

These data therefore extend on the findings reported by Higgins et al. in showing that not only can priming specific trait labels affect the encoding of behavior but also that priming behavioral exemplars of a trait can increase the accessibility of a general schema associated with the trait, and therefore can affect the way in which other more ambiguous behaviors are interpreted. Let us now turn to some additional issues associated with the effects of category accessibility and the processes that underlie them.

Generalizeability of Priming Effects

The study by Higgins et al. (1977) demonstrated that exposure to favorable or unfavorable traits had no effect on evaluations of the target person unless they were applicable for encoding the target's behavior. This indicates that priming affects judgments of a person only through its mediating influence on the interpretation of information about this person. However, once the information has been interpreted and the person is assigned an attribute implied by this interpretation, the assignment may be perceived to have implications for other traits that are not directly related to either the information about the person being judged or the items contained in the initial priming task. The judgment that someone possesses the trait being primed (e.g., "hostile") may lead to a more general representation of him as an exemplar of a prototypic person with this attribute (i.e., a "hostile person"). This classification may lead the person to be assigned other traits that are not descriptively implied by this attribute but are contained in the schema of a person who possesses it. (Thus, for example, although hostile behavior is not typically relevant to intelligence, a "hostile person" may nevertheless be inferred to be unintelligent, or to possess other undesirable qualities by virtue of their presence in the prototypic schema of such a person.) In fact, this appears to be the case. In the study by Srull and Wyer (1979) cited earlier, ratings of the target person with respect to traits that were evaluatively similar to the primed attribute but descriptively unrelated to it were affected in much the same way as ratings of the target with respect to the primed attribute itself. Thus, although priming a concept does not have direct effects on judgments on a person along dimensions to which the concept is inapplicable, once the information about a person is encoded in terms of a primed concept, the effects of this encoding may be quite widespread.

Effects of Time Delay

There often may be an appreciable length of time between the activation of a concept and the acquisition of information to which the concept is potentially relevant. Moreover, a period of time may elapse between the acquisition of information about a person and judgments based on this information. The question therefore arises as to how priming effects are influenced by these time delays.

The formulation proposed in this chapter makes quite clear predictions concerning these effects. First, once a trait schema is used and then redeposited on top of the attribute bin, it will be retrieved for use in interpreting information to which it is applicable as long as no other relevant schemata are used in the interim and thus are stored on top of it. However, the likelihood of using other applicable concepts increases with time. Therefore, the effect of priming a concept on the interpretation of information is likely to decrease over the interval between the priming task and presentation of this information.

Different considerations underlie the effects of a delay between the receipt and encoding of stimulus information and a judgment based on it. As long as the original stimulus information is retained in the Work Space, both this information and the encoded representation of it may have direct effects on judgments. However, once the Work Space is cleared, only the encoding of the information is available for use in making judgments. Because the likelihood of the Work Space being cleared increases over time, the effect of the encoding of the stimulus material, and consequently the effect of priming, will *increase* with the time interval between the presentation of information and judgments based on it.

There is support for both of these predictions. In Srull and Wyer's (1979) study, stimulus information was presented either immediately, 1 hour, or 24 hours after subjects had performed the priming task. Priming effects on judgments decreased consistently over time, although they sometimes were still evident after a period of 24 hours. A second study (see Wyer & Srull, in press) also found decreased priming effects under these conditions. In the latter study, however, additional conditions were run in which the stimulus information always immediately followed the priming task, but the time interval between the acquisition of this information and judgments of the targets was varied. In this case, the effect of priming on judgments of the target increased consistently as a function of time, being more extreme 1 week after the stimulus information was presented than it was immediately. Similar increases in priming effects as a function of the time delay between stimulus presentation and judgments were also reported in the study by Higgins et al. (1977).

The Temporal Locus of Priming Effects— The Role of Processing Objectives

In discussing the research described previously, we have assumed that priming effects on the interpretation of the behavioral information presented occurred at the time this information was first received. However, it is also possible that the encoding of information does not occur until subjects are called on to make a judgment of the person to whom the information refers. That is, the original behavioral information may be stored in memory in roughly unadulterated form until a judgment based on it is requested, whereupon it is retrieved, encoded in terms of whatever concepts happen to be most accessible at the time, and a judgment made on the basis of this encoding.

One implication of this latter line of reasoning, however, is that priming should affect judgments when it occurs *after* the stimulus information is presented as well as before. This possibility was investigated in a later study by Srull and Wyer (see Wyer & Srull, in press). This study was conceptually identical to the initial study by the authors in which the number of items in the priming task and the interval between priming and stimulus presentation were varied. However, in this study, the priming task was presented after the presentation of the stimulus information and not before. In contrast to the earlier study, neither the number of priming items nor the time delay manipulations affected judgments. In fact, there was no evidence of any priming effects whatsoever. This strongly argues against the possibility that in the conditions we have constructed, the stimulus information is encoded at the time a judgment is made. Rather, the accessibility of various cognitive categories appears to influence the way in which information is interpreted at the time it is first received. Once the information is encoded and stored in memory, judgments are based on this encoding and not on a reinterpretation of the original information in terms of concepts that are available at the time. Note that this conclusion is similar to that drawn on the basis of research by Higgins et al. (1977) cited earlier in this chapter.

This does not mean that the interpretation of information is never affected by concepts made accessible after the information is received. In fact, according to the formulation we have proposed, the critical factor is not what concepts are accessible at the time of stimulus presentation per se, but rather, what concepts are accessible at the time the information is encoded in pursuit of processing objectives to which these concepts are relevant. In the studies reported earlier, these processing objectives (to form an impression of the target person) were introduced before the behavioral information was received, leading the behaviors to be encoded in terms of impression-relevant traits at the time they were read. However, suppose that the behavioral information is first presented under instructions to remember the material. In this case, there is no reason to encode the material in terms of traits at the time it is presented. If after receiving the information subjects are then asked unexpectedly to form an impression and judge a person described by it, they may then recall the behaviors and encode them in terms of whatever concepts are salient at *this* time. Under these conditions, the insertion of priming after presentation of the stimulus information (but before the statement of processing objectives) may have more effect.

Indirect Evidence of Priming Effects on Social Judgments

The studies just described theoretically concern the effects of priming general concepts assumed to be contained in the attribute bin on the encoding of person information. Similar considerations should apply in the case of concepts and schemata contained in other bins. Although this possibility has not been explored directly, several suggestions of it pervade the literature. Research by Salancik and his colleagues (Salancik, 1974; Salancik & Calder, 1974; Salancik & Conway, 1975) is particularly noteworthy. For example, Salancik and Calder found that subjects' attitudes toward religion were significantly more highly correlated with demographic factors when behavioral items were responded to before the attitudes were reported than when this order was reversed. Presumably in the process of responding to the behavioral items, event schemata associated with these behaviors were moved to the top of subjects' "self-bins" and subsequently used as a basis for reporting their attitudes.

Using a quite different procedure, Salancik (1974) asked students near the end of the semester to generate open-ended responses to a set of items about their classroom behavior. In one condition, items were completed following the stem "in order to" (e.g., "I raise my hand in class in order to . . . "), whereas in the second condition, they were completed following the stem "because I" (e.g., "I raise my hand in class because I . . . "). The author reasoned that responding to items in the first condition would lead subjects to use extrinsic incentives as bases for explaining their behavior (e.g., ". . . in order to let the teacher know who I am," " . . . in order to get a good grade," etc.). In contrast, responding in the second condition should lead subjects to use intrinsic incentives (e.g., " . . . because I want to learn the material"). Thus, in terms of the conceptualization proposed here, "in order to" subjects should have a preponderance of extrinsic incentives near the top of the bin associated with the class, whereas "because I" subjects should have a preponderance of intrinsic factors on top. Therefore, the first group of subjects should be more likely to use extrinsic factors as a basis for their subsequent judgments of the class than should the second. This appeared to be the case. After completing the questionnaire, subjects were asked to rate how well they liked the course, and these ratings were subsequently correlated with final course grades (an extrinsic factor). This correlation was .94 in the case of "in order to" subjects but near zero (-.16) in the case of "because I" subjects.

The Effects of Initial Representations of Persons on Subsequent Judgments of These Persons

The proposed formulation implies that once a representation of a person has been constructed, this representation will tend to be used as a basis for subsequent judgments of this person. Moreover, the effect may be quite independent of the direct implications of the information on which the representation initially was based. This possibility becomes particularly interesting when the implications of the representation for the judgment to be made are unrelated to, or even inconsistent with, those of the original information received.

The representation of a stimulus person on the basis of information about him may be a schema consisting of several interrelated features, or possibly a simple judgment of the person that has been formed on the basis of such a schema. Studies by Carlston (Chapter 3, this volume) and Lingle and Ostrom (1978; see also Ostrom, Lingle, Pryor, & Geva, Chapter 2, this volume) both provide evidence of the effects of prior judgments on subsequent ones, and work by Lee Ross and his colleagues (for a summary, see Ross, 1977) provides indirect evidence of the effect of more complex representations. Because these various studies differ in detail, we review them briefly with specific reference to the formulation we have proposed.

The Effects of Initial Judgments on Subsequent Ones

In the study by Carlston (this volume), subjects initially read six behavioral descriptions of a target person that implied that this person was either (1) both kind and dishonest, or (2) both unkind and honest. In some cases, each description had implications for only one of the two traits, whereas in others, each description had implications for both traits simultaneously. (An example of the latter type, which conveyed unkindness and honesty, described the target as telling his girl that he thought her new hair style was unattractive.) After receiving this information, subjects rated the person with respect to one of the two traits to which the information was relevant (either kindness or honesty). Then, either a few minutes or several days later, they again rated the target person, this time along dimensions pertaining to the other trait, as well as along other evaluative dimensions. If subjects base their final judgments on the implications of the original behavioral information, these judgments should not differ as a function of subjects' initial ratings. However, suppose that in making the first judgment, subjects construct a representation of the target on the basis of a prototypic schema of a person who possesses the trait to be judged (e.g., a "kind" person schema). This schema presumably contains other attributes that are apt to be evaluatively similar to the trait assigned to the target on the basis of this judgment. If this is true, and if subjects recall their representation of the target rather than the original behavioral information to use as bases for their final ratings, there should be a positive relation between the favorableness of these ratings and the favorableness of their first judgments.

The foregoing predictions were supported when subjects' initial judgments were relatively extreme and thus had clear implications for the final ones. However, in some conditions of the study, in which each behavioral description had implications for both traits simultaneously, many subjects' initial ratings of the target were relatively neutral. These subjects' final judgments were consistent with the implications of the original information for the trait they were rating. This, however, does not necessarily mean that they based their final judgments on this information. As Carlston suggests in this volume, these subjects may have spontaneously encoded the original information as it was received in terms of the trait to which the interpolated judgment did not pertain. This may have led their initial judgments along the opposite trait dimension, a compromise between the direct implications of the information presented and the implications of their spontaneous encoding of it, to be relatively neutral. However, these subjects may have subsequently disregarded this neutral rating when making their final judgment because it had unclear implications for this latter judgment, and relied instead on their spontaneous encoding of the original material. A supplementary experiment reported by Carlston, in which the evaluative implications of subjects' spontaneous descriptions of the target based on the original information were used as a basis for predicting their final judgments, supports this line of reasoning.

In addition, the effect of initial judgments on final ones increased over time. This effect, like the increased effects of priming over time obtained by Higgins et al. (1977) and Wyer and Srull (in press), is predicted by the formulation we have proposed. That is, when judgments are made a long time after the original information is processed, the original information is likely to be cleared from the Work Space, and the judgment is consequently based only on the encoding of it retrieved from Permanent Storage. Thus, the encoding has relatively greater effect. Recall data strengthen this interpretation. Specifically, subjects' initial judgments of the target person were recalled with a high degree of accuracy even after a week had elapsed since making them. In contrast, behavioral information that was irrelevant to these initial judgments (e.g., information relevant to honesty under conditions in which kindness was initially judged, or to kindness when honesty was initially judged) tended not to be recalled. Thus, behavioral information that is not relevant to the initial processing objectives appears not to have been encoded and stored in the bin associated with the target person, whereas the encoded behavior and the judgment based upon it is stored and ultimately retrieved.

A second study, by Lingle and Ostrom (1978; see Ostrom et al, Chapter 2, this volume), suggests that more general occupational judgments may also be used as a basis for subsequent ratings of persons, again independently of the information initially received about these persons. This study is of additional interest because response times rather than judgments per se were used to identify the effects. Subjects first judged a stimulus person's suitability for a given occupation on the basis of attributes describing that person. The number of attributes presented was systematically varied. To make the initial judgment, subjects presumably must retrieve a prototypic schema of a person in the occupation to be rated (i.e., an occupational stereotype) and compare the configuration of attributes presented to those comprising the stereotype. Because the comparison process presumably takes longer when there are more attributes to be interpreted and compared with the prototypic schema, the time required to make this judgment should increase with the number of attributes presented. This was in fact the case.

After making these first occupational judgments, however, subjects then rated the target person's suitability for a second occupation that required characteristics either similar or dissimilar to those required by the first occupation. If subjects base these second ratings on the original attribute information, the time required to make these judgments should also increase with the number of attributes in the set. In fact, however, response time was less when the second occupation was similar to the first than when it was dissimilar and, in both cases, was independent of set size. This suggests that subjects did *not* base their second judgments on a reassessment of the implications of the original attribute information, even when the two occupations were dissimilar. Rather, they apparently based their second judgment on a comparison of the previously formed schemata associated with the two occupations being considered, generating similar judgments if the features of the two schemata were similar and different judgments if they were dissimilar. The greater response time in the second case may simply have been due to the greater time required to compare two schemata with relatively different features (cf. Wyer & Carlston, 1979). Additional studies reported by Ostrom et al. (this volume) support these basic conclusions.

From the perspective of the formulation proposed in this chapter, the fact that the original information seemed to have no influence at all on the final occupational judgment is somewhat surprising. Because the time interval between the stimulus information and the second occupational judgment was short, the original information should have been available in the Work Space at the time the second judgment was made. It is conceivable, however, that subjects who are implicitly required to make judgments rapidly may not attempt to reevaluate the implications of the initial information as well as the encoded representation of it but may rely only on its representation. Future research that varies both the number of judgments to be made and the time allowed for making them is needed to clarify this issue.

Effects of Overt Responses on Subsequent Judgments and Behavioral Decisions

The studies cited earlier suggest that once a judgment of a stimulus is made, it may affect subsequent responses to the stimulus independently of the information upon which it was initially based. However, as we noted earlier, it is often important to distinguish between subjective judgments of a stimulus and ratings of the stimulus along response scales of the sort used in psychological experiments. These ratings may be partly a function of situation-specific assumptions about the position of the response scale in relation to the particular range of stimuli to be considered. Thus, if subjects expect to rate stimuli with predominately positive values along an evaluative scale, they may subjectively position their rating scale to include only positively valued stimuli. Their rating of any given stimulus along the scale may consequently be more negative than it would be if the stimulus had been presented in the context of others with predominately negative values. These "contrast" effects may not reflect differences in subjective judgments of the stimuli but rather may be due to differences in the "language" used to report these judgments (for an elaboration of these response processes, see Upshaw, 1969, 1978; Wyer, 1974).

However, once a stimulus has been rated, this rating may be stored in memory on top of a bin corresponding to the stimulus being judged. Therefore, if the stimulus is considered in the future, this rating may be retrieved and its implications interpreted independently of the conditions that produced it. Thus, suppose a stimulus has been rated relatively unfavorably as a result of its presence in the context of a series of desirable stimuli. If this rating is subsequently recalled, it may lead the stimulus to be responded to less favorably on an absolute basis than it would otherwise.

Although research directly bearing on the implications of this possibility for the study of person perception has not been performed, a recent study by Sherman, Ahlm, Berman and Lynn (1978) is of considerable interest. In this study, subjects first rated the importance of a target concept (recycling trash) in the context of either important social issues or unimportant ones. As expected, these contexts had a contrast effect on ratings of the target; that is, recycling was rated as more important in the context of trivial issues than in the context of important ones. Once these ratings were made, a confederate posing as another subject spontaneously indicated that she happened to be involved in a recycling project and was recruiting persons to volunteer help. Subjects who had rated recycling in the context of trivial issues volunteered significantly more help than those who had rated it in the context of important ones.

In interpreting these findings, it is necessary to consider a second set of conditions in which subjects initially rated only context issues but did *not* rate the target issue. Here, the importance of the context issues had precisely the opposite effect on subjects' helping behavior; that is, subjects helped *less* when they had previously rated trivial issues than when they had rated important ones. This finding is important because it rules out an interpretation of the first set of data as due to the effects of context on subjective perceptions of the importance of the target issue (if this were the case, the contrast effect of context on helping should have been manifested regardless of whether the target issue was formally rated). In any case, these findings are also consistent with the formulation proposed. When a specific judgment of the target issue had not been made, subjects apparently based their decision to help on general concepts that were made salient by the context issues they had rated. Thus, their willingness to help increased when the issues considered were of high social importance. However, when subjects made an explicit rating of the target issue, the implications of this *rating* served as a basis for their subsequent decision to help, independently of the contextual factors that influenced their initial rating.

Self-Perception Processes

Although much of the research cited previously concerns the effects of a prior judgment or rating of a stimulus on subsequent reactions to the stimulus, other types of representations may have similar effects. For example, a person who manifests some behavior toward a stimulus object may encode and store a representation of this behavior and its implications on top of a bin pertaining to this object. To this extent, subsequent judgments of the object may be based on this representation rather than on other potentially relevant information.

This possibility is formally recognized by Bem (1967, 1972) in his theory of self-perception. According to this formulation, a person who is asked to report his attitude toward an object is likely to base this evaluation on the implications of his most recent behavior toward the object, independently of other previously acquired information that may be relevant to the judgment. Many well-known studies suggest that this is indeed the case (e.g., Bem & McConnell, 1970; for a summary, see Bem, 1972). Other implications consistent with the formulation proposed here are worth noting. First, the encoding or interpretation of one's behavior, rather than the behavior per se, presumably provides the basis for judgments to which the behavioral information is relevant. Thus, a person who volunteers to advocate a position publically may subsequently interpret this behavior by invoking a prototypic schema of persons who freely speak out on issues in which they believe, whereas a person who is forced to advocate the position may interpret the behavior with reference to a prototypic schema of someone who does not favor the position and therefore has to be bribed or coerced into doing so. Thus, as demonstrated in numerous other studies of role-playing effects on attitudes (for a summary, see Zajonc, 1968), behavior should have greater effect on judgments in the first case than in the second.

On the other hand, the proposed formulation implies that these effects will be greatest when only the behavioral information is accessed for use in making judgments. When other relevant material is stored on top of the bin associated with the object being judged, or is available in the Work Space as a result of its recent use for other purposes, the effects of behavioral information may be diminished. This is suggested in a study by Snyder and Ebbesen (1972). Here, subjects wrote an essay advocating a position on an issue with which they did not initially agree. However, some subjects were asked to collect their thoughts on the issue before being told they would write the essay whereas others were not. To attain these processing objectives, the first group should theoretically access information about the issue (presumably supporting their initial opposing position) and transfer it to the Work Space. This material may remain there even after the essay is prepared and thus may be available for use as a basis for subsequent judgments. In contrast, subjects in the second group may have only information about their behavior and its implications in their Work Space upon completion of the essay. To the extent that subjects' ratings of the target issues are based on material in the Work Space, the effect of essay writing on these ratings should be less in the first case than in the second. This is in fact what happened.

Persisting Effects of False Information

The preceding analysis of self-perception phenomena has several additional implications. If a person's behavior in a given situation has been interpreted or explained in terms of a prototypic schema associated with the type of behavior and the conditions surrounding it, this representation may be used as a basis for subsequent judgments, independently of the original information that led the schema to be constructed. In fact, it may continue to have an effect even after the original information has been discredited.

Research by Lee Ross and his colleagues is worth noting in this regard. In one study (Ross, Lepper, & Hubbard, 1975), subjects first received either positive or negative feedback about their accuracy in distinguishing between real and bogus suicide notes. It seems reasonable to assume that this information stimulated subjects to retrieve characteristics from their "self-bin" in an attempt to interpret this information, thus leading them to construct a self-schema of themselves as good or bad judges. Later, all subjects were told that the information they received about their performance was false and bore absolutely no relation to their actual performance. Subjects were then told they were about to perform a similar task to the first one and were asked to predict how well they would do. Subjects who had been falsely told they were good judges and then were debriefed predicted they would do better on the second task than did subjects who had been told they had performed poorly and then were debriefed. These results are thus consistent with the hypothesis that subjects constructed a self-schema to explain the original feedback information and used this self-schema as a basis for predicting future performance, independently of the discredited information on which the schema was based.

Results with similar implications were reported by Ross, Lepper, Strack, and Steinmetz (1977) in a study where subjects judged persons other than themselves. Specifically, they first received background information about a clinical patient and were asked to explain why the person might have either committed suicide or donated money to the Peace Corps. Some subjects were told at the outset that the behavior to be explained was hypothetical and that the experimenter actually had no knowledge of the patient's subsequent activities. Other subjects were initially led to believe that the behavior they explained had actually occurred, but were subsequently debriefed. Then, all subjects were asked to predict the likelihood that the patient would actually manifest each set of behaviors, including the one they had previously explained. Regardless of experimental condition, subjects predicted the behavior they had previously explained to be more likely to occur than behaviors they had not previously considered. Although there are other possible explanations for this finding,[3] it is again consistent with the general notion that once subjects have constructed a representation of a person, they tend to use this representation and its implications as a basis for subsequent judgments. This study is also important, however, because it demonstrates that this will be true even when there is full awareness that the original information was false.

Conclusions

The research cited in this section provides consistent support for the general hypothesis that once new information about a person or event is encoded or organized in terms of previously existing concepts, this encoding is used as a basis for subsequent judgments independently of the information on which it was originally based. Moreover, once this encoding of the information has occurred, its influence in relation to the original information presented increases over time. The initial encoding of the information may be influenced by prior experiences that fortuitously make concepts potentially applicable for interpreting the information easily accessible. Moreover, once persons are judged on the basis of information about themselves, this judgment may come to function autonomously of the original material and thus may affect future responses to the target along still other dimensions. In combination, the research suggests that over a period of time one's judgments of persons and predictions of their behavior may come to be based on cognitions about the persons that are only remotely related to the information that was originally acquired about these persons. The processes underlying these phenomena appear easily interpretable in terms of the theoretical formulation we have proposed.

CONCLUDING REMARKS

In this chapter, we have proposed a preliminary formulation of information processing that can be used to integrate much of the current literature in social cognition and that has many additional implications for the phenomena to

---

[3]For example, because subjects were given no indication of why they were asked to explain the particular behavior they were asked to consider, they may have assumed it was selected because the experimenter personally thought it was likely to occur, regardless of whether he knew for a fact that it did occur. Accordingly, they may have complied with this implicit expectancy.

which this literature pertains. Although there are many ambiguities in the model in its present stage of development, these ambiguities appear likely to be eliminated as the model becomes more refined and as additional research is performed to test the specific assumptions underlying it. Concepts borrowed from existing formulations of cognitive functioning (Rosch, 1973, 1975; Smith et al., 1974; Schank & Abelson, 1977; Wyer & Carlston, 1979) may be able to be incorporated effectively into the model as it continues to develop. However, the specific model we have proposed here is incidental to the main objectives of this chapter and of this volume as a whole. The chapters of this volume exemplify a general conceptual approach to the study of social cognition that will, we believe, have a major impact on the field of social psychology in the years to come. The concentration on fundamental psychological processes that have broad implications for an understanding of social perception may ultimately tie together many of the fragmented, microtheoretical concerns that have traditionally pervaded work in impression formation, attribution, interpersonal attraction, and person perception. Although the chapters in this volume have not provided definitive answers to many of the questions of concern in these areas, they do, we believe, exemplify a provocative and fruitful approach to their future investigation.

ACKNOWLEDGMENTS

This paper was supported by National Science Foundation Grant BNS 76-24001 to the first author, and USPHS Training Grants MH-14257 and MH-15140 to the second author.

REFERENCES

Abelson, R. P. Script processing in attitude formation and decision-making. In J. S. Carroll & J. W. Payne (Eds.), *Cognition and social behavior*. Hillsdale, N.J.: Lawrence Erlbaum Associates, 1976.

Abelson, R. P., & Reich, C. M. *Implicational molecules: A method for extracting meaning from input sentences*. Paper presented at the International Joint Conference on Artificial Intelligence, Bedford, Mass., 1969.

Anderson, J. R. *Language, memory, and thought*. Hillsdale, N. J.: Lawrence Erlbaum Associates, 1976.

Anderson, J. R., & Bower, G. H. Recognition and retrieval processes in free recall, *Psychological Review*, 1972, *79*, 97–123.

Anderson, J. R., & Bower, G. H. *Human associative memory*. Washington, D. C.: V. H. Winston, 1973.

Anderson, N. H. Cognitive algebra: Integration theory applied to social attribution. In L. Berkowitz (Ed.), *Advances in experimental social psychology, Vol. 7*. New York: Academic Press, 1974.

Anderson, N. H., & Hubert, S. Effects of concomitant verbal recall on order effects in personality impression formation, *Journal of Verbal Learning and Verbal Behavior*, 1963, *2*, 379–391.

Anderson, R. C., & Pichert, J. W. Recall of previously unrecallable information following a shift in perspective. *Journal of Verbal Learning and Verbal Behavior*, 1978, *17*, 1–12.

Baddeley, A. D. The trouble with levels: A reexamination of Craik and Lockhart's framework for memory research. *Psychological Review*, 1978, *85*, 139–152.

Baddeley, A. D., & Hitch, G. J. Recency reexamined. In S. Dornic (Eds.), *Attention and performance VI*. Hillsdale, N. J.: Lawrence Erlbaum Associates, 1977.

Barclay, J. R. The role of comprehension in remembering sentences. *Cognitive Psychology*, 1973, *4*, 229–254.

Barclay, J. R., Bransford, J. D., Franks, J. J., McCarrell, N. S., & Nitsch, K. Comprehension and semantic flexibility. *Journal of Verbal Learning and Verbal Behavior*, 1974, *13*, 471–481.

Bartlett, F. C. *Remembering: A study in experimental and social psychology*. Cambridge: Cambridge University Press, 1932.

Bem, D. J. Self-perception: An alternative interpretation of cognitive dissonance phenomena. *Psychological Review*, 1967, *74*, 183–200.

Bem, D. J. Self-perception theory. In L. Berkowitz (Ed.), *Advances in experimental social psychology, Vol. 6*. New York: Academic Press, 1972.

Bem, D. J., & McConnell, H. K. Testing the self-perception explanation of dissonance phenomena: On the salience of premanipulation attitudes. *Journal of Personality and Social Psychology*, 1970, *14*, 23–31.

Bobrow, D. G., & Norman, D. A. Some principles of memory schemata. In D. G. Bobrow & A. Collins (Eds.), *Representation and understanding: Studies in cognitive science*. New York: Academic Press, 1975.

Bousfield, A. K., & Bousfield, W. A. Measurement of clustering and of sequential constancies in repeated free recall. *Psychological Reports*, 1966, *19*, 935–942.

Bower, G. H. Cognitive psychology: An introduction. In W. K. Estes (Ed.), *Handbook of learning and cognitive processes, Vol. 1*. Hillsdale, N. J.: Lawrence Erlbaum Associates, 1975.

Bransford, J. D., & Franks, J. J. The abstraction of linguistic ideas. *Cognitive Psychology*, 1971, *2*, 331–350.

Bransford, J. D., & Franks, J. J. The abstraction of linguistic ideas: A review. *Cognition: International Journal of Cognitive Psychology*, 1973, *1*, 211–249.

Brown, H. B. An experience in identification testimony. *Journal of the American Institute of Criminal Law*, 1935, *25*, 621–622.

Cohen, C. E. *An information processing approach to social perception: The influence of a stereotype upon what an observer remembered*. Unpublished doctoral dissertation, University of California, San Diego, 1976.

Cohen, C. E., & Ebbesen, E. B. Observational goals and schema activation: A theoretical framework for behavior perception. *Journal of Experimental Social Psychology*, 1979, *15*, 305–329.

Collins, A. M., & Loftus, E. F. A spreading-activation theory of semantic processing. *Psychological Review*, 1975, *82*, 407–428.

Craik, F. I. M. Depth of processing in recall and recognition. In S. Dornic (Ed.), *Attention and performance VI*. Hillsdale, N. J.: Lawrence Erlbaum Associates, 1977.

Craik, F. I. M., & Lockhart, R. S. Levels of processing: A framework for memory research. *Journal of Verbal Learning and Verbal Behavior*, 1972, *11*, 681–684.

Crowder, R. G. *Principles of learning and memory*. Hillsdale, N. J.: Lawrence Erlbaum Associates, 1976.

Ebbesen, E. B., & Allen, R. B. Cognitive processes in implicit personality inferences. *Journal of Personality and Social Psychology*, 1979, *37*, 471–488.

Franks, J. J., & Bransford, J. D. A brief note on linguistic integration. *Journal of Verbal Learning and Verbal Behavior,* 1974, *13,* 217–219.

Harris, R. J., & Monaco, G. E. Psychology of pragmatic implication: Information processing between the lines. *Journal of Experimental Psychology: General,* 1978, *107,* 1–22.

Hastie, R., & Kumar, P. A. Person memory: Personality traits as organizing principles in memory for behaviors. *Journal of Personality and Social Psychology,* 1979, *37,* 25-38.

Heider, F. *The psychology of interpersonal relations.* New York: Wiley, 1958.

Higgins, E. T., & Rholes, W. S. "Saying is believing": Effects of message modification on memory for the person described. *Journal of Experimental Social Psychology,* 1978, *14,* 363-378.

Higgins, E. T., Rholes, W. S., & Jones, C. R. Category accessibility and impression formation. *Journal of Experimental Social Psychology,* 1977, *13,* 141-154.

Hinrichs, J. V. A two-process memory-strength theory for judgment of recency. *Psychological Review,* 1970, *77,* 223-233.

Johnson, M. K., Bransford, J. D., & Solomon, S. K. Memory for tacit implications of sentences. *Journal of Experimental Psychology,* 1973, *98,* 203-205.

Jones, E. E., & Goethals, G. R. *Order effects in impression formation: Attribution context and the nature of the entity.* Morristown, N. J.: General Learning Press, 1971.

Kintsch, W. *Memory and cognition.* New York: Wiley, 1977.

Klatzky, R. L. *Human memory: Structures and processes.* San Francisco: W. H. Freeman, 1975.

Kosslyn, S. M. Can imagery be distinguished from other forms of internal representation? Evidence from studies of information retrieval time. *Memory and Cognition,* 1976, *4,* 291-297.

Kosslyn, S. M., & Promerantz, J. R. Imagery, propositions and the form of internal representations. *Cognitive Psychology,* 1977, *9,* 52-76.

Lingle, J. H., & Ostrom, T. M. Principles of memory and cognition in attitude formation. In R. E. Petty, T. M. Ostrom, & T. C. Brock (Eds.), *Cognitive responses in persuasion.* Hillsdale, N.J.: Lawrence Erlbaum Associates, 1980.

Loftus, E. F., Miller, D. G., & Burns, H. J. Semantic integration of verbal information into a visual memory. *Journal of Experimental Psychology: Human Learning and Memory,* 1978, *4,* 19-31.

Loftus, E. F., & Palmer, J. C. Reconstruction of automobile destruction: An example of the interaction between language and memory. *Journal of Verbal Learning and Verbal Behavior,* 1974, *13,* 585-589.

Loftus, G. R., & Loftus, E. F. *Human memory: The processing of information.* Hillsdale, N. J.: Lawrence Erlbaum Associates, 1976.

Markus, H. Self-schemata and processing information about the self. *Journal of Personality and Social Psychology,* 1977, *35,* 63-78.

Massad, C. M., Hubbard, M., & Newtson, D. Perceptual selectivity: Contributing process and possible cure for impression perseverance. *Journal of Experimental Social Psychology,* 1979, *15,* 513-532.

McGuire, W. J. A syllogistic analysis of cognitive relationships. In M. J. Rosenberg, C. I. Hovland, W. J. McGuire, R. P. Abelson, & J. W. Brehm (Eds.), *Attitude organization and change.* New Haven: Yale University Press, 1960.

Meyer, D. E., & Schvaneveldt, R. W. Facilitation in recognition between pairs of words: Evidence of a dependence between retrieval operations. *Journal of Experimental Psychology,* 1971, *90,* 227-234.

Miller, N. E., & Campbell, D. T. Recency and primacy in persuasion as a function of the timing of speeches and measurements. *Journal of Abnormal and Social Psychology,* 1959, *59,* 1-9.

Moyer, R. S. Comparing objects in memory: Evidence suggesting an internal psychophysics. *Perception and Psychophysics,* 1973, *13,* 180-184.

Murdock, B. B. *Human memory: Theory and data.* Potomac, Md: Lawrence Erlbaum Associates, 1974.

Newtson, D. Foundations of attribution: The perception of ongoing behavior. In J. Harvey, W. Ickes, & R. Kidd (Eds.), *New directions in attribution research, Vol. 1.* Hillsdale, N. J.: Lawrence Erlbaum Associates, 1976.

Newtson, D., & Engquist, G. The perceptual organization of ongoing behavior. *Journal of Experimental Social Psychology,* 1976, *12,* 436–450.

Newtson, D., Rinder, R., Miller, R., & LaCross, K. Effects of availability of feature changes on behavior segmentation. *Journal of Experimental Social Psychology,* 1978, *14,* 379–388.

Norman, D. A. (Ed.) *Models of human memory.* New York: Academic Press, 1970.

Norman, D. A., & Bobrow, D. G. On data-limited and resource-limited processes. *Cognitive Psychology,* 1975, *7,* 44–64.

Norman, D. A., & Bobrow, D. G. On the role of active memory processes in perception and cognition. In C. N. Cofer (Ed.), *The structure of human memory.* San Francisco: W. H. Freeman, 1976.

Osgood, C. E., & Tannenbaum, P. H. The principle of congruity in the prediction of attitude change. *Psychological review,* 1955, *62,* 42–55.

Paivio, A. *Imagery and verbal processes.* New York: Holt, Rinehart & Winston, 1971.

Peterson, R. G., & McIntyre, C. W. The influence of semantic "relatedness" on linguistic integration and retention. *American Journal of Psychology,* 1973, *86,* 697–706.

Postman, L. The present status of interference theory. In C. N. Cofer (Ed.), *Verbal learning and verbal behavior.* New York: McGraw-Hill, 1961.

Rogers, T. B. Self-reference in memory: Recognition of personality items. *Journal of Research in Personality,* 1977, *11,* 295–305.

Rogers, T. B., Kuiper, N. A., & Kirker, W. S. Self-reference and the encoding of personal information. *Journal of Personality and Social Psychology,* 1977, *35,* 677–688.

Rosch, E. On the internal structure of perceptual and semantic categories. In T. E. Moore (Ed.), *Cognitive development and the acquisition of language.* New York: Academic Press, 1973.

Rosch, E. Cognitive representations of semantic categories. *Journal of Experimental Psychology: General,* 1975, *104,* 192–233.

Rosenberg, S., & Sedlak, S. Structural representations of implicit personality theory. In L. Berkowitz (Ed.), *Advances in experimental social psychology, Vol. 6.* New York: Academic Press, 1972.

Ross, L. The intuitive psychologist and his shortcomings: Distortions in the attribution process. In L. Berkowitz (Ed.), *Advances in experimental social psychology, Vol. 10.* New York: Academic Press, 1977.

Ross, L., Lepper, M., & Hubbard, M. Perseverance in self perception and social perception: Biased attributional processes in the debriefing paradigm. *Journal of Personality and Social Psychology,* 1975, *32,* 880–892.

Ross, L., Lepper, M. R., Strack, F., & Steinmetz, J. Social explanation and social expectation: Effects of real and hypothetical explanations on subjective likelihood. *Journal of Personality and Social Psychology,* 1977, *35,* 817–829.

Rothbart, M., Evans, M. & Fulero, S. Recall for confirming events: Memory processes and the maintenance of social stereotypes. *Journal of Experimental Social Psychology,* 1979, *15,* 343–355.

Royer, J. M. Remembering: Constructive or reconstructive? In R. C. Anderson, R. J. Spiro, & W. E. Montague (Eds.), *Schooling and the acquisition of knowledge.* Hillsdale, N. J.: Lawrence Erlbaum Associates, 1977.

Rumelhart, D. E., & Norman, D. A. Accretion, tuning, and restructuring: Three modes of learning. In J. W. Cotton & R. L. Klatzky (Eds.), *Semantic factors in cognition.* Hillsdale, N. J.: Lawrence Erlbaum Associates, 1978.

Rumelhart, D. E., & Ortony, A. The representation of knowledge in memory. In R. C. Anderson, R. J. Spiro, & W. E. Montague (Eds.), *Schooling and the acquisition of knowledge.* Hillsdale, N. J.: Lawrence Erlbaum Associates, 1977.

Salancik, G. R. Inference of one's attitude from behavior recalled under linguistically manipulated cognitive sets. *Journal of Experimental Social Psychology,* 1974, *10,* 415-427.

Salancik, G. R., & Calder, B. J. A non-predispositional information analysis of attitude expressions. Unpublished manuscript, University of Illinois, 1974.

Salancik, G. R., & Conway, M. Attitude inferences from salient and relevant cognitive content about behavior. *Journal of Personality and Social Psychology,* 1975, *32,* 829-840.

Schank, R., & Abelson, R. *Scripts, plans, goals, and understanding: An inquiry into human knowledge structures.* Hillsdale, N. J.: Lawrence Erlbaum Associates, 1977.

Sherman, S. J., Ahlm, K., Berman, L. & Lynn, S. Contrast effects and their relationship to subsequent behavior. *Journal of Experimental Social Psychology,* 1978, *14,* 340-350.

Smith, E. E., Shoben, E. J., & Rips, L. J. Structure and process in semantic memory: A featural model for semantic decisions. *Psychological Review,* 1974, *81,* 214-241.

Snyder, M., & Cantor, N. Testing hypotheses about other people: The use of historical knowledge. *Journal of Experimental Social Psychology,* 1979, *15,* 330-342.

Snyder, M., & Ebbesen, E. B. Dissonance awareness: A test of dissonance theory versus self-perception theory. *Journal of Experimental Social Psychology,* 1972, *8,* 502-517.

Snyder, M., & Uranowitz, S. W. Reconstructing the past: Some cognitive consequences of person perception. *Journal of Personality and Social Psychology,* 1978, *36,* 941-950.

Sperling, G. The information available in brief visual presentations. *Psychological Monographs,* 1960, *74,* 1-29.

Spiro, R. J. Remembering information from text: The "State of Schema" approach. In R. C. Anderson, R. J. Spiro, & W. E. Montague (Eds.), *Schooling and the acquisition of knowledge.* Hillsdale, N. J.: Lawrence Erlbaum Associates, 1977.

Srull, T. K., & Wyer, R. S. The role of category accessibility in the interpretation of information about persons: Some determinants and implications. *Journal of Personality and Social Psychology,* 1979, *37,* 1660-1662.

Taylor, S. E., & Fiske, S. T. Salience, attention and attribution: Top of the head phenomena. In L. Berkowitz (Ed.), *Advances in experimental social psychology, Vol. 11.* New York: Academic Press, 1978.

Tulving, E. Episodic and semantic memory. In E. Tulving & W. Donaldson (Eds.), *Organization of memory.* New York: Academic Press, 1972.

Tulving, E. Ecphoric processes in recall and recognition. In J. Brown (Ed.), *Recall and recognition.* London: Wiley, 1976.

Tulving, E., & Bower, G. H. The logic of memory representations. In G. H. Bower (Ed.), *The psychology of learning and motivation, Vol. 8.* New York: Academic Press, 1974.

Tulving, E., & Pearlstone, Z. Availability versus accessibility of information in memory for words. *Journal of Verbal Learning and Verbal Behavior,* 1966, *5,* 381-391.

Tversky, A. Features of similarity. *Psychological Review,* 1977, *84,* 327-352.

Tversky, A., & Gati, I. Studies of similarity. In E. Rosch & B. B. Lloyd (Eds.), *Cognition and categorization.* Hillsdale, N. J.: Lawrence Erlbaum Associates, 1978.

Upshaw, H. S. The personal reference scale: An approach to social judgment. In L. Berkowitz (Ed.), *Advances in experimental social psychology, Vol. 4.* New York: Academic Press, 1969.

Upshaw, H. S. Social influence on attitudes and on anchoring of congeneric attitude scales. *Journal of Experimental Social Psychology,* 1978, *14,* 327-339.

Wells, J. E. Strength theory and judgments of recency and frequency. *Journal of Verbal Learning and Verbal Behavior,* 1974, *13,* 378-392.

Winograd, T. Computer memories: A metaphor for memory organization. In C. N. Cofer (Ed.), *The Structure of human memory.* San Francisco: W. H. Freeman, 1976.

Woll, S., & Yopp, H. The role of context and inference in the comprehension of social action. *Journal of Experimental Social Psychology*, 1978, *14*, 351-362.

Wyer, R. S. *Cognitive organization and change: An information-processing approach.* Potomac, Md: Lawrence Erlbaum Associates, 1974.

Wyer, R. S. The role of probabilistic and syllogistic reasoning in cognitive organization and social inference. In M. Kaplan & S. Schwartz (Eds.), *Human judgment and decision processes.* New York: Academic Press, 1975.

Wyer, R. S., & Carlston, D. E. *Social cognition, inference and attribution.* Hillsdale, N. J.: Lawrence Erlbaum Associates, 1979.

Wyer, R. S., & Hartwick, J. The role of information retrieval and conditional inference processes in belief formation and change. In L. Berkowitz (Ed.), *Advances in experimental social psychology, Vol. 13.* New York: Academic Press, in press.

Wyer, R. S., & Podeschi, D. M. The acceptance of generalizations about persons, objects and events. In R. Revlis & R. E. Mayer (Eds.), *Human reasoning.* Washington, D. C.: V. H. Winston, 1978.

Wyer, R. S., & Srull, T. K. Category accessibility: Some theoretical and empirical issues concerning the processing of social stimulus information. In E. T. Higgins, C. P. Herman, & M. P. Zanna (Eds.), *Social cognition: The Ontario Symposium.* Hillsdale, N. J.: Lawrence Erlbaum Associates, in press.

Zajonc, R. B. Cognitive theories in social psychology. In G. Lindzey & E. Aronson (Eds.), *Handbook of social psychology, Vol. 1.* (2nd ed.) Reading, Mass.: Addison Wesley, 1968.

Author Index

A

Abelson, R., 16, 25, 28, 32, *49, 51,* 104, *118,* 198, 217, *224,* 227, 234, 238, 239, 246, 247, 249, 259, 280, *295, 299*
Adams, N., 26, *52*
Ahlm, K., 291, *299*
Ajzen, I., 22, *45,* 164, *176*
Allen, R. B., 15, *47,* 189, 191, 193, 195, 196, 197, 199, 200, 204, 206, 208, 213, 219, *222, 223,* 233, *296*
Anderson, C., 165, 166, *176*
Anderson, J. R., 3, 5, 12, 19, 29, 31, 34, 35, 37, 42, *45,* 62, *86,* 155, 167, 168, 172, 175, *176, 177,* 233, 254, *295*
Anderson, N., 23, 29
Anderson, R. C., 227, *295*
Appley, M. H., 30, *46*
Asch, S. E., 23, 38, 43, *46,* 57, 60, 63, *86,* 121, 123, 126, 127, 148, *152, 176*
Atkinson, R. C., 5, 10, 11, 35, *46,* 169, 170, 175, *176, 177,* 206, *222*

B

Backman, C. W., 105, *119*
Baddeley, A. D., 11, *46,* 148, 170, *152,* 255, 271, *295*
Bahrick, H. P., 35, *46*

Bandura, A., 179, *222*
Banks, W. P., 36, *46*
Barclay, J. R., 261, 277, *296*
Bartlett, F. C., 66, *86,* 95, *118,* 158, 161, *176,* 261, *296*
Battig, W. F., 36, *50*
Baumgardner, M. H., 65, 66, 78, 80, *87*
Bem, D. J., 215, *222,* 292, *296*
Berlyne, D. E., 109, *118*
Berman, L., 291, *299*
Berscheid, E., 215, *222*
Bever, T. G., 31, *46*
Bjork, R. A., 58, *88*
Bobrow, D. G., 191, *224,* 231, 241, 246, *296, 298*
Bois, J., 3, 17, *50,* 180, 182, 184, 186, *224*
Boies, S. J., 11, *51*
Boring, E. G., 38, *46*
Bousfield, A. K., 35, 36, *46,* 138, *152,* 166, *177,* 268, *296*
Bousfield, W. A., 35, 36, *46,* 138, *152,* 166, *177,* 268, *296*
Bower, G. H., 3, 5, 6, 11, 12, 29, 31, 33, 34, 35, 37, 42, *45, 46,* 62, *86,* 166, 168, 172, 175, *177,* 231, 233, 235, 254, *295, 296, 299*
Braly, K. W., 59, *87*
Bransford, J. D., 95, 96, *118,* 216, *222,* 244, 261, *296, 297*

Subject Index